LUCIUS LYON:

An Eminently
Useful Citizen

Lucius Lyon

LUCIUS LYON:

An Eminently Useful Citizen

By Kit Lane

Pavilion
Press

P.O. Box 250
Douglas, Michigan 49406

LC # 91-60196

ISBN 1-877703-21-4

Frontispiece: This portrait of Lucius Lyon is a copy of an ambrotype taken the year before his death. The copy was made by the Hamilton Studios, Canal Street, Grand Rapids, about 1890. It is used courtesy of the Michigan Historical Collections, Bentley Historical Library, University of Michigan, Ann Arbor.

Dedication

To Lucius Lyon who lived it --

To Caroline P. Campbell who preserved it --

To Carolyn Erickson Suding who helped present it --

With heartfelt thanks.

Table of Contents

My motto is,
"Labor to be useful."

Lucius Lyon

1

"An Eminently Useful Citizen"

In his four volume history of Michigan Charles Moore wrote of Lucius Lyon: "No man in Michigan crowded more into a comparatively short life. To him public place meant simply opportunity for work; he was a firm friend, a good politician, a man of the highest integrity, and an eminently useful citizen. Had he been an orator probably he would have left a great name. As it is, only those who take the pains to become acquainted with his actual work with ever know how much of a debt the state owes to him."

In a biography written in 1896, his nephew George W. Thayer commented in the flowery prose of the times: "Fifty years ago Lucius Lyon was one of the well known public men of Michigan. Today but a small fraction of its inhabitants know that such a man was in the past, one of its most useful and influential citizens during the closing years of its territorial existence and one of the foremost of those who assisted in placing her among the jewels that have, from time to time, been added to the setting in that national crown of civil liberty that was marvelously constructed by the 13 original states of the American Union."

Lyon was useful in many areas of Michigan's history, when it was Michigan Territory and reached westward to the Mississippi River and beyond, during its long fight for admission to the Union, and later as it grew into the young State of Michigan.

He surveyed much of the Lower Peninsula of Michigan, and a large section of southern Wisconsin, doing his task well and honestly, in contrast to workers in some areas whose surveys, drawn in the cozy confines of the nearest tavern, continue to cause land title conflicts well into the 20th century.

He served in the U. S. Congress as a territorial delegate defending the best interest of the rapidly growing Michigan Territory, and he was one of the first delegates to be concerned with the interests of those settlers west of Lake Michigan.

Lyon was an influential member of the first Michigan Constitutional Convention which created the document by which the territory hoped to become a state. He took that document to Washington and as a not-yet-seated senator from the not-quite State of Michigan labored long and hard for full state status. In 1843 he again accepted public office serving as representative from the second Michigan Congressional district.

As a land speculator he purchased thousands of acres in Wisconsin and across the Lower Peninsula of Michigan, founding several villages (including Schoolcraft and Lyons). He was among the founding fathers of many other settlements (including Grand Rapids, Kalamazoo, and Ypsilanti in Michigan; Cassville and others in Wisconsin). Not content to simply draw the lines and sell plots to prospective settlers, Lyon sought internal improvements wherever he went, building mills, dams, canals and bridges. He was part of a group which built the first water system in the City of Detroit.

As an elected official, and later as an appointed Indian commissioner, Lyon worked hard to settle problems arising from misunderstandings with the native Americans and was instrumental in organizing treaty negotiations with the government.

The son of a farmer, as soon as his Michigan land was ready, Lucius Lyon planted many acres of Lower Peninsula farmlands to cash crops and experimented with other potential agricultural products. He was among the first in Michigan to explore the importance of a sugar beet industry.

An early teacher in Detroit, Lyon was one of the first trustees of the University of Michigan and founder of a lyceum in the City of Detroit which was responsible for bringing Douglass Houghton to Michigan.

In the federal office of Surveyor General he worked hard to get the final areas of the new state surveyed, to check out the work previously done, and to organize records before turning them over to state officials.

The population of Michigan in the 1820 census, shortly before Lyon's arrival, was 8,765. By 1830 it was 31,639, and by 1840, 212,267 people lived within the boundaries of the state. A large share of these people were simple farmers and shopkeepers, who wanted only to clear and plant their plots of land or to make their small businesses profitable. There was a small group of Michigan men, nearly all with at least one hand in the political process, who guided the growth of the new state and touted its benefits to businessmen and settlers looking for a new home in the west. Lucius Lyon was one of these.

He knew most of the rest of the early Michigan men. He traveled with Lewis Cass and was rumored to have been in love with Cass's daughter; he once boarded with the family of Indian agent Henry Rowe Schoolcraft and was himself landlord to John Allen (founder of Ann Arbor and other communities); he courted the sister of Michigan's first state governor Stevens T. Mason and locked legal horns with early fur trader and Grand Rapids founder Louis Campau.

8

Perhaps he is best summed up in the frank assessment contained in the 1881 *History of Kent County.* "Mr. Lyon was not a brilliant man, nor rapid in his mental action; but, by being patient, carefully observing, and deliberately considering all subjects which were submitted to him, he generally reached a correct conclusion, and was especially able to make practical applications of results. Thus, in his favorite line of study, natural and mechanical science, he became a proficient, and a peer of those who had enjoyed superior educational advantages. The extent of his knowledge and his capacity for action were sometimes obscured by his modesty. From the unpretentious and silent man, but a tithe of that influence and achievement was expected which he was found to have wielded and accomplished. He was amiable, benevolent and religious; and, in after life, found rest, satisfaction, comfort and joy, often fervently acknowledged, in that form of Christian faith taught by Swedenborg. From his first appearance in public life, until his death, a consistent Democrat, he was unwavering in his political principles and associations. . . . In conclusion it may be said that to no other statesman whom Michigan has produced and sustained in office does she owe more than to the citizen Lucius Lyon."

* * * * *

Soon will toll the knell of summer,
Fleeting as the busy wind.
Autumn is a speedy comer,
Joy or grief to leave behind.

Then since time in all its power,
Will not stop nor stay behind,
Let us seize the present hour
Mend the heart, improve the mind.

by Lucius Lyon
(about 1825)

An 1869 map of western Chittenden County, Vermont

2

New England Roots

Lucius Lyon was born on a farm near Shelburne Falls, Vermont, about six miles from Burlington in Chittenden County, on February 20, 1800. He was the oldest of eight children born to Asa and Sarah (Atwater) Lyon.

His father was a farmer but with a difference. In an 1896 biography Asa Lyon is described by a grandson as "a robust athletic man, over six feet in stature, large in frame weighing 225 pounds, stately in bearing, faultless in form and feature; with a mental vigor above his neighbors."

Sarah (Atwater) Lyon, the mother of Lucius, was a daughter of Ambrose and Sarah Atwater of Cheshire, Connecticut, where she was born, February 11, 1777. She is described as "from an excellent family, having more than usual prominence in their neighborhood." With eight children surviving her, including a three-day-old daughter, she died September 28, 1813. The following spring, on March 27, 1814, Lucius's father was married to Mary (Hawley) Lyon, the widow of Timothy Lyon. She was born at Tinmouth, Vermont, March 11, 1777. The couple had one child, George H. Lyon, born November 15, 1817. Mary died June 17, 1836, and May 18, 1837, Asa took as his third wife, Mary (Atwater) Smith, the sister of his first wife, and widow of Peter B. Smith of Burlington, Vermont.

Lucius Lyon left Vermont in 1822 and was so enthusiastic about what he found that he wrote many letters back east urging friends and family to join him in Michigan. His father was invited on several occasions to invest his future various land deals and move to Michigan but he always remained rooted to his New England home. However, Asa and his third wife, Mary (Atwater Smith) Lyon, visited Michigan twice. On the first visit in 1839 they did not see Lucius who was away in Wisconsin most of the summer serving as Indian commissioner. The second trip occurred in the summer of 1850, and it was on the way home that year, while they were visiting part of the Smith family in Rochester, New York, that Asa died suddenly September 22, 1850.

Lucius had seven full brothers and sisters, one half brother, and others of a more distant family relationship:

11

1. Pamelia (sometimes spelled Pamela) was the oldest sister, and second-oldest child of Sarah and Asa Lyons She was born October 14, 1801, and married to Nathaniel Thayer at Burlington, Vermont, December 3, 1823. On December 8, 1831, "the matrimonial connexion between Nathaniel Thayer and his wife proving unhappy," a bill of divorce was granted by the Supreme Court at Burlington. Two Thayer sons, Lucius Alexander Thayer, born August 21, 1824, and George Washington Thayer, born September 27, 1827, were brought to Michigan and became special charges of their famous uncle. Washington would eventually be his heir and biographer. Pamelia also moved to Michigan about 1848.

2. Merab. the third oldest child, was born October 29, 1803, and married to Truman Palmer of New York in 1834. She resided in New York State until her death of consumption August 9, 1837, in Portage. She left one daughter, Sarah Cecilia Palmer.

3. Orson, born July 26, 1805, moved to Michigan Territory in 1830 at the request of his brother Lucius, to assist with the task of surveying the territory. He worked mainly on lands in Illinois, Wisconsin and Iowa.

4. Lucretia, born October 20, 1807, was a special friend and confidante of her brother Lucius. It is through many of his letters to her, which were carefully saved, that the modern generation has insight into his thoughts and activities and into the history of some of the settlements he founded. She moved to Michigan in 1840 and lived more than 50 years in Grand Rapids.

5. Altha, born September 9, 1809, died March 9, 1817, at the age of seven.

6. Esther, born September 7, 1811, was married in 1832 to James W. Tabor. They moved to Michigan in 1836 at Lucius's request and took charge of his farms in Ionia County.

7. Sarah Atwater Lyon was born September 25, 1813, three days before the death of her mother. The baby lived less than a year and died February 20, 1814, on her eldest brother's fourteenth birthday.

George H. (records kept by Lucretia record his middle name as Homan, often spelled Heman, a common surname in that portion of Vermont; it has come down in his family as Homer) Lyon, son of Asa and Mary (Hawley Lyon) Lyon, was married to Phoebe M. Russell in New England in 1840 and eventually, after the death of his half-brother Lucius, went to Michigan with his son.

In addition, Mary, the second wife of Asa Lyon, had several children who bore the last name of Lyon by her first husband, Timothy

Lyon, who died March 9, 1813. A note found in the papers of Lucretia Lyon indicated that these children were no blood relationship to Asa, but Lucius, writing in 1838 about Truman H. Lyon, describes him as a cousin. The two families, that of Asa and Sarah (Atwater) Lyon and that of Timothy and Mary (Hawley) Lyon, lived only a short distance apart in or near Shelburne in Chittenden County. The 1810 census shows them separated by about 15 households. The two groups of children were about the same age and would have grown up together and gone to the same schools. When the families merged, the oldest children, Lucius and Lorain, were 14 and 19, respectively, and the youngest surviving children in each family, Lenora and Esther, were both two. Several of the members of the second Lyon family came to Michigan where they and some of their offspring figured prominently in the early settlement days. The eight children of Mary and Timothy Lyon who grew to adulthood, and their birth dates are listed below:

1. Lorain, March 17, 1795, later Mrs. Heman A. Barstow
2. Lavina, August 4, 1798, later Mrs. Joseph Irish
3. Truman Hawley, February 24, 1801
4. Dan, May 10, 1803
5. Edward, June 12, 1805
6. Leicester (or Lester), February 5, 1808
7. Mary, December 17, 1809, later Mrs. Gaius Deane
8. Lenora, February 13, 1812, later Mrs. David Irish

Mary (Atwater Smith) Lyon, the third wife of Asa also had a number of children by her first husband, Peter B. Smith. These included:

1. James Smith
2. Tory Smith, born November 12, 1798
3. Sidney Smith, born May 10, 1800
4. Eliza Smith, married Philander Davis in 1837

In addition to siblings, and step-siblings named Lyon, there were others in the Lyon family (both that of Asa and the branch that Timothy belonged to) and the Atwaters (the family of Lucius's mother) who came to Michigan to seek their fortune in the west. These include cousins Isaac Newton Higbee, George A. Robinson, Homer A. Barstow, and Luman R. Atwater, and an uncle, Ira Lyon, who arrived in Michigan possibly as early as 1828.

In the 1810 census of Chittendon County, Vermont, the Asa Lyon 2nd household includes two males under 10, one 10 to 16, one 16 to 18, and one 26 to 45, and two females. In the 1820 census, taken after

13

the elder Lyon had married the second of his two wives, and several of her children had joined the household, the count included one male under 10, two 10 to 16, one 16 to 18, and one over 45. There were nine females, three under the age of 10, one 10 to 16, three 16 to 26, and one 26 to 45. Hired men and servant girls were included in the household count during a census.

In the margin of the family Bible there is a note that Asa, Lucius's father, was "Distinguished by the appellation of A. Lyon 2nd there being an older man in Shelburn, Vt. by the same name." In October of 1833, Lucius wrote his sister, "Tell me whether old Mr. Asa Lyon is still living in Shelburn, that I may know how to address father. I don't know exactly why it is, but I always feel a little dislike when I place '2d' after his name. I think he ought to be No. 1. I wish he had been a colonel or a general or a judge or a 'squire' that he could have been distinguished in some other way." The elder Asa, a brother of their grandfather, died in September of 1836, and Lucretia wrote Lucius, "You need not annex No. 2 to Father's name anymore."

Although he was frequently urged to move west Asa, father of Lucius, refused to leave Vermont and even asked on his death bed that his body be returned there for burial. Asa apparently enjoyed the married state, and tended to remarry quickly following the death of a spouse, sometimes to the embarrassment of his children. Mary (Hawley Lyon) Lyon died June 17, 1836. On August 19, 1836, Lucretia wrote Lucius, "It is yet uncertain whether Father will live long in his present situation of loneliness or whether he will seek him out another companion and partner to cheer his declining years -- Think, however, that I have seen some indications of the latter choice. . . Your advice may be beneficial in this case -- "

Lucius's response was quick, and probably about what she expected. In a letter dated September 5, 1836, he addressed Lucretia, "I notice what you say about Father's inclination to marry again, but it seems to me impossible that he should so soon entertain a notion of that sort . . . before his late amiable and estimable wife is got fairly cold in her grave. A decent respect for appearances, if nothing else, ought to prevent it." Asa agreed not to rush into it, but both of his families of offspring named Lyon approved his intended when they found it was "Aunt Smith," Mary (Atwater) Smith, the widowed sister of his first wife. He proposed and in a letter dated November 5, 1836, Mary Smith responded, "I mentioned your proposal to my children they had not made the least objection to it. I have now made up my mind in favour of your request to spend the remainder of my days with you. . . " Because her son, Sidney, had left for Michigan, and was intending to sell his New York home where she had been living, Mary wrote Asa

14

recommending that he come earlier than he had anticipated, so that her living situation could be arranged. He left Vermont in mid-January of 1837 for the matrimonial engagement.

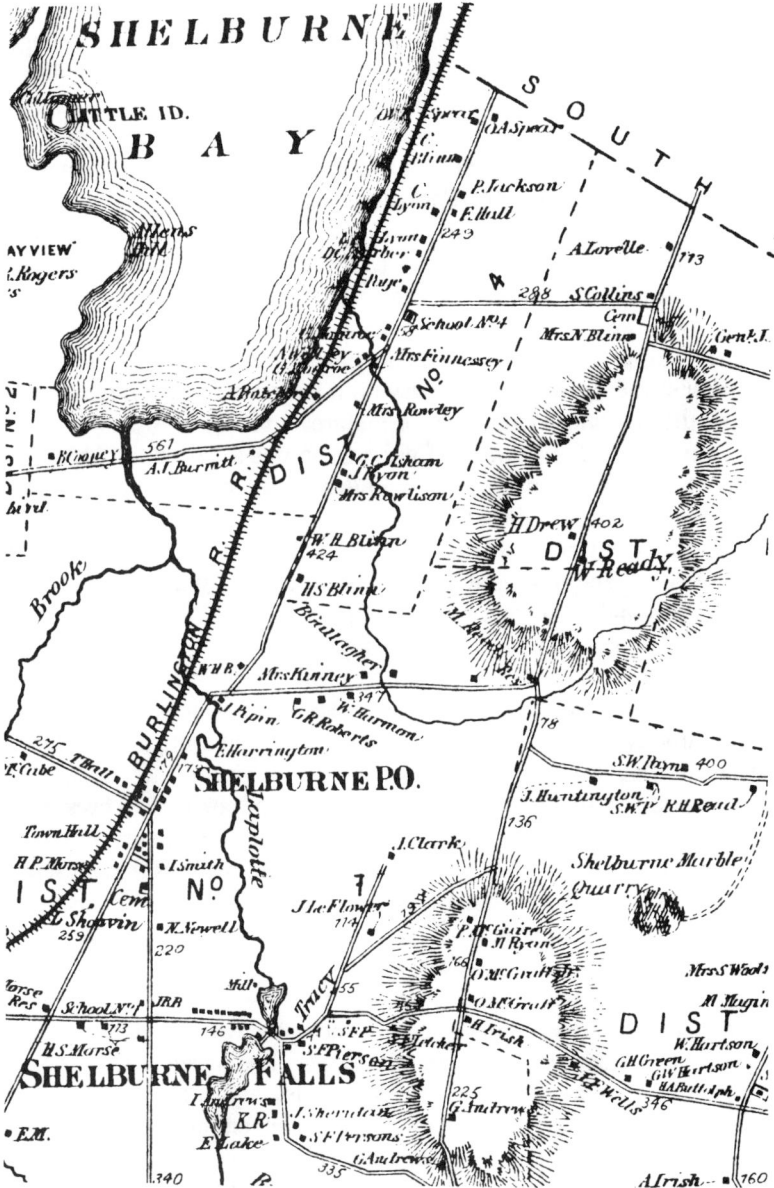

Shelburne and Shelburne Falls in 1869.

Chittenden County is on the western edge of Vermont, across Lake Champlain from New York State. About six miles south of Burlington there is a natural bay. The settlement of Shelburne is within sight of this bay, on an old road which runs the length of western Vermont. Shelburne Falls is less than a mile to the east. Both villages were named for the Second Earl of Shelburne, William Fitzmaurice Petty, who lived 1737-1805. The Battle of Shelburne Blockhouse occurred on March 12, 1778, and local patriots were successful in fending off an attack by Indians and Tories, in one of the backwaters of the fight for independence. The settlement grew around a dam and sawmill constructed in 1786. To the east is Shelburne Pond, a small lake of about 600 acres, which is the source for Muddy Brook. The pond was an early fishing spot, noted for fine pickerel and bass fishing. In the earliest days the town name was usually spelled Shelburn, and several other variations are common. The Shelburne post office was opened in 1814. Shelburne is best known today for a large museum complex which houses buildings and artifacts from the area's past.

In physical appearance Lucius Lyon was a particularly big man for his day. Bert Klopfer, in the Fuller series on Michigan history describes him: "He was 5 feet 11 inches tall, weighed about 200 pounds and was portly but not fleshy. His head and face were large, complexion light and florid, and hair light brown. His voice was kind, manners grave and dignified and his habits were exemplary."

Lyon's nephew, George W. Thayer, who admits that he thought his uncle "nearly perfect" said in an 1896 biography: "He was a man of distinguished appearance and where unknown, would be noticed and inquired about among any body of men of which he might be one. In stature, he was about five feet ten inches, weight a little under two hundred pounds, features regular, face large and attractive, eyes grey, hair a soft silky brown, forehead wide, head very large, very neat and particular in dress, rather slow in movement, impressive in bearing, courteous in manners, pleasant in voice, agreeable in conversation, especially with his acquaintances. He was not an orator nor easy public speaker, never being able to overcome the embarrassment felt when he addressed public assemblages, which he avoided as much as possible. As a writer he was able, expressing his thoughts with ease, force and clearness. He was temperate in all things. He never used profane language. In public station he had equipoise, clear discernment, far reaching judgment. In politics he was neither scheming nor artful. As a man of business he was rather sanguine. He planned and entered upon many large enterprises, some of which, had he possessed greater caution, would have appeared to him less promising of success. His mind was broad and comprehensive, his nature most generous. . . ."

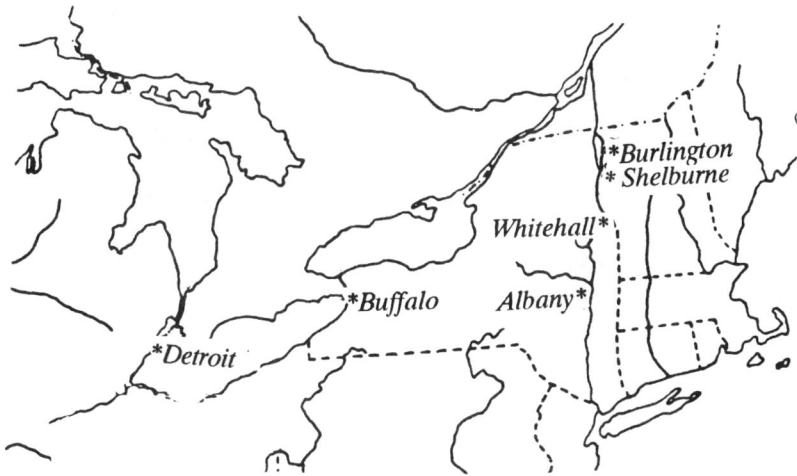

Route of Lyon's journey to Detroit

According to a 1915 biography, as a child Lucius was "quick, active and resourceful and diligent, and possessed a retentive memory." He attended an academy at Shelburne Falls and afterwards at Burlington. During a portion of this time, to provide some income, he taught in a nearby district school. Between the ages of 18 and 22 he obtained instruction in land surveying and practical engineering from John Johnson, a well-known civil engineer, in Burlington. Having received the best education available without attending a university, a situation his father could not afford, Lucius began looking about for a place to settle and begin his life's work.

In 1822, at the age of 22, Lucius decided to seek his fortune in the west. It is possible that he considered Michigan from the beginning, on the recommendation of Ezra Mack of Shelburne, who gave him a letter of introduction to Solomon Sibley of Detroit, an early territorial delegate to Congress from Michigan Territory and later a judge on the territorial court. The letter is a brief note that appears to be written hastily on a small scrap of paper, frayed perhaps by being carried in a pocket. It is dated "Shelburn April 24th 1822" and reads, "Dear Sir. Allow me to recommend to your notice Lucius Lyon who is one of our most respectable young men. His intentions are to settle in your part of the country. Any favors you may confer on him will be duly acknow-ledged. (signed) Ezra Mack." Mack lived in Shelburne not far from the Lyon family. In 1810 the two households were registered on the same census page.

17

Lyon left Vermont by boat on Lake Champlain to its head at Whitehall, and by stage to Albany, New York, where he spent some time gathering additional information on the west in general, and Michigan in particular, the latest trends in surveying and engineering, and available employment. In Albany he met up with John Farmer, a former teacher in an Albany school who had recently been hired as principal of a school in Detroit. Farmer signed on young Lyon as an assistant. A job in his new home already secured he left Albany by stage to Buffalo and boarded a sailing vessel to Detroit. (Later, the trip from Albany to Buffalo could be made on the Erie canal.)

As the story of that voyage was related to a Masonic gathering in Burlington, Vermont, in 1851, Lyon had failed to inquire before he boarded the boat about the cost of the passage and after the boat was under way he discovered that he lacked $2.50 of having enough money to purchase a ticket to Detroit. A stranger nearby overheard his predicament and on discovering that they were both Masons (Lucius having joined the Washington Lodge while he was in Burlington), the stranger volunteered his financial aid saying, "I have $10 left; I will divide with you -- here is five." Lucius took the money and made careful note of the name and address of his benefactor. There are two versions of the end of the story. In one, Lucius obtained the cash and repaid the Masonic brother when the boat docked in Detroit, but then lost track of his name and address and was never able to find him again. In the version written by his nephew in an 1896 biography, Lucius lost the name and address before the money could be repaid, and, despite repeated efforts to identify and locate the man, was never able to repay the debt. "He could only give like unselfish assistance when opportunity offered," the nephew observed.

3

Educator

If the shipboard story is to be believed literally, Lucius Lyon arrived in Detroit with no money in his pocket, but with at least one letter of introduction to a prominent Detroiter and the promise of a job.

The Detroit he found in 1822 was an old settlement by midwest standards. It had been founded by the French in 1701. However, physically, it was almost entirely new having been devastated by a major fire in 1805. The growing village was only six blocks wide, bounded on the south by the Detroit River, on the west by the Cass farm, and on the east by the Beaubien and Brush farms. With those constraints, all growth was forced to occur on the northern edge. Following the fire a new and better Detroit had been mapped, but by 1822 this plan had been realized only to about Congress Street on the north. When the new territorial capitol was completed in 1824 north of Congress, it was only accessible by footpath. The settlement was still very French in language and in character.

Lewis Cass, originally from New Hampshire and later Ohio, had been territorial governor since 1813. He had previously served as a brigadier general and military administrator during and after the War of 1812, and was often addressed as General Cass. He was appointed Governor of Michigan Territory by President James Madison in 1813 replacing William Hull, who was to be court martialed because of his surrender of Detroit to the British in 1812. Cass was thought of as an able man, and probably had a better grasp of what was happening in the territory than anyone, but he was frequently out of Detroit tending to business, especially with the Indians, and during these times the secretary of the territory was acting governor. William Woodbridge, a fervent member of the Whig party and a professional politician, was appointed secretary of the territory in 1814 and held the post until 1828, when he manipulated an appointment to the territorial court. Many at that time, and others with the benefit of historical perspective, have written that Woodbridge so thoroughly dominated territorial politics, especially when Cass was away, as to constitute an early sort of boss rule. However, his influence tended to wax and wane according to the fortunes of his political party. Of little consequence during Michigan's fight for statehood (a largely Democratic effort), he still had enough influence to be elected governor of Michigan in 1839.

REFERENCES
A. Capitol
B. Penitentiary
C. Catholic Church
D. Council House
E. Episcopal Church
F. Old Market
G. New Market
H. Presbyterian Church
I. Public Wharf
J. Bank of Michigan
K. Mansion House
L. Methodist Church
M. U.S. Arsenal
N. University of Michigan
O. Log Scales
P. 1st House of Moses Brady
Q. Mason House 1835
R. Brush Farm House

PLAN of DETROIT by John Mullett Engraved & Published by J.O. Lewis MD

ADAMS AVENUE

GRAND CIRCUS

MADISON AVENUE

MACOMB AVENUE

WASHINGTON AVENUE

MIAMI AVENUE

WOODWARD AVENUE

Fort Gratiot Road

Part of BEAUBIEN FARM

BRUSH FARM Intended road

MICHIGAN

MONROE AVENUE

CAMPUS

Part of GOV. CASS FARM

La Fayette Street

Fort Street

Pierce Street

Cass Street

Wayne Street

Shelby Street

Griswold Street

MARTIN

Bates Street

Congress Street

Larned Street

AVENUE

Commons Sewer

JEFFERSON AVENUE

Woodbridge

Randolph Street

Atwater Street

DETROIT RIVER

Map of early Detroit drawn about 1830. At that time the settlement was hemmed in by the Cass farm on the west and the Brush and Beaubien farms on the east. Lyon lived first at the Mansion House (the square building in the lower left corner).

Solomon Sibley was born in Massachusetts in 1769 and had arrived in Michigan in 1797 after a short stay in Ohio. In some historical

20

accounts he is credited with being the first person of American citizenship to permanently settle in Detroit. He was the territory's first representative to the Legislative Council of the Northwest Territory, and he had known Cass in Ohio. Following his service as territorial delegate to Congress, Sibley was named to the territorial court by President John Quincy Adams. He is described by an early settler as "quite short, very stout, very deaf, a most venerable, excellent, plodding slow careful judge . . . with long, gray hair, large projecting eyebrows and heavy set jaws." Sibley may have been related to the Mack family, including Ezra Mack who had given Lyon a letter of introduction. Stephen Mack, son of Solomon Mack, who had come to Michigan from Massachusetts via Vermont, was a business partner with Sibley in the founding of Pontiac, and in establishing limestone quarries in Monguagon Township. Stephen was also the first Yankee merchant in the city of Detroit, opening the Mack & Conant Store in 1799. Colonel Andrew Mack was Detroit customs collector 1829-39, and he held several local political offices including mayor of Detroit in 1836.

Lucius Lyon, the eager young man from Vermont found quick acceptance in the political-social scene of early Detroit. The first mention of his name in the history of the city occurs in October of 1822 when Melvin Dorr, who was serving as clerk to the territorial court, submitted his resignation with the recommendation that his deputy, Charles C. Trowbridge, be named his successor. There were three judges serving at that time: A. B. Woodward, John Griffin and James Witherell. Silas Farmer wrote in his 1890 history of early Michigan, "It should be borne in mind that Judge Woodward seldom consulted Judge Witherell upon any question, as the latter was so practical and straightforward that he could never agree with him. Judge Griffin on the contrary, was easily persuaded by Woodward, and therefore the appointments and decisions of the court were really made by Woodward."

Farmer goes on to relate that the appointment of the deputy clerk Trowbridge to the vacancy had been approved with generally unanimous consent by the members of the bar in Detroit, and that recommendation, along with the resignation of Dorr, was presented to the court. "In the evening the judge called at the office where the deputy was making up the records and complimented the young official upon the handsome testimonial he had received from the members of the bar, intimating that, as a matter of course, the appointment would be given him. 'By the way,' said the judge as he was leaving, 'I have a young friend, Lucius Lyon, just arrived from Vermont, who is in want of employment; I wish you would make him your deputy.' Mr. Trowbridge replied that he should prefer to perform all the labor himself, and save the expense of a deputy. The next morning in cheerful voice, he read the records of the preceding day, which, being signed, as approved by Judge Woodward, were handed back with this order: 'Mr. Clerk, enter, as the order of the court, that the resignation of Melvin Dorr is accepted, and that John Woodward of Harrisburgh, Pennsylvania, is appointed clerk, and that Jonathan Kearsley, of Detroit, is appointed clerk pro tem., until the arrival of the said John Woodward.' If the roof of the old Indian council-house had fallen, it could not have been a greater surprise to Judge Witherell, to the bar, and to the disappointed deputy. John Woodward proved to be the father of the judge, an old man on the verge of the grave. He died at Erie, Pennsylvania, on his way to Detroit."

Trowbridge, a son-in-law of Solomon Sibley, went on to be mayor of Detroit, cashier of the state bank, and Whig candidate for governor in 1837. As a victim of Judge Woodward's stubborn, sometimes irascible and unpredictable nature he had plenty of company. Popular opinion was decidedly against Woodward and in 1824 he resigned and left Detroit.

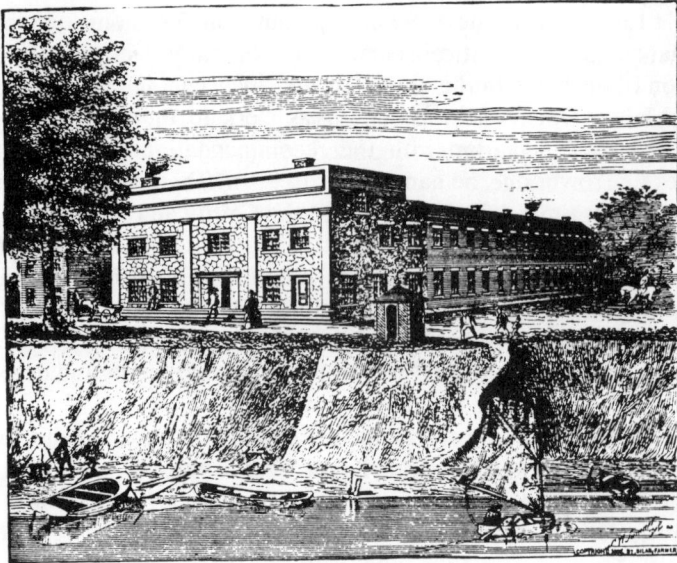

The Mansion House

The fiasco of the new appointment was covered in some detail by the *Detroit Gazette* in the October 25, 1822, issue where the account began with a quote from Shakespeare, "Gracious Heaven, thou usest thy strong sulphureous bolt against the unwedgeable gnarled oak, rather than the soft myrtles, but man, vain man, dressed in a little brief authority, most ignorant of what he is most assured -- his glossy essence, like an angry ape, plays such fantastic tricks as to make the angels weep." The editor went on to comment at the head of the story that in Shakespeare's description of an unjust judge, "we have so striking a comment upon our own observations and experience in our own town."

One of Lucius's first homes in Michigan was the Mansion House, a stone hotel near the banks of the Detroit River, on what would later be the northwest corner of Cass Street and West Jefferson Avenue. It had been built after the great fire of 1805 which destroyed most of the city. In the Farmer history of Detroit it is recorded that James May gathered up the rubble from the chimneys of ruined houses after the fire and constructed the hotel. Another account states that it was built from stone salvaged following the destruction of the first Fort Shelby. The two-story stone building was purchased by Judge Woodward who leased out the hotel portion to various innkeepers, keeping quarters for his personal use. This was most likely where he met Lucius Lyon, the new arrival from Vermont.

When Lyon stayed at the Mansion House it was run by Major John Whipple, an old captain in General Anthony Wayne's army. A bill among Lyon's papers indicates that for seven and a half week's lodging from February to April, 1823, he paid $28.57, plus an additional $7.14 for candles, $21.43 for horsekeeping, and $37.16 for "sundrys."

In 1825 he described his quarters in Detroit in a letter to his sister, Lucretia: "So here I am, seated at a large and substantial pine table, on one side of which, against a partition, stands a homely book case of the same material, where the greater part of my knowledge is arranged in rows, for I must confess that like many of the would-be sages of the times I have more knowledge in books than in brains.

"I have in my room three chairs, a looking glass on the window and a few feet back stands my bed. . . . The broad expanse of the delightful river lies open before the window in full view. Turning to the left the eye is arrested by the city buildings in that direction, and as I glance along the main street I observe but here and there a solitary taper burning through the sullen gloom of night. The watch dogs bark. The crickets chirp and creak. . . . "

One of Lyon's early acquaintances in Detroit was the Henry Rowe Schoolcraft family. Schoolcraft was an Indian agent, and scholar who had married a part Indian woman, Jane Johnston. For a few years they moved from their post at Mackinac and resided in Detroit where Lucius lived with the family when he was not in the woods surveying. In July of 1828 he described Schoolcraft to his sister in a letter as "author of several valuable works with whom I board."

Although it would appear that school teaching was not Lucius

Lyon's first choice as a life's work he had already had some experience at it back in Vermont, and probably enjoyed the innovative methods in the school that he and John Farmer ran. In a sense the Lancasterian school was an early part of the University of Michigan. On August 26, 1817, a school, styled the Catholepistemiad Michiganensis, was founded in Detroit. A board was set up to administer it and on September 12, 1817, the board approved an act to establish a Classical Academy, a school that was generally equivalent to a high school with some primary subjects. A building was approved to house the educational endeavors and the cornerstone was laid September 24, 1817, for a 24 x 50 foot, two story building on the west side of Bates near Congress Street in downtown Detroit.

COPYRIGHT 1880. BY SILAS FARMER.

Bates Street Schoolhouse in Detroit

Six months after the Classical Academy began operations a primary school, to offer instruction in "Reading, Writing, Arithmetic, English Grammar and Elocution" was approved by the University regents. There was much debate in educational circles and in the columns of the *Detroit Gazette* about the Lancasterian method of education. The basic ideas of the system had been worked out by Joseph Lancaster (1778-1838), an English educator and member of the Society of Friends who came to the United States in 1818. His plan organized corps of older boys who served as monitors to oversee and instruct the younger students. The teacher would come in direct contact with older pupils, who in turn carried the education they received to the lower classes which were organized into different levels to receive it. One of the main advantages of the Lancasterian system was its economy. With the assistance of the monitors it was said that one teacher could instruct as many as 1000 students. The school was especially thought useful to prepare students for the millennium (the return of Christ and the end of earthly society) which many at this time thought imminent.

Lancaster wrote in *Improvements in Education*, "Any boy who can read, can teach; and the inferior boys may do the work usually done by the teachers, in the common mode; for a boy who can read, can teach, although he knows nothing about it; and in teaching, will imperceptibly acquire the knowledge he is destitute of, when he begins to teach, by reading." The students were graded into small groups of ten to twelve. The first class learned the alphabet, the second was taught words of two letters; the third class, three lettered words; and so on through the fifth class where "syllabick" reading was begun. Letters were taught by an older student who traced a particular letter in damp sand, the pupil retraced the same letter until the motion carried over and he could reproduce the letter unaided. Because of the teaching medium the young pupils were often referred to as "sand scratchers." Those who did their lessons well were given a prize or reward and the upper level student who taught them received a similar reward. When a student had learned all a particular class had to offer he moved on to the next.

The act setting up the primary school "on the Lancasterian principle" was passed April 12, 1818. The first teacher was Lemuel Shattuck, a native of Connecticut, who arrived in June. The school opened August 10. Shattuck is recognized as a teacher of exceptional ability who adapted the educational ideas of Lancaster to fit the situation.. An early pupil records the workings of the Detroit version of a Lancasterian school. One of the major differences in Detroit was that the school was co-educational.

"This school had two distinct departments, one comprising the common English branches, on the ground floor, the room divided in the center, like church pews. The sexes sat on separate sides and seated in classes of ten or twelve, facing each other at a double desk. Beginning with the sand scratchers each class was presided over by a scholar taken from a higher class seated at the end of the desks to preserve order and give instruction for the day or week. There were broad aisles on the outside in which around half circles the classes recited their lessons to the instructor, standing within the circle with a pointer. The lessons for the juveniles on placards were upon the wall; all the classes reciting at the same time, it being a school graded into classes. At the entrance end, between the doors, upon a raised platform, were seated two monitors, a young gentleman and a lady from the high school, with desks and chairs, overlooking the whole room, keeping order, giving instruction, and receiving reports from those presiding over classes and probably receiving pay. The principal, Mr. Shattuck, over all; quietly entering the room, passing around, giving instructions, sometimes carrying a small rattan, or raw-hide, but seldom used, except to tap a pupil on the shoulder when found playing or dozing. . . . The languages were, with mathematics and higher branches of English taught in the upper room where Mr. Shattuck presided."

In 1821 Shattuck returned East but prior to his departure was authorized by the Board of Trustees on October 8, 1821, to write to educator William A. Tweed Dale of Albany, New York, asking his assistance in locating a teacher familiar with the Lancasterian methods. It was apparently Dale who put them in touch with John Farmer and Major A. Edwards, one of the trustees, made a special trip to New York to complete the arrangements that would bring Farmer to Detroit. As Farmer was preparing to leave for the west he was introduced to Lucius Lyon and before leaving Albany he hired him as his assistant. If he followed the arrangements begun by his predecessor this would have meant that Lyon was the male monitor on the lower floor.

Recitation Time at a Lancasterian School

In 1822 there were nearly two hundred students. Farmer and his assistant (or assistants) probably had their hands full. Neither man remained long in the teaching profession. Lyon left as soon as a surveying job could be procured in 1823, and Farmer resigned in 1824 to become a full time map maker. The Lancasterian experiment was abandoned after six years. In 1827 the Board of Trustees resolved that as the funds were insufficient for the support of a Classical School, the teacher was thereafter to continue the school at his personal risk. After

26

that date there was official action granting the use of the school building free of rent to such persons as were deemed competent teachers.

When plans were realized for an educational institution of higher learning, Lucius Lyon was named, March 18, 1837, to the first Board of Regents for the University of Michigan. The board included John Norvell, a fellow senator; Isaac E. Crary, the first Congressional representative of the State of Michigan; John J. Adams, who kept records at the capital; Henry R. Schoolcraft, Indian agent and friend; Major Jonathan Kearsley, a hero of the War of 1812 who was later mayor of Detroit; Samuel Denton, an Ann Arbor physician; politicians Gordon C. Leach, Seba Murphy and George Whittemore; and Dr. Zina Pitcher who had been associated with Lyon and Schoolcraft in publishing the *Journal of Education of Detroit*.

Lyon resigned from the board with a letter to Governor Mason July 10, 1839, "Finding it impossible in the midst of my numerous other engagements to attend punctually the meetings of the Regents of the University . . . in order that my place may be filled by some one better qualified than myself, who can give that attention to the interests of the institution which its importance demands."

Although he had only a very limited amount of education beyond the common school and never attended any college or university, Lyon valued education and continued his own throughout his life. In 1826 he wrote his sister Lucretia, then a young lady of 18, concerning the subjects important for her to include in her school curriculum. The two often communicated in verse and he couches his advice in rhyme:

And now, my dear sister, as I promised to write,
Concerning your studies, I will do it tonight.

My advice is but short, few words will contain it,
Still fewer be used to expound or explain it.
Stick close to your English, make perfect in that,
Then French and Italian, if chances are pat;
There's music and drawing should ne'er be neglected,
And fancy and needlework never rejected.

As for Greek and Latin, they cost so much time,
To obtain a good knowledge in prose and in rhyme,
That one hardly gets paid for the trouble one's taken,
The pleasure he's lost and the studies forsaken.

After discussing his health, the fruit available in the city, and the arrival of a letter from Vermont, he closes with this couplet describing his letter:

> Though its doggerel for wisdom can't vie with Confucius,
> It may serve to remember the friendship of
> Lucius.

Lucius Lyon also supported continuing education and joined with Lewis Cass, H. R. Schoolcraft, H. Whiting, William Ward, A. S. Porter, J. L. Whiting and W. L. Newberry in 1830 in an attempt to revive the Lyceum of Michigan, an organization interested in scientific, literary, benevolent and patriotic projects. A lyceum often was established in a community to set up a lecture series for the education and entertainment of the adults. An earlier lyceum, originated in 1818, by A. B. Woodward, William Woodbridge, Charles Larned and J. L. Whiting was no longer active. The second lyceum was short lived as well but produced some excellent lectures, many later published.

In a letter back home Lyon explained that the object of the lectures was "to prevent the pesky old bachelors and gay young belles, puny young beaux and prim old maids from suffering so much from ennui as to cut their throats during the long season that by mud and water, frost and snow, they are almost cut off from the world."

In 1830 Lucius Lyon made a journey to the Van Rensselaer Polytechnic School at Troy, New York, on his way to Washington, D. C., to secure a lecturer on the natural sciences. The story often related in connection with this visit is that Lyon was conversing with Professor Amos Eaton, the head of the institute, and made his request. The gentleman rose from his chair and opened a nearby laboratory door to reveal a very young man inside and indicated that this was the man Lyon wanted. The visitor from Michigan was momentarily flustered, feeling that the professor was joking, or insulting him, by offering him a boy instead of the expert he had requested. However, once he had a chance to meet Douglass Houghton, and hear his story he agreed that the young man was an excellent choice. Houghton had completed his degree at that institution as a teenager and at the time of Lyon's visit, was an assistant professor. The same autumn, Houghton, then twenty-one years old, appeared in Detroit to enter upon a career. His lecture series was a great success, the young man not only knew his subject, but he was an excellent speaker, and the natural sciences had never been more popular.

His friendship with the young geologist was useful in 1845 when Lyon was appointed surveyor general and was able to help Houghton get the contract for a combined geological, mineralogical, topographical and magnetic survey of the 4000 square miles of government land in the Upper Peninsula. Houghton died on that expedition October 13, 1845.

Not content merely to organize, Lyon may have himself been a lyceum lecturer. In January of 1831 he wrote Samuel Williams, clerk in the surveyor general's office, for some technical information. He said that he had been asked to deliver a discourse on land surveying for the lyceum.

Lewis Cass

Schoolcraft was also a big mover in Detroit's second lyceum, and when asked to lecture in 1831 replied, "No duty is more important than that which diverts a town from idle gratifications and fixes its attentions on moral and intellectual themes." He spoke on natural history, in the group's usual meeting place, the upper chamber of the old Indian council house, and his lecture was later published. When he moved back to the Upper Peninsula, the second lyceum ceased activity.

About the same group of people founded The Historical Society of Michigan, July 3, 1828, in a meeting at the Mansion House. Lewis Cass was president, H. S. Cole and John Biddle, vice-presidents, and other officers were Thomas Rowland, Henry Whiting, C. C. Trowbridge and J. L. Whiting. Some sources list Lucius Lyon as a charter member. The first series of lecturers were Lewis Cass, Henry Rowe Schoolcraft, John Biddle, and Henry Whiting, all of whom spoke to the group in apparently annual meetings 1828 through 1832. Their lectures were printed as *Historical and Scientific Sketches of Michigan*. It was probably at this time that Lyon recorded several pages of recollections from Jonathan Kearsley, who had lost a leg during service in the War of 1812. Kearsley was receiver at the U. S. Land Office in Detroit for more than 30 years beginning in 1819. He served as mayor of Detroit in 1829 and was a city recorder in 1827 (a post that put him second in command to the mayor, and included presiding over an early version of Recorder's Court). Following publication of the collected lectures the society was largely inactive until 1857.

Lucius Lyon's first oath as a surveyor signed in 1823.

30

4

Deputy Surveyor

Although he was glad for the schoolteaching job that gave him employment on his arrival in Detroit, Lucius did not see education as his future career. A number of sources, including a history of Detroit written by John Farmer's son, Silas, note that Lyon taught at the early school, but his tenure must have been brief. He wrote to Solomon Sibley, January 16, 1823, "I am employed in the Quarter Masters Department and not having much to do have commenced a study of the French Language. . . "

However, the major portion of the letter to Sibley dealt with a recent problem with surveying in Michigan, and hints that the young man from Vermont would like to change his line of work. "The business of surveying goes on rapidly in this Territory -- Mr. Wampler carried through about three and a half tiers of townships from Lake Huron to the Saganau [an early spelling of Saginaw] surveys, when finding the surveying rather bad, he quit and about the first of December came in to Detroit, and from thence proceeded to Ohio, in order as he said to persuade the Surveyor General to pay him for what he had done, and release him from the contract, or if not, to wait until winter to perform it. . . .

"Now the truth is, not finding his job a very good one . . . he determined to quit it and work on better ground. Accordingly he gave his compass to one of his hands who last year could not (if I am correctly informed) write his name, and directed him to proceed to subdividing Townships between Pontiac and Saganau whilst he went to persuade the Surveyor General to conform to his designs. . . Mr. Wampler has said that he could do as he had a mind with the S. Genl -- The foregoing circumstance confirms it -- Such management ought not to be tolerated. . . . I hope that hereafter the surveying of this territory may be done by Surveyors residing in it -- I should myself like extremely well to have a good Job of surveying to do next season and as there are several who calculate to go to Chillicothe about the time that they suppose the S. G. will receive his instructions, it might perhaps be for your interest if he should not receive them until about the time that you arrive there or if you should bring them. . . ."

Sibley was then territorial delegate to Congress, and Lyon seems to be advocating that the orders and appropriations for surveying in

31

Michigan not be revealed by mail but brought to the surveyor general's office in Chillicothe, Ohio, on Sibley's way home from Washington, with the hope that Lyon could have a chance at being on hand at the right time to get a contract.

He had studied surveying as part of his schooling in Burlington, prior to leaving Vermont. In 1822 and early 1823, apparently in addition to his other work, he joined Joseph Fletcher and John Mullett who were surveying private claims along the Detroit River. In 1828 when some question arose about the work he wrote that he had actively participated in the work on the 22 claims made by Mr. Fletcher, "I accompanied and assisted him in preparing his plan of operations and in the execution of the work on the ground and in making his returns."

By the time he wrote Sibley he had already contacted the surveyor general and asked that a portion of the work in Michigan be allotted to him. In November of 1822 Lyon wrote a friend: "The Territory of Michigan in its full extent comprehends all the territory of the United States north of the Ohio and east of the Mississippi. . . But a small part of the Territory is yet surveyed and I have not been able to obtain a job from the United States yet, but have a fair prospect of obtaining a district of ten townships to survey on the opening of spring, which at three dollars per mile will amount to 1,800 dollars, out of whch I can save something pretty handsome."

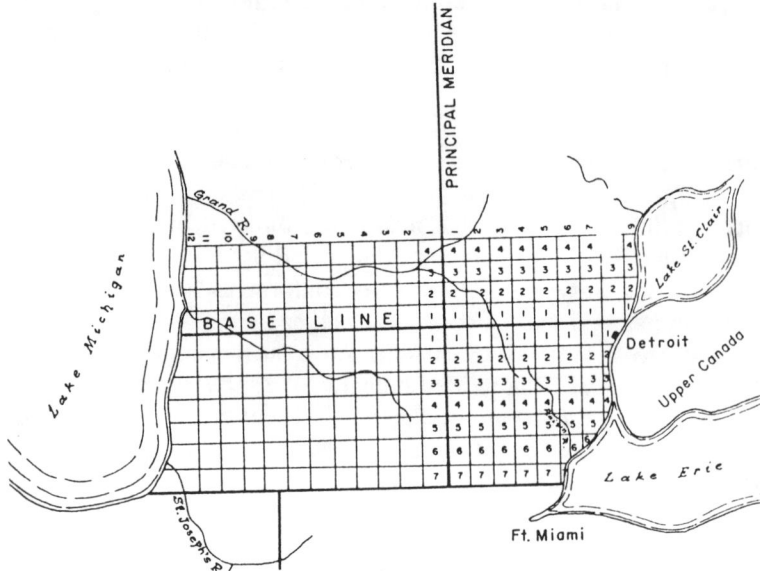

Southern Michigan showing the principal meridian and base line.

Surveying was considered an exciting and lucrative position for a young man. In 1829 Cadwallader Washburn of Galena wrote, "If I can obtain a surveyor's post, I would not sign up for the best office in John Tyler's gift." George Washington, the father of the United States, had been a surveyor. Although fees received for the task did not give instant riches, it was enough money to allow investment in lands, which was the way to wealth, and a chance to choose the best lands by on-site inspection.

NORTH.

6	5	4	3	2	1
7	8	9	10	11	12
18	17	School 16 Section	15	14	13
19	20	21	22	23	24
30	29	28	27	26	25
31	32	33	34	35	36

WEST.   EAST.

SOUTH.

At the corners of each section, four trees are marked (one standing on each section) by the Surveyor, with the number of the township, range and section, thus:

T 7	T 7	T 7	T 7
R 14	R 14	R 14	R 14
S 14	S 15	S 22	S 23

A model township.

The Ordinance of 1787, often called the Northwest Ordinance, provided for the development of land beyond the original states and required that in advance of sale (and ideally before occupation) the land should be laid out in orderly townships and sections. At regular intervals, designed roughly to coincide with expected state boundaries, a baseline running east and west and a meridian running north and south were established, and the intersection of these two lines formed the basis for the survey. Townships, six miles square were further divided into 36 sections.

The numbering system went right to left, dropped down a row and went on left to right. Section 16 was designated the school section and all proceeds from land in that section went for the support of the public schools. When the early surveyors determined the township lines, and the section lines, they marked each place where four lines met. Four trees would be blazed and marked with the Town number (the number of townships that a particular township was north or south of the base line), the Range number (the number of townships that a particular township was east or west of the meridian), and the Section number (the number of that section within the township). If the trees were not exactly on the corner there would be an additional note that the line was three feet east or two rods north of the marking. Where there were no trees, corners were marked with mounds of earth, or rocks, centered by a stake carrying the same information. Settlers lost, or wandering in the woods in search of land, could navigate by the survey markings when they were fresh.

In 1823 Lyon received his appointment as a deputy surveyor. He took his first oath, "to faithfully and accurately" execute the duties of a deputy surveyor on July 2, 1823, before Thomas Rowland, Wayne County justice of the peace. Lyon's first assignment was near Fort Gratiot in St. Clair County, where the city of Port Huron was later established. He had been given five townships to survey, and Sylvester Sibley, son of Judge Solomon Sibley's brother Nathaniel, had five townships nearby. They were just setting out when Lyon wrote William Woodbridge, July 8, 1823, asking that Woodbridge assist him in checking whether there were any private claims filed for the area. In the same letter Lyon noted that when the Fort Gratiot area work was finished, he was to map "the meander of L. Huron North of this."

There is some evidence that the position for both Lyon and Sylvester Sibley was procured with the backing of Solomon Sibley and Territorial Governor Lewis Cass. Both the elder Sibley and Cass wrote letters to Surveyor General Edward Tiffin, in the fall of the year addressing the hope that Tiffin would see fit to give the young men "further employment as surveyors." Sibley goes on to point out that the new workers "after deducting all xpenses will not have received much profits for their labor." He suggests that the surveyor general assign bigger districts, since some of the expenses would be the same with bigger districts, and the payment would be larger. Tiffin continued to assign work in five township lots.

34

A map of surveyed lands drawn in 1822 by Lucius Lyon
for Lewis Cass, probably to show off his mapmaking skills.

In the winter and spring of 1824 Lyon continued his survey
work in St. Clair County and Lapeer County just to the west. The work
finished, he left for Vermont on his first trip home since his departure.
He remained until August spending several weeks at Middlebury taking
scientific studies, including geology, to better outfit him for his work in
the field.

35

On his return in the fall Lyon was named, with W. A. Fletcher, and B. F. H. Witherell, as a "disinterested person" to view a proposed extension of Detroit's Jefferson Avenue to the northeast. The three were named "viewers to judge of and report of the utility and the inutility, convenience or inconvenience which would result to the public as well as to individuals if such road should be opened." In November of that year the committee reported that they felt the road should be completed as far as the old Moran farm. Their report was protested by many of the landowners in the area and the matter dropped. The following spring the county commissioners, in a sudden and possibly illegal decision, voted to complete the entire road, and a second suit was filed to remove the decision on the question from the county commission to the territorial court. Signers of the second petition included Antoine Dequindre, Charles Moran, Dominique Riopelle, and several members of the Campau family. It is possible that Lyon's involvement in this squabble had some bearing on his later problems with Louis Campau during the early days of the Grand Rapids settlement.

Early in 1826 there were complaints from some Michigan residents concerning the quality of survey work being done there. Surveyor General Edward Tiffin, in a letter to George Graham at the General Land Office, enumerates and defends each of his surveyors and hints that part of the problem was due to altered surveys done by "designing men." About Lucius Lyon he wrote: "His knowledge of the theory and practice of surveying is very good; and he has performed his work well and to my entire approbation. He is a young man whose character I believe is irreproachable. To his abilities as a surveyor, he superadds very respectable acquirements in the sciences of mineralogy, geology, and botany; all of which may be useful to him in his profession as surveyor of public lands."

In the winter of 1825-26 Lucius Lyon and John Mullett completed some preliminary surveys in what would later be Allegan County, in western Michigan, running township borders for the easternmost row of townships in the county, and a preliminary survey of the Grand River. Land records also show that Lyon ran section lines for a township in Monroe County near the Raisin River.

In April of 1826 during work on the Grand River Lucius met up with Rix Robinson, a fur trader located at what he calls "Forks, Grand River", probably the junction of the Thornapple and Grand River where the town of Ada later grew. He purchased supplies from Robinson costing "$8.7 1/2." The items included 40 pounds of sugar, 2 bushels common corn, 5 sturgeon, and 1 pair of "mockasins" and Robinson drew up a bill of sale. At the bottom of the bill was appended a note, "To Messrs. Newberry, Dequindre, or any person from Detroit, will oblige me by paying Mr. Robinson account for above. . . I will account them on sight for the same." The signature was "Lucius Lyon, U.S. D. Surveyor."

About the first of August 1826 he fell ill and remained in Detroit unable to work even though he had been assigned several townships. In a letter dated December 21, 1826, and datelined Ypsilanti, he wrote Tiffin: "As I have not yet commenced my survey I think proper to inform you of the fact that you may not be disappointed if my returns should not be made by the time specified . . . Twice I have started out to commence my Survey, and have been compelled to return on account of ill health. -- I am on my way out for the 3rd time and my health is now so far improved that I think I shall be able to proceed." He predicted that the job would be completed in April, and asked for the honor of doing the Bois Blanc Island survey if that was to be on the schedule for summer. In a letter to Samuel Williams, clerk in the surveyor general's office, September 27, 1826, he described his problem as "billious fever."

Also in September Lyon wrote his 19-year-old sister Lucretia that because of his illness, and board and doctor bills that amounted to over $200, he would not be able to send her money to go abroad to school, but thought the proceeds of his Ypsilanti farm "where three or four men are constantly employed in clearing and ploughing," might improve the situation the following year.

In 1826 and 1827 Lyon also did work in Clinton County, just north of where Lansing would later be built. The first season he ran the township lines in the southern half of the county, and returned later to do section lines in Bengal and Riley Townships, and perhaps others. Another project in 1826 was the north and west boundary of Eaton County while John Mullett ran the line on the south. Eaton County is located immediately south of Clinton County, and east of Ingham County. The 1826-27 season also included work in Eaton and Ionia Counties.

In 1827 he worked on township and private claim lines on the Rouge River, west of Detroit, at the same time directing some planting at his Ypsilanti farm. During the summer he went north to Bois Blanc Island, near Mackinac Island in the straits, for a small survey. It was not as enjoyable as he has anticipated. He reported in September that he had been troubled by high water and "almost impervious thicket with which the island is covered." He had been instructed to have the commander of the garrison at Fort Mackinac designate a woodlot, but the officer declined to do so until after the islabnd was surveyed. Then he visited Bois Blanc with Lyon and the two of them marked off the woodlot "with very conspicious boundaries." Lyon also wrote Lucretia in

37

August that the survey had been an unprofitable one.

In 1828 surveying work was light. He wiled away the early part of the year in Detroit writing and researching an article on surveying which he sent to *The Journal of Science and Arts* published by Yale professor, Benjamin Silliman, a frequent correspondent on scientific subjects, whom he may have met in the East. Lyon's article, published in the July, 1828, edition is entitled:

ART. VI.—*Observations on Surveying Instruments, and the means of remedying their imperfections; by* LUCIUS LYON, *Surveyor and Civil Engineer—(with a print.)*

Detroit, Michigan Territory, Jan. 26th, 1828.

MAGNETISM is the well known name of a mysterious power, manifested only by its effects, and of whose ultimate cause we are ignorant.

Among its effects, none is more important, than that which results from the application of one of its familiar properties, to the art of surveying.

By no other means at present known, can lines be run, new lands be laid off, estates subdivided, their boundaries 'o- fined and the local position of   os 2   ned. *

The article draws on Lyon's five year career as a deputy surveyor and while admitting that, "By no other means at present known, can lines be run, new lands be laid off, estates subdivided, their boundaries defined, and the local position of places ascertained with so much facility as by the magnetic needle," the main point of the article is that there are a number of things that would cause this needle to err.

He recommends an "improved elevating compass" to provide more flexible aim in hilly country and the journal includes a diagram of such a compass designed by Benjamin Platt of Columbus, Ohio. Lyon adds that continuing and careful checks of the precise variation of the needle from true north should be undertaken. He gives figures for a number of readings that he and John Mullett had taken at different places in Michigan, at various seasons, and notes that there is often a variation from what the surveyor knows to be north even when there are no iron deposits nearby which might unduly influence the needle. He also compares English and American instruments used for surveying. The second half of the article discusses some of the ways that a needle can become magnetized causing aberrant readings:

38

The common method of carrying the compass for convenience and for the protection of the glass, particularly in the woods, is to throw it over the left arm, with its face towards the body, holding one sight-vane in the hand, while the other lies across the arm above the elbow.

In this position, one part of the glass will frequently come in contact with the covering of the body ; and I have found by abundant experience, that it is the part thus excited, which, in a dry atmosphere, very often produces the aberrations of the needle so much complained of, the cause of which has generally been considered so inexplicable.

I believe, that in nine cases out of ten, where local attraction is suspected, the surveyor need not look beyond his instrument for the cause.

Sometimes from this cause, when the compass is set, and the needle let down on to the centre-pin, it will swing hastily around to a certain position, where it will suddenly stop, and rem⸗⸗ for sev⸗⸗⸗l minute⸗ ⸗til th⸗ ⸗⸗⸗⸗⸗ment ⸗ ⸗⸗s to

Athough his name was correct on the article, the budding young author must have been chagrined when he turned to the index and read:

As February began, and still he received no contracts, Lyon began to doubt the fortune to be gained as a surveyor. He wrote to Tiffin, February 7, 1828, "Having understood that a survey of some part of the country bordering on the St. Joseph and Lake Michigan has been ordered Mr. Mullett and myself have for some time past been anxiously waiting in the hope of receiving contracts and instructions. As we are not allowed to survey for the U.S. out of this Territory, and from our peculiar situation, that business is our sole dependence, we view every opportunity, appropriation and arrangment for surveying in the Territory with a deep interest. . . ." He goes on to point out that in addition to the other problems connected with a change of occupation, that they had invested in many instruments that would be useful only to surveyors.

The following week an angrier letter went out to Tiffin, expressing disappointment that the St. Joseph County job had been given to someone who offered to do it at a reduced price, and asking for a chance to work in the Fox River area of Green Bay. This elicited a letter from Tiffin setting out new reduced surveying rates of $2 per mile.

On February 27, 1828 Lyon wrote Territorial Governor Lewis Cass deploring the new rates and commenting, "The inevitable consequence of such a reduction will be that the work will be badly done in the field, however well it may appear on paper."

Canals and railroads were the big projects of the day. Discouraged, and seeking work, possibly a new field of work, he headed for Washington "looking on to grow wise." There he watched while a Michigan canal project was defeated in Congress. Then he moved on to Pennsylvania and Maryland to assist in the laying out of a railroad and to aid investors in locating a canal. He had his first ride on the railed cars in Pennsylvania and wrote, May 11, 1828, "Yesterday for the first time, I took a ride upon the railroad which extends from Lehigh at this place, nine miles in a westerly direction. We were drawn up by a horse eight miles, on to the summit level, in about an hour, but came back according to the law of gravitation . . . in thirty five minutes in a truly republican style, without any adventitious aid from either horses or servants." He had planned a trip back to Vermont to visit the family as part of his eastern sojourn but wrote Lucretia sadly, "as I am now wholly out of profitable employment I find it absolutely necessary to study economy in my expenses."

After Lyon left Michigan, an assignment from Tiffin's office tried to reach him and forwarded to Washington, upon receiving it Delegate A. E. Wing sent it back to Detroit. Eventually, a letter caught up with Lyon in Pennsylvania and he wrote Tiffin from Pittsburgh, June 12, 1828, that he had just received the contract and "shall proceed immediately to Detroit and thence to Prairie du Chien with all possible expedition to execute the work which you have had the goodness to assign to me."

Back in Detroit for the first time in several months, Lucius wrote Lucretia on July 4th that he was leaving within the hour for Green Bay aboard a vessel that was also carrying Governor Cass, Henry Rowe Schoolcraft, and several members of the legislative council. At Green Bay he would part from the others and "go up the Fox River and down the Ouisconsin to Prairie du Chien on the Mississippi river where I am ordered by the government to survey some few private land claims. From the prairie I contemplate going down the Mississippi River, stopping at the lead mines of Fever River and at St. Louis, and up the Ohio to Cincinnati and thence home through the State of Ohio." There were no maps of the western portion of Michigan Territory so, with the aid of a pocket compass he took courses and distances of the Fox-Wisconsin River route and later joined his findings with others. This was given to a mapmaker who published, in 1829 or 1830, the first "approximately correct" map of the country between Green Bay and Galena. In January of 1829 a rough sketch was forwarded to Delegate A. E. Wing with a note that Lyon regretted not having sent it before "as formation of a new territory has been under consideration of the House."

This assignment in Wisconsin was the first surveying done in that part of the territory and was ordered to set the boundaries of some private land claims held by French fur traders, voyageurs and their descendants. The land had been granted to the claimants by the federal government in the early 1820s, but the boundaries had not been surveyed. Lyon's first stop was the 648 acre, wedge-shaped claim of Augustine Grigon, between the Fox and Wisconsin Rivers, near the portage. The majority of the private claims were at Prairie du Chien, near where the Wisconsin River empties into the Mississippi, in the southwest corner of what would later be the State of Wisconsin.

After completing his work at Prairie du Chien, Lyon met up with Morgan L. Martin, a lawyer he had first met in Detroit and renewed acquaintance with as he passed through Green Bay on his way to the prairie. The two decided to join forces for a tour through the lead mines of the Galena area. They proceeded by boat down the Mississippi on what Morgan later described as "a primitive sort of steamer. There were two vessels like Mackinaw boats, with a platform between and a shed built on that -- it was, in fact, a steam catamaran." This was the early days of steam in the west and the two boats that formed the catamaran may have been Mississippi keelboats; not Great Lakes Mackinaw vessels, both are widebeamed wooden vessels with points on both ends. The steam engine was located in the middle and the paddlewheel positioned to the rear of the platform, between the two boats that formed the hull.

After a stay in Galena itself, they continued on what Morgan called "a decidedly novel trip" through the mining region north of Galena. Most of the area they traveled through was located in what was officially Michigan Territory, north of the northern border of Illinois. Morgan wrote, "Our first objective point was Dodgeville, where Henry Dodge had started a diggings. We found his cabins surrounded by a formidable stockade and the miners liberally supplied with ammunition. The Winnebagoes had threatened to oust the little colony, and were displaying an ugly disposition. Dodge entertained us at his cabin, the walls of which were well covered with guns. He said that he had a man for every gun and would not leave the country unless the Indians were stronger than he. At Platteville was John H. Rountree, who, with his men, lived in tents. We did not see Rountree himself, at that time, but were much impressed with what was pointed out to us as his claim. There was a hole some twenty feet square and four or five deep, the bottom of which was a solid body of lead. There was a family at Blue Mounds living with Ebenezer Brigham; they were, with Brigham, the first settlers at the place. Brigham was not at home, but the man with a family was, and entertained us in his cabin, which was used as a hotel

41

when occasion required. We spread our blankets upon the bare ground, which was the floor of our hostelry, but slept quite as soundly as one might in the best chamber of a palace hotel. . . .

Chandler's 1829 map of a portion of the leadmine district.

"There were fully two thousand men in the country north of Galena, and we frequently came up with little groups of two or more, trudging painfully along with their bundles slung over their shoulders, or perhaps encamped by the wayside; while to come upon a couple of rough fellows sitting on a log or stone, playing old sledge for each other's last dollar, was no uncommon experience. We rode through the country with our horse and buggy, -- hired at Galena, -- with perfect ease and freedom, and met with no semblance of opposition from either white man or red."

On the trip Lyon and Morgan mapped settlements, mines, Indian villages, trails and other landmarks, and gave the notes to R. W. Chandler of Galena who, in 1829, published a map which served as a guide to hundreds of miners and settlers.

Lyon arrived back in Detroit near the end of October having traveled 2,400 miles via Michillimackinac, Green Bay, Prairie du Chien, St. Louis, Louisville, Cincinnati and Chillicothe, Ohio, then the location of the surveyor general's office where he would have gone to file his report and collect his pay. During his stop in St. Louis, he met William Clark, former governor of Missouri Territory, who was superintendent of Indian affairs for the region. Clark, with Meriwether Lewis had completed a historic exploratory trip from the Mississippi to the Pacific Ocean in 1805-7.

In a letter to his sister in July of 1828, Lyon had written that his plan was to return to Detroit but briefly in October, then leave for a three month surveying trip "to the western part of the peninsula of Michigan, near Lake Michigan." The new assignment was near the St. Joseph River, by the shores of Lake Michigan. In preparation for this task he wrote Tiffin in April of 1829 that "scarcity of provisions at St. Joseph's will make it necessary to take them from this place around the lakes by water (the roads being bad)." As if to emphasize the remoteness of his travels his letters carry exotic addresses, "Powatigen" (an early name for Niles), "Cogwatique" (near St. Joseph) and October 10, 1829, in a letter datelined, "Wilderness of the St. Joseph" he wrote, "'The groves were God's first temple' says Bryant, but temples do not often make the most desireable dwellings -- I know these please me not. However well I might like occasionally to visit them with horse and hounds and sounding horn (though by the by I am no nimrod) . . . I have been totally exiled from all society for the last three months with prospect of the like privations for six months to come. . ." He complained that he had grown "as thin as the ghost of a greyhound," and that his time in the woods had done little to turn his thoughts to religion, instead, "I begin to sigh for the flesh pots of Egypt, and now while feelings of manhood run high, if I were to meet a beautiful female in the sylvan shades, it is difficult to calculate precisely whether reason and religion would not bend before the besetting sin of the Israelites."

In 1829 Lyon also became involved in building a lighthouse at Fort Gratiot under contract to the government. The lighthouse was to replace an earlier structure that had been damaged by a storm in September of 1828 and caved in completely the following December before it could be repaired. The contract, awarded to Lyon in April of 1829, was for $4,445 for a brick lighthouse 25 feet in diameter, with a focal plane of 69 feet, and a dwelling for the keeper. George McDougall was the genial, portly keeper of the Fort Gratiot light from 1825 to 1842, working in both the old and new lighthouses although area histories point out that he seldom performed the lamplighting duties

43

personally because his portly figure was a tight squeeze on the cramped lighthouse staircase. Lyon would have met McDougall during the earlier surveys of the area and the two corresponded for many years, especially when Lyon was in Congress, when a pay raise for lighthouse keepers was a recurring theme.

Lyon had hoped that building the lighthouse would be a source of additional income for him, but by the time it was built there was little profit in it. While the work was underway he continued his surveying activities and was rarely on site, depending on the supervision of general agent, Jeremiah Moss, which added to the expense. Lyon kept track of things with frequent correspondence and personally recommended that Z. W. Bunce be hired to do the woodwork. The Fort Gratiot light stands at the foot of Lake Huron where boats enter the narrow swift-flowing St. Clair River on their way to Lake St. Clair, the Detroit River, and Lake Erie. The height of the lighthouse was increased to 86 feet in 1861, and it was automated in 1933. In 1991 it was still operating, the oldest functioning lighthouse on the Great Lakes.

The Fort Gratiot lighthouse, a detail from an early watercolor.

By a treaty with Congress completed in 1829 the resident Indians ceded much of the land that is now southern Wisconsin. With no surveying assignments to sustain him, Lyon went to Washington in April of 1830 with Lewis Cass on territorial business relating to the treaty. Lyon wrote John Johnson April 27 that he was headed for a survey on the upper Mississippi, "the whole, however, depends upon an appropriation by Congress, which is not yet made." The appropriation apparently received approval, and he was assigned the task of surveying the boundary between the ceded and unceded lands west of Lake Michigan and east of the Mississippi River.

Traveling the country by horse and wagon, as he and Martin had done in 1828, was something of a novelty to a Michigan surveyor more used to dense woods and swamps and he decided to try the method for long distance travel. A Galena, Illinois, newspaper, *The Mining Journal*, in its August 7, 1830 issued related: "Lucius Lyon, Esq., of Detroit, is now engaged under instruction from the secretary of war in surveying and marking the boundary between the ceded, and unceded lands west of Lake Michigan, and east of the Mississippi, agreeable to the stipulations of the Treaty of Prairie Du Chien, of 1829. . . Mr. Lyon and Mr. Kercheval arrived this place, in a light pleasure wagon, which we believe is the first that has ever come through from Detroit by way of Chicago and the branches of the Rock River. They met with but few and very slight obstructions; the country is all the way open, and will admit of one of the finest roads in America. The Distance from Detroit to this place is about 500 miles."

By now his brother, Orson, had joined him in the field to complete the steps that would give him full surveyor qualifications. They started the survey ten miles north of the cluster of cabins at Chicago and installed a six-inch square wood post at the lakeshore. Then the survey party continued northwest to the Rock River and on to Blue Mounds, east to Lake Mendota, and north to Portage. Their map shows all land from the survey line west to the Mississippi River, and south of the Fox and Wisconsin Rivers. Lyon added some of the features that he and Martin had mapped in the lead mine region and other features built by the Indians. The map was so complete, showing buildings and sometimes even garden plots, that it has been used by Indian scholars to reconstruct Indian life of the early 1800s.

When the work was completed, he went to Washington, via New York, and Baltimore, to settle accounts with the War Department, making his way through Ohio and Pennsylvania where, having no other work on the horizon, he stopped for several "public entertainments and private and parties." He wrote Lucretia, "The truth is I have had nothing to do, and have been so busy doing it . . . that I have never found leisure to write before." On his way back to Michigan he stopped in Troy, New

York, to pick up Douglass Houghton who had agreed to go to Detroit to teach and give lectures for the Lyceum Association. Lucius wrote his sister from Howard's Hotel in Troy, November 24, that ". . . my young professor has gone on before me; of which, by the way, I will not complain, for as he was poor I had been induced when I saw him four or five weeks ago to offer to bear all his expenses out of my own pocket." Houghton arrived in Detroit, according to traditional accounts, with one dime in his pocket.

Lyon spent most of 1831 in the woods of Allegan County on the western side of the Michigan peninsula, with a short trip to the Grand River area to survey a pre-emption claim for Louis Campau that would later be the subject of great controversy. The regular work, however, was delayed by cold weather and other factors. He lists a few of his troubles in a letter to the new surveyor general, Micajah T. Williams, a personal friend, dated Detroit, July 26, 1831: "Sir, at a time when I may, and ought to be expected to make complete returns of my survey, I am sorry to say I have only to reiterate apologies. When I last wrote, I had little doubt but I should be able to finish by the first of the present month, but the country where I was engaged was very thickly wooded, and when the leaves came out, and musquitoes and flies were constantly and incessantly annoying us every moment, day and night, I found it impossible to make but slow progress.

"The season has been wet; my men suffered so much with sore feet, that they were unable to go on more than every other day, and finally finding it impossible to keep them in the woods at any price, I was obliged to leave my work again unfinished and return; with the intention of resuming it in the fall, when it will take me about six weeks to complete it. . . ." He adds that his health has been very poor through the summer and that he will travel to Washington with Governor Cass "to consult some more able physician than this place affords."

Lyon and Cass arrived in Washington the first week in August, having made the trip from Detroit in seven and and half days, "the shortest passage ever made between the two places" he wrote John Johnson in Vermont. Cass had just been appointed Secretary of War, a position that also put him in charge of most Indian affairs, and he had hoped to give Lyon the job of surveying some boundaries. However, he learned, on arrival in Washington, that his predecessor had already assigned the task to another surveyor. Lyon wrote Johnson that Cass had told him "to proceed immediately in person to St. Louis and ascertain whether any thing had yet been done, and if not to countermand the order. . ." He added, "I have some warm and strong friends here who would assist me to any thing in their power in the way of office and I can now have my choice out of four clerkships in the departments, the

46

highest of which is $1500 salary, but I want no situation of the sort at all -- I had much rather be independent at home than dependent here."

No records remain indicating whether he made the trip to St. Louis, but Lyon returned to Allegan County and what would later be Ottawa County in 1831 and was engaged in running township and section lines. To enable others to do the section lines after he had completed the township borders he wrote in December of 1830 that he would leave notes on the variation of the needle from true north marked on one of the bearing trees on the corner of Section 35 and 36 of each township. In addition to the details of the survey work, many of Lyon's official notes to the surveyor general's office contain a lot of geological notations, history, and local gossip of the land being surveyed. When the survey of Otsego Township, in eastern Allegan County was completed in January of 1831, the following description was included:

> "The township of which the foregoing are the field-notes is a fine tract of land for a new settlement. Three families have already located themselves within it, and more are coming in the spring. So that before the close of next summer this township will probably contain thirty families.

> "Sections twenty-eight, thirty-one, and thirty-three contain some groves of valuable pine-timber, which is much needed in the oak-opening country to the south and east.

> "A Mr. Turner Aldrich is now erecting a saw-mill on Pine Creek, in the northwest quarter of section twenty-eight, and, it is understood, is designing to cut off most of the pine before the land comes into market. In this, however, the inhabitants about here feel an interest in preventing the waste of this timber, and hope he will be disappointed by the early sale of the land.

> "Mssrs. Sherwood & Scott are also making preparations to erect a saw-mill and grist-mill on Pine Creek, near its mouth, on section twenty-one.

> "There is also a mill-site on Gun River, in section twenty-four and the south part of section thirteen; and another good one on the Grand Rapids of the Kalamazoo River, in the west part of section twenty-three; and another in sections five and six, on a stream running southwest in the Kalamazoo River.

> "Water power is abundant. The soil of the land

47

is generally good, the surface rolling, and in some places hilly. The timber is beech, sugar-maple, oak, ash, lynn, black-walnut, with iron-wood, and in some places briars and vines. Everything considered, this township may well be designated first-rate.

"Of its geology and mineralogy little can be said. No rock appears in sight in the township, though in many places there are deep ravines and favorable places for observation. A deep stratus of earth covers the whole. But if an opinion may be formed from the configuration of the surface and the character of the pebbles seen, the underlying rock is probably calcareous sand-rock. No metals are found, but several springs indicate the existence of iron-ore."

Lyon returned to Allegan County, and completed the sectional lines in Salem Township in 1832. This was at least his third trip to Allegan County where he was well known among early settlers. The first settler in the county, William G. Butler, landed in 1829, near what would later be Saugatuck on Lake Michigan near the mouth of the Kalamazoo River, and several families arrived shortly afterwards on the western side of the county. Lucius Lyon spent so much time in the county in 1830 and 1831 that an 1889 history of the county lists him as an early settler, along with Giles Scott, Dr. Samuel Foster and Hull Sherwood, all of the Otsego area. During his stay Lucius may have accepted the hospitality of the Giles Scott family. The first white child born in Otsego, a son to the Giles Scott family in the winter of 1830-31, was named Lucius Scott.

At this point in his surveying career Lucius Lyon was working for a number of different government departments. The Indian boundaries were under the auspices of the Department of War which handled Indian affairs. The county and township lines were directed by the surveyor general's office which had the responsibility for preparing new lands for sale. He also occasionally did small plats for individuals. His next trip west added another kind of government task.

When Illinois had applied for statehood in 1818, the original bill fixed the northern boundary 10 miles north of the southernmost extremity of Lake Michigan at a latitude of 41 degrees 39 minutes. During the hearing on the statehood question Nathaniel Pope, then territorial delegate, appealed for a more generous portion of lakeshore and recommended a boundary 41 miles farther north. This change was approved and the admission of Illinois was passed with a northern boundary at the latitude 42 degrees 30 minutes. This change increased the area of Illinois by 8000 square miles and brought the site of the future City of Chicago within the state. At this time there was little doubt about the position of the northern boundary of the state (although Wisconsin would raise some questions when it anticipated statehood in 1842), but since the boundary had not actually been surveyed there was a good deal of speculation about exactly where this line was located in the rolling countryside of the lead mine district.

Setting the boundary became a major issue. In the February 13, 1830 issue of *The Miners' Journal* of Galena a writer grumbled, "More than one month of the present session of Congress has passed . . . and not a word on the subject of ascertaining and surveying the Northern Boundary of Illinois seems to have escaped the lips of either Senator or Representative from Illinois or elsewhere. Missouri can have her northern boundary determined, and why not Illinois?" The following week, "to afford some relief" the newspaper reported that D. R. Davis, "a gentleman of very respectible mathematical accomplishments," had run a portion of the line and that Governor Cass had directed the authorities of Michigan to respect the line "until something definitive shall be done by the Government."

The March 13 issue carried a copy of a bill that would ascertain "the true northern boundary lines of the states of Ohio and Illinois," with a provision that no compasses or magnets be used in surveying the line.

By 1831 the federal government had approved a survey of the northern boundary of Illinois and made Lucius Lyon a commissioner to perform the task. Since travel expenses and equipment purchases were the responsibility of the individual surveyor there was some effort by officials who assigned the contracts to see that each surveyor had sufficient work to pay his expenses. It was partially to this end that Elijah Hayward, commissioner of the General Land Office, wrote the surveyor general in August of 1831 that he would like also to give the running of the meridian line to Lucius Lyon of Michigan "in whose fidelity and capacity all confidence may be placed." He also advised Williams to give Lyon as many other townships to survey "as he is willing."

Thus in 1831 and 1832 Lyon was actually doing three tasks at once: The work on the northern boundary of Illinois, the northward extension of the meridian, and the township surveys. Since the Illinois boundary line was not to depend on compasses and magnets because of the fear that mineral deposits of the area would cause the needles to deviate from the magnetic north (the surveyors called it local attraction), it was important that the surveyors be able to get an accurate fix on the sun and stars, much as navigators do on the sea. Their instrument for this task was a solar compass being developed by William A. Burt who did much of the surveying work in Michigan.

To establish the location of the 4th meridian the surveyors first ran the line from its previously surveyed point at the Illinois rapids of the Mississippi north into Iowa. Then they recrossed the Mississippi into the State of Illinois, passed practically through Galena and extended it northward to about where they expected the meridian would intersect the northern boundary of Illinois.

The trip did not start well. The problems Lyon had encountered in western Michigan seemed trivial compared to those that now assailed him. On October 16, 1831, in a letter datelined "Foot of the Illinois Rapids, Lasselle Co., Ill." Lyon wrote Micajah T. Williams:

"Every thing has gone wrong with me since I left Cincinnati -- I was detained at Louisville five days for a Boat, and at St. Louis had to wait eight days for Col. McKee to make out instructions for the extension of the 3rd and 4th principal meridians, and when I was ready to start from there, there was no boat going up the River, and I was obliged to furnish my own conveyance by land. The rain had lately fallen in great quantities, and after swimming almost every little stream on the road, I arrived here about a week ago, and have since been diligently engaged in searching for my starting point on the 3rd meridian which I found yesterday. And now, on examination, I find that my compass had been so much damaged in crossing some of the Streams, that, before I can make much progress, I expect to have to send 150 miles to Galena, for another. . . ."

One of the problems with the Illinois boundary survey was that work could not be prosecuted unless both commissioners were present, Lucius Lyon representing the federal government and Michigan Territory, and Hiram Rountree, the commissioner appointed by the State of Illinois. Rountree did not like to go out in cold weather for fear that a storm would strand him in the field. Lyon wrote him several letters and finally succeeded in getting him out the first part of November only to be thwarted by rainy, cloudy weather. Finally the clouds parted and they had a brief work period. Lyon wrote in November, "this is the first day that we have been able to see the sun to make an observation for latitude, and, judging from the past, it is very doubtful whether we shall soon see it again."

By the first week in December he was able to report that they had "at length" determined the latitude on the banks of the Mississippi and had raised a stone monument marking the beginning of the line. The same day that he made his official report he wrote a private letter to Williams, apologizing for the slow progress on the surveys but explaining: "It is almost impossible to get Mr. Rountree to come out at all this season -- He is an excellent man, but having been brought up at the south, he is as afraid of winter as a Barn Swallow, and about as hard to keep in a cold climate. In truth, the prospect is not very cheering for the most hardy -- Even those who love to skate, ride in sleighs upon the ice, and hunt deer on snow shoes, begin to shiver and gather themselves into the warm places. . . ."

The northern boundary of Illinois also served as the baseline for the lands of Michigan Territory west of Lake Michigan, the area that would eventually be the State of Wisconsin. After Rountree left, Lyon continued his work on township lines and the extension of the meridian which did not depend on the sun. Even this work was interrupted in October by snow and cold weather that made travel difficult and froze the ground so solidly that mounds could not be constructed on the townline corners without the use of a pickax. Records show he returned to western Michigan and ran some township lines in Allegan County, finishing in January of 1832, then returned to Illinois in February.

Although the ground was still frozen the survey crew began the township lines in Wisconsin which would open that area to settlement, and continued the northward extension of the meridian. The Illinois border had by then been surveyed to a point about ten miles to the east where it crossed the meridian a few miles south of what would later be Hazel Green, and, at that point, on February 16, 1832, Lyon and his four-man crew began work at "Baseline, T1N, R1W, NW Ter." On March 28, 1832, Lyon wrote that he was in Collet's Grove, 10 miles north of Galena running township lines but could only chop holes in the frost with an ax to set posts at the corners "and leave them to be found and mounds raised around them when the earth should be thawed."

Finally, in April, full-scale survey work began, on May 23 the exterior lines of Township 1, range 1 were completed. This would later be designated Hazel Green Township, in the southeastern corner of Grant County. By then the Black Hawk War had begun, making it dangerous for white men wandering about alone or in small groups. The uprising was led by a Sauk warrior named Makabaimeshekiakiak or Black Sparrow Hawk, usually called Black Hawk. He had moved with his people from Rock River near the Mississippi, to the Missouri area. Faced with Sioux opposition and a shortage of food, part of the tribe had returned to the Rock River in 1832 to plant corn. The settlers saw this as a hostile move. Illinois called out the militia and the battle was on. The call was put out for troops in Illinois, Indiana, and on the peninsula of Michigan Territory. Things were especially tense in northern Illinois where the Indians had always resented the white man's seizure of the lead mines, previously a source of income for the tribes, and where a group of white miners, following a night of drinking, had abducted and abused a number of Indian women in 1827. The well-stocked and armed cabins housed farmers, families, and travelers who scurried in from the mines and the woods to a place of safety.

Edwin Jerome was working with a surveying crew led by John Mullett, at the time Lucius Lyon was surveying lands from the Illinois state line northward and adjoining the fourth principal meridian. Jerome wrote later, "Our work was founded on his, running east to the Indian boundary line at Sugar river. At each tier of townships, Mr. Lyon left a letter on the northeast corner post of the town, telling us of the progress of his work and the progress of the Indian war. The day after the memorable Stillman battle with Black Hawk we were crossing the Blue Mounds with a town line leading us near the residence of Mr. Brigham, meeting here an Indian half-chief who had just arrived from the Menominee camp with the details of the battle stating the slain to be three Indians and eleven whites. The long shaking of hands and the extreme cordiality of the Indian alarmed Mullett for our safety, but he locked the fact in his own bosom, and went nearly five miles east with our line and camped; the next morning we went two and a half miles south and brought up an unfinished line, and formed and built a mound for a town-corner.

"On completion of this mound, Mullett gave the first hint of his fears by raising himself to full height, saying, 'Boys, I am going in; I'll not risk my scalp for a few paltry shillings.' This laconic speech was a frightful electric spark to the whole company. My own sensation was as if every hair of my head instantly became a porcupine quill, raising my hat in air, myself from the ground, my head sore as a boil.

"The Indian trail from Galena to Fort Winnebago passed here, which Mullett instantly struck into on a dog trot, followed by his frightened men, seeing a foe in every imaginary sound or rustle of prairie grass, bounding involuntarily to right or left to avoid the rushing legions of Indians. . . . "

The terrified group of surveyors eventually reached Galena, where hundreds of miners had hurried for protection and were helping the residents construct a fort on the hill with blockhouses on two angles. Lyon, too, abandoned his part of the work. He wrote Micajah Williams from Galena in a letter dated, May 18, 1832, "The State boundary cannot be established now until the Indians have been humbled and compelled to sue for peace." Shortly afterwards he left for Washington with a letter from Lieutenant Colonel William Campbell of the 27th Regular Illinois Militia for President Andrew Jackson.

Black Hawk surrendered August 27, 1832, although the battle had moved from the lead mine district several weeks earlier. The

September 19. 1832 issue of *The Galenian* carried the news, "Lucius Lyon Esq., returned to Galena on Sunday evening last. He will remain in this neighborhood until the arrival of Hiram Rountree Esq. to complete the Northern boundary of the State of Illinois."

Galena preparing for the Black Hawk War. The Nicholas Dowling house, at right, still stands in downtown Galena.

At this point there was a futher delay because of a cholera epidemic that swept the area. Workers could not be hired at any price. The disease was a side effect of the Black Hawk War and spread quickly through gathered troops, settlers, and Indians. In a letter dated October 13, 1832, Lucius wrote Lucretia from Galena, "My health is better now than it has been in three years before. The atmosphere where the cholera rages and people die suddenly and rapidly, as is the case here now, seems to suit me best." Cholera was not the death sentence it had been in earlier days. Physicians had experienced considerable success treating it with calomel and opium when caught in the early stages. Lucius continued in the letter, "Strange that people will be so careless when first they feel the symptoms. An acquaintance and friend of mine, one of the richest and most influential men in this part of the State, has been ill for three days, but was visiting and doing business all the time. I was with him four hours ago doing business at his office. He sent for the physician two or three hours later for the first time and now, while I am writing, I hear he is dead! The doctor says he has had the cholera for three days, but its first stages were so mild and so little painful or troublesome that the patient himself was not at all aware of the danger of his situation."

The wait for Rountree extended into the first week of November when Lyon received a letter from Illinois governor John Reynolds that Rountree had resigned as commissioner because of ill health and been replaced by a Mr. Messenger. On November 3, 1832, Lyon wrote the governor: "The occurrence of the event that has caused the resignation of Mr. Roundtree I very much regret, both on his own account, and because as we had commenced, I had fondly hoped we should complete, the establishment of the boundary line together.

"In the appointment, however, of Mr. Messenger, the State has from his practical knowledge and reputed scientific acquirements, a sufficient guaranty for the correctness of the work . . . He is now with his party progressing eastwardly on the line, about twenty-five miles from this place. I left him yesterday and tomorrow shall return to continue with him through to Lake Michigan. Any communication that may be forwarded after this will probably reach us soonest if sent to Chicago.

"Mr. Braley has not yet arrived, but will probably overtake us in a few days and I hope now, notwithstanding the lateness of the season, we shall yet be able to complete the survey this fall."

Finally on January 23, 1833, under the heading: NORTHERN BOUNDARY, *The Galenian* was able to report, "This very desireable, and long wished for object, we are happy to be able to say, is at length accomplished. The commissioners, together with A. M. Braley, Esq., assistant astronomer, are now in Galena. We learn from the commissioners that the length of the line from the Mississippi river to Lake Michigan is 144 miles and strikes the lake 40 miles north of Chicago."

The surveyors had returned to Galena to make the report, and for a social respite. The frontier town, on the banks of the Fever River, was one of Lucius Lyon's favorite settlements. In May of 1833, when he had been in the area for more than 19 months, he wrote Lucretia, ". . . if my interest and what little property I have lay here I could be content, I think, to settle down here for life, though in doing so I should, according to your estimation, place myself beyond the pale of civilization. He had studied and enjoyed the society of the frontier but warned Lucretia, "Were you to come here, however, you would find yourself under mistake, as persons generally do who come from the old states. The people here, and of the new states generally, are people of the world. Many of them are and have been acquainted with the society of our eastern cities, and by mingling with society and persons from all parts of America and of the world, their views are consequently enlarged, while they lose in a great measure those local feelings and prejudices that characterize persons of narrow minds and a limited education. Such persons look with pity on the 'green horn' that comes on from the east, and whose whole knowledge having been gained from books alone, not infrequently seem to think themselves a superior order of beings." He acknowledges that the men of the district far outnumber the women and relates to Lucretia, tongue in cheek, a plan that he and a friend had devised "to collect from Connecticut and some of the old states a cargo of young ladies, a whole steamboat load, which he intends to dispose of here at a handsome advance on the original cost and charge of transportation."

Lyon could not have bought land in this area, except for village lots, if he had desired it and had had the means. Because of the lead and other metals in the area, much of the land around Galena was designated "mineral lands" and remained under federal control until 1847. In this system the land could be leased, but not sold. It was also part of the agreement that the lessee mine his land continuously, delivering ore at least once every month to a government designated smelter, who retained 10 percent of the finished product as the government's portion. A few years later, when "agricultural" land was available for purchase, Lyon was a big investor in lands in southern Wisconsin. According to the law, land could only be sold for agricultural purposes if there was no potential for mining the property, but there were no rules set down as to how the mining potential was to be determined. One ruse recorded in traditional history was to lead a blindfolded man over the acreage in question, and then get him to honestly declare that he had visited the land and seen no minerals.

Even after the Illinois line was completed Lyon remained in the Illinois-Wisconsin lead region for several months completing surveying work there. It was in mail picked up in Galena that he heard of his nomination as Territorial Delegate for Congress. In May he shouldered his surveying equipment and returned to Michigan for the turmoil of a political campaign.

5

Territorial Delegate to Congress

In 1819, in response to petitions from citizens of Michigan Territory for some federal representation, Congress passed a bill authorizing election of a non-voting delegate to the U. S. House of Representatives. All white males who had resided in the territory for one year prior to the date of the election and who had paid a territorial or county tax were eligible to vote.

In setting up this system Congress was not sticking strictly to the provisions of the Northwest Ordinance, which required a male population of 5,000 free adult males before the process of organization could begin. Instead they were apparently truly responding to the petitions of some of the people and to a series of letters that had appeared in a Detroit newspaper. In response to the same stimuli Territorial Governor Lewis Cass had put the possibility of a Territorial Council on the ballot in February of 1818. The measure had been soundly defeated, primarily because the settlers, especially the French-speaking population, felt it would be an unnecessary expense.

The first elected delegate to Congress from Michigan Territory was William Woodbridge of Detroit who was also secretary of the territory. He resigned as delegate in 1820 and Solomon Sibley was selected to succeed him and served until 1823. That year a bitter contest for the delegate seat was carried on between Austin E. Wing, sheriff of Monroe county; John Biddle, clerk of the land office in Detroit; and Father Gabriel Richard, a Roman Catholic priest from Detroit, who was one of the first professors of the University of Michigan and had founded the first newspaper in the Michigan Territory. Richard was finally the winner, the only priest to serve in Congress, where he was criticized by some for his humble dress and heavily accented English. In 1825 the same three candidates slugged it out and Wing was elected. In 1827, under similar circumstances, Wing won again. The following election Wing declined to run, and Biddle was sent to Washington. In 1831 Austin Wing was returned to office.

The 1830 federal census revealed that the total non-Indian population in the territory was 31,639. Of this number 27,378 resided in the area that would later become the State of Michigan. The area was inching toward the 60,000 residents needed to petition for statehood.

A number of political situations influenced the election held in

1833 to select a delegate to Congress. Party lines were shifting and the former Whig, Austin Wing, ran as a National Republican. A major political controversy nationwide was the opposition to secret societies, most notably the Masonic order. With Wing's feeling on this matter still uncertain to the majority of voters (the Whigs supported Masonry, the National Republicans did not), William Woodbridge was nominated as an Anti-Mason candidate. He was also supported by some old Whigs.

The Democratic Republican party held a convention in Ann Arbor on February 12 and the 46 delegates, all supporters of Andrew Jackson for the presidency, nominated Lucius Lyon as their candidate for territorial delegate. His residence at the time was given as Kalamazoo County making him the first west Michigan man elected to Congress, but he was well known in Detroit and in most other areas of the territory. The convention voted to make the nomination by ballot, without nominating speeches; the tally of the first ballot was Lucius Lyon, 25; Darius Comstock, 10; John P. Sheldon, 9; and Austin E. Wing, 2. The nomination was then made unanimous.

The remainder of the convention was spent presenting and voting on resolutions calling for immediate permanent organization of the Democratic party, decrying the "odious misrepresentations" of opponents relative to the policies of Andrew Jackson, and asking for a new territorial census. One resolution also recommended "with pleasure and confidence to our fellow citizens, Lucius Lyon as a sound and consistent democratic republican, possessing useful talents in an eminent degree, an integrity never yet questioned, and a minute and accurate knowledge of the Territory and its interests, which cannot fail to render him a valuable and efficient representative; and we solicit from our fellow citizens throughout the Territory a united and cheerful support for the democratic republication candidate for congress."

The candidate himself was off on a surveying trip in the western portion of the territory. It was mid-May, nearly three months after the convention, when Lyon called for his mail in Galena, Illinois, and received word of his nomination. He wrote his sister, May 24, 1833: "I am about completing my business here and shall leave this part of the country to return to Detroit in about three weeks. By some letters and papers received a few days ago from the peninsula, I learn that I have been nominated by a general territorial convention as a candidate for Delegate to Congress. You will see some notice of it in the last "Galenian" which I have forwarded to father. Whether I shall be elected is of course now very doubtful. All things, however, look tolerably fair at this time. The election will take place on the second Monday in July next."

*A young Lucius Lyon from a portrait done
about the time he was first elected to office.*

According to an 1888 biography, in 1832 the voters of the
territory, dissatisfied with Wing, began talk that "the office should at
that time above all other times be filled by one intimately acquainted
with every part of the territory, and that there was just one man in it
besides Gov. Cass, who had such acquaintance. This talk was duly
communicated to Mr. Lyon, but it caused no other action on his part
other than to say that he would be glad to receive the nomination if
offered him. Even after nomination he kept at his work in the field, only
doing such political work as came in his way without hindrance or
interruption to his business."

After Lyon's nomination the editor of *The Galenian* wrote in
the March 19 issue, "We heartily congratulate our democratic friends
and neighbors of Michigan Territory, on the nomination, by the
democratic territorial convention of our worthy friend, Col. Lucius Lyon.
. . . The circumstances under which the nomination was made, by the
delegation from the peninsula, while the nominee was traveling the
woods and prairies with his compass, and far from the place of meeting
of the convention, is evidence positive, of the high estimation in which

he is held by his fellow-citizens in the eastern section of the Territory; and must be truly gratifying to himself, and to his friends in the west."

Lyon probably did his candidacy no harm in the west by revealing that in the month of March, 1832, he had found a quantity of lead ore on the east bend of the Mississippi between the Platte and Gratiot Rivers in Iowa County, Michigan Territory (later the southwestern corner of Wisconsin). The Galena newspaper announced the find in the April 16, 1833, issue and continued, "The further examination of the locality of this discovery with a view to its extension was prevented by the Indian war and other circumstances until last winter. Miners feel it will prove to be one of the most valuable sections of the mineral region."

It is one of the legends connected with Lucius Lyon that his heavy vote in the lead mine district was the result of a party thrown by him for the miners and other voters of the district. Edwin Jerome wrote in his account, "Incidents of the Black Hawk War," that it was at Galena "the writer witnessed the levee given by the Hon. Lucius Lyon that secured his election to Congress by giving him the 600 votes of the lead mine district." The people of Galena were not eligible to vote in the election since they were south of the territorial border in the State of Illinois, but the settlement served as a gathering place for lead miners from the entire area. Other sources record the site of the fete as Mineral Point, just north of the Illinois line.

In the June 7, 1833, *Galenian* a long letter appears, datelined Mineral Point and signed "Iowa County":

"Who shall represent the Lead Mines in the next Congress? This question is one which should be asked and answered with great candor; for much, very much, concerning the prosperity of this country, depends entirely on the interest taken, and influence used by the Delegate in Congress. . . . Who will be most likely to interest himself in our favor? Can we expect it from those whose whole interest is a thousand miles from this, and who, *sneeringly* join with those who say that we residents of the mines are the cause of all the Indian disturbances, and hence deserve no credit for the achievements of the last summer's campaign?"

Several paragraphs later he concludes, "The interest of Mr. Lyon is identified with ours in the Territory west of Lake Michigan. He has been for some time past, a resident among us and intends, so soon as the lands are sold, to become a free-holder among us. He is already engaged in mining and so far, has proved himself to be a *digger* of the first order."

(According to a later communication the letter to the newspaper signed "Iowa County" was written by Lyon's friend and supporter Addison Phileo who reported in August that the diggers "nearly all went right" despite an individual who went to Mineral Point to electioneer against the "wormwart called Lyon.")

Back on "the peninsula" (the land that later became the Lower Peninsula of the State of Michigan) a fierce battle of words was raging. Lyon arrived in Detroit near the end of May, 1833, and, according to an item in the May 29 *Democratic Free Press*, was designated by the Secretary of War to accompany Captain Talcott of the Corps of Engineers "in performing the service required by the Act of Congress of the 14th July 1832, which act provides for the taking of certain astronomical observations preparatory to adjustment of the northern boundary of Ohio. The settlement of the boundary is a matter of deep interest to our whole territory and we are gratified that Mr. Lyon has been invited to attend to it." However, having determined that little could be done before he was due to leave for Washington, Lyon wrote August 17, 1833, resigning the task. Unable to secure the services of Lyon, Captain Andrew Talcott turned to Lieutenant Robert E. Lee, a 28-year-old graduate of West Point who had specialized in engineering, to do much of the actual survey work on the line. Lee was a close friend of Captain Talcott's and they were related by marriage. Lee's wife, Mary Anna Custis, and Talcott's wife, Harriet Hackley, were cousins. Lee was to rise to military prominence during the Mexican War and would later command the Army of Northern Virginia for the Confederacy during the American Civil War.

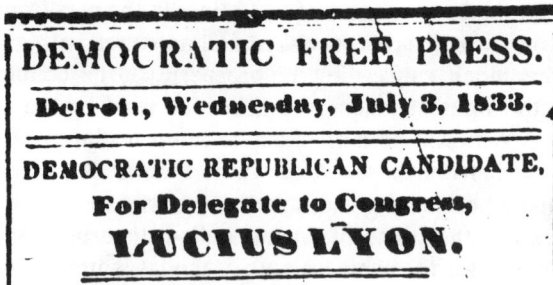

DEMOCRATIC FREE PRESS.

Detroit, Wednesday, July 3, 1833.

DEMOCRATIC REPUBLICAN CANDIDATE,
For Delegate to Congress,
LUCIUS LYON.

The Democratic Free Press supports its candidate.

While Lyon was in the west on business, the *Detroit Journal and Advertiser*, which supported Wing, ran a series of accusations, couched in the form of pointed questions and signed only by the pseudonym "Examiner." They implied irregularities in the sale of land in Kalamazoo

County, at Grand Rapids, and at Prairie Ronde (near Schoolcraft) that may well have had some truth to them. In some instances the questions related to activities that were not strictly illegal but showed Lyon taking advantage of his job as surveyor. Other points involved ethical questions that seem clear violations to the Twentieth Century observer but would not have been questioned under the less developed codes of the early 1800s. Just before the election Lyon wrote a letter which was printed in the newspaper responding to the accusations, but only in vague, general terms. He concluded his long letter with ". . . there is no act of my life, however unimportant it may have been, about which I would desire the least concealment, I hold myself in readiness at all times, to meet, fully and satisfactorily, all charges that may or can be made."

Some of his friends and persons identified in the published letter replied refuting with additional specifics some of the questions asked by the "Examiner." Both accusations and replies were published fully in the *Democratic Free Press*, but the entire incident was timed by the supporters of Wing to give the Democrats insufficient opportunity to respond. Still feeling uncertain about the outcome of the election the Wing supporters circulated a rumor that Lyon truly did not want the office, and, when he returned from his work in the west, would decline to run. The *Free Press*, in its June 26, 1833, issue, called the rumor "unqualifiedly *false*" and noted that it was started by "a gentleman from Monroe who now holds at least two lucrative offices under the government." This is probably a reference to A. E. Wing himself.

On the other side of the election the supporters of William Woodbridge, the anti-Mason candidate, emphasized the Masonic membership of Lyon in Vermont. The Democratic party declined to come out fiercely on either side of the Masonic question choosing instead to base their platform and choice of candidates on what they said were more important issues. They did however point out that Lyon had in the past supported anti-Masonic candidates and proposals. On the eve of the election, fearing inroads by the Wing organization, the Democrats sent runners to large population areas to whisper the "news" that Lyon was, indeed, anti-Mason.

The election was held July 8 and returns were received slowly. For some time after election day the results were uncertain. It was not until the first week in August that John P. Sheldon arrived with official returns from Iowa County. They gave Lyon 182 votes to 24 for Wing. In the final tally Lyon received 2,775 votes; A. E. Wing, 2,179 votes; and William Woodbridge, 1,803. There were five votes for Calvin Britain, and one each for William Welch, Henry Smith and Samuel Adair.

The *Schenectady Whig*, a newspaper of New York State, wrote:

"This result is highly gratifying as it was at this election that a regular organization of parties was had in that territory, and, if we mistake not, the first decided contest between those parties took place. The contest was a warm one, and has resulted in the triumph of democracy."

The *Cincinnati Republican* wrote: "We are delighted to learn that Lucius Lyon the Democratic candidate has been elected delegate to Congress by a handsome majority. Such intelligence is really refreshing this hot weather."

Michigan Territory as Lyon took office in 1833.

In September a letter from Clinton County politicians inviting him to a public dinner to celebrate his victory was published in the *Democratic Free Press* along with a reply that it would not be possible for him to attend because of a busy schedule, then added: "With the promise that my best exertions shall not be wanting in aid of what I conceive to be the interest of the Territory, you will permit me, gentlemen, to decline your kind invitation thus leaving it for time to determine whether, so far as relates to myself, the result of the late election is a subject for public gratulation or regret."

John P. Sheldon, former editor of the *Detroit Gazette*, who had done some friendly editorial doctoring to the reply above, penned a letter of advice to the new delegate: "I can well imagine that you are overwhelmed now-a-days with demonstrations, professions, and advice -- of the latter forgive me if I pour out a little upon you. Do not let your usual good nature forsake you upon any occasion -- hear every body out, and then let your best judgement direct you. I have no fear that the machinations and cunning of our political or personal foes can ever persuade you to adopt, or in any way countenance the 'buying-up of the opposition,' as it is called in a late Illinois paper. . . . Good nature and friendly, sociable and neighborly treatment is all that our opponents are entitled to expect from us as a party."

A friend, Samuel Williams, was even more graphic in his description of political rivalries. He wrote Lyon, as he prepared for his first session: "I suppose you will have some rare fun now and then by the warfare between the 'Scots and Picts.' Only I hope they will not serve each other as the two black snakes that some wag tells us about; which meeting in their travels, very naturally seized each other by the tail and commenced devouring each other, and finally had swallowed down each other, until there was nothing of either left."

Lucius Lyon took his seat in Washington as Delegate to Congress from Michigan Territory in December of 1833 at the age of 33. The House met at that time in the old House chamber, the area that would later become Statuary Hall. The central section of the Capitol, including the rotunda and the first dome, had just been completed in 1829 connecting the House and Senate chambers.

Andrew Jackson was inaugurated as president in 1829 at the age of 66, the first president from west of the Appalachian Mountains and he was, in general, supportive of the territories and young states in the west. He was especially fond of Stevens T. Mason who went to Michigan in 1830 when his father John T. Mason was appointed secretary of Michigan Territory under Territorial Governor Lewis Cass. Mason proved more enthusiastic about the work in Michigan than his sire, and he was named secretary of the territory when his father resigned and left for Mexico in the summer of 1831. When the territorial governor was out of town, and between appointments, the secretary was acting governor. This was often the case with young Mason, who served for a short time prior to the appointment of George B. Porter as governor in August of 1831, and for more than a year following Porter's death in 1834. Stevens T. Mason was just 19-years-old at the time of his appointment as secretary of the territory and is often referred to as Michigan's "boy governor."

Lucius Lyon's career as territorial delegate was marked by efforts to introduce legislation for internal improvements that would benefit the Territory of Michigan. On the national level it was a period when Congress was still exploring what improvement projects should be the province of the national government and which should be left to the states. In 1830 President Jackson had vetoed a road bill with the declaration that he was opposed to federal support of internal improvements that were not of national importance. As a territory Michigan was a special case. The officers of the territory were appointed

63

by the federal government, and, although the Territorial Council had some power on a strictly local basis, most of the important issues concerning the territory were decided by Congress where the citizens had only a non-voting delegate in the House, and no representation at all in the Senate. Though Lyon fought valiantly for a variety of projects, few were accomplished.

The U. S. Capitol building in 1833

In the 1833-4 session he tried introducing most of his chosen projects in a single resolution near the beginning of the Congressional year. On December 17, shortly after he was seated as a delegate, he introduced a motion to: consider a ship canal to connect the navigable waters of the River Raisin with Lake Erie; survey the flats of Lake St. Clair, and the mouth of the St. Clair River; build a pier at the mouth of the Clinton River; approve an appropriation for constructing a harbor at the mouth of the St. Joseph River on Lake Michigan; and appropriate monies to defray the expense of surveying the obstructions to navigation of the St. Joseph and Kalamazoo Rivers "as far up as the said streams may be considered navigable." The complex bill died in committee.

He tried shorter, one issue, proposals. In December he introduced a motion to inquire into the construction of certain proposed roads in Michigan Territory, especially one from Saginaw to Mackinac and on to Sault Ste. Marie. In February he made a request for an appropriation to pay for military service claims growing out of the Indian disturbances in the Territory in 1832; and also that month he presented a bill to establish certain postal routes. In March bills introduced including one asking for the grant of a township to establish a seminary in Oakland County, a post route through Adrian and other settlements that would intersect with the Chicago road at Hillsdale, and a petition for a road from Fort Gratiot to the Grand River and thence to intersect with the Detroit-Chicago road. Some of the proposals in his first bill were reintroduced as individual motions.

Harbor improvements and lighthouses on the Great Lakes were a major effort. A bill making appropriations of $16,000 for a survey of the harbor at the mouth of the St. Joseph River had passed both houses of Congress in an earlier session, but the appropriation for the Michigan harbor had been left off by a temporary clerk during the copying of the final law. In an effort to get the appropriation, which has previously been approved, in February of 1834, Lyon sent both the before and after versions of the bill to Joel B. Sutherland, Chairman of the Committee on Commerce, with the note: "It will be seen that he only copied the first page of the bill and never looked over to see what was on the next page; and by reference to the law as it passed, it will be seen that the title of the law is, 'An act for improving the Navigation of certain Rivers in the Territories of Florida and Michigan, and for Surveys,' and yet in the body of the act there is not a word said about Michigan at all. The loss of appropriation last year, it seems to me should give us a strong claim upon the liberality of your committee at the present."

He worked hard for lighthouses at the mouth of the Kalamazoo and Grand Rivers noting, "If Light Houses are not built there, such is the uniformity of the Shore of Lake Michigan at those points, that it will be (as it is now) impossible ever to find and get into a harbour there in the night time, however violent the storm may rage on the lake. The consequence must be that vessels and Steam Boats while waiting, during the night, will be in great danger of being driven on shore and dashed to pieces; This has been the melancholy fate of no less than three lake vessels in that vicinity within the last three years, and the wrecks have caused the loss of the lives of several of our most valuable and respectable citizens."

A continuing theme in the Congressional session of 1833-34 was the need to settle the question of the boundary of Ohio, to prepare for a new state, and to set up the remaining Michigan Territory as a separate territory with future plans for a statehood of its own. When Ohio had applied for admission to the Union in 1802, the boundary line between the proposed state and Michigan Territory had not been fully surveyed. According to the fifth article of the Ordinance of 1787 the line was to be established at the southernmost point of Lake Michigan and brought eastward until it intersected Lake Erie. Uncertain quite what this would include Ohio had written into their constitution a provision that if this line did not fall north of Maumee Bay, it could be slanted northeastward to include the mouth of the Maumee River, and the growing city of Toledo within the State of Ohio. Congress admitted Ohio to the Union, but did not formally approved alteration of the boundary. There were several surveys done during the next 30 years but none of the proposals received Congressional approval. When Michigan applied for admission to the Union the boundary question could no longer remain unsettled.

On March 6, 1834, Lyon presented a resolution to establish a separate territorial government west of Lake Michigan and to recognize the line established by the fifth article of the Ordinance of 1787 as the southern boundary of Michigan. To expedite debate the following month he presented a resolution to have the secretary of war send to the House the report of Captain Andrew Talcott on the observations made by him during the past season.

There were a number of factors, far beyond the control of those from Michigan Territory, which caused opposition in Congress to the idea of forming a State of Michigan or even of dividing the growing Michigan Territory into two administrative divisions. Lyon summed up some of the problems in a letter May 19, 1834, to his friend John P. Sheldon, former Detroit newspaper editor, who had recently been appointed to the land office in Dubuque:

"Your valued favor of the 23rd . . . had come in good time to be made use of in the Senate where an attempt will soon be made by Mr. Kane to get up the new Territory bill. . . . A majority in the Senate uniformly express the opinion that this bill is not at present necessary and that it will not pass. They are opposed to doing anything that will allow the President the least extension of patronage, in making appointments. I believe, however, when it comes to the test they will not dare to vote against the measure in sufficient numbers to defeat the bill, even though they may care to do so.

"I am at a loss to know whether the Senate will adopt Genl. Tiptons amendment to the bill reported for taking a census of the Territories of Michigan and Arkansas, so as to allow those Territories to go on and form constitutions and State Governments in the event of their being 60,000 inhabitants. It will be a bitter pill for the majority to swallow for, as they very plainly see, it will have the affect to bring into the Senate four new Senators who will probably be opposed to them in politics, yet those of the leaders . . . who are looking forward to higher stations than they now occupy will hardly dare to risk their popularity in those new States by opposing their admission -- I think the amendment will be carried and unless the bill for the admission of Michigan should be trammelled by some august provision relative to her southern boundary, it will probably pass both Houses. I however very much fear that the Senate will so trammel it."

In the Senate the bill was sent to the Judiciary Committee for a recommendation, largely on the question of whether Congress had the power to change the boundary lines that had been provided in the Northwest Ordinance. Lyon wrote William Woodbridge in May of 1834 that he had checked on the status of the bill and asked to address the committee concerning it, and noted little progress. But things changed suddenly. "I am now in hot water here on account of a decision against us on the boundary question by the Judiciary Committee of the Senate. That commission is composed of Mr. Clayton of Delaware, chairman, Mr. Bibb of Kentucky, Preston of South Carolina, Smith of Connecticut and Bell of New Hampshire and on Monday morning last the chairman rose in his place and reported that after careful examination of the subject and the different arguments and papers on both sides the committee were <u>unanimously</u> of the opinion that Congress has the power to establish the Northern Boundary of Ohio as proposed in her constitution, and that it is expedient to do so. . . . I happened to be in the Senate the moment when the report was made and thunderstruck to hear it, for nothing could be farther from my expectations." He adds that the boundary bill with the committee recommendation will probably pass the Senate, "but I am certain I can kill it in the House."

Lyon moaned to Sheldon after the committee recommendation was announced, "The committee do not say that the State of Ohio has the least claim to the tract of country which it is proposed to give her, but that it is <u>expedient</u> to fix the boundary as she asks it. The committee also say in their report that they 'have carefully examined the arguments and papers on both sides of the question,' when it is now well known that they never looked into a book, or a single document on the subject, but adopted a report which <u>Mr. Ewing wrote for them</u>, on a subject which not one of them knew any thing at all. I am completely disgusted with such proceedings on the part of a committee from whom I had certainly a right to expect an impartial examination of the subject, before they should report. I wish to God I could be permitted to speak for half an hour in the Senate. I would give them such a blowing up that they would repent of this in dust and ashes." Ewing was a senator from Ohio.

With the vote pending in the full Senate Lyon, unable to address the assembled senators, put up a last ditch written defense. In the Lyon Papers at the Clements Library in Ann Arbor there are several copies of a sort of form letter. The handwriting of the letter is Lyon's. The still-existing copies of the letter read: "The proposition to cut off a part of Michigan and attach it to the State of Ohio, is now urged with such zeal and perseverance in the Senate, and is a measure which, if carried, will do so great injustice to that Territory and to the State now about to be formed there, that I feel no apology is necessary from me for troubling you with the enclosed communication." The enclosed communication was a printed pamphlet, possibly with a copy of Talcott's map, which reiterated at length the legal and geographical circumstances surrounding the boundary dispute between Ohio and Michigan. In the pamphlet he wrote that he never thought the committee would "deem it expedient to take any thing from what will be the *small* and *weak* State of Michigan, to add to the *great* and *powerful* State of Ohio, unless the *legality* and *equity* of the claim shall be clearly and unequivocally made out. . . ." He pointed out that the proposed northern boundary of Ohio had not been adopted in any of the five times the proposal had been introduced to Congress beginning in 1802.

Stevens T. Mason

A copy of this pamphlet was included by Acting Governor Stevens T. Mason with his address to the Legislative Council, September

1, 1834. At the time Mason said: "I need not recur at this time the argument by which our right to our southern boundary, as claimed by Michigan, has been and may be incontestably maintained, but simply refer you to the able, unanswered and unanswerable views of our delegate to Congress last session, a copy of which is herewith transmitted to be spread upon your journals, there to remain whatever may be the final decision of the question, as an indelible record of the unrighteous and unwarrantable claim of Ohio."

Lyon was probably relieved to be able to communicate with the senators in written form. Though he was an eloquent writer, he was a reluctant public speaker. But he could speak out when necessary. His knowledge and understanding of the boundary question, along with his awareness of how important the question was to his constituents, brought him to his feet in the House, June 11, 1834, with a motion for a first reading on a bill that would fix the northern boundary line of Ohio at the line specified in the Fifth Article of the Ordinance of 1787.

According to the *Congressional Globe* William Allen of Ohio moved to postpone the bill until Thursday and make it a special order of the day. "Mr. Lyon objected to that motion saying he hoped the bill would take the regular course. Mr. Allen opposed at length a consideration of the bill at this time because he felt that passage of the bill at this session would be to the great injury of interests in Ohio.

"Mr. Lyon rose to reply but his remarks were overruled by the Chairman who announced the special order of the day: the Kentucky contested election."

The following day the debate warmed up. As the second item of the day Lyon made a motion to refer the bill settling the boundary between Ohio and Michigan to the Judiciary Committee. In remarks intended partially as an answer to Allen's speech of the day before, Lyon said that the boundary controversy had arisen in 1802 or 1803 when Ohio was admitted into the Union. It had frequently come before the House and its committees and the pretensions of Ohio had been uniformly disregarded. During the present session the subject had come before the Committee on Territories, which had reported against the claim of Ohio. It was impossible for the House to make the necessary investigation; but it should be referred to one of the standing committees for their report upon the law and facts.

Samuel Vinton, representative from Ohio, said that the arguments on the part of both Ohio and Michigan had been reported by the Committee on Territories three months ago. He added that he felt it was "highly important" that the subject be disposed of during this session noting that the location of a line of canals in progress in Ohio depended on a settlement of the controversy.

Others jumped into the fray. John Ewing of Indiana advocated the motion to commit "at length." Lewis Williams of North Carolina "contended that the House should postpone the bill to a day certain and make it the special order." Joseph Vance of Ohio proposed reference of the bill to a select committee composed of a member from each state and said it was "exceedingly important that the question be settled before Michigan was admitted." Amos Lane of Indiana said the internal improvements of Indiana and Ohio made immediate settlement necessary.

Lyon stated that he had no objection to a committee composed of one member from each state but felt that the committee would be rather large, and Ohio would have the advantage, as one of her members would be on the committee, and Michigan would have no representative because it was still a territory. Senator Vance countered with a proposal to omit Ohio from the select committee.

Roger L. Gamble of Georgia advocated the reference of the bill to a select committee as it involved "questions of considerable intricacy and importance" and Ratliff Boon of Indiana called for the order of the day which was -- the Kentucky Contested Election.

Two days later Lyon introduced, and his colleagues passed, a resolution to have the clerk of the House print maps of the area.

With a lull in the boundary question Lyon was free to speak on another bill which was one of his special interests. The motion would increase salaries paid to territorial judges. In March he had written Lewis Williams, chairman of the Committee on Territories, pointing out that the duties of the judges had increased. In the beginning they held a session once a year in Detroit and they were able to make their salaries pay the "necessary and actual expenses of living and supporting themselves." However, as the settled country pushed west, more work had been placed on them "such as to allow the judges no rest whatever." He recommended as a "reasonable allowance" about $1,800 annually. This proposal, with a modified pay scale which left most territorial judges earning about $1,500 annually, passed.

The same day a bill to aid in the construction of "certain roads in the Territory of Michigan" was also passed, despite the efforts of Speaker of the House James K. Polk to have it tabled.

One of the last acts of the 1833-34 session was to greatly increase the expanse of land administered by the government of Michigan Territory. The western boundaries were extended beyond the Mississippi River and north to the Canadian boundary. The states of Iowa, Minnesota, and portions of North and South Dakota were later formed from this territory.

As Lyon had predicted, the bill establishing the northern boundary of Ohio failed in the House. In the Senate the anti-Michigan forces had held full sway. He wrote John P. Sheldon just after Congressional adjournment, July 5, 1834:

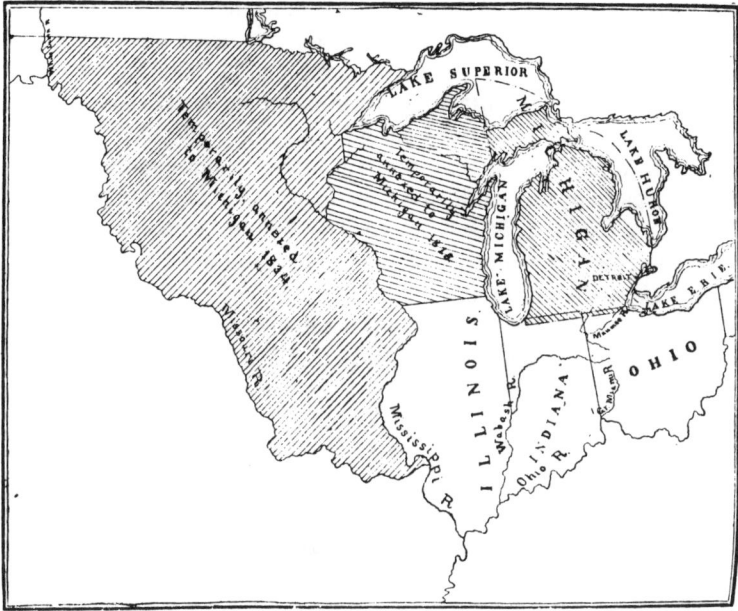

Michigan Territory in 1834

"The bill for authority of the people of the East Division of Michigan to form a constitution and State Government -- the bill for the establishment of a new Territory West of Lake Michigan, and the bill to provide for taking a census of the people of the East Division of Michigan were all laid on the table in the Senate by the efforts of Poindexter, Clay, Ewing and Calhoun, who were decidedly opposed to all these measures. They would not even allow us a census lest that should show that we are entitled to demand as a right what we can now only ask as a favor. . . . The only way for us to get either a State Government or a new Territory is to form the whole Territory East of the Mississippi into a state and demand admission into the union. . . . I am sure the council will feel disposed to take efficient measures in this matter if the Governor will but call them together, and I last night saw Gov. Cass who will today write him a private letter. If he does there is no danger of his hanging back for Gov. P[orter] would crawl any where to please him. . . ." Plans were complicated the day after the letter was written by the sudden death of Governor Porter in Michigan.

Lyon spent the summer shuttling about the territory, mostly in western Michigan, and as harvest season approached prepared to return to Washington. He wrote John Johnson in Vermont, September 15, 1834, "I look for a more tranquil session than the last one was, and for a firmer union and more unshaken confidence among the friends of the measures of the administration than was manifested last winter. . . . Michigan is now in an interesting position and we shall before long have politics enough of our own without minding much about our neighbor - - Our Legislative council has just adjourned after passing a law for taking a census next month and should we find that we have 60,000 inhabitants we shall probably proceed next summer to form a constitution and state Government with our southern boundary as defined in the Ordinance of Congress of 13 July 1787 -- This will bring us directly into conflict about boundaries with Indiana and Illinois [he means Ohio], and Congress will probably not admit us into the union without a good deal of difficulty. Should we be refused, we shall remain a sovereign and independent state out of the Union, and without any connexion whatever with the United States Government, any more than with Canada -- I look for a novel state of things in about 18 months."

No one expected the problems leading to statehood to be prolonged or difficult. President Jackson in attempting to replace Governor Porter, looked at a number of candidates including John H. Eaton, former secretary of war, who had recently been named Territorial Governor of Florida, but who wrote from the heat of a Florida summer that he would prefer the job in Michigan. Jackson declined to nominate Eaton for the post. He wrote Francis P. Blair that he was reluctant to bring Eaton's name before the Senate a second time in the same year and added, "I doubt whether it would be in his interest to be passed, for Michigan will be a state, in a year or so, and Florida will not. . . . "

On November 5, 1834, Jackson submitted the name of Henry D. Gilpin of Delaware to Congress for approval as Michigan Territorial Governor. The Senate launched a long investigation, focused on his activities as one of four federal bank directors. During this process Stevens T. Mason continued to serve as acting territorial governor. He wrote Lyon, in a letter dated, November 24, 1834, that he was anxious for the arrival of Governor Gilpin so that he could visit Washington. "I shall consider it a duty to remain long enough at home after his arrival to enable him to obtain all the necessary information connected with the Indian and executive department, and to see him on the right tack with the Legislative Council. . . . I think he need not fear the Senate. There is a point beyond which even that body dare not go. They have attempted to sacrifice him at the shrine of their idol, but should they reject him as Governor of Michigan, the very marble halls of their sanctuary will mourn the misguided policy of the chief priest of Mamon." The Senate rejected the appointment on February 2, 1835, in a close vote.

Lyon wrote President Jackson in February recommending that no further nomination be made "as the time is now near at hand, when the People of the eastern division of Michigan are to form for themselves a constitution and state government, under which they will elect their own governor as well as other officers. . . . Mr. Mason, the acting Governor, is deservedly popular and will, I believe, continue to have their confidence and support." Mason continued in the position until September of 1835 when he was replaced as territorial secretary and acting governor by John S. Horner, because of his inflammatory remarks and behavior during Michigan's fight for statehood. By then it was fairly clear that he would be elected governor of the new state.

Shortly after the Congressional session began Lyon received a brief note from Stevens T. Mason, dated December 5, 1834, that "a bill was reported on Monday calling a convention. You shall hear from me fully on this matter in a day or two." Later that month Mason wrote that the original bill he had mentioned had been thrown aside and that the Legislative Council elected instead to adopt one proposed by Judge James D. Doty, which "confines the selection of delegates to the peninsula of Michigan and extends the right of suffrage to all free male persons bona fide residents of the territory at the time of the election." He adds, "I think it will become a law."

Most of the session of 1834-35 was spent jockeying for position on the impending question of Michigan statehood. On December 12, Territorial Delegate Lyon addressed a letter to John M. Clayton, chairman of the Senate judiciary committee, "I beg leave that whenever it shall be taken up I may have the privilege of appearing personally before the committee to exhibit information which they have never received and which I trust will satisfy them of the injustice and inexpediency of legislating at all on this subject." Clayton responded the following week that the committee was prepared to hear testimony on the boundary on December 18. The letter added, "Notice will be given to some of the Ohio delegation to attend also."

They met on the appointed day, and according to a letter written later by S. F. Vinton, representative from Ohio: "I was deputed by the Ohio delegation to go before that committee and argue the question for Ohio. It was argued for Michigan by Mr. Lyon, who was a delegate for the territory. It was elaborately argued by both of us. When the argument was closed Mr. Preston [William Preston, senator from South

Carolina] inquired how much territory lay west of Lake Michigan. The answer was that the country had never been surveyed, but was supposed to contain more than a hundred thousand square miles. He remarked that the peninsula of Michigan was an unequal division of the remaining territory, and that the country west of the lake was too large for one state. He put his finger on a map, which hung before him, and drew it along the very line which now forms the boundary between Michigan and Wisconsin, and remarked that he thought that would be a fair division of the country.

"Mr. Lyon protested strongly against that suggestion. He said they did not wish to extend the state beyond the limits of the Lower Peninsula; that for a greater part of a year nature had separated the Upper and Lower Peninsulas by impassable barriers, and that there never could be any identity of interest or community of feeling between them."

The day after his appearance before the Senate judiciary committee Lyon wrote a letter to the *Free Press* enclosing a copy of the proceedings by which Tennessee in 1796 had joined the union and noting, "The case will furnish a strong precedent if we choose to follow it, but I think there is now a disposition manifested by Congress to do justice in all but the boundary question, at least. I fear the political influence of Ohio will be too strong for us."

The bill from the committee reached the floor of the Senate and on January 6 preparation for a third reading was ordered. Lyon petitioned the Senate, "Understanding that a 'bill to settle and establish the northern boundary of the State of Ohio,' in such manner as to cut off and give to that state a large tract of the best portion of the Territory of Michigan (together with a very important harbor at the west end of Lake Erie) has been reported and is now under consideration by your Honorable body, the undersigned, Delegate in Congress from said Territory, deeply impressed with a sense of the inexpediency and injustice of this measure, and feeling it his duty to use all the means in his power to oppose it, respectfully requests the privilege of appearing before your Honorable Body to make such statement of facts in relation to the subject as he humbly conceives, if correctly understood, must have an important bearing on the passage of the bill under consideration. It is with great diffidence that the undersigned submits this request, but he trusts that the importance of the subject, and the fact that his hundred thousand constituents are unrepresented in your Honorable Body, may be considered sufficient apology for so doing."

However, before any arrangements could be made, the bill was brought to the floor, this time for a third reading. Ether Shepley of

Maine, said that he believed "with regard to this bill many gentlemen were acting under erroneous impressions," and asked to give the Delegate from Michigan "an opportunity of laying before the Senate certain statements and facts relating to the subject." To do this it was necessary to suspend rule nineteen which, Shepley said, "forbids the admission upon the floor of any person interested in any discussion."

John C. Calhoun of South Carolina pointed out ominously, that such a suspension of rules required unanimous consent of the Senate, and William R. King of Alabama said that if that is the rule, then it had been "most flagrantly violated" in the past. George Poindexter of Mississippi said he was "disposed to extend as much indulgence as possible to the Delegate from Michigan. That the bill was one of great importance to his constituents." He moved to lay the bill aside to give the Delegate time to lay his views before the Senate "in writing, or otherwise."

The Ohio senator said he "did not object to hearing the Delegate but did strongly object to laying the bill on the table. He was opposed to any delay. The subject had been before the Senate for two years already." The motion by Shepley lost, and the bill which set the northern boundary of Ohio in favor of Ohio was read for a third time and passed.

Advice and opinions on the boundary issue flowed into Delegate Lyon's Washington mailbox from all quarters. Anthony McKey wrote him in December, "I can inform you that out of Toledo and its immediate vicinity there are but few, very few, individuals who do not anxiously desire to remain in Michigan. This I know by personal conversation with a great many. . . . " On the other side of the proposed state, L. J. Daniels, who resided at Schoolcraft for a while but had large interests in the west wrote, "The western part of the territory (Wisconsin) are deadly hostile to coming in with us. . ." He recommended a bill "setting off all west of Lake Michigan leave the Sault and Mackinaw attached. . . and let our constitution be formed without any action of Congress on the subject. In this way you will give universal satisfaction to the Wisconsin Territory, &c &c. . ."

A letter from Captain Talcott, who had made a special survey of the boundary line in 1834, settled the question as it related to actual land measurement. He stated that his survey discovered that a line from the southernmost point of Lake Michigan would not only be far south of Maumee Bay, but that "the result would seem to destroy all probability that a due east line from the south bend of Lake Michigan will intersect the boundary of the United States on Lake Erie."

Lyons introduced the usual bills for internal improvements including lighthouses at the mouths of the Detroit, Kalamazoo, and

Grand Rivers; a road from Fort Gratiot to Grand Rapids, and across Wisconsin; a bill establishing an Indian school on Mackinac Island; improvement of the harbor at St. Joseph, and a light house in the straits of Michilimackinac. But there were other bills that apparently had as an ulterior motive, the establishment or recognition by Congress of Michigan's jurisdiction over some of the territory claimed by Ohio. These include December 24, 1834, a bill giving authority to sell certain lands "at Toledo in Michigan Territory" which had been granted for the use of the University; on January 12, 1835, the establishment of a post route from Whitesford in the County of Monroe to South Bend, Indiana, and "from Toledo to Dundee, both in the County of Monroe in said Territory"; and on February 20, 1835, a railroad bill that dipped into the disputed area.

The railroad bill was a proposed amendment to one which had been sent to the house by the Committee on Territories and included a railroad in Florida Territory. As debate was beginning to escalate quickly, as it always did when matters pertaining to the boundary were brought up on the floor, Joseph M. White, Territorial Delegate from Florida, said that "he understood that the railroad in Michigan was connected with the disputed boundary question; he therefore hoped that the delegate would withdraw the amendment and attach it to one of his own bills; as it would be calculated to embarrass the bill in which his (Mr. W's) constituents were particularly interested."

Recognizing in White another non-voting territorial delegate crying in the wilderness Lyon replied that, "he could see no force in the objections of the Delegate from Florida. The boundary question had nothing to do with it. He understood that members from Ohio intended to resist the amendment because one end of the proposed road touched upon a tract of country claimed by the State of Ohio. He thought that an objection of that character was an illiberal one . . . but in order to avoid a long debate and according to a promise which he had made the Delegate from Florida, not to throw any embarrassment in the way of the passage of the bill, he would withdraw the amendment."

In early 1835 nominations were to be made for the territorial delegate election, and Lyon had apparently refused to allow his name to be entered. John S. Barry wrote him February 6, that he hoped that the rumors he had heard that Lyon would not run were not true, "though in pecuniary point of view it is probably in your interest to decline public office . . . still I think in the circumstances now existing in this territory, that the Democratic Party have a claim on you which, for slight, cause, you ought not to withhold." Lyon must have explained that by the time the territorial delegate was to take his seat in December of 1835, he expected that he would no longer be a resident of the territory, residing instead in a State of the Union.

The one bright note was from a House select committee appointed to consider the Ohio boundary bill. Lyon wrote Woodbridge on February 5, that they "have reported in our favor." He lists the members of the committee as "Messrs. J. Q. Adams, Horace Binney, Dickerson of New York, Thomas of Maryland, J. Y. Mason of Virginia, Bynum of North Carolina and Murphy of Alabama. All but Binney concurred."

One attempt to actually discuss the Ohio boundary question on the floor of the House on February 9 during debate of a bill to establish the Territory of Wisconsin had brought long intense debate and complicated parliamentary maneuvering. At that time the whole boundary question of Michigan Territory and the established states was compounded by the first of efforts by residents west of Lake Michigan (in the area that would eventually be Wisconsin) to get back from Illinois the land between the original line at the foot of Lake Michigan and the northern boundary at a latitude of 42 degrees 30 minutes which had been allowed Illinois when it gained statehood in 1818. The whole complicated boundary question was firmly referred back to committee where it languished until after the session adjourned March 3, 1835.

As the members of the House were preparing to leave for home, Lucius Lyon visited John Quincy Adams and thanked him for his support. Adams wrote afterwards in his diary:

> *March 18.* -- In the evening Mr. Lyon called, and spent an hour with me. The legislature of the State of Ohio have passed an act directing their Governor to take possession of the disputed territory by force; and the legislative council of Michigan have resolved to make resistance also by force. . . . He said I had been the only cause of the failure of the bill in the last House, and that the People in the Territory of Michigan were grateful to me for it.
>
> Yes, grateful. I know what that means. Never in my life have I taken in public controversies a part more suicidal to my own popularity than on the present occasion. The people of Ohio, Indiana, and Illinois will hate me with perfect hatred for crossing their interests. The people of Michigan, while the question is at issue, may pass cold resolutions of approbation or of thanks to me for espousing their cause, and then forget me. I

place in perpetual opposition to me, and to everything that I propose or support, twenty-nine members of the House and six of the Senate; and for all this and its consequences I have no compensation in prospect but the bare consciousness of having done my duty.

John Quincy Adams

6

Constitutional Convention

Having done what he could to pave the way for statehood Lucius Lyon rushed home from Washington to work on a constitution for the new state.

His official residence at this time was Bronson (later the City of Kalamazoo) and while still in Washington he had received an urgent letter from Thomas C. Sheldon, dated March 15, 1835, which read in part: "Not knowing but you might arrive at Detroit before I could get there, I have deemed it proper to state that your presence in this county previous to our Election is absolutely desirable, if not very necessary. The opposition held a meeting yesterday at Prairie Ronde for the purpose of nominating their candidates, as delegates to the convention. The delegates of the Democratic party of this county assembled here on the 9th Inst. agreeable to public notice, every town was strongly represented. Yourself, L. J. Daniels & Lovell Moor were nominated as the Democratic Candidates. Your particular friends Abm. Edwards Welsh (there is the Rub) -- Lovell, Belcher, Doct. Brown, Jim Smith Humphrey, & all their forces are up and doing. Poor Willard Van Dewarken & myself as also Mr. Ransom have to stand the blowing. We are called all sorts of hard names, all of which cannot I think affect the result. You unquestionably will be elected . . . They will I think find that the size of their caliber is all together too small on this occasion. . . Make tracks for Bronson by way of Gull Prairie thru Comstock, Bronson, P. Ronde &c, by so doing you will just exactly do what will be right and proper."

It would appear that Lyon did not leave Washington in time to get to Kalamazoo County before the election, but he was elected anyway. April 15, 1835, Sheldon wrote from Detroit, announcing that Lyon had been elected "by allmost an unanimous vote of Kalamazoo" as one of the delegates. William H. Welch and Hezekiah G. Wells of Schoolcraft were also elected from Kalamazoo County. Sheldon closed his letter, "I have just learnt that Governor Lucas has concluded to abandon his foolish project of taking possession of the disputed ground -- make haste home you are very much wanted."

Lyon received congratulations on his arrival home, from P. R. Toll of Centreville, who added, "I am highly pleased to see that we are to have such men to form for us a constitution, we want sir, a constitution that is truly Democratic and such an one can only be formed by Democratic republicans, who are so, not only in name, but in principle, having been thoroughly educated in the republican schools of <u>Jefferson</u> and <u>Jackson</u>." Just prior to the opening of the convention Lyon was invited to a public dinner. The 23 signers of the invitation wrote that they wanted to express, "the approbation of the manner in which you have discharged the important public duties recently confided to you."

Prior to leaving for Detroit Lyon had apparently written to former territorial governor Lewis Cass, who was Jackson's secretary of war, inviting him to participate in the writing of the new constitution. Cass replied from Washington, April 29, "As to any interference of mine in the proposed Constitution of Michigan, it appears to me it would only provoke invidious remarks, and lead to no useful result. . . ."

Michigan's Territorial Capitol at Detroit

The convention met in Detroit in the chambers of the Legislative Council in the Territorial Capitol which had been built in 1824. The library of the Council was ordered open for their use. The Council had already made provision that the convention expenses would be paid by a tax levied on the counties according to the assessed valuation of the property within the county. Some sources indicate that both Lucius Lyon and John McDonell of Wayne County had been offered the president's post of the convention and had declined to serve. The official journal of proceedings, published in 1835, shows only that John Biddle, a Whig from Detroit, was named president by resolution as the first order of business on the first day, May 11, 1835.

Harold M. Dorr, who collected and analyzed the proceedings of the convention a century later, wrote that he felt that "Lyon's influence was unsurpassed by that of any other delegate." Dorr continued, "Lyon's position of influence in the Democratic party is not at once under-standable." He notes that following his successful candidacy for Territorial Delegate in 1833, defeating Woodbridge and Wing, Lyon's leadership was well established and he was widely known and well liked throughout the central counties of the Territory. "Thrown into close relationship with [John] Norvell during the greater part of his political career, Lyon consistently refused to 'close' with him on any of his deals, and they were never on friendly terms. Norvell was ambitious to dominate the Democratic organization, but was frustrated by Lyon's influence with the conservative wing of the party. . . . " Dorr noted that Lyon, who never enjoyed public speaking, participated relatively little in the debates, but he rendered valuable services in committee meetings, and by advising less-informed delegates. "More important," Dorr con-cluded, "he matched Norvell in cunning and adroitness in directing the course of the proceedings."

At the first session Lyon was named, with John McDonell of Wayne County, Ross Wilkins of Lenawee County, Isaac Crary of Calhoun County and Randolph Manning of Oakland County, as a committee to report rules for governing the convention. They returned at 10 a.m. the following day with a list of rules which the convention accepted. The rules included a provision that the president would give the call to order "upon the appearance of a quorum," and that "No member shall be referred to by name in debate." Decorum was main-tained by a rule that stated, "While the president is putting a question, no member shall walk out of or across the house; nor when a member is speaking, shall any member be engaged in conversation." Most of the rules were borrowed from rules usually governing procedure in legislative bodies.

Further borrowing from the political scholarship of others was expedited on the second day when delegates passed a motion that 20 copies of the constitutions of the several states of the U. S. be obtained for their reference. The major part of the work of the convention was done in a series of committees selected to make recommendations for specific areas of the new constitution, and in special committees appointed to research specific questions. Lyon was appointed to the committee on the legislative issue and served as chairman. He also sat on the committee on expenditures, concerned with the cost of the convention.

It was partly a discussion of costs that caused one of the biggest controversies of the opening days -- whether to ask Detroit clergy to offer prayer at the beginning of each session. The debate dragged on for several weeks, according to newspaper reports, mostly on the point that a clergyman invited to give the prayer should be paid at the rate of $3 per prayer. A counter motion proposed the daily prayer, but with no provision as to who would make it. Eventually the question was dropped and the convention turned to the business at hand.

On May 19 Lyon offered a resolution that a committee of seven be appointed "to inquire into the expediency of changing the name of the proposed state of Michigan, to Huron." Ross Wilkins of Lenawee County, according to a newspaper account, was "decidedly opposed even to an inquiry upon the subject. Michigan had gained honors under that name, and he was unwilling to change it. He was as unwilling to change the name of Michigan as to change his party.

"Mr. Lyon replied that the gentleman was perhaps one of those who mistake names for things. For his part he was not one of that number. His feelings were as in favor of the name as much as those of any man. All he possessed, and whatever success had attended him, identified themselves with the name of Michigan. It was true she had gained honors under the name; but would those honors be taken away by adopting the name of Huron? It was a mere question of expediency. This was not the establishing of the ephemeral name of a day. It was to last for ages, he trusted, until time should be no longer. Many great states had been named from lakes and rivers in their vicinity, or within their borders. We were near the lake of that name, and we alone could properly adopt it. It had been proposed to call the territory about to be established west of Lake Michigan, by the name of Huron, which would be there entirely misapplied. It was therefore, at least a fair subject of inquiry, since we are immediately upon Lake Huron, whether it would not be expedient to prefer that name for the future state, and leave the name of Michigan for the territory." He went on to point out that Huron was much shorter than Michigan, "containing but five letters in its formation." As a final argument he added that the word Huron was "certainly to every ear who appreciates such matters more euphonious than the barbarous and cragged name of Michigan."

John Norvell of Detroit said that he was opposed to changing the name. He agreed with Wilkins "that the name of Michigan was associated with many precious recollections in the minds of the people of this peninsula. It had, in fact, become a classic name." However, he felt it would be useful to adopt the resolution of inquiry that Lyon had proposed because, "It might elicit much desirable information; it might shed interesting light upon the origin and history of Michigan." He also recommended choosing Lyon to be on the committee, as "No member was better qualified." The resolution was not approved.

The following day Jeremiah Riggs of Oakland County moved to reconsider the vote of the committee of inquiry about changing the name. The newspaper account related, "His object was to obtain information upon the subject which could not be otherwise obtained. Many would be gratified to hear the reasons which might exist in favor of the proposition. No delay or interference with other duties would happen from the inquiry, and he regretted that the vote had been so hastily passed over."

"Mr. Lyon said it was not a matter of course that the state would be called Michigan. It was necessary that a name should be adopted for the future state, whether that of Michigan or another. That the state does not necessarily take the name of the territory, it was only necessary to refer to the State of Alabama, which was formed from the Mississippi territory. The question is whether we, who are but about one third of the territory, shall adopt the name or leave it to the other two-thirds." But he added that his object had been gained in having called attention to the subject, and he was perfectly satisfied whatever disposition should be made of it. Wilkins said that he regretted that he had moved for the disposal of the subject so hastily, although he still strongly supported retaining the name of Michigan.

The resolution to appoint a committee to consider the change from Michigan to Huron was withdrawn, and then immediately reintroduced by William Woodbridge. This resolution passed and on May 21 Lyon, along with Riggs, Welch, Norvell, Elijah F. Cook and Samuel White of Oakland County, and Rufus Crossman of Washtenaw County were chosen to serve as a committee relative to the adoption of a name for the new state. There is no committee report included with official convention papers but the final version of the constitution states clearly that the new state was to be called Michigan.

Lyon also served on a committee to make recommendations for the design of a Great Seal for the new state. On June 21 they presented a drawing created by Lewis Cass, who had apparently considered the question for some time. A description of the device was read to the convention, and the drawing was left on the table for a day so delegates could examine it for themselves. The description read: "A shield shall be represented on which shall be exhibited a peninsula extending into a

Lake, with the sun rising, and man standing on the peninsula with a gun in his hand. On top of the shield will be the words TUEBOR and underneath in a scroll will be the words, SI QUAERIS PENINSULAM AMOENAM CIRCUMSPICE. There will be a supporter on each side of the shield, one of which will represent a Moose and the other an Elk. Over the whole, on a crest, will be the EAGLE of the UNITED STATES with the motto E PLURIBUS UNUM. Around will be the words GREAT SEAL OF THE STATE OF MICHIGAN A.D. MDCCCXXXV."

An 1837 rendering of the Great Seal of Michigan

("Tuebor" has been translated "I will defend." The longer Latin inscription means roughly, "If you seek a pleasant peninsula look around you." The seal has been in use by the state since that time and remains essentially the same although minor details vary as new versions are drawn. The date on the bottom has remained MDCCCXXXV, the year Michigan wrote the Constitution and applied for statehood, rather than MDCCCXXXVII, the year the State of Michigan was actually admitted to the Union.)

Probably remembering the rule against using names in debate, or considering Cass's expressed opinion to Lyon prior to the start of the convention that he did not wish to interfere, President Biddle told delegates, "A distinguished friend of the Territory" had presented the device which was proposed to the convention as the state seal. Ross Wilkins rose to move the question on the understanding that the person who had presented the design was Lewis Cass. The device was adopted and a resolution passed "that the president of this convention tender to the Hon. Lewis Cass the thanks of this convention . . . for the handsome state seal presented by him to the forthcoming state."

The question of locating the state capitol was delayed until a future date, and after a small skirmish for the honors of temporary capital it was decided to let it remain in Detroit utilizing the buildings that had been provided for the territorial government. The convention had rejected a proposal to outlaw imprisonment for debt after January, 1840, and another to bar members of the clergy from running for public office. William Woodbridge had also failed to get included a provision that would require candidates for governor to be at least 35 years old (which would bar Mason from the office for several years). The delegates anticipated the coming women's movement by several decades on May 30 when during a debate on a Bill of Rights article they voted to change, "Every man has a right to worship Almighty God according to the dictates of his own conscience," to every "person."

On May 20 the convention, by a rousing 81-0 vote, passed an article that stated: "Neither slavery nor involuntary servitude shall ever be introduced into this state, except for the punishment of crimes of which the party has been duly convicted." It was one of the provisions of the Northwest Ordinance that slavery not be allowed in states formed from the territory, but apparently convention delegates wanted to make their feelings clear.

They had a much more difficult time deciding just who would be entitled to vote in the new state. In the voting for constitutional convention delegates the electors were required to be free white males at least 21 years old who had lived in the territory three months or more. The electors did not have to be citizens, but the delegates they selected did. McDonell made a motion that white males over 21 be allowed to vote in the new state and the question was immediately asked whether this also disenfranchised Indians and half-breeds. McDonell replied, "The word white was used in contradistinction to the black alone, and though the Indian was copper-colored, he was not to be classed among the latter."

Norvell, with some sarcasm, suggested that Indians should be allowed to vote without taxation or restriction, a move that would at least show consistency. According to the newspaper, Lucius Lyon said "he was certainly in favor of such a modification. In all general elections it make the popular vote of Kalamazoo County of consequence."

Lyon, according to a letter he wrote in December to a friend in New Orleans, was among those who sought to require citizenship for the electors. He pointed out, "The whole subject, so far as the elective franchise goes, is completely within the control of the states, and needs no action of Congress. Congress has no right to interfere in any manner whatever with the states in saying who may and who may not vote.

Giving a man the right of voting does not make him a citizen, nor does the fact of his being a citizen entitle him to a vote. If so, negroes and women and boys would have the right."

In the end it was decided that the right to vote would be restricted to white male citizens over 21 who had lived in the state six months, and white males over 21 who were residents of Michigan at the time of the signing of the Constitution.

This was one of the specific compromises that the *Michigan Sentinel*, published in Monroe, mentioned in its June 20, 1835, issue with special congratulations for the work done during the convention. The paper said:

"This arrangement has been brought about by a mutual interchange of sentiment among brethren of the same principle -- and by means of a creditable and honorable concession to some extent, of the *majority* to the views of the *minority* for which the latter have every reason to be thankful. Much credit is due to several gentlemen for the manly and conciliatory measures resorted to in bringing the matter to a favorable issue -- among the rest, I may be permitted to name (in addition to your own delegation) Messrs. Lyon and Welch (of Kalamazoo), Wilkins (of Lenawee), Briggs, Moore and Mundy (of Washtenaw) McDonell and Ten Eych (of Wayne), Cook (of Oakland) and several others of the delegations from the western and northern counties."

Delegates on June 23 had rejected a section that stated: "All officers, executive, legislative, and judicial, holding their offices and appointments in this territory by virtue of acts of Congress of the United States have a right under the authority of the United States to continue the exercise of their respective official function until the admission of this state into the Union, and until superseded under this Constitution." The vote was 4-59 with only Woodbridge, David White of Monroe, James Odell of Cass and Louis Beaufait of Wayne County voting in the affirmative.

According to Article 12 as finally adopted, the first election was to be held on the first Monday in October, and on Tuesday, the following day. At the same time the new constitution would be voted on by having voters write "yes" or "no" on the ballots. If the constitution was ratified, the first meeting of the Legislature was to be in Detroit on the first Monday in November, 1835.

As business wound down there was a lively debate concerning how many copies of the new constitution should be printed and in what languages. The first proposal was 800 copies in English and 200 in French. Another proposal introduced by a Washtenaw County delegate recommended 3,500 in English, 1,000 in French and 500 in German. In the end, primarily because of budgetary limitations, the Michigan Constitution was printed only in English.

The final vote was taken June 24 and the new constitution was adopted 75-2 with only Townsend E. Gidley of Jackson and William Woodbridge voting no. One of the last resolutions of the convention was approval of a proposal to have rooms in the territorial capitol set up for accommodation of the Senate and House of Representatives of the new state.

The original copy of Michigan's first Constitution
after its rediscovery in 1915.

The first constitution of Michigan has been hailed by many as its best. It is a short document with a brief preamble which has echoes of the Declaration of Independence and states, "The time has arrived when our present political condition ought to cease and the right of self government asserted. . . ." There are 13 articles. Article One, largely a Bill of Rights, began with the statement that "All political power is inherent in the people." The original document which was signed by delegates, was lost for many years although the pen they had used to sign the paper was placed in the cornerstone of the new capitol in Lansing. In 1915 Mrs. Caroline P. Campbell was given permission to search the archives for it, and discovered the paper, ragged and much-worn, in a tin tube in the vault. It was restored and bound for preservation.

Stevens T. Mason, as secretary and acting governor of the territory, a federally appointed official, was not a delegate to the convention, and made no official addresses, but he sat in on most sessions and did some manipulating behind the scenes. He was nominated during the summer as the Democratic candidate for governor of the new state. On September 10, several weeks before the scheduled election, Mason received a letter from Washington signed by Secretary of State John Forsyth, dismissing him as a territorial official for failing to preserve "the spirit of moderation and forbearance." This action was based mainly on Mason's activities during the brief armed, but nearly bloodless, conflict as both Ohio and Michigan sought to exert political control of the strip of land that both claimed near Toledo. John S. Horner was named secretary and acting governor and arrived in Detroit September 19. He was alternately harassed and ignored.

The people of Michigan went to the polls October 5 and 6, 1835, and voted 6,299 to 1,359 to accept the new constitution. Even before all of the statewide vote was tallied, they voted again for governor, lieutenant governor, state representatives, state senators, and a single member to represent them in the U. S. House of Representatives.

Shortly after the constitutional convention adjourned Lyon left for western Michigan to look after business interests in Schoolcraft, Kalamazoo, and Grand Rapids. He wrote his sister, Lucretia, October 9, 1835, in a letter from Bronson (Kalamazoo) "Within a week or two I shall make a journey to Detroit and remain there until after the meeting of the first State Legislature on the first Monday of next month, when two Senators are to be chosen to represent the State of Michigan in the Congress of the United States. From all appearances now my prospect is fair for one of these seats, which is as high as I can ever hope to attain, for there is no higher office in the United States excepting that of President."

The possibility of being elected to the Senate could not have been a total surprise for Lyon. In May, shortly after he had completed his term as territorial delegate, he received a letter from J. Jay Langdon who wrote from Washington, "I am happy to hear of your election as a member of your convention and shall be more so this winter to see you transferred to the other end of the capitol."

He had another supporter in Washington. Mrs. Josiah F. Polk, who ran a boarding house often frequented by federal office holders, wrote prophetically, November 4, 1835, "I saw Mr. Rice the other day who says you will not be a delegate any more but will most probably be appointed by the Michigan Legislature to the Senate of the United States. This is what I have been hoping for and I shall rejoice to see -- but I fear you will find difficulty in getting a seat for a session or two."

In his inaugural address Governor Stevens T. Mason, upheld Michigan's right to form a state government but recommended that the Legislature pass few laws until statehood was approved by Congress. The first Michigan Legislature convened on November 2, 1835, in Detroit, and, following the recommendation of the governor, passed on only seven proposals in its first session. The acts were mostly involved in fiscal matters and organization, but on November 10 the State Senate nominated Lucius Lyon and John Biddle as U. S. Senators. Lyon was elected to one Senate seat with enthusiasm but the House rejected Biddle, a Whig who had received the second highest vote for Governor. Unable to agree, the two houses of the Legislature met in joint session. Lyon related later to H. D. Gilpin, "John Norvell Esq. was elected in joint meeting of the houses by a majority of seven votes over Maj. John Biddle. There were but three persons voted for. The Democratic Party were divided between Mr. Norvell and Maj. Biddle and the contest between the friends of Mr. Norvell and those who were opposed to him has been exceedingly violent -- so much so that I fear the bitterness of feeling engendered between them will remain and divide the party. Gov. Horner is here and would maintain the Territorial Government in opposition to that of the State if he could find any body to accept office under that tenure. As it is, he is wholly without power . . . Nobody blames him for he acts in obedience to instructions from the State Department. We are all desirous to avoid trouble and for that reason though we believe we have a right to self government, and though we have a government of our own fully organized and ready for action, we yet mean to wait patiently and do as little as possible until we see what Congress will do."

Following selection of the two senators the Legislature then adjourned until February 1, 1836, in the hopes that Michigan would be a state of the Union by then. With barely time to pack their bags Lyon and Norvell (postmaster of Detroit who left, but did not resign, his appointment) were off to Washington to be there when Congress was scheduled to convene on December 7.

7

Senator from Michigan

The new senator sprang quickly into action. Even before leaving Detroit he penned a letter to Amos Kendall, postmaster general, recommending Sheldon McKnight to take the place of Norvell in the Detroit post office; to S. R. Hobbie, assistant postmaster general, enclosing a proposal for establishment of a private mail route from White Pigeon to Constantine and a post office at Constantine; and a note to the Young Men's Society of Detroit thanking them for the "evidence of regard" shown by his nomination as an honorary member of that organization.

From Detroit on November 15 he wrote to Edwin Crosswill at Albany, "I shall leave here in a few days for Washington City. I have the pleasure to inform you that I have been elected, by the unanimous vote of both houses of the legislature, now convened in this place, to a seat in the Senate of the United States whenever Michigan may be admitted into the Union. . . . I hope it is not true, as reported here, that New York is going against our proceedings in forming a State government and against the admission of Michigan into the Union. Such a course would most effectually break up the Democratic party here, and besides would do us the greatest injustice as a people entitled to the rights of self government. Michigan has petitioned year after year for the passage of an act authorizing her to form a State government, a request always heretofore granted the new states whenever asked by them, and long before they had as great a population as Michigan has had for the last three years. At length, finding that by her census taken last year, a considerable excess over the number necessary according to the fifth article of the compact contained in the Ordinance of 1787, which guarantees her the right in the most solemn manner, she has proceeded as did the state of Tennessee, by the spontaneous action and voice of her whole people carefully to form for herself a constitution and State government and she now asks, by every consideration of legal as well as moral right, to be recognized by Congress as one of the twenty-four states of the Union."

Following the adjournment of the State Legislature Lyon wrote from Detroit to H. D. Gilpin who had been rejected as territorial governor in February, in a letter dated November 16, 1835: "The Legislature will convene the first Monday in February, by which they

90

expect Congress will have acted on the admission of the State and also the question of boundary -- What the decision will be on the latter I am at loss to form an opinion -- I hope Michigan will not be sacrificed to political considerations connected with the election of the president, but from what I hear, I fear this will be the case. If so there will be serious work here whenever Ohio shall attempt to take possession of the county. The Wolverines as we are sometimes called, will be slow to give up the territory in dispute until there shall be a judicial decision against them."

Lyon arrived in Washington Sunday, November 29, 1835, after "a fatiguing journey of eight days." One of his first acts was to write a confidential letter to John Horner, secretary and acting governor of the territory. Lyon wrote that he had delivered some personal letters Horner had entrusted to him and then met with Secretary of War Lewis Cass and President Jackson, "Both the President and the Secretary of War supposed that you had gone to Green Bay to meet the legislative council. I told the latter that it was your intention to have done so, but he would perceive it was a case of some difficulty for you to decide on in the absence of all instruction or even an intimation from the state department on the subject. On the one hand, the law of Congress made Detroit the seat of government for the Territory of Michigan and required the residence of the Governor to be there, and on the other, the . . . Legislative Council had passed a law which was approved by your predecessor providing for the next meeting of their body at Green Bay. Under these circumstances it was very desirable that you should have received intimation of the course to pursue, but as none was given you felt inclined to comply with the provision of the council and go to Green Bay if you could do so without being accused of deserting your post at the seat of government and thereby subject the administration to censure. Indeed, I said, I believed you would have gone in any event had not some person here wrote to you that the President would expect you to remain at Detroit. To this he replied that 'Whoever wrote so wrote a falsehood' and added, 'it was impossible for the government to notice at all any inchoate proceedings of this sort, and that you were purposely left to act as circumstances might render proper.' He however, seemed satisfied with the course you had adopted and remarked that you had nothing to do but remain as quiet as possible and await the action of Congress on the admission of Michigan as a state, which he said he thought would take place in about two or three weeks after the commencement of the session."

Lyon added that President Jackson had said he was waiting for the official copy of the constitution together with the census and law providing for the convention, and that when they were received he would transmit them to both houses with a special message similar to the one sent by President George Washington in the case of Tennessee in 1796. "Everybody here thinks that nothing but our Ohio boundary difficulty and the provision in our constitution which will conflict with the boundary of Indiana can prevent the immediate admission of the State into the Union. I can judge better on this subject when I shall have seen the members who are now fast coming in. My own impression is that we shall not get our seats before February."

On December 6 Lyon wrote E. D. Ellis of Monroe, "I find the members of Congress as well as the cabinet as favorably disposed toward the admission of Michigan into the Union as could be expected. It will probably be made a party question but I think the State will be recognized as early as February. Ex-President Adams and John Y. Mason will take charge of the matter in the House of Representatives, and Messrs. Benton, Grundy and Wright in the Senate. You need have no fear that we shall be sent back and the people required to make the constitution over again. Nobody here thinks of such a thing."

On December 9, President Andrew Jackson sent a message to Congress in which he stated the facts of the boundary dispute, outlined the precedent of Tennessee which had formed its state government prior to admission to the Union without an enabling act of Congress, and said that the decision was to be left to Congress. On December 10, Senator Thomas Hart Benton of Missouri presented the credentials of Senators Lyon and Norvell and moved that seats be given them on the floor of the Senate until Congress could act on admission of Michigan to the Union. The motion was tabled while a select committee of five considered the request.

Six days later Benton moved again "to extend the courtesy of the Senate to the gentlemen elected as Senators from Michigan, so far as to assign them seats on the floor. . . ."

Senator Henry Clay of South Carolina opposed the motion with thunderous rhetoric. As the reporter from the *Congressional Globe* reported the speech: "Mr. Clay, for one, was not prepared to vote for this resolution. For what purpose (asked he) were they to put those gentlemen on the floor. Not, he presumed, to take a part in the proceedings of that body; not for the purpose of voting with them -- certainly not. Why, then, (asked he,) are we to admit them, and if admitted, to what extent would be their rights on that floor? . . . He was opposed to admitting them on the floor on principle, till it was decided that Michigan should be admitted into the Union. But it had been asked to admit those gentlemen as an act of courtesy only. What courtesy? Because they were Senators from Michigan? We could not do otherwise (said Mr. C.) admit these gentlemen on the ground of courtesy, than we could admit any other gentlemen. . . . He was opposed to the resolution, because it would, in some measure, admit them as Senators by implication, and thus commit the Senate."

State of Michigan } S.S.

This shall certify to all whom it may concern, that at an election held by the Legislature of the State of Michigan on the 10th day of November A.D. 1835, Lucius Lyon, was duly chosen a Senator, to represent said State in the Congress of the United States. In testimony whereof I have hereunto set my hand, and affixed the Great seal of the State, this 18th day of November in the year of our Lord one thousand eight hundred and thirty five.

By the Governor of the State:

Stevens T. Mason.

A reduced facsimile of Lyon's senatorial credentials.

Senator Benton replied that it was simply a question of what was decent and proper. As the *Globe* reporter recorded his remarks,

"When a gentleman brought a letter to him from a respectable source, he at least asked him to take a seat until he read it; and here (said he) these gentlemen have brought a letter from a State, *de facto*, signed by a high official functionary, and we are to hesitate before we extend to them an act of common courtesy!" He said that giving them a seat on the Senate floor did not commit the Senate, and pointed out that when his own state, Missouri, was admitted, the senators had been sent back after having had seats assigned to them. It was suggested by an Alabama senator, that Lyon and Norvell be seated outside of the bar. The motion to seat them was then laid on the table.

The two pieces of paper which Lyon and Norvell took to Washington are not designed to impress. Both still exist in the State Archives of Michigan. Lyon's is written on a standard-sized piece of rough paper by Stevens T. Mason himself using his "executive" script. He had a beautiful, copper-plate handwriting when serving as clerk for another official, but his executive handwriting was bolder, with more character. On the left of the paper was impressed the official seal of the State of Michigan, hastily cast following the Constitutional Convention. On the back are two notes, separated by a double line. The handwriting on the first might be Lyon's. The notes beneath the line were added later, and are in a different hand (perhaps two different hands):

24 Cong?
1 Sess.}

Credential

of Hon. Lucius Lyon

_____

1835 Dec.r 11 – read
1837 Jan. 26 rec.d &
took Seat

Norvell's credential, written five days earlier, is on a legal-sized piece of paper written in a fancier script by K. Pritchette, secretary of state. It was signed by Stevens T. Mason and there is a large blob of wax on the left hand side, but no evidence that there was ever an attempt to affix a seal to it. One slight difference of wording in Norvell's credential is that the words "in the year of our Lord one thousand eight hundred and thirty five" are followed by "and the Independence of the United States the Sixtieth." The back of Norvell's paper bears the same words, in the same script as Lyon's, substituting his name in the top line.

On December 22 Benton asked leave to change the wording of his motion and submitted, "That Mr. Lyon and Mr. Norvell, who claim to be Senators of the United States, be received as spectators and that chairs be provided for that purpose on the floor of the Senate, until the final decision of the Senate shall be given on the application to admit Michigan into the Union." He said that this was similar to the motion that had been adopted when the senators from Tennessee were seated prior to that state's admission to the Union.

Senator Thomas Ewing of Ohio pointed out that Mr. Lyon, "on account of being a Delegate to the other House," was entitled to the privileges of members of that branch of Congress. He also had no objections to admitting Mr. Norvell as a spectator to take a seat on the benches in the gallery.

Senator William Hendricks of Indiana said he always regretted an appeal to his liberality of comity for anything he could not grant. "What is the case? A man comes into my house; he tells me that he has come for the purpose of appropriating to himself a part of my house, or of despoiling me of a portion of my goods, and that he has means in train by which he will, in his opinion, speedily accomplish these objects; but inasmuch as it will be more convenient to him to attend to this work of spoilation within the house than out of doors, he asks that, through comity, I would assign him a seat, and permit him to remain until he can finish his work. . . . He had but one course to take and that was to resist the admission of Michigan as a State of this Union at every step, until she expunged from her constitution her unfounded claim upon the territory of Indiana."

After several hours of speeches on both sides, the would-be senators from Michigan were allowed seats outside of the official Senate area.

Lyon wrote C. K. Green, December 27, 1835, "I need not write you about our prospects as a State. You will see by the debates that they are not very flattering. The including a portion of Indiana within our limits, I fear, will lose us the disputed tract between Michigan and Ohio. Had we bounded our state on the south by Ohio and Indiana without saying where that boundary should be fixed all would have been well; as it is, two to one, we lose all."

In some ways the two senators and the representative from Michigan were able to function in a nearly normal manner. They were allowed Congressional franking privileges, could investigate matters for citizens, pass on post office requests and recommend men for federal appointments. However, as political opinion polarized, even simple tasks became more difficult. Lyon wrote A. E. Wing, a former territorial delegate, on December 27, 1835, "Situated as we are here now, without the privilege of a seat on the floor of either house, our opportunity is not very good to forward business of any kind, for, by some portion of the members of both houses, it seems to be thought rather indelicate and improper in us to make ourselves at all active in any way until the recognition of the State, which from present appearances is not likely to be very soon, if at all, unless we relinquish all claim to the disputed territory. . . . So the probability is that before Congress acts on the question of our admission into the Union, that body will do all in its power to cut off from us everything that is asked for by others."

The disputed territory.

Michigan fairly readily conceded the area to Indiana, the legal question was different. The border change had been specifically outlined and accepted by Congress. In Ohio the change had been made contingent on the assent of Congress, and that assent had never been given. On the strict basis of law the decision clearly favored the Michigan claim. But the problem went beyond the legalities of the question. The behavior of Ohio had so riled the populace and politicians of Michigan that they defiantly refused to permit any compromise on the boundary question. Lyon wrote in January of 1836, "The committees of both houses are to sit shortly on our boundary question and the aspect of affairs just now is very unfavorable for Michigan. There is very strong probability that both houses will pass a bill for cutting off from Michigan and giving to Ohio all she asks. This they will probably do before acting on our application for admission as a state, and will make one dependent and conditional upon the other. Then when it shall be proposed to us to change our constitution so as to conform to the new boundary, the question will arise, shall we do so? Or shall we not, at least so far as Ohio is concerned, rather remain a state out of the Union? I say, for one, we shall. We shall never acknowledge the power of Congress to take from us the tract claimed by Ohio. It is enough to submit to the unconstitutional action of that body in giving part of our territory in Indiana -- more than this we cannot bear, especially as there can not be found in either house a single member, except from the states interested, who will say that state has any legal claim."

John Quincy Adams, who continued to support Michigan with thrilling oratory, was discouraged by the members of Congress who refused to even consider the legal question. He wrote later, "Never in the course of my life have I known a controversy of which all the right was so clearly on one side and all the power so overwhelmingly on the other."

Lewis Cass, as a cabinet officer, had no official capacity in the controversy, but as a former territorial governor and a man with easy access to the presidential ear, he was prominent behind-the-scenes. Cass had always professed himself a close friend of Lucius Lyon and on a personal level this was certainly true. However, as the political machinations multiplied concerning statehood it was Cass, in Washington, and Mason, back in Michigan, who kept up a two-sided correspondence of strategy. In a letter to Cass in August of 1835, Mason admonishes him, "communicate this only to Mr. Norvell." During the entire period that Michigan was operating as a state-outside-the-Union, Lyon continued in correspondence with people like H. D. Gilpin, rejected candidate for territorial office, and later John S. Horner, who replaced Mason as secretary of the territory. This may have been a contributing factor to their caution.

A second factor was a falling-out that occurred between Mason and Lyon. In some way the contents of a letter that Mason had written to Lyon in the winter of 1834-35, outlining why he thought the appointment of Colonel Andrew Mack as governor of Michigan Territory would not be a good idea, had been seen by others. In an angry letter dated January 4, 1835, Mason wrote, his script large, black and slanting, "That letter was written in the spirit of disinterested friendship and as I supposed to a friend who was entitled to my confidence. . . .

Write to me frankly. If there are any circumstances attending this transaction calculated to lessen its aggravating representation, let me have them. If you have done this with the <u>secret</u> intention of injuring me it will readily occur to you what the injured feelings of every gentleman would be on such an occasion. . . ." Lyon quickly replied that if the letter had been seen it was without his permission and added other protestations to smooth things over. In a letter dated January 25, 1836, young Mason accepted the apology and theorized ". . . there is a bad and evil spirit existing somewhere, trying to break all ties between us. Let them work, and if you will deal by me as I shall by you, I think we can weather the storm. Recollect that frankness is the greatest security for friendship; you shall have it from me, and I expect it from you." Then adds, "One thing is certain there is no retreat for us; we are on the billows with our vessel of State, and it is easier to reach the point of destination than to get back to the place of departure."

Feeling more comfortable with the written word Lyon sent a thick report to the committee on territories. The report included a detailed analysis of the surveying questions involved as well as the historical and moral questions.

But the outlook was grim. Lyon wrote a friend in Detroit, January 3, 1836: "Things look unfavorable at present, though nobody here thinks of requiring Michigan to go back to a territorial government, nor does anybody find fault with the constitution, except of that part relative to boundaries." Things got a little more complicated when the terms of the Michigan Supreme Court justices expired. Territorial justices were appointed by the President. If Michigan was a state, the selection would be handled at that level. The first effort was to simply put off appointments until after Michigan was admitted to the Union. When this did not seem feasible, the Michigan delegation met with the President to see if they could mutually agree on candidates. Another appointment that was touchy was that of the postmaster of Toledo, the major settlement in the disputed area. In January of 1836, Lyon wrote to a friend, "Will you write us who should be appointed postmaster at Toledo in place of S. B. Comstock who has resigned. . . . We want some competent man of good character and standing in the community who will at least be so much on the side of Michigan as not to date his post bills, 'Toledo, Wood county, Ohio' . . . as they have been heretofore." At one point he received a letter from Postmaster General William J. Barry (who was married to Stevens T. Mason's aunt), asking his opinion of a request to remove the "post master of Toledo, Michigan Territory, upon the ground of his having assumed to determine without an order from this department, the location of his office as being in the State of Ohio, and his having taken an improper part in the controversy now pending, between that state and Michigan Territory, which has created much excitement and dissatisfaction among the people." Lyon recommended delay.

The State Legislature was scheduled to reconvene on the first of February. On January 31, 1836, Lyon wrote a letter of advice to Charles W. Whipple, "Tomorrow I suppose you will again take your seat in the legislature, but whether the two houses will immediately adjourn again to await the action of Congress on our application for admission into the union, or continue in session and proceed to prepare the different subjects of legislation for their final action at the proper time, is a matter about which I am not well informed. The President himself and all our leading political friends here think it best for the legislature to adjourn and wait the action of Congress until the close of the session or until the admission of the State into the union, but if not admitted before the adjournment, they will then have no objections to our going on in our own way and enjoying the rights of self government as well as the people of the original states."

At the opening of the Legislature, Mason told the assembled would-be lawmakers, "The essence of freedom is self government. . . . It would afford the highest satisfaction to announce our acceptance into the Union. . . . However, I am compelled to state that the application remains without the final action of Congress and that its ultimate fate is yet unknown."

After receiving a copy of Mason's message in February, Lyon, from his vantage point in Washington, wrote, "I fear your remarks . . . will occasion us a good deal of trouble and I will tell you how. It is now absolutely certain that Congress will never consent to our admission into the union without a change of boundaries, at least so far as our southern boundary is concerned, and if we remain out of the union the President will consider it his duty to enforce the Territorial government with all the power at his disposal. This, united with the force that we should have to encounter from Ohio, would make resistance almost hopeless if we should attempt it. I don't say that we ought to submit, let the odds be what it may against us . . . but it is my impression we shall be compelled to submit by the strong arm of power."

The proposal of the Ohio boundary had again been referred to the judiciary committee, and on March 1, 1836, they reported in favor of Ohio. According to a letter written later by Samuel F. Vinton of Ohio, the committee added to the report a comment that "If Michigan be not sufficiently large, it is easy to remedy that objection." Senator Preston was still on the committee and, it is supposed, renewed his suggestion to include additional land to the north. At the same time two messages from the President concerning aspects of the question were referred to a select committee, and that committee presented a report March 22, 1836, establishing the southern boundary of Ohio, and giving Michigan the Upper Peninsula. The idea of linking the peninsula between Lakes Huron and Michigan, and that between those lakes and Lake Superior was not an altogether new idea, even when first proposed by Preston in 1834. From 1816 to 1818, after Indiana attained statehood but before Illinois entered the Union, the boundaries of Michigan Territory were quite similar to those eventually approved for the State of Michigan. Lyon first mentioned the possibility of additional territory in a letter dated February 4, 1836, to Col. D. Goodwin of Detroit. "I thank you for the suggestions . . . relative to an addition to the State of Michigan on the west, provided Congress should break up our boundary on the south. The matter has been fully discussed here and I have no doubt the committee will be willing to give us all the country west of Lake Michigan and north and east of the Menominee river of Green Bay and the Montreal river of Lake Superior, thus giving us the great part of the coast of that lake, which may at some future time be valuable. This seems to be the division fixed on in case our southern boundary should be broken up, which I yet hope will not be done. If it should be, however, I for one shall go in for all the country Congress will give us west of the lakes. It will only require the consent of the legislature to receive it, according to the doctrine which maintains that Congress can cut and carve the territory as they choose, and if that doctrine is to prevail, we will take advantage of it and let the 'Devil take the hindmost' as gamesters say."

Michigan Territory 1816-1818

Although he was probably one of the few people arguing the question who had actually visited the Upper Peninsula, Lyon was not entirely won over to the idea. He wrote a friend in Galena, February 18, 1836, "The corruption and management of the delegation in Congress from Ohio and Indiana is about to deprive Michigan of the country claimed by the former state, and to compensate us in some measure, the committee will probably give us a strip of country along the southern shore of Lake Superior, where we can raise our own Indians in all time to come and supply ourselves now and then with a little bear meat for delicacy."

The question of the border with Ohio was not just a matter of boundaries to many Michigan residents. In a letter dated March 15, 1836, E. D. Ellis, a senator in the Michigan legislature, wrote, "If you can get the bill through before Congress for our admission, so as to accede to Michigan all except Indiana and the district of country south of the Maumee River, without the Indian country, and a recognition of the propositions contained in the Ordinance appended to our Constitution upon the condition that the same shall be accepted by the people of Michigan, either by a direct vote at the polls, or in a special Convention to be called for that purpose -- it may be well. If not, my advice is, that you say to Congress that you are no longer the agent of Michigan, but shall at once return home. You must know, that neither our Representatives in Congress or in the Legislature, have the power to barter away our rights to Ohio, and that agent who advocates such doctrine can no longer expect to enjoy the confidence of the people of Michigan, who know their rights and dare assert them." It was pointedly addressed to "Hon. Lucius Lyon, Senator-elect from Michigan."

While the boundary question was still pending, a petition was sent to members of Congress, Vinton of Ohio later wrote, "remonstrating against the boundaries it proposed to established and charged that the country on the Ohio border had been bartered away by the Michigan delegation for that beyond the lake. Mr. Buchanan (afterwards president) made a speech on that bill in which he adverted to that charge. He said: The paper undoubtedly conveyed the meaning that the senators and representatives of Michigan had been willing to barter away the territory of the state. Now, if he had ever met with three pertinacious gentlemen in his life, it was these very men, one of whom he was proud to call his friend. The line, the irreversible line, fixed by the act of 1803, and by the ordinance of 1787, was the burden of every song they sung. He should as soon have thought of obtaining the consent of a man to deprive himself of his life, as to have dreamt of obtaining the consent of these three gentlemen to a relinquishment of this line. He would do them justice to say, that if any member of the senate had ever heard them express the slightest willingness to accept the boundary proposed in this bill, he had been more fortunate than himself. He asked any senator to say whether he had ever heard from them any such intimation."

As the sessions ground on it became clear that nothing would budge on the question of the southern border, and Lyon seemed more resigned to permitting the alteration on the south and adding territory elsewhere. After noting that both Norvell and Crary, his colleagues in Congress, were opposed to the addition and would try to prevent it, Lyon wrote on February 21, 1836, ". . . it seems to me if we are to lose so much on the south we ought at least to have something on the west and north. . . . It can certainly do us no harm if it does no good. . . . If we lose on the south and gain nothing on the north and west, we shall be poor indeed." Three days later in a similar letter written to C. K. Green he concluded with, "My course here is straight forward and whether it leads me through a bog or over mountains I shall follow it and follow it alone if my company have left me."

Lyon wrote on March 2, 1836, "Reports have been made against us in both houses on the boundary question, in the senate yesterday and in the house today. Congress will certainly decide against us." On March 12, he wrote angrily to Z. Pitcher in Virginia, "I send you a copy of the report of the judiciary committee of the senate on our boundary question. It agrees with the report of the committee of the house and both show beyond all question that practically there is no such thing as morality or honesty in politics. . . . We shall probably be allowed to come into the union if we surrender our rights, but the union of gamblers and pickpockets, to a poor traveller who has just been robbed, is hardly to be desired."

Wearied by the stubborn refusal of those around him to see the inevitability of accepting a change in southern boundaries Lyon wrote to Colonel Goodwin in Detroit, March 27, 1836, "It is now. . . considered doubtful whether Michigan will come into the Union at all. It is supposed here that neither the legislature nor the people in convention will ever consent to the change of boundaries which Congress proposes and until they do so it is certain that we shall not come in. . . . The opposition to the administration, it is now ascertained, are determined to oppose us at every step and force us back into a territorial government to begin all things anew, in the hope that at the next election their party may have the majority."

By April the bill for admission, with the changed boundaries, had passed the Senate and was being readied for debate in the House. Lyon wrote Thomas C. Sheldon, April 3, 1836, "Humiliating as these terms are they are the best that can possibly be obtained and our political friends in Congress have had to fight hard for us to carry the bill through even bad as it is. I perceive that some of our political friends in Michigan have held a public meeting in Detroit, passed resolutions and signed a paper insinuating against the delegation here for an attempt to barter away the country claimed by Ohio. All I have to say to them is, in the language of Crockett, 'they are barking up the wrong tree this time.' Every member of Congress knows their insinuations are exceedingly unfounded and unjust. We shall, of course, not take our seats this session."

To make the area's political status even shakier, in May of 1836, the Territory of Wisconsin was organized, leaving Michigan outside of the functioning territorial government, but still outside of the Union. Edward D. Ellis of Monroe, wrote, May 15, 1836, "We can choose Presidential Electors and go on prudently with our government. As to the bill pending; I think Michigan would veto it by a vote of two-thirds -- after an angry and unpleasant controversy about a matter in which there ought to be unanimity."

Bills for statehood for both Michigan and Arkansas were approved by Congress on June 13, and signed by President Jackson on June 15. On the same day Congress passed an act to distribute surplus money in the federal treasury to the states after the start of the new year. The money was to go to States of the Union; none was to be given to any territories. It was estimated that Michigan's share, if it attained statehood before that time, would be nearly a half million dollars.

Governor Mason called a special session of the Legislature for July 11, and election for delegates to a Convention of Assent was scheduled for the second Monday in September. The Convention was held in Ann Arbor and on September 30 the Congressional compromise for statehood lost by a vote of 28-21. Many, including Lucius Lyon, who had worked the hardest for the agreement, were disappointed. Shortly after the results were announced many citizens and some lawmakers, having expended their fury at the injustice of the situation, began to understand its inevitability. They realized too that if the assent to the boundary change could be arranged before the first of the year, Michigan could still receive a share of the surplus federal money. This did not give them much time.

Near the end of October the Democratic Party of Wayne county urged meetings in all counties at which the people should call spontaneously for a new election and a new convention to put an end to what Major John Garland called, "the anomalous position of Michigan." Mason found what he considered a loophole in the laws allowing this, and a circular was sent to the counties calling for an election the first week in December and a meeting to convene in Ann

Arbor on December 14. On that day 78 delegates from 18 counties moved quickly to accept the Congressional proposal, and John R. Williams and Hart L. Stewart were chosen special messengers to carry the resolution to Washington. Because it met in the middle of a northern winter this convention of assent has been known popularly in Michigan history as the "frostbitten convention."

There were no rapid communications in 1836 and Lucius Lyon, down in Washington, was not immediately aware of events in Michigan. On December 23, 1836, he wrote anxiously to Alpheus Felch, "We have as yet heard nothing from our second convention upon the action of which it is expected the President will issue his Proclamation declaring Michigan a state, and only eight days remain between this and the first of January -- I fear we shall be too late to save our share of the surplus."

The breathless messengers arrived, and, had Congress not been in session, Jackson probably would have proclaimed Michigan a state, as he had promised at the close of the spring session. Instead, on December 27, he sent the resolution and a report of both conventions of assent to Congress. In his message he noted that the act setting up the procedure for becoming a State "does not prescribe by what authority the convention should be ordered, or the time and manner of which it would be chosen . . . I deem it most agreeable to the intent of the law, and proper for other reasons, that the whole subject be submitted to the decision of Congress." And added, "The importance of your early action upon it is too obvious to need remark."

In the Senate the message was presented by Felix Grundy of Kentucky, head of the Judiciary Committee, who attempted to hurry its passage by recommending an immediate third reading. Senator Thomas Ewing of Ohio called this, "a rather strange request," and John C. Calhoun of South Carolina stated that there were "facts and principles involved that required the gravest examination and deliberation." He recommended a delay until Monday, January 2.

Senator Benton observed wearily, "The subject of Michigan's admission to the Union has been before the Senate for upwards of five years, and he apprehended that no question relating to it could come up but what had already sufficiently been discussed." The bill was sent back to committee by a vote of 22-15. The main question was the method of calling the second convention and the wording of the preamble that was deemed offensive by some senators. Calhoun did declare from the floor of the Senate that if the haste on the bill was the result of a fear that Michigan would lose its share of the federal surplus that some means would be devised by Congress to give the new state a full share even if it entered the Union after January 1.

In the House John Quincy Adams pointed out that in 1835 a

House committee had voted six to one that the State of Ohio had no right to the disputed territory but that they believed that Michigan was entitled to it "by every law, human and divine." He paid a brief tribute to the efforts of Lucius Lyon by noting that in previous sessions there were 29 members (19 from Ohio, 7 from Indiana, and 3 from Illinois) speaking against the measure, and a single individual, representing the Territory of Michigan, "who had to sustain the rights of his constituents by the powers of speech alone, for he had no vote."

The bill was returned to the floor of the Senate where it met further delaying tactics. On the fourth of January Calhoun proposed an amendment which would repeal the conditions that Congress had put on statehood for Michigan, a move designed to cause lengthy debate. Weary with the question the senators voted down the Calhoun motion and instead voted 27 to 4 to engross the bill for a third reading. On January 5 the bill to admit Michigan to the Union was passed by a vote of 25 to 10. Senators voting against the measure were Richard H. Bayard of Delaware, John C. Calhoun of South Carolina, Henry Clay and John Jordan Crittenden of Kentucky, John Davis of Massachusetts, Joseph Kent of Maryland, Samuel Prentiss and Benjamin Swift of Vermont, Samuel Lewis Southard of New Jersey, and Gabriel Moore of Alabama. Senators Thomas Ewing and Thomas Morris of Ohio did not vote on the question.

Back in Michigan, John Almy, a member of the state legislature from Grand Rapids, fretted, "The legislature is waiting in breathless suspense to hear what is to become of the administration question. If the question is disposed of agreeable to our wishes and hopes, we can then go on with confidence and legislate to some purpose."

Mark Norris, who was associated with Lyon in an Ypsilanti mill and farm, wrote sympathetically that he notices by the paper that Michigan "is not admitted yet. . . . When we saw the President's message on the subject we were in hopes we should have been admitted without further discussion, but I think we may say, as did the frog when he lost his tail, I wonder what next?"

The House approved admission on January 25, by a vote of 132 to 43. The no votes included eight from Ohio, six from Kentucky, five each from Pennsylvania and Massachusetts, four from South Carolina, three each from Maine, Virginia and Maryland, two from New York, and one each from New Jersey, Georgia, Alabama, Delaware and North Carolina. President Jackson signed the bill the following day and Michigan became the twenty-sixth state of the United States of America. Because of the circumstances Michigan was permitted to receive a share of the surplus federal revenue, amounting to just under $400,000.

With noticeable haste the signed act was brought to the

meetings of the House and Senate. In the Senate Felix Grundy, interrupted debate on a land bill, the *Congressional Globe* reported:

MICHIGAN SENATORS.

On motion of Mr. GRUNDY, the bill was here laid on the table, to allow him to make a motion with regard to the qualification of the Michigan Senators.

A message was then received from the President of the United States, by Mr. ANDREW JACKSON, Jr., his Secretary, stating that the President had signed the bill for the admission of the State of Michigan into the Union on an equal footing with the original States.

The credentials of the Hon. JOHN NORVELL and the Hon. LUCIUS LYON, elected by the Legislature of the State of Michigan on the 10th November, 1835, to represent that State in the Senate of the United States, were read by the Secretary; and,

On motion of Mr. GRUNDY, the usual oath to support the Constitution of the United States was administered to Messrs. NORVELL and LYON by the Vice President, and they took their seats in the Senate.

Discussion then proceeded on a new land bill provision to allow settlers to enter a section of land in the name of any of their children between the ages of 12 and 21, the patent not to issue until the child becomes of age. The first vote the new senators participated in was on a portion of a banking bill to require that banks issue notes of not less than $20 in denomination if their notes are to be received as payment for public dues. Lyon voted "yes."

The following meeting Grundy called the new senators from Michigan forward and said it was necessary to determine what class of the senate each would belong to. The election of senators was staggered, and when Arkansas was admitted their two new senators had drawn to determine what class they belonged to, thus, to keep the classes to as nearly equal size as possible, the choice available to the new senators was narrower. Slips of paper were placed in an empty ballot box and Norvell and Lyon drew for position. Lyon received the term which was scheduled to end in 1839; Norvell's term would extend to 1841.

The Hon. M. Sterling wrote, January 30, "Permit me to congratulate you on your final and glorious triumph! The Papers of this morning announce to us that you and Norvell have attained your seats at last -- So all is settled and well settled and Michigan and its friends have triumphed most gloriously."

Lyon also received a letter from cousin Sidney Smith, who had recently moved to Michigan. "We have just got the news of the admission of Michigan into the union & that our Representatives have taken their seats. They must rejoice, after standing so long knocking for entrance. I congratulate you & your colleagues on the result."

Two days after they were seated Lyon was back at work promoting Michigan interests. On January 28 he presented a petition from the inhabitants of Niles and New Buffalo asking for an appropriation for a harbor and lighthouse at the mouth of the Galien River on Lake Michigan. Possibly remembering his frustrating days as a non-voting territorial delegate in the House, unable to speak in the Senate, he also championed the interests of Wisconsin Territory. On January 30 he asked the committee on finance to make an appropriation of $2,159.72 to defray the expense of the legislative council of the Territory, and on February 22 he introduced a bill to improve Milwaukee Harbor. He let Norvell do the honors with an omnibus Michigan lighthouse request on February 7, and on February 15 Lyon presented a petition to completed the military road from Detroit to Mackinac, and thence to Fort Brady on Lake Superior.

Much of the 1837-38 Congressional session was tied up in debate over the admission of Texas to the Union, a controversial question mainly because the northern states feared it would extend slavery into the west. Early in the session Lyon presented a petition from a number of Michigan citizens that Texas not be admitted.

According to the index of the *Congressional Globe* Lyon introduced no bills that year, but he did get involved in a heated debate with Senate giants John Calhoun and Henry Clay over a pre-emption bill, a law which usually gave an advance settler the privilege of buying the lands on which he had settled at a minimum price before the government put the land up for auction. Calhoun objected to the bill because he said that the general effect of the bills was to allow speculators to go in and seize the best lands in anticipation of a pre-emption bill covering the area and he was further opposed because it put the sale of lands under the control of party politics.

The *Globe* reported, "Lyon, rising to reply to Calhoun, remarked that the latter was mistaken . . . that if he had had the advantage of personal observation . . . he would be in favor of pre-emption. There was, said Lyon, only one class of politicians who had any reason to oppose pre-emption laws, and Calhoun was not of that class. No doubt, certain speculators had combined to keep settlers off some good lands, but that they had done so with all good lands was untrue. There were

107

thousands of acres of unoccupied land on both sides of the Mississippi in Wisconsin Territory, and he knew the hospitable and generous character of the people there too well to believe than any person going there with the intention of becoming an actual settler in the country would be treated badly by those already there. It was true, Lyon went on, that settlers west of the Mississippi had formed pre-emption societies. Such a society had also been formed in Michigan, he said, but there was nothing very wrong in that. They contemplated no force, no violence, either at the public sales or elsewhere. Any person choosing to bid against the settlers would be free to do so, as though no society had been formed. The members merely pledged among themselves that they would not disturb each other in the possession of their own improvements.

"The lands in Wisconsin had for a long time been held from sale, said Lyon. Had they been put on the market as soon as they were wanted for settlement, there would have been no need for the formation of these societies, for every man would then have bought a piece for $1.25 an acre. The price would have been no more than that because no land, however good, could be worth more if it lay in advance of settlement, especially any considerable distance in advance. Settlement and improvement were what increased land values. And yet, he continued, these settlers had been denounced by Senator Clay as land pirates, plunderers, and robbers. Did they deserve such epithets? Whom had they robbed? Certainly, not the government. . . .

"It had been said, Lyon went on, that these settlers were trespassers and intruders, that they violated the laws in settling on public lands before those lands were put on sale, and that therefore they ought not to receive the protection and encouragement of pre-emption laws. But the only laws they had violated, he protested, were laws which did injustice to every poor man who was unable to purchase land and so sought a home where he could support himself and his family, laws which were unreasonable and unnecessary and which opposed the moral sense of the people and could not be enforced with a standing army of 100,000 men. There was, he repeated, but one class of politicians who could find any good reason for these laws, and that class was made up of the supporters of the American System, a system which wanted a public land policy whose effect would be to confine the population within the old states, where the poor man would be compelled to become the tenant of some wealthy landlord and place his children in a factory, instead of seeking a home in the fertile lands of the west."

Clay responded by reading from the field notes of surveyors of the Black Hawk purchase which stated that the land was generally settled by intruders and complained that the surveyor's progress had been interrupted by threats. In reply to Lyon's assertion that it was settlement that gave land its value, Clay said it was rather fertility of the soil, its natural advantages, and its capacity to yield a profitable return. The bill passed, and Lyon, whose dislike of speaking in public was well-known, must have felt gratified to have taken on two famous political orators to such good advantage.

As the national economy struggled, money for internal improvements dried up and many of the canals, railroads, and other projects begun in the early 1830s languished unfinished. On April 25, 1838, Lyon wrote William Woodbridge of Detroit, who had apparently inquired about some project, "The state of the treasury is such that there is not the slightest prospect that any new work will be begun or provided for this year, and it is even doubtful whether appropriations will be made to carry on the works, harbors &c, already begun." Woodbridge had continued an important political figure in Michigan history and would be elected governor in 1839. He was an early Michigan acquaintance, and although they represented the extremes of the political spectrum, he and Lyon had always treated each other with careful courtesy. The letter is signed:

With unfeigned respect,
I am, Dear Sir,
Your most Ob't. Serv't.
Lucius Lyon

The question of slavery was being agitated more actively. On its admission Michigan had been paired with Arkansas to maintain the balance between slave and free states. As a senator Lyon received several petitions calling for the abolition of slavery in the District of Columbia and against the annexation of Texas which, it was feared, would spread slavery westward. January 7, 1838, Lyon replied to Nathan M. Thomas, an abolitionist from Schoolcraft and an organizer of the Liberty Party, "I am well convinced, from all the observation and reflection I have given the subject . . . in anxiously watching it for the last 10 years, that any attempt from the North to abolish or ameliorate the condition of slavery at the south can only tend to establish it more firmly! This every body knows, here, it has done already, and from the very nature of man, it must always do it. What think you the people of the State of Michigan would do if the people of South Carolina were to attempt either to dictate to or advise her to change any of her laws or institutions because they believed them sinful? Should we not spurn such advice and tell the people of South Carolina to mind their own business -- that it was for us, and for us alone to judge of and regulate our own institutions? And should they still annoy us with their opinions and requests would not the effect be to make us more firm, nay even obstinate in adhering to and supporting what at first we cared very little about, and what, if left to ourselves, we might have changed or abolished altogether?" He recommended that instead of government action those who felt they should fight against slavery should go directly to the people who live in the slave areas, and if that does not work they should go to those areas to live themselves."

If Senator Lyon had been only a rare voice in the session of 1837-38, he came to Washington in December of 1838 determined to be heard. In contrast to the single mention of his name in the *Congressional Globe* index the previous year, the index of the 1838-39 session lists 32 references. He looked a little like a man running for office.

Although Lyon was sometimes reluctant to admit it, he wanted very badly to continue in the senate. He wrote Mary Tott, January 19, 1839, "What slaves we are here! And yet, how anxious most of us are to retain our places. My own term expires on the 3rd of March next, and two years ago I did not believe anything could induce me to remain here beyond that time; but having consented to become a candidate for re-election, I now feel almost as anxious for success as ever I did."

Inflated currency and land values had put men under debts that they had no hope of paying off in their lifetimes. To provide an alternative they could apply for Congressional "relief", a form of early bankruptcy. Lyon presented many such bills during this session for individuals as well as legislation to adjust some specific land claims. He served on the committee for private land claims, the committee of roads and canals, and the committee for patents and patent office.

On December 28 he spoke out in favor of a bill to provide for pre-emptive rights in the sale of land in the lead mine region. The *Congressional Globe* reports, "He knew men who had spent many years of their lives, and ten or fifteen thousand dollars of their capital in improving these mineral lands, who would, if the bill became a law have to enter into competition with other purchasers for their own improvements."

In January he introduced a bill that would confirm the claims of Francis La Venture, Ebenezer Childs and Linas Thompson to the lands on which a portion of the village of Milwaukee, Wisconsin Territory, had been built.

In February he presented a memorial from John P. Richardson and 19 others to establish military posts in Oregon Territory. "Mr. Lyon said if Congress would pass a law granting to each immigrant one thousand acres of land, a sufficient number of enterprising young men would go there to defend the country from attacks from any quarter. These young men would be of their number; and he was acquainted with them, and knew them to be young men of character and respectability." At that time there was fear of attack on Oregon settlers both from the Indians and from the British who were disputing the territory's northern boundary.

Also in February Lyon introduced a petition from several young men who were occupants and cultivators "but not housekeepers of personal residence" in Kalamazoo County, asking that Congress modify the existing law giving them the right of pre-emption. The same month he presented a proposal from the Michigan Legislature that the state be allowed to locate other lands in lieu of those granted them for their university, when the lands granted had already been claimed as pre-emptions by actual settlers, and to continue pre-emption rights of deceased settlers to their women and children. Petitions were also presented from Israel V. Harris who asked the establishment of a post road from Kent County through Tallmadge in Ottawa County to Muskegon County, and a petition asking for an appropriation to establish a harbor at Port Sheldon, Ottawa County.

On February 20 he addressed the question of money to complete the roads begun in Michigan by the federal government before statehood. Lyon pointed out that he had presented such a bill when Michigan entered the Union and a year later, but both had been defeated. He said it was "precisely what every other new State in the Union had received and no more. . . . Now something else must be done. . . . He was determined not to relax his efforts to effect the object so long as he should retain a seat in the body, and if he could not do it one way, he would try another." His proposal was to attach the request to a bill for military roads in Arkansas. It did not succeed.

The undercurrent of all this activity was the expiration of Lyon's term at the end of the session in 1839, and his hopes for re-election. United States Senators continued to be elected by state legislatures until a constitutional amendment for popular election was passed in 1913. To get the election it was first important that he assist in electing a Democratic legislature. He worked hard for that result, even foregoing a trip to New York in the fall of 1838 for the wedding of Governor Stevens T. Mason and Julia Elizabeth Phelps. He wrote Mason from Detroit, October 20, 1838, "I arrived here this evening from Kalamazoo on my way to New York to be present at your wedding but, after passing an hour or two at your house, have changed my determination. Your father addresses me by all means to remain in the state till after the election and do all the good I can for the democratic cause." Following the election both houses of the Michigan Legislature had Democratic majorities, but the party itself was so fragmented that there would be great difficulty in taking advantage of the numbers, and no one faction was able to elect its candidate.

As early as September of 1838, William A. Richmond, a Grand Rapids friend and colleague who was serving in the Michigan Senate wrote: "I would 'not intrude' but would merely 'suggest' that the idea of your being the candidate for Governor next fall may not be a bad one. . . . The Legislature of next winter may not be as Democratic as you and I might wish, in that case a Whig might get elected Senator. But by no means give up your present position. Let nothing drop which may be tortured into a deinclination by those anxiously wanting to seize upon a word or expression to that effect."

There were insinuations thrown around that Lyon had arranged for a road that would go to Lyons, a settlement in Ionia County that he had an interest in. There were rumors that John Norvell, who still had two years to run on his Senate term and was the leader of a Democratic faction that usually opposed Lyon, had written a letter in his favor. Lyon wrote denying any knowledge of the action, "Mr. Norvell knows that I neither solicit or desire his interference in my behalf, for no one knows better than I that he can do me no good."

A letter, dated January 30, 1839, from E. F. Cook, was confident of Lyon's election. He wrote that he had just returned from a caucus and "There are many candidates in the field and a strong opposition prevails, but will undoubtedly be defeated. Your friends are fierce and determined that on Tuesday next 'We will meet the Enemy & he shall be ours.'"

Richmond, from his seat in the Michigan Senate saw it differently, "If you fail in getting the election it will be attributable to the over zeal of your friends, some of whom are too warm to please -- and sometimes too boisterous to influence."

As late as February 4, 1839, Lyon replied to an apparently optimistic letter from Sheldon McKnight, "You seemed to be of the opinion, when you wrote, that I would be re-elected, and I hope that your opinion may prove to be well founded; but I confess I have come to a different conclusion." The same day Isaac Q. Adams was writing a letter to Lyon which said cautiously, "There is still some chance of your election," and listing the arrangement of votes in the 10 ballots that had been taken that day.

On February 7, Warner Wing was nominated in the Michigan

Senate. The next day five dissenting Democrats permitted the nomination of Whig John Biddle in the House. Confusing an already muddled situation was the fact that Wing was a member of the Michigan Senate. There was some feeling that the U. S. Constitution prohibited a member of the state legislature from receiving a civil appointment from the legislature. The opposition was led by William Woodbridge who had himself been roundly criticized for serving as territorial delegate to Congress while at the same time continuing in his federal appointment as secretary for Michigan Territory. The constitutional question split the Democratic vote. Those who felt it not a problem voted for Wing; the others supported Randolph Manning.

In late February there was still hope that a compromise candidate could be agreed upon, and Joseph Vickery wrote, "No result of the election of the U. S. Senator is yet known, it is confidently believed, however, that John Biddle will be the man. Sir I fear your pretended friends have deserted you -- Judge Ransom instead of putting forth all his strength for your re-election has himself been a prominent candidate. I think T. C. Sheldon has done all he could but he has had a host against him."

Partly, it would appear, to rationalize their own votes against Lyon as senator, some of his friends began to promote him as a gubernatorial candidate to succeed Mason, whose popularity had dropped dramatically and who wanted only to get out of Michigan as quickly as possible. Colonel Daniel Goodwin of Detroit brought this idea forward as early as the first week in January. Lyon's friend, Sheldon McKnight, wrote January 9, "Goodwin is not acting fairly towards you. We prefer to see you elected to the U. S. Senate . . . you will be just as 'available' there. He is urging the members to hold you back for Governor."

Another friend, Thomas Fitzgerald, wrote in mid February, "If you are defeated now, or rather if you should not be elected, you must be elected our next Governor -- if we can elect you."

As the end of his term approached, the Legislature was still unable to agree on a successor, but Lyon, at least, seemed out of the running. On February 24, 1839, he wrote to S. H. Webb of Detroit, "The result of the senatorial election so far as I am concerned, has not disappointed me, because I knew something of the men who figured in the matter, and I had reason to believe that I should be, as I have been, the victim of treachery and lies. I do not find fault with this, nor can I very much regret it. I shall be at home now and be able to attend to my false friends as well as open enemies. . . . I have done my duty here and my whole duty, honestly and faithfully, so that in retiring from my public station I can look back without even a wish that I had acted differently in anything that I have done. If the Legislature or the people find fault it is because they are imposed upon by those who have selfish motives of their own."

When Congress recessed in March of 1839, the Michigan Legislature had still not been able to agree on his successor and Lyon rushed home to urge them not to adjourn "without agreeing on some one to supply my place. The risk is too great to postpone an election till next year." But the House refused to approve anybody but Warner Wing, and the Senate refused to concur. The legislature adjourned without agreeing and by the time they reconvened in January of 1840, the Democrats had lost their chance. The November elections had changed the political makeup of both houses, and the Whig majority selected Augustus Porter. Lyon wrote Edward Lyon, January 24, from Detroit, "I arrived here the day before yesterday just in time to go to the house of A. S. Porter, Esq., and drink a glass of wine with him in company with the throng who went to congratulate him on his election that day as my successor in the Senate of the United States, to serve six years from the third of March last. He is a consistent Whig, and personally an honest, intelligent and clever man, though not much more of a speaker than I am myself."

Lyon had also refused to be a candidate for governor. As he explained later to a friend, he had asked that his name be withdrawn because his private affairs required "my whole time and attention for the next year or two in order to relieve me of embarrassments," and secondly because he saw, "or thought I saw that a good many professed Democrats and some of them professed friends of mine were ready to treat me again as they had done before in the attempt to elect a United States Senator; and I did not wish to place myself in the humiliating and mortifying condition of being a second time abandoned by my own party."

However, he quickly learned that a politician, even out of office, is considered fair game in the press. In the September 2, 1840 issue the *Democratic Free Press* of Detroit wrote, that the *Advertiser*, Detroit's Whig newspaper, had "falsely characterized ex-Senator Lyon with offering and declining bets &c on board the *Missouri* on Saturday last. We are authorized by Mr. L to say that the entire article does not contain a single particle of truth as it relates to him." They chided the rival paper for attacking a private citizen.

In the waning days of his senatorial career Lyon was charged with the task of procuring for Michigan a portrait of the Marquis de Lafayette, the French nobleman and soldier who as a young man had assisted America with its Revolution, and who, in more mature years, became a driving force in the political revolution of his own country.

The resolution for the portrait had been offered in the Michigan legislature by John Almy of Kent County in 1837. There was also to be a portrait of George Washington.

The portrait of Lafayette that Lyon bought is a copy of one that was painted by French artist Ary Scheffer and presented to the United States January 20, 1825 during a visit of Lafayette just prior to the celebration of the 50th anniversary of the American Revolution. The Scheffer portrait hangs in the House of Representatives at Washington D.C. The copy was made by Washington portrait artist and copyist Alexander Simpson. It is said that he had the advantage of having Lafayette in the city while he worked on the painting and that the work received such favorable attention that it was exhibited in the Capitol rotunda and in the Washington council chamber.

Lyon located the portrait through the services of George Templeman, a Georgetown antique and art dealer. When purchase of the painting was being contemplated, Templeman sent a copy of a letter from Thomas L. McKenney, who had interceded for the artist to get permission to copy the painting. McKenney wrote that Lafayette who was visiting the United States saw the copy before it was quite finished. "The Genl was so much delighted with the artist and so impressed with his genius -- on the spot he invited him to visit France and make Lagrange his home. . . ." A second testimonial letter that Templeman sent was from Thomas Carhey of Washington who stated that he had been invited with several other gentlemen to view the finished copy, along with the Scheffer painting. "None of us could tell the copy from the original."

It is not known which came first, the availability of the portrait, or the Legislative idea, but the transaction was apparently completed before Lyon left Washington, and, following his return, he wrote Templeman on June 30, 1840: "When I was in Washington in April your son informed me that you were having a box prepared to put up the portrait of Lafayette in and forward it to me. I have not yet, however, heard of its arrival and I now write to enquire whether you have forwarded it? If so, when and how? If you have not forwarded it, I hope you will put it up carefully and forward it immediately to the care of Edward Lyon, National hotel, Detroit."

The portrait arrived in Detroit in September of 1840, coming from Georgetown to Detroit on the boat *George Washington*. It was hung in the National Hotel for a time and then hung in the Michigan Capitol in Detroit. It was moved with the rest of the furnishings to Lansing in 1847. An old legislator related in 1894 that he remembered the Lafayette painting sitting on top of a bookcase in the state library with no frame. In 1867 attention was drawn to the picture by Senator Andrew Howell of Adrian, and the Senate approved a resolution to have the portrait reframed and hung "in a conspicuous place in the senate chamber." It was placed to the right of the rostrum where it remained until 1980. The portrait is full length and shows Lafayette as a mature man, dressed in a black suit, with brown overcoat, and a top hat and cane in his right hand. The light from the sky illuminates his face and the land and water behind the figure.

The Lafayette portrait presented to the Michigan capitol.

It is such an excellent copy (some said Simpson's copies were often better than the original) that there was confusion for many years about the artist. Some declared that the painting was actually by Scheffer. A story grew up that the wily Lewis Cass, who for several years was Minister to France, when he was asked by the government to arrange for the portrait for the U. S. Capitol, managed to negotiate a two-for-one deal with the original artist. During restoration work on the painting, however, an inscription was found on the back which identifies the painting as a copy "from Scheffer by Simpson."

During an earlier effort to ascertain the facts of the picture's origin a researcher asked George Washington Thayer, nephew of Lucius Lyon, if his uncle had thought that the work was by Scheffer, or was a copy "from Scheffer." Thayer said he was not sure and added, "Uncle Lucius admired Lafayette greatly. However, he knew nothing about art, and neither do I."

When Henry Holt researched the story of the Lafayette portrait in 1894, he wrote that although there had been a resolution presented in the legislature for an appropriation of $1,000 to pay for the proposed portraits of Washington and Lafayette, the bill never actually completed passage and there is no bill or receipt to indicate that the State of Michigan paid for the picture. Thayer said that it was the family's understanding that the portrait had been purchased by Lucius Lyon and presented to the State of Michigan. (Lyon may have paid for it with land. George Templeman and his brother for nearly a decade owned several village lots in Lyons.)

In 1989 the painting was refurbished and sent on a national tour as part of an exhibit marking the Centennial of the French Revolution. When the tour was over, the portrait was returned to its former place in the freshly restored Senate chamber. Balancing the Lafayette portrait, at the left of the rostrum, is a full length painting of Austin Blair, governor of Michigan 1861 to 1865.

8

Indian Commissioner

As a surveyor Lucius Lyon worked much of the time in land occupied by, or surrounded by, Indians. In 1828 he was sent west of Lake Michigan to survey boundaries set up by Indian treaties, and some of his maps of Indian lands west of Lake Michigan show intimate detail of the land and its uses, marking each Indian hogan, meeting house, and many outbuildings.

Some of his earliest and closest friends in Michigan Territory were men closely involved in dealing with the Indians. Lewis Cass (affectionately known to the Indians as Os-Kotchee, Big Belly) had negotiated Indian treaties as far back as 1819. Lyon had lived with Henry Rowe Schoolcraft and his half-Chippewa wife, Jane, in Detroit in 1828, and purchased supplies from Indian trader Rix Robinson on an early surveying expedition. As a territorial delegate in the years 1833-35, and from 1835 to 1839 as a U. S. senator, Lyon was in the thick of the land buying and treaty negotiations that extinguished the Indian title to nearly the entire land mass of the State of Michigan.

In the fall of 1835 the Department of War, which administered Indian affairs, had asked Henry Rowe Schoolcraft to inquire about whether the Indians north of the Grand River would be willing to sell their lands. He found them so willing to make the deal that some of the chiefs started at once for Washington on their own. John S. Horner, who had just replaced Mason as acting governor of the territory and was totally unfamiliar with Indian affairs, refused to authorize the trip. Taking one of the last vessels of the season out of Michigan Schoolcraft arrived in Washington in mid-December, and he and Secretary of War Lewis Cass, and senator-elect Lucius Lyon undertook to make the arrangements on their own, with the unofficial assurance that the government would be so pleased with the result that they would eventually fund the expenses.

Lyon wrote Rix Robinson, December 25, 1835, "Mr. Schoolcraft, who has lately arrived here, has just informed me that he wrote you yesterday about having a delegation of Indian chiefs north of Grand river come on here soon for the purpose of making a treaty with the government for the sale of their lands. . . . I take the liberty to request that you will bring or send on here such chiefs and other persons as you may judge necessary to have the Indians fully represented and at the same time to effect a treaty with them for the whole peninsula if possible. I have no doubt whatever you may think proper to do will meet the wishes of the government and that you will be paid for it, though there is as yet no appropriation for that purpose and on that account it is very desirable that the expenses of the treaty be as light as possible."

Indian Treaty Cessions

Correspondence continued throughout the winter deciding what chiefs were needed and who would accompany them. By February some had arrived in Washington, but Schoolcraft, who by now had been appointed official Indian commissioner to effect the treaty, decided that some important bands were unrepresented and sent north for additional chiefs. One delegation refused to come without Rix Robinson; therefore, his travel expenses were also authorized. He traveled south with two stage coaches full of Indian chiefs, outfitted in the odd assortment of Indian and European clothing that the Indians wore when thrust into white society. A story is told in a later biography of Robinson that on the way to Washington they stopped at a tavern in the interior of Indiana, where Robinson ordered dinner for everybody. Just when the food arrived the stage coach drivers announced that they were ready to go, and, as they were carrying U. S. mail, they would not wait. Robinson was forced to pay a full, even inflated, price for the dinner, which no one had had the time to eat.

"On their way back when nearing the same place he would not for a whole day let them eat; the chiefs complained of hunger; his only reply was, 'tighten your belts.' A short time before arriving at the tavern, he got up beside first one driver and then the other. The chink of silver could have been heard. They arrived there. He ordered as before, adding that his Indians were very hungry. . . . The food was set before them. Robinson said, 'Loosen your belts.' It disappeared in a minute; they called for more, the girls brought it, the landlord rushed distracted to the door, but no stages were driving up, nor were there any signs of any; more food was the call; all that was cooked was brought up, then the cold meats and everything eatable was brought and eaten up; finally their appetites were satisfied, but the famine in that house was awful. . . . The whole secret of the matter was, Mr. Robinson had penetrated the innkeeper's secret and overbid him with the drivers."

The collected Indian chiefs, Schoolcraft, Robinson, and interpreters, with occasional visits from Secretary of War Cass, and not-yet-seated Senator Lyon, met in the Masonic Hall in Washington and negotiations continued for several weeks. The Indians, who had only a vague understanding of ownership, were willing to sell their rights in the lands because the game was beginning to fail in many areas, and treaty money from the government was their only method of raising cash to pay outstanding credits to traders. But agreement among chiefs was achieved only slowly. Lyon wrote A. E. Wing, March 19, 1836, "Mr. Schoolcraft is here holding a council with a delegation of Chippewa and Ottawa chiefs for the purchase of all the northern part of the peninsula of Michigan. Their answer yesterday was that they would not sell and the present prospect is discouraging. Yet I think their objections will be overcome and that the United States will get the lands."

The treaty was signed March 28, 1836, and ceded to the United States all Indian lands in the Lower Peninsula of Michigan, north of Grand River and west of Thunder Bay, and about six million acres of the Upper Peninsula, extending from Drummond Island through the Straits of St. Mary, west to the Chocolay River on lake Superior and south to Green Bay. Limited reserves were set aside for the principal villages of the Indians, and they were given permission to occupy any portion of the land until it was actually needed for settlement. The total cost was to be $1,601,600 including payments to teachers, missionaries, blacksmiths, and farmers, and funds for medicine and vaccines, and monies for annuities.

Henry Rowe Schoolcraft

Lyon sent an article to the *Detroit Free Press* which outlined the major provisions of the treaty and concluded, "The treaty, so just to the Indians, so favorable in its terms for the United States and so important to the best interests and prosperity of Michigan has been effected by Mr. Schoolcraft with the approbation and aid of the secretary of war and in the face of difficulties and embarrassments which no person of less superior qualifications could have overcome. Michigan ought to be grateful for their services. Of the country purchased about 4,000,000 acres extending from the Grand river north is known to be fine land for settlement and within a very few years we shall, no doubt, see towns springing up at the mouths of all the rivers flowing into Lake Michigan for a hundred miles north of Grand River, if not all around the lower peninsula. The upper peninsula is known to contain vast forests of the very best pine, which is even now much wanted in Ohio, Indiana, Illinois and the southern part of Michigan and Wisconsin, and must very shortly furnish the material of a highly valuable trade."

This article about the Indian treaty also marks the first public use of the expression "upper peninsula" which would shortly figure so prominently in Michigan's boundary disputes during the fight for statehood.

The ink was not dry on the treaty when Lyon suggested to Cass that while the Indians were in a selling mood the United States should purchase the reservations set aside for the Indians in the Treaty of Saginaw of 1819. Lyon wrote C. C. Trowbridge, March 27, 1836, that Cass had replied ". . . he had no authority to invite a treaty with them involving the expenditures of money . . . but if the chiefs interested would come on here and propose to sell, the government would give them a fair and liberal price and in case a treaty should be made all necessary expenses would be paid by the government." Lyon further asked Trowbridge if the banks "would not advance money to pay the expenses of the chiefs coming on here should they be anxious to come." They came and the result was a treaty signed May 20, 1836, but later rejected by the Senate and replaced by another signed January 14, 1837.

There is some evidence that the chiefs enjoyed their sojourns in Washington and sought to visit "the Great White Father" whenever they had an excuse and could get the government to pay their passage. Although the Pottawatomi tribe agreed to leave the land they ceded in an earlier treaty and most members of that tribe would be forcibly removed between 1838 and 1840, there arose some question about whether the Treaty of 1836 called for the removal of the Indians, or simply their relinquishment of the ownership of the lands. In reply to a question from missionary Leonard Slater of Kalamazoo County, Lyon wrote March 14, 1836:

"I have consulted the Commissioner of Indian Affairs, T. Hartley Crawford, on the subject touched upon in your letters and am of the opinion that the Chippewas and Ottawas who made the treaty in 1836 for the sale of the country in the northern part of Michigan cannot be forced to remove west of the Mississippi unless they choose to go there. They will have to leave their reservations within the five years mentioned in the treaty but they may buy lands of the government as other people do and remain in the country, or they may go wherever they please. Should they conclude to buy lands and cultivate them in the

122

State of Michigan, most of them settling near together, there would probably be no objections to furnishing them farming utensils, teams, etc., mentioned in the treaty; but if only a small portion of them remain it would be difficult to do so. . . . In relation to the visit which you think of making the President with the chiefs, the commissioner deems it entirely unnecessary and will not pay any portion of the expenses if they come."

During the Congressional session of 1838-39 Lucius Lyon had made several inquiries at the Indian Affairs Department on behalf of half-breeds and others in the Wisconsin area to determine when the money promised to them by treaty would be distributed and about other matters. By April when it was apparent that re-election to his Senate seat was not likely, he agreed to an appointment as Indian commissioner. In this manner he could earn some extra money during the summer and stay out of reach of his creditors. Lucius wrote his sister Lucretia from Detroit in a letter dated April 25, 1839, "I have within the last few days accepted the appointment (tendered me by the Secretary of War) of commissioner to apportion and distribute the money (amounting to about $100,000) to be given to the Half Breeds of the Chippewa Indians under the treaty of 1837, and I am to leave here, with my secretary to the commission, on the 15th of June and meet the Indians at La Pointe in Lake Superior, on the 10th of July."

His compensation would be $8 a day "spent in the actual execution of this duty," and $8 for every 20 miles of travel from his residence to La Pointe, an Indian gathering place near the south end of Madeline Island in Lake Superior north of the bay where the city of Ashland, Wisconsin was later built.

The payment to half-breeds was a part of the Treaty of St. Peters concluded July 29, 1837, with Chippewa chiefs in Wisconsin territory. By this treaty the Indians ceded to the United States a large tract of land in Wisconsin and what would later be eastern Minnesota. Included among other provisions of the treaty was $100,000 to be given to those who were the product of one Indian parent and one European-American. A large percentage of these white parents were of French origin, many connected with the fur trading industry.

The distribution of money was complicated by a three year old murder case. In the summer of 1836 a Chippewa half-breed named Alfred Aitkin was killed by a full-blooded Chippewa. Other half-breeds apprehended the Indian and turned him over to the government for trial, but he was acquitted. The half-breeds were displeased with this outcome and wanted the Indian returned to them so he could be tried according to Indian custom, a circumstance which would probably result in his immediate execution.

Superintendent of Indian Affairs, T. Hartley Crawford, wrote Wisconsin Territorial Governor Henry Dodge that the courts had ruled that it was a case where "an Indian killed an Indian on Indian grounds" and the case therefore did not come under territorial jurisdiction. Crawford noted that this brought up the question about whether a half-breed is an Indian, but no one was ready to made a decision on that issue. A federal hearing was convened in Washington to review the ruling, and the conclusion was that having been once acquitted of the charge of murder, the Indian could not be legally jeopardized again for the same offense. The letter from Crawford to Dodge, a copy of which was sent to Lyon, advised the governor that the Indian Affairs Agency would "rely on your strenuous endeavors to avert the threatened mischief . . . and the attention of yourself and Bushnell is specially directed." Crawford recommended that they threaten to withhold the payments due both the Indians and half-breeds until the issue was settled, and the idea of revenge had been given up.

Lyon felt that Crawford's proposal was not a good solution, and wrote him in a letter dated July 16, 1839, "I have had several conversations with persons well acquainted with the half-breed Indians with whom I am commissioned to treat and I much fear that I cannot prevent them from carrying their threat of revenging the murder of Alfred Aitkin into effect by threatening to withhold payment of the money . . . as it is intimated to me in my instructions.

"They are a proud sensitive people who are anxious to be recognized by the Government as citizens of the United States and to receive protection from its laws. This they evidenced by delivering up the murderer of Alfred Aitkin to the civil authorities instead of punishing him according to Indian customs by taking his life themselves. . . . I very much fear that an attempt on my part to withhold the money . . . would only tend to exasperate them and precipitate commission of the very act which it is part of my mission to prevent." He suggests that they ask an American colonel who had organized a group of half-breeds into an army regiment in nearby Michigan to speak to them on the issue.

But by the time Lyon's letter reached Washington, Governor Dodge had asked Daniel Bushnell, deputy Indian agent, to use his influence with them. On July 20 Bushnell addressed the assembled half-breeds. He admonished them that if they expected the protection of the laws of the United States they would have to abide by the decision which had been made under these laws. He told them nothing would be gained by taking the life of the alleged killer and hinted that the money to be distributed under the treaty might be delayed, or withheld, until the question was peacefully resolved. After a short conference the half-breeds gave their pledge not to seek the life of Aitkin's killer, "to cover the dead" was the Indian expression, and the examination proceeded.

Upon arrival at La Pointe, Lyon went to work hearing claims of half-breeds and Indians. There were 189 petitions heard over the course of about two months. Two questions had to be addressed in each case. There had to be some proof of the parentage of the person in question, and there also had to be proof that the Indian parent was a member of the tribe covered by the treaty. Each petition was written out on a separate piece of paper and stated the facts of the case, usually including a family tree, place of birth and residence and tribal (and often clan) affiliation. There was also appended a note of the disposition of the case. Petitions were written, in rare instances, by the claimants, but more often by P. H. Brown of Frederick Town, Maryland, who had been assigned as clerk for the project, Indian agent Bushnell, or Lyon himself.

A number of petitions were submitted from white traders who claimed that the Indians or half-breeds owed them money, and from traders and settlers who claimed their property had been destroyed by the Indians. These claims were also considered, and several disallowed for lack of evidence, including a claim of $48,058 brought forward by the old American Fur Company. Nearly all of the 189 petitions were retained by Lyon and form part of the Lyon Papers in the Clements Library.

The process was nearly complete by mid-August and Lyon wrote Schoolcraft from La Pointe, in a letter dated August 18, 1839, "I have nearly finished the examination of half-breed claims and shall be ready for the payment in three or four days. I have not time to make out a list of those entitled to share the hundred thousand dollars, under the 3rd article of the treat of the 29 July 1837 in time to send you by the vessel which will take this letter to St. Mary's . . . but will leave the list with Mr. Bushnell. . . . The half-breeds as well as the Indians are now nearly all here, in waiting, and will soon be in a starving condition."

As the money was paid out to the half-breeds, Indian traders were on hand to cash in on the windfall. Lyon, who saw all money with respect to how much land it would purchase, wrote Robert Stuart, as he was wrapping things up, November 17, 1839: "After the half breed claims and the claims for debt were all decided, the money paid on the former and the certificates for the latter all delivered and receipted for, seeing the claimants disposing of their funds to Mr. Crooks for what I considered a very inadequate compensation, I offered publicly to give any claimant ten per cent annual interest on all the money he would place in my hands, and to give him good security, if required, for the payment of principal and interest at the time that might be agreed upon. The result was that some few of the most intelligent claimants, who had not disposed of their funds, offered them to me on the terms proposed."

The summer at La Pointe planted two other ideas in Lyon's active mind. In February of 1840 he wrote a long letter to R. D. Turner, head of the commerce committee in the Michigan House of Representatives, concerning the resources of Lake Superior and the importance of building a ship canal around the falls of the St. Mary's River. This would not only open the northern fisheries, woods, and potential mining areas to shipment by water, Lyon said, but he also felt that the canal would be important "in the event of war with England or with Indian tribes of the northwest, and would be a great service to the whole United States on account of the facilities it could afford for the transportation of troops and military stores. It is in fact emphatically a national work, and ought to be and I trust will be constructed by the general government."

The second thought that grew as a result of his six weeks at La Pointe was less optimistic. Lyon wrote in the same letter, "Having, when in Congress, taken an active part in procuring the extension of our boundary to the northwest" he had visited the area to view the land for himself. He said that the land suitable for agriculture, the rivers, and the potential for minerals were "more favorable than I had ever anticipated." However, he added that he had looked over the situation of rivers, lakes and other landmarks mentioned in the boundary line description and found them "not quite as anticipated. It is therefore probable that a question of some importance may hereafter rise between Michigan and Wisconsin in relation to this boundary, and I mention this subject here that the legislature may be apprised of it."

The issue did arise and the line was redescribed in the Wisconsin enabling act of 1846, and in greater detail in the Michigan Constitution of 1850. Suit was filed by Michigan in the U. S. Supreme Court in 1923 charging that the surveys of 1840-7 were not in accord with the descriptions, but the court, in 1926 confirmed Wisconsin's title on the basis of possession and sovereignty. A further decree of the Supreme Court in 1936 confirmed the earlier decision and defined in greater detail the boundaries that fall in the Great Lakes and bays adjoining them.

9

Land Speculator

Lucius Lyon was a surveyor and saw all of the best land in the Territory of Michigan as it passed under his transit. There were times he could scarcely contain himself. He wanted all of his old friends to come and buy land too, and he had acres of the very best land for settlement, lumbering, and investment that they could choose from. In 1822, when he was first heading out he wrote to a friend back in Vermont, "This section of the United States has been much undervalued. Michigan has been considered but little better than the waste land of the United States, but when the country was explored and surveyed, though but a small part of it is surveyed, it was found to possess as good a soil and greater advantages than the famed Ohio."

The life of a land speculator was often disappointing, and the market unpredictable. The change in the route of a railroad, the defeat of a proposed canal were just two of the circumstances totally out of the control of the land owner that might have serious repercussions on the price of a certain piece of land or determine whether it was marketable at all. But if he bought smartly and things went well, frontier land could be very profitable. As an example of the latter circumstance, Lyon recorded among his papers an instance where he purchased a selection of lots in what would later be called Wisconsin Territory with his own funds on June 11, 1836. On July 20, just over a month later, he sold these lands to Spear Nicholas and Co. of Baltimore for the sum of $39,606.84. After deducting interest and the expense of conveying the property Lyon realized a clear profit of $21,367.

In addition to the social prestige of wealth Lyon was looking forward to being able to care for his extended family as a responsibility befitting an eldest son. He wrote Lucretia in 1836, after the death of their stepmother, that he hoped to be able soon to be able to furnish his father with money to live, "without the necessity of attending to any business whatever." He tells Lucretia to ask if she ever needs money for herself, little brother George, or the Thayer boys. "I never keep much money on hand; but I have landed property which is worth at least two hundred thousand dollars, and its value is still increasing, so I expect to be able to realize enough every year to support myself, and by good management, all my brothers, sisters, nephews, &c who need it. . . ."

Each asterisk on this map marks the site of land owned by Lucius Lyon at some point in his land-buying career in southern Michigan.

Lyon was certainly aware of the highs and lows of fortune that might be anticipated. In 1830 during a visit to Washington he wrote John Johnson with whom he had studied engineering in Vermont, "The new Surveyor General, William Lytle, a few years ago was the most wealthy man in the western states being worth four or five hundred thousand dollars, all of which he made by surveying and dealing in lands -- He has lost now all but about thirty or forty thousands by heavy endorsements for his friends . . . in consequence of which he has accepted the appointment he now holds, in place of his predecessor Gov. Tiffin who was removed for want of Jacksonism." Lyon's own case would strangely parallel the misfortunes of Lytle.

In addition to purchasing land on his own account, Lyon organized companies in which he usually retained a share, he bought land outright for others, and for still more he served as consultant, discovering areas that he felt would make profitable investments. He rarely purchased directly from the government, because such sales required cash, but usually bought from individuals on contract. In some cases he made the purchases from early settlers who had occupied the lands and thus acquired pre-emption rights to large tracts.

Some time prior to 1833 Lyon had made the acquaintance of the Bronson family from New York. In August of 1833 he received a long letter from Arthur Bronson giving Lyman. J. Daniels and Lyon sweeping powers to invest in western lands on behalf of Bronson and Charles Butler, also of New York. Bronson wrote during a visit to Detroit, "There are few persons to who I should be willing to give this large credit, placed at the disposal of their judgment, and there are none in this Territory with whom I could make the arrangements contained in my propositions with such entire confidence and satisfaction as with you and Mr. Daniels acting together." On October 24, 1834, Lyon signed a contract with Isaac Bronson, Arthur's father, to invest $24,000 in real estate "west of Lake Michigan and between said lake and the Mississippi River and, if deemed advisable in the States of Illinois, Indiana and Ohio and the Peninsula of Michigan." Lyon was to hold a half interest in the investment, his portion to be paid in later out of the proceeds of the sales. Under this agreement, the more land Lyon purchased for Bronson, the deeper he was in debt to him. The debt was secured by the land itself. Shortly afterwards he began buying land for Arthur's brothers, Frederick and Oliver Bronson.

Eastern investors were unpopular in some areas because they drove the price of land up in their ignorance, so the Bronsons and Lyon went to some pains to keep their relationship a secret. Arthur Bronson warned in a letter written December 13, 1834, "Do not mention my name in connexion with the Michigan and Illinois Canal or the railroad."

He said that a Chicago newspaper had recently run an article ascribing a recent project "to Wall Street." However, the Bronson name has been perpetuated in Michigan on street signs in some of the settlements their investments made possible. There is a prominent Bronson Street in Grand Rapids, and also in Ada. In addition to mutual investments Lyon sometimes borrowed money from the Bronsons for purchases in his own name.

Prior to their connection with Lyon and Daniels, the Bronsons had had an agreement with C. C. Trowbridge and Elon Farnsworth to invest in western lands. Trowbridge wrote later in his memoirs, "I had met Mr. Bronson on Wall Street, New York, when he asked me playfully for advice as to whether he should sell certain stocks. I, as playfully, said, 'Yes, and bring the money to me west and sow it broadcast.'" Although the original remark was apparently in jest, Bronson later sought out Trowbridge and Farnsworth and made a contract with them to invest funds, not to exceed $50,000 in western lands for five years, after which they would divide the profits. The business took more time than Trowbridge and Farnsworth felt they could spare so they canceled the contract after $30,000 had been invested. The land they bought had produced $80,000 and they shared in a tidy profit. It was at this point, with negotiations only partly complete with Robert Kinzie of Chicago for a one-fourth portion of the Kinzie addition to the city, that Lyon and Daniels, with some assistance from Benjamin B. Kercheval, stepped into the business.

The Bronsons were serious businessmen, and they had frequent disagreements with Lyon and others who were making investments for them. Detroit historian George C. Bates describes Arthur Bronson as "the closest, most penurious rich man in New York." There are several instances where the Bronsons met with Lyon in Washington to discuss face-to-face a particular problem which they did not wish to consign to the mails, and on at least one occasion they demanded his presence in New York City when they feared there was a shortage in the books. Charles Butler, who was co-investor in several projects and who was also apparently the recipient of blunt accusations and curt notes, wrote Lyon confidentially July 2, 1835, "I hope that your contract with our friend Bronson will soon be closed and that you will be at liberty to unite with me in some good investments. I propose to raise a fund for you of from 60 to 100,000 or some such as you can profitably invest. . . ." At the time Lyon replied that in two months he would be able to go with Butler, if the Bronsons would allow his brother, Orson, to do their investing in the west. Before the end of the year, however, Lyon had acquired a large indebtedness to Arthur Bronson as a result of a Grand Rapids transaction. Later the death of Isaac Bronson further complicated matters.

Orson also wrote that he couldn't afford to do business "at that small share of profits." Indebtedness to the Bronsons was to become a major part of Lyon's economic difficulties beginning in the late 1830s.

Other frequent business partners were Thomas C. Sheldon, former sheriff of Detroit; his brother, John P. Sheldon, one-time editor of the *Democratic Free Press* and later land agent in Wisconsin; Epaphroditus Ransom of Kalamazoo, later governor of Michigan; Judge James D. Doty, later of Wisconsin; E. P. Hastings and C. C. Trowbridge.

Shortly after Lyon began his Michigan Territory investments land was selling at an unprecedented rate. Thomas C. Sheldon, who ran the land office at White Pigeon and later, Kalamazoo, wrote in April of 1836, "You will hardly credit the Statement when I say that $467,913.15 has been Recd. at this office the last quarter -- very near a half million in ninety days and that to be in the months of January, February and March of all seasons in the year, the most unfavorable for the sale of public lands -- What will become of us when the navigation opens, and business fairly commences the Lord only knows."

During these years of boom it seemed a real affront to those involved with land that an establishment as successful as Michigan was by appearance could not achieve a more ready welcome into the Union. Isaac Barnes of Geloster (named for his three sons GEorge, CarLOS, and LesTER, later Richland) in Kalamazoo County, wrote February 28, 1836, "So great is the press of business at the land office at Bronson that the purchaser is sometimes detained two or three days before he can obtain his papers -- Many second and third hand sales have been made this winter to very good advantage -- Thus our young state is advancing in wealth and importance not withstanding the . . . views which some of our neighbors take of us."

Lyon's investments, both on his own behalf, and for other Michigan and Eastern investors, spanned the lower peninsula of Michigan and extended into Wisconsin and Illinois. The descriptions below of lands which Lyon invested in or developed cannot possibly be complete, but they cover the major investments and give some idea of the scope of his undertaking.

Ypsilanti

One of Lyon's first land investment ventures was Ypsilanti, in Washtenaw County, directly west of Wayne County where Detroit is located. The community was begun in 1822 by Augustus Brevoort Woodward, who served as chief justice of the territorial supreme court, 1805 to 1824, before assuming a similar position in Florida territory. In

1825 Lucius Lyon bought 700 acres of the judge's land for $2,300.

Lucius wrote his father in September of 1825, "Judge Woodward laid out a village on this ground, believing at some future time it would be a place of some importance. There was not then an inhabitant in that part of the country, now the population is considerably dense along the river above and below this place and is every day increasing. At a tavern three-fourths of a mile distant they frequently have from ten to twenty lodgers in a night, although the accommodations are of the poorest kind. The advantages of this situation are, in my estimation, greater than those of any other place within 100 miles of Detroit. It is on a navigable river [the Huron] about 22 miles from its mouth, in the midst of a fine country. A leading road, one of the greatest in the territory which has just been laid out and which will probably be finished in two or three years, passes through it. It is the best site for a mill in that part of the country."

Judge Woodward, known as a deep thinker in early Michigan, had suggested the name for the town to honor two current heroes, the Ypsilanti brothers -- Alexandre and Demetrio. The two were Greek patriots leading the revolt of their countrymen against Turkish rule. The Greek struggle for independence aroused popular sympathy in the United States and in the early 1820s public meetings and rallies on behalf of the Greek patriots were common events in Detroit. Lucius explained to his father that it was pronounced "as if written Ipsilanti," He then goes on in some detail outlining a plan whereby his father could sell his Vermont home and farm and invest over $3,000 in the new settlement. The elder Lyon was apparently unconvinced.

Between surveying jobs, in the latter half of the 1820s, Lucius Lyon also established a small farm on a part of his Ypsilanti land. He wrote Lucretia in the spring of 1827, "I shall probably spend the summer at Ypsilanti farming." He was in Ypsilanti in October of 1826 when Daniel B. Brown, who would shortly settle in Ann Arbor, encountered him on the road to Detroit, and the two rode in together. Lyon owned at least one house in Ypsilanti, near the mill, and may have lived there for a brief period. Later, a cousin, George A. Robinson, ran a general store at Ypsilanti and in 1834 entered into a partnership with Elijah Ellis. The two young partners considered a move to Schoolcraft because "in Ypsilanti there is too much competition and we can get no foothold" but two months later Robinson bought Ellis out and he reported that alone he hoped to do quite well. Robinson later moved to Lyons, then to Ada, and eventually worked in the salt mining operation in Grand Rapids.

Lyon's partner in much of the Ypsilanti investment was Mark Norris, Ypsilanti postmaster, who stayed on-site and tried to make the project work. Both were investors in the Detroit and St. Joseph Railroad which would pass through Ypsilanti. The railroad development began in 1833 and Norris wrote Lyon, then just beginning his first term as territorial delegate in Washington, "A railroad from Detroit to St. Joseph would cut 5 or 600 miles of Dangerous navigation in supplying the particle regions west with goods and receiving in exchange the growth of a country boundless as the ocean, and fruitful as the garden of Damascus. And now Sir, the citizens of the Territory are looking for and Expecting that the 'young Lyon of the West' will do his best to accomplish this object."

An 1825 plat of Ypsilanti. Lyon and Norris purchased the land previously owned by Judge Woodward (lower left).

In 1835 Lyon made a deal with Norris that he and Isaac Bronson would purchase Norris's half interest in the mill privilege, two mills, two dwelling houses, and all unsold village property and other lands for $5,000, and then rent the mills back to Norris for a period of two years. Norris agreed to the terms at least partly to gain the support of the Bronsons and Eastern money to build the railroad, "If we are to have a railroad in Michigan," he wrote in September of 1835, "we must build it ourselves . . . and you must not be backward in this Good Cause. I rely on you and your influence with the Bronsons to bring them into harness."

Norris worked to bring the tracks their way and have the depot erected on their property. He wrote February 23, 1836, "I have surveyed several routes into the village, but all of the different lines run across the Land I sold you, so that they cannot shun our land." But before the railroad was actually constructed it was taken over by the state, shortly after Michigan was finally admitted to the Union, and the new commission located the depot elsewhere. They also planned a water station for the bank of the river but Norris wrote December 22, 1837, "The engineer was sent and he understood he had the power to change the site if he did not like it, and he was dissatisfied with it and commenced erecting a water station upon your and my land." The engineer prepared the site and collected materials and then got orders to put it by the river where the directors had previously told him to. Norris's letter continued, "He started to move it, but became so disgusted with it that he quit the whole and went to Detroit. I then commenced and have erected a water station where the engineer thought the best place with the faint hope of having the decision of the commission reversed. Most likely you will think me a great fool and probably I am, and shall be confounded, and it will be called Norris's Babel, for it some what resembles the one built at Bable."

But on Christmas Day he wrote triumphantly, "The commissioners have reversed their decision and made the water station, depot &c on our land. It was more than I expected a few days ago." The first train entered Ypsilanti February 8, 1838. It arrived without incident although the engineer and fireman in charge were so bent on impressing the officials on board that they burned out the flues of the engine on the return trip, and all the distinguished guests were compelled to walk the last leg of the journey back to Detroit.

With business looking up, Norris sought to get the help of Lyon and Bronson to build new mills, "our old mills are about done," or to buy them out. On November 21, 1837, he wrote, "Can I have the mill another year or two? I have had a millwright in constant employ repairing ever since last March and nothing but a constant tinkering will keep them together -- If you do not wish to improve, and I cannot buy of you, I will sell to you." He offered them $10,000 to purchase their interest in the mill property, including buying back the portion he had sold them two years earlier. Lyon accepted with a show of reluctance, "Your offer to buy or sell," he wrote, "seems to be a fair one, but in reality the advantage is all on your side, for situated as I am you are aware I could not afford to pay more than three-fourths as much as you could." Norris's first contract was canceled when the bank refused to accepted $1,400 of the money he presented for the first payment. It was the height of the wildcat banking era, when much of the currency was suspect and personal notes were also being refused when the bankers knew their signers to be insolvent, but he later renewed the offer on slightly different terms. Late in 1838 Isaac Bronson died and the contract obligating Norris to buy the land from Lyon and Bronson was turned over to the executors of the Bronson estate.

Chicago

Even among the rapidly growing settlements in the American west Chicago is remarkable. From a handful of settlers clustered around a wooden stockade in 1830, its population rose to 4,470 in 1840, and had reached 29,000 by 1850. Just as this growth was beginning, possibly as early as 1826, Lucius Lyon, who was surveying on the southwestern edge of Michigan Territory, became interested in land speculating. In the company of L. J. Daniels, who was part of the Schoolcraft venture, Lyon bought a number of parcels at the first public auction of lands in Chicago. Most of this land was sold within a very short time to Eastern speculators; some of it may have been bought with their funds or at least at their direction. Arthur and Isaac Bronson, and Charles Butler of New York City, were among Eastern investors who made a good profit from land purchased by Lyon and Daniels and others at Chicago. Arthur Bronson wrote many and voluminous letters, and in a missive dated August 24, 1833, he notes that he is forwarding ten previously written letters to Lyon in Illinois. At that time purchase was pending of two parcels in the middle of what would be the City of Chicago. Bronson states that under already completed agreements he and the other investors will "lend or procure for you on your Bond and Mortgage, on the property purchased at that place any sum for the purpose not exceeding $5000 in which purchase it was understood we were to share one-quarter each, to your one half, unless you take one-third interest in the Kinzie purchase, if made by us, in which case we were not to participate in your one third share of that property." He asks Lyon to help Benjamin Kercheval, another Bronson agent, in his selections at a school section auction scheduled for October, and adds, "If you wish (and I should advise you to do it) to bid at the public sale of the town section you are at liberty to do so. . . ." The first village plat of Chicago was laid off in 1830, with no Lake Michigan shoreline. In 1832 an 80 by 100 foot lot sold for $100. One Chicago city lot, at the corner of what would be South Water and Clark Street, was sold for $100 in 1832, for $3,000 in 1834, and for $15,000 in 1835. The Bronsons made considerable profit on their Chicago investments but complained constantly that it could be more. Eventually both Arthur and Frederick spent time in Chicago personally dealing with business there. As early as the summer of 1833 they felt that soaring land prices were making Chicago investments look less promising and Arthur wrote, "The result of an examination of our finances and our prospective engagements at Chicago and elsewhere has brought us to the conclusion not to invest any more for the present at Chicago." They began instead investing in prairie land in Illinois and Wisconsin. According to correspondence it was during this time that they discovered several valuable areas of land in Michigan including large tracts of prairie. There are several letters to Lyon from Arthur Bronson which are postmarked White Pigeon Prairie, the site of an early land office in Michigan nearly within sight of the territory's southern boundary.

Mount Clemens

In 1835 Lyon bought lots in the village plat of Mount Clemens, the county seat of Macomb County, from Christian Clemens who had platted the original village in 1818 on the Clinton River near an old Moravian settlement they called New Gnadenhutten. The land, bought for the Bronsons on February 9, 1835, consisted of 60 building lots and was bounded on the south by Front Street, on the west by New Street, on the north by Court Street, and on the east by Market Street. In January of 1836 Lyon explained to Isaac Bronson that the Mount Clemens property was worth about $4,000 when he purchased it, and would be worth at least $5,000 now "though this is low because the legislative council has granted a railroad charter between Mount Clemens and some point west which will greatly increase the value of property at that place." The settlement was also to be the eastern terminus of the Clinton-Kalamazoo Canal which was begun July 20, 1838. Stevens T. Mason turned the first spade of earth and 150 people attended a dinner served in a bower erected on the public square. Mount Clemens was originally incorporated as a village in 1837, but in the economic panic that quickly followed, the charter was not implemented, and the settlement did not apply for incorporation again until 1851. The lands that were purchased for Isaac Bronson were retained by his son, at least as late as 1839.

An early plat map of Mount Clemens

Washtenaw County

In addition to lands in the village of Ypsilanti and farm land nearby Lyon owned at least one other plot of land in Washtenaw County. This was a 17 acre parcel near the later settlement of Saline. It was purchased in 1830 from S. Orange Risdon. In January of 1836 Risdon wrote him in Washington trying to convince him to sell it to Philander Howe for $650, or to exchange it for other lands.

Battle Creek

In June of 1831 Sands McCamly visited the southern portion of Kalamazoo County and was impressed with the land around what would later be Battle Creek. When he arrived at the land office in White Pigeon which served that portion of the territory, he discovered that others had expressed an interest in the land. J. J. Gurnsey of New York, was one of the parties, and Lucius Lyon and Robert Clark, government surveyors, had made note of the locale as an excellent one to start a town. The two surveyors sold their right to bid against the others for

$100 cash. This was apparently not a true pre-emption right, merely a promise not to enter the bidding and drive the price up; it may be that they were also asked to keep quiet about the excellence of the location.

A deal was made with J. J. Gurnsey, and he entered 837.44 acres in Battle Creek Township, including the water power potential on the river, with the understanding that McCamly and Daniel G. Gurnsey would share the cost equally with him. Gurnsey also had a cabin built on his property to secure the claim that was the first house in Battle Creek. The families were to meet in Detroit the following October when the original purchaser was to quit claim an undivided third of the entire tract to each of the other two. Each would then place $2,000 in the bank and move to the area to oversee the birth of the new town. McCamly reached Detroit at the appointed time, and so did J. J. Gurnsey and his brother-in-law and their wives. The women said they had been to look at the place and couldn't possibly live there.

McCamly, discouraged, moved to Nottawa Prairie in the southern part of Calhoun County and later to the Marshall area where his efforts during the cholera epidemic of 1832 made him something of a local hero. J. J. Gurnsey went back to New York and sold some of his land to Nathaniel Barney and some to his brother Ezekial. Still believing that the location was a good one, McCamly returned to the Battle Creek area in 1834, bought out the Gurnsey relatives, and began development of the site. He built a canal, the first sawmill, and a factory for "practical furniture." In pioneer annals McCamly is called the "real founder of Battle Creek, its best friend and benefactor." He later served in the first senate of the new State of Michigan.

When Lyon ran for territorial delegate in 1833 one of the accusations leveled at him was that he or his agents had received "hush" money from men wishing to purchase land at public sales in exchange for a promise not to bid against them. This may have been one case the accusers had in mind.

Schoolcraft

Lyon wrote his sister from Bronson, later Kalamazoo, in a letter dated October 19, 1833, about his business interests in Bronson and added, "I also own the village of Schoolcraft, on Big Prairie Ronde, about twelve miles south of this, in the same county, one of the pleasantest and most beautiful places in any country. It is situated on the east border of an island of about 700 acres of wood land, in the center of a high and fine, rich and beautiful prairie containing about 20,000 acres. Description is useless. The village I named after my friend,

Henry R. Schoolcraft of Mackinaw, in this Territory, who is well known to the scientific world, both in America and Europe, as a distinguished traveler and writer. It was laid out about two years ago and now contains two stores, a large public house and about 300 families. They purchased their land about three years ago for a dollar and a quarter an acre. Besides the village plat, I own about 220 acres adjoining it, which would bring $12 per acre (cash) any day. I look upon this country as my future residence, at least for three or four years, and perhaps forever."

The new village was to be located in the middle of Prairie Ronde, a nearly round treeless area which covered half of one township and a third of another. In the center of this "round prairie" was a grove of trees rising like an island from the surrounding grasslands. These openings in the woods were considered valuable lands by the early settlers because they did not have to be cleared of towering forest trees before planting crops.

The settlement at Schoolcraft had scarcely begun in April of 1832 when the residents were roused late at night by a rider from White Pigeon calling out the county militia. He told them that the Indians in Illinois had risen and were slaughtering inhabitants, had taken some military posts in Chicago. Indeed the whole country was in danger. E. Lakin Brown, a partner of the Smith brothers, was given the community's fastest stallion and was sent to Kalamazoo (then Bronson) to inform militia officers.

Brown wrote later, "I saddled and mounted and started about midnight, very dark, rode to Bronson, and in front of the store hailed [Major Hosea] Huston, crying: 'The Indians are upon us!' Huston came to the window half dazed. I explained matters to him and went on to Gull Prairie, getting there just at daylight. I left the express with Colonel [Isaac] Barnes, got some breakfast and started home." A few days later Brown left with the other troops from Schoolcraft, but, when they arrived in Niles, they received notice that the army under General Jacob Brown was about to start out and had no provision to spare. Since they were not needed, the men returned home. Brown said later, "For this experience in war, besides a month's pay, I afterward received bounty warrants, first for forty acres of land and then for 120 more."

According to the *Kalamazoo County Tract Book* Lucius Lyon purchased five parcels of land in what would be Schoolcraft Township on June 6, 1831. This was twelve days before land in that area was available for purchase by any other than previous settlers. The purchase of lands on Prairie Ronde prior to the public sale was one of the irregular land deals mentioned in 1833 when the opposing party was trying to discredit Lyon during the election campaign for territorial delegate.

At that time James Smith, for many years a major land holder in Schoolcraft, attempted to answer these charges by explaining that he had been to Prairie Ronde in early June, had selected several lots and then had gone to the land office to enter them. "I found that the land officers had not yet arrived; I called upon Mr. McGaffey, lawyer of the place, and he informed me that Maj. Edwards, the Register, had recently written him that they should be there to open the office the next week Monday. I left with Mr. McGaffey the money and numbers to enter said lots. Maj. Edwards arrived at White Pigeon the Saturday after. There was then a great concourse of people waiting impatiently to enter land -- it was in the afternoon. Maj. E. at the time of his arrival informed all those who wished to purchase land to hand in their applications, and where there were no collisions, the papers would be made out to be delivered. My application from some cause, (I presume accident,) not being handed over -- Mr. Lyon applying for the same lots, received his papers for them. In the course of the same week, I called upon Mr. Lyon, stating to him the circumstances of the case. He observed that he had made application for the same lots some time previous to the office being opened -- that he had no knowledge of any other person wishing to enter them. The Register made the same statement. Mr. Lyon and myself then agreed that our applications should be considered as having been presented at the same time; and we agreed in the division of said lots, to the perfect satisfaction, I believe, of both parties."

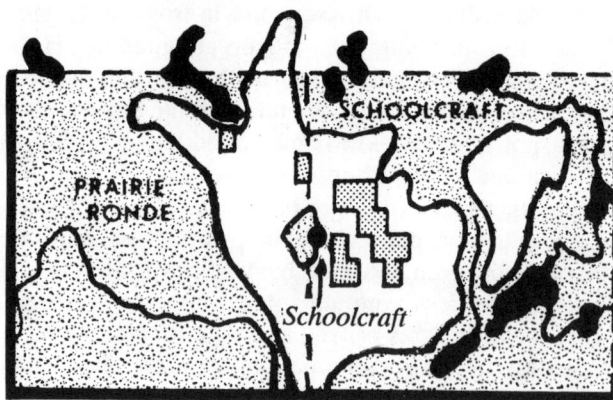

A map of the two townships in the southwest corner of Kalamazoo County showing lakes and streams, and the natural prairies. The light area at right is Gourdneck Prairie, the one in the middle, centered by the grove of trees and the settlement of Schoolcraft, is Prairie Ronde. Outlined plots on the larger prairie indicate the boundaries of land owned by Lyon.

140

In an 1840 affidavit, when some of the citizens of Schoolcraft were trying to fend off a relocation of the main road of the village, they described its beginnings. "In 1831 a company of persons, viz. Messrs. Smith and others established themselves in this place in the mercantile business. In the same year Lucius Lyon purchased land where School-craft now is, and laid out the Village, a concurrence of interests consequently took place between Lucius Lyon, proprietor, and Smith & Co., in the growth of the place. . . . Smith and Co. built a large town house . . . to be made a central point of business, now the Big Island Hotel." In 1833 the Smiths purchased 40 acres south of the village and west of Main Street. Lyon acquired land to the east of the original village, which had previously been reserved as university land, and platted it into lots. With added settlement on the east the main north-south road where the hotel was located was abandoned and a new main street established to the east.

Most of the early settlers of Schoolcraft were from Vermont. James Smith was part of a large Smith family which came to the prairie at an early date and ran a store and hotel. He is not the James Smith who was a first cousin (later step-brother) of the Lyon family, although they may have been more distantly related, but the name is a common one, and a kinship is not mentioned in written communications that have survived. The James Smith who settled in Schoolcraft was in charge of selling lands owned by Lucius Lyon for several years, and held power of attorney to purchase lands for him as well. Despite the glowing testimony in the newspaper the two did not get along well, and in November of 1835 serious charges of mismanagement of Lyon's affairs in Schoolcraft by the Smiths were made by other interested parties.

In April of 1834 Lucius received a letter from Ira Lyon, an uncle, notifying him that he had moved to Michigan and was living near Pontiac. It was about this time that discontent with the way the Smiths were handling things surfaced and Ira was asked to move west to take charge of the Schoolcraft project. His power of attorney from Lucius to sell land to settlers is dated October 17, 1835. The Smiths remained. Ira wrote in November of 1835, that in order to earn operating funds, he had contracted to hew 12,000 rails for James Smith.

By February of 1834, Lyon was developing the farming on his Schoolcraft land. He wrote one of his fellow investors that the materials for a proper fence for the farm would cost $835, and that a contract had been let for the spring plowing. In November of 1835 he wrote that he had harvested a fine crop of wheat and oats. In 1835 he purchased lots two and 11 of the Schoolcraft plat, both with houses on them, from Albert. E. Bull.

It was on the wheat fields of Prairie Ronde that the Moore-

Hascall harvesting machine was tested and which was the setting for the last chapter of James Fenimore Cooper's novel *Oak Openings* that describes the machine in action.

The village lots and farmland around Schoolcraft was taken over in early 1840 by Arthur Bronson during the settlement of his father's estate putting in limbo nearly every parcel of land that had been sold by Lyon or his agents. After visiting the settlement in 1842 Bronson relented and said that he was willing to relinquish claim to any village lot which had been sold prior to December of 1835, the date of the first mortgage.

Kalamazoo

The first land which Lyon bought in the vicinity of the later settlement of Kalamazoo was in August of 1830 when he purchased a parcel in section 15 from Nathan Harrison. The following year he bought additional lands in the future village and several other parcels in the countryside surrounding. On September 1, 1832, Lucius Lyon and Justus Burdick completed an agreement concerning ten parcels of land, totaling 541 acres, along the Kalamazoo River in Kalamazoo County, Arcadia (later Kalamazoo) Township. Some of this land had been purchased from the earliest settler, Titus Bronson, and some from others. Six of these parcels, 355 acres, were to be owned by Burdick alone, and the remaining four, 186 acres, were to be held jointly with the understanding that Burdick retained the right to buy out Lyon's interest for $1277 should he so desire at a later date.

Titus Bronson had lived in Ohio and Ann Arbor and had visited the site of Kalamazoo some time prior to arriving as a settler in June of 1829. Even then he probably stayed in his quickly built shelter only until cold weather, retiring for the winter to a farm on Prairie Ronde. In January of 1831, the village site was selected as county seat for Kalamazoo County. Shortly afterwards Titus Bronson and others recorded a plat calling the new settlement Bronson.

Justus Burdick was from Vermont, living first in Woodstock, later in Burlington. He had been urged to come west by former Vermonter Elon Farnsworth. Burdick had met Lucius Lyon during a trip to Detroit and Lyon had prevailed upon him to visit Kalamazoo County. After the purchase of land was formalized, Justus Burdick returned to Vermont and sent his brother, Cyren, to look after interests in Michigan. (Justus returned to Michigan with his family in 1837, and lived in Kalamazoo until his death in 1849.)

In August of 1834 Thomas C. Sheldon, former sheriff from

Detroit, and, more recently, land office receiver at the White Pigeon land office (later moved to Kalamazoo), joined them as the third proprietor of the village.

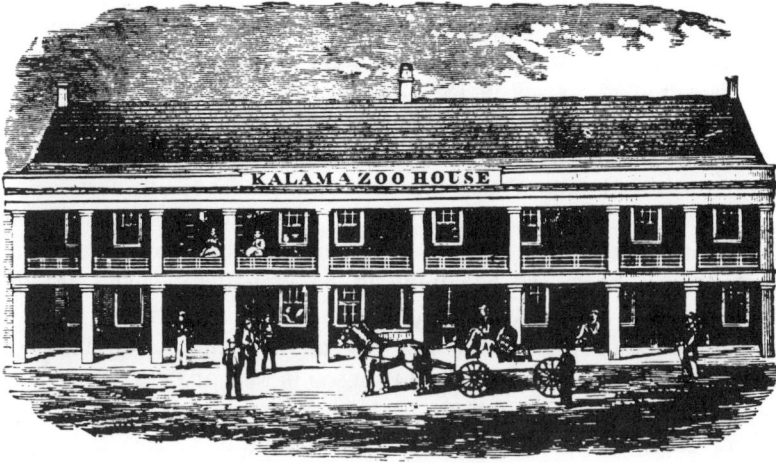

The Kalamazoo House

One of the earliest improvements to the town plat was the building of the Kalamazoo House, a hotel which would serve as a stopping place for would-be settlers and others interested in the purchase of land. It was a two-story frame structure, 30 by 40 feet, with a two-story veranda in front built by an Allegan county contractor. A Kalamazoo County history later reported that the day the frame was to be raised, "which was on Saturday, there were not hands enough to do the work; but on the following day (Sunday), when everybody was supposed to be resting, the able bodied men were collected from far and near, and the frame went up." In 1834 the official plat of the settlement was slightly altered so as to make one of the main streets bend to bring travelers from the south to the Kalamazoo House. Ownership of the hotel changed frequently, title sometimes being vested in Burdick, sometimes in Burdick and Lyon, and later with Burdick, Lyon and T. C. Sheldon. By 1842 all had relinquished their interest to others.

Lyon wrote his sister Lucretia, in a letter from "Bronson, Kalamazoo Co., Michigan Territory, October 19, 1833. The place where I now write is the seat of justice for one of the richest and most productive counties in our Territory and although there are now but two stores and about a dozen dwelling houses, it will in a few years be one

143

of the finest villages in the western part of the peninsula. It is situated on the southwest side of the Kalamazoo river about 50 miles above its mouth and about 140 miles west from Detroit. I own one-third of the village plat and about 160 acres of land adjoining, which must in a few years be very valuable."

All did not progress smoothly, however. In December of 1833 Cyren Burdick wrote Lyon that they were having trouble with William Harris, who had arrived in 1830 and is credited with building the first real cabin in the village (the structure that Bronson originally lived in was more of a shanty). Cyren complained that ". . . he asserts claims and cuts timber on land that he does not own. The difficulty has an unfavorable effect on the settlement of this place. Many persons are wishing to purchase but do not wish to receive a title which is doubtful. Lots in this place are beginning to be in better demand and the peaceable and undisturbed control of the whole is desirable."

Colonel A. Edwards, who was contemplating a stage line from Detroit to St. Joseph, wrote from Bronson in May of 1834, "This village is improving, several buildings are being constructed at this time and several more will be shortly. I like the situation much and the country for miles about it."

Arthur Bronson was sometimes asked to be the go-between for the Michigan investors and printers in New York. In June of 1835, he sent three proof copies of a map of Bronson for correction and approval and was sufficiently impressed with the project to note that "Mr. Sheldon suggested that an interest might be available . . . on favorable terms." Six hundred copies of the corrected map were forwarded in July with a bill for $60.63.

There is some evidence that Lucius Lyon was seriously contemplating a permanent residence in the settlement. While serving as territorial delegate in Washington in April of 1834, he received a letter from a contractor offering to build a house. A letter from T. C. Sheldon in April of 1836 carries the note that John Almy of Grand Rapids would furnish the "neatest and cheapest plan for your house -- I had better defer it until you come here." Also in the Lyon papers is a detailed proposal for a house to be built in "Bronson," but no evidence that construction was ever begun.

On March 2, 1836, an act was approved by the state legislature to change the name of the village from Bronson to Kalamazoo. In a letter dated, March 25, 1836, Kalamazoo investor Epaphroditus Ransom asked Lyon who was representing Michigan in the U. S. Senate to have the name of the post office changed as well. "The importance of this change must be apparent to the Dept. it should have been changed sooner, had not the namer of the town and village here attended. There is a Post Office by name of <u>Bronson's Prairie</u> in Branch Co. There has always been much confusion of the mails, on that account." Many historians also feel that the change was an effort by investors to distance themselves from original settler Titus Bronson, an honest but somewhat eccentric pioneer. If there is a family relationship between Titus, and Isaac Bronson and family, it is distant. Titus Bronson came originally from Connecticut.

The economic prospects of the growing village were further enhanced in June of 1836 when the U. S. land office was moved from White Pigeon to Kalamazoo. On September 16, 1836, Lyon sold what interest he had left in the Kalamazoo project to Justus Burdick and decided to concentrate on his growing settlement at the rapids of the Grand River.

As late as March of 1846 Thomas C. Sheldon and General Burdick asked Lyon to help them wind up affairs of the Kalamazoo Corporation, "There is no way we can close our differences," Sheldon wrote, "short of your personal appearance."

Grand Rapids

Lyon did a special survey in 1825-26 to determine the meander of the Grand River. However the area that would become the City of Grand Rapids, Kent County, was not surveyed in preparation for settlement until 1831 when he and John Mullett completed the task. Lyon's responsibility was town seven north range twelve west; Mullett's survey included town seven range eleven.

During Lyon's political campaign of 1833 there were claims of irregularity in the purchase of the land that later became downtown Grand Rapids. Lyon was accused of pulling strings to get Louis Campau full pre-emption benefits and then purchasing half of his land. The unsigned letter, published in a Detroit newspaper, also accused him of surveying the fractions "so as to cover all the water power on the south side of the river."

In response, a supporter, A. S. Dygert, replied by letter in a subsequent newspaper that he had spoken to Campau about the deal and that Campau had said he was "highly satisfied with everything that Mr. Lyon had done on the matter -- said he had acted with the utmost honor, fairness and liberality in assisting him to obtain a pre-emption right, at much trouble and expense to himself, when the time allowed by law had so nearly expired that Mr. Lyon was obliged to send to the Surveyor General's Office at Cincinnati expressly for the purpose -- that he could not have purchased the land at that time without the aid of

Mr. Lyon -- and that he felt now and had always felt under great obligations for his kindness." A letter in the files of the surveyor general's office dated April 30, 1831 confirms Lyon's assistance to Campau.

Two years later the issue surfaced again. At that time A. S. Cotton, who had served on Lyon's surveying gang in 1831, gave testimony that "Mr. Lyon left his survey on the Kalamazoo River and with his whole party and baggage travelled through the woods to Grand River expressly to survey the lot claimed by Campau so that he, Campau, could obtain a preemption in the purchase of said land before the expiration of the preemption law then in force.

"When we arrived at the Grand Rapids where Mr. Campau then and now resides he stated in a conversation with Mr. Lyon in my presence that he was not anxious to purchase all the land that his preemption claim would cover, but was desirous to secure about an acre on which his house stood so that he might trade with the Indians without the risk of being driven away by Mr. Slater, the Missionary at the Rapids, who, Mr. Campau said, threatened to buy his land from under him because, as I understood, Campau was in the habit of selling whiskey to the Indians.

"He also seemed to fear that the Americans, or Whites, by coming on and settling the country, would destroy his Indian trade, and he seemed to calculate on leaving the country whenever that should take place, he told Mr. Lyon he might have the whole of his claim, excepting the land where his house stood (for his trouble and expense in surveying it and procuring preemption) by paying the Government price for all but the acre aforesaid, or a spot large enough for a garden.

"This proposal, voluntarily made and first suggested by Mr. Campau, Mr. Lyon accepted, went on to survey the land, and after the survey of the Fractional Township, in which it lay, was completed he, Mr. Lyon, at the request of Campau, sent Aaron Adams, one of his chainmen, to the Surveyor General's office at Cincinnati to carry the field notes of the survey and bring back the plat of the Township before the expiration of the preemption law. . . .

"I understood Mr. Lyon advanced the money to Mr. Campau to pay for his preemption in pursuance of the aforesaid arrangement, and thought at the time and so, I believe, our whole party thought, that this amount together with the trouble and expense he had incurred would make the land offered him by Mr. Campau cost him all it was worth.

"It was well known to me and to all who composed Mr. Lyon's party at that time that Mr. Campau could not have obtained a preemption at all, under the law then in force, without the assistance which Mr. Lyon rendered him, and whatever may be his feelings now, since the land has become valuable; he at that time seemed satisfied with what had been done."

Campau traveled to White Pigeon to make his purchase September 20, 1831. The parcel contained about 72 acres including most of what was later downtown Grand Rapids and was roughly bounded by Michigan Street on the north, Fulton on the south, Division Avenue on the east and the river on the west. The cost was $1.25 per acre or about $90.

The following summer Lyon took title to about half of the tract from Campau. His land extended from midway between present-day Lyon and Pearl Streets north to Michigan and east to Division. Eurotus P. Hastings was included in the original deed and subsequent dealings would indicate that there were several silent partners including the Bronsons. In addition to the land purchased from Campau, Lyon and friends purchased 135 acres in section 34 and other lands in section 30 before 1834. Their land acquisitions would eventually box in the Campau settlement.

Although Bronson held some land in Grand Rapids and wanted to buy more, especially certain parcels from Louis Campau, he was not successful in attempts to purchase into the major project. In August of 1833 he reported to Lyon that he and L. J. Daniels had been trying to purchase the two-thirds interest owned by C. C. Trowbridge and E. P. Hastings but were having a hard time coming to terms because Trowbridge and Hastings wanted to include some land they held nearby and were demanding a large cash downpayment. Bronson termed their demands "altogether inadmissible" and explained, "A large expenditure will be required to render the Rapids profitable at an early day which I should think it unwise for us to incur. We must wait the lapse of time and the operations and expenditures by others and cannot afford to pay a large price in anticipation of what the property may hereafter possibly be worth."

Later in 1833, Trowbridge wrote Lyon that he had bought the interest of Hastings. "I am afraid," Trowbridge wrote in December, "you will think me a little wild. I gave him cost and $1200 in dicker for his share of the Grand Rapids purchase. What do you think of it?. . . . The place is attracting attention. A gentleman of New York called . . . who said he had a capital of $4000 and that he intended to go there next spring with a store, and he wants to know what we intended there. . . . We could only say that our plans were not yet mature." Sometime prior to the summer of 1835 Nathaniel O. Sargeant, a former shoe and boot salesman from Detroit, bought a half interest in the project.

Louis Campau had his settlement platted and called it the

Village of Grand Rapids, after the large (in French *grande*) rapids on the river at that point. The principal street of the settlement was Monroe, laid out along an old Indian trail that led to the trading post. Lucius Lyon and his fellow investors laid their land out in regular lots with a north-south orientation. On February 8, 1836, a plat of this land was recorded at Kalamazoo as the Village of Kent, taking its name from the county in which it was located which had been named for James Kent, a New York State jurist.

Relations between the two town proprietors were strained. In a letter dated October 12, 1835, Lyon refers to Campau as "a jealous, selfish and troublesome Frenchman." The situation was not improved when it was discovered that Sophia de Bec Campau, wife of Louis, had not signed the deeds for the lands her husband had sold to Lucius Lyon, and later would not do so when asked. Lucius wrote one of his fellow investors, Arthur Bronson of New York, in November of 1835, "I ought to also inform you that the wife of Louis Campau Jr., of whom I purchased the fraction which we own together, has never relinquished her right of dower in said land and refused to do so." Lyon filed suit in court to obtain clear title. (This difficulty was eventually smoothed over by giving the lady two lots. Mrs. Campau then signed the paper clearing the title on the rest of the plat.)

The two contiguous settlements, with roads which either intersected on the diagonal, or not at all, created some confusing traffic patterns that still affect travelers in downtown Grand Rapids today. Campau owned the land from Pearl Street halfway to Lyon Street and proceeded to plat a row of town lots that closed off entry to his settlement down Canal Street, the main street of Kent, which ran parallel to the river. According to traditional accounts he is said to have told Lyon, "If you want to come into my plat you will have to go around by Division Street."

This ruse was partially defeated when Campau sold lots one and two to Abram S. Wadsworth for a sawmill. Since the mill wheel extended out into the river, Wadsworth discovered that he did not need both lots and sold a strip to the Kent investors who promptly cut Canal Street through to Pearl. However, two right angle turns were still required to get to Monroe. (It was not until 1873 that several buildings were razed to give Canal Street a smoother access to Monroe.) To make other through streets more difficult, Lyon and his partners, or Campau, or both, saw to it that lot boundaries between Lyon and Pearl Streets did not line up, making it difficult for future generations to bring the three north-south streets on Lyon's plat between Canal and Division through to Pearl Street.

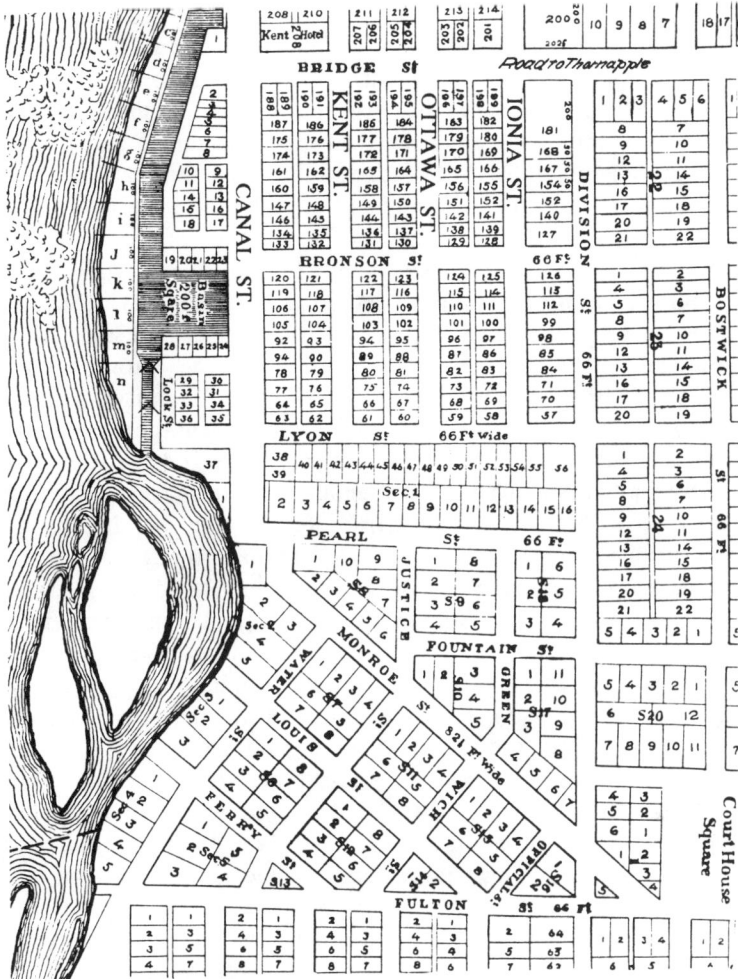

Campau's settlement of Grand Rapids ran from just north of Pearl Street to Fulton on the south. Lyon and friends owned the settlement of Kent, bounded on the south by a line midway between Lyon and Pearl Streets and continuing to the north of Bridge Street. The canal, showing the proposed (but never built) locks, is at upper left. The canal, the river between the two islands and the shore, and much of the river shoreline that shows in this map was later filled to provide additional building sites in downtown Grand Rapids.

By October of 1835 development of industry was well under way. That month Lyon wrote investor Arthur Bronson that he had paid $500 for himself, and given a $500 draft for Bronson to Nathaniel O. Sargeant as their share of the expense already incurred in the construction of the canal which would bypass the rapids and furnish waterpower for the mills. "Mr. Sargeant has with him an excellent engineer and about 50 men . . . and will probably have the excavation nearly completed before winter sets in. The expense of the excavation alone is estimated at $5,000." (See chapter 11.)

Shortly afterwards landowners along the canal asked for joint ownership of the project, and Bronson, who had purchased some river-side land, balked at the idea. It is possible that his earlier rebuffs affected his decision. In December of 1835 when Lucius was still in Washington serving as territorial delegate Bronson went there from New York and met with him to discuss the project. The next day, Lyon wrote N. O. Sargeant in Michigan, a partner and on-site manager, "Arthur Bronson reached here from New York city last night. As he did not assent to our agreement, I commenced negotiations to buy him out and have effected a purchase of all his interest in Grand Rapids for $21,000."

In July of 1836 while Lyon was checking on some property in St. Joseph, he received a letter from George A. Robinson with the news, "Almy says Mr. Sargeant has sold the whole of his interest in the Town of Kent to a gentleman by the name of Carroll for the sum of eighty-three thousand dollars and that money was paid Thursday last. -- Mr. Carroll is down here." Charles H. Carroll was from New York but frequently visited Michigan, and retained an interest in Grand Rapids for many years. Other investors who were officially on the books at this time included John Almy, judge and engineer; and William A. Richmond.

Almy had been especially concerned that accommodations be constructed for prospective land owners and visitors and wrote in October that they planned to erect in the spring "a large and commodious public house on the . . . north side of the 100 foot street leading down to the canal. Such a house is much needed. . . " The hotel was opened for business in 1837 at the corner of Bridge and Kent Streets and first called the Kent Hotel, later the Grand River Exchange, and about 1845, after the first bridge across the Grand River was completed nearby, it became the Bridge Street House.

Just when money was needed most the supply seemed to dry up. Prices had gone so high that land sales dropped off dramatically. A new law that required gold for the purchase of federal land added to the investors' problems. William A. Richmond reported, November 24, 1836, "Upon an examination of the financial concerns, I find that the Treasury

150

circular and some other <u>Panic</u> <u>fiend</u> has penetrated even into the wilderness, and that even Kent feels the pressure -- yes, we want funds."

But plans pushed forward, the investors seemed especially eager to prove that the financial setback had been only temporary. In December engineer John Almy wrote, thanking Lyon for "a package of Fifteen Hundred dollars" and added a note, "I hope you will not be called upon by me again for any more funds. No, it is to be hoped that you will begin to receive something from this property. I begin to feel more at ease, believing as I do that things are now in a very good train for the ensuing years business. . . "

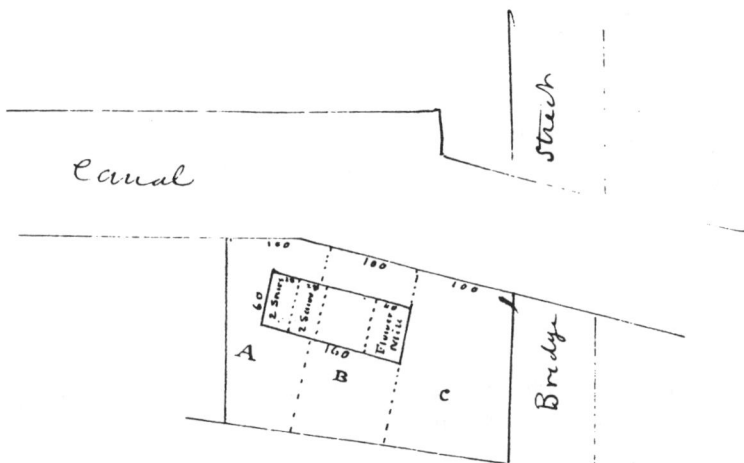

The above is a diagram showing the situation of the mill building on Lot a b v c Now I estimate the building and water sufficient to put in operation as much Machinery as the building will accommodate together with the ground it stands on to be worth at least $25,000. the then Lease L v. C. unincumbered and about 40 feet of Lot A north of the mill clear _ _ .

Contemplated Grand Rapids mill.

In the same letter Almy sent a drawing of mill buildings that would provide space for a Kalamazoo man who proposed to make a downpayment of $4000 for enough of the mill building and waterpower to run two saws, ". . . they to finish their portion, taking the building as it is now." Almy wrote, "Now it is my opinion that we had better take this offer. Especially considering the source from whence it comes, their character and standing and means to do business, and the probable

151

bearing it will have on the remaining part of our interest. . . . If it is deemed important to have a saw mill of our own that we should take the next space sufficient for 2 saws and have them ready for our own use by the time the water is let into the canal. The balance of the building I should think had better be appropriated for other purposes. Say 40 feet of the south end would make a flouring mill large enough for 4 runs of stone, this should be worth say $6,000 as it now is . . . there will remain about 70 feet which had better be filled up for various branches of business that require the aid of water. . .

"Our Public house is now open and full of Boarders and strangers, everything looks promising, sales are good and we shall be able to do what I did not believe could be done this fall, that is to sell Lots at the rate of $50 per foot. I have made one sale at this price. There are now several persons in the place who have come for the Express purpose of purchasing and also to become citizens -- let me but see one year more and I will show what can be done in the way of building a city -- "

Almy adds that he has just been returned to the state legislature and will attend to getting a bank charter and a bridge charter, and begin plans for incorporating the settlement as a village.

Later that year, for additional funds, Almy advised the sale of village lots at auction "say at Washington." He recommended that they not sell the downtown lots, but those "a little remote from the present scene of active operations." He says if Lyon and other owners feel that the sale is a good idea he will make a list of lots and also a map "not however embracing the whole plat but so much of it as would show the Lots for sale to occupy a more central position. . . "

By 1837 Richmond, who seems to be the investor most in favor of moderating their expenditures, wailed, "The extravagant and unreasonable plans for improvement have rendered their completion impossible, and the property of the place will have been advanced by less calculation and show, and more of the reality." Their dreams form much of this description in an 1838 gazetteer:

> GRAND RAPIDS, a village, the seat of justice for Kent county, located on the south bank of the Grand river, at the Grand Rapids. The presbyterians and episcopalians have each organized churches and settled ministers. It contains a church for catholics, a printing office that issues a weekly newspaper, two banking associations, court house, 12 stores erected or erecting, three commodious hotels, four practicing physicians, and six lawyers. A Branch of the University has been located here. The fall in the river is fifteen feet, and, by employing the entire volume of water, an immense hydraulic power can be obtained, and there is

every reason to believe that it will become a place of much note for manufacturing. A large mill, called the "Mam moth mill," believed to be the largest and most expensive in the western States, when completed will be in length 160 feet, 60 feet wide, and five stories high. The first two stories are of stone, the wall is 4 feet thick and 20 feet high. About $20,000 have already been expended upon it. The entire expense, when completed, will be $50,000. It is intended for the manufacture of lumber and flour. Three saws and two run of stone have just commenced operation. A charter has been granted to a company to connect the opposite banks of the river at this place by a bridge, the estimated expense of which is $15,000. It has great natural and prospective facilities for commercial intercourse, not only with the interior but likewise with foreign markets. It is approached to the foot of the rapids by steamboats from the lakes, and from their head to the village of Lyons, steamboats are continually plying. A canal is constructing to connect the waters of the head with the foot of the falls. Several roads laid out and in contemplation will connect it with different parts of the State. The principal one completed leads to Detroit. When the line of rail-road from Grand river to St. Clair is finished, the "Great Western" thoroughfare may be said to pass through it. Salt springs and gypsum have been found, within a few miles, of a good quality. The conveniences for building are numerous. Pine lumber, building stone, lime stone, water lime stone, and materials for brick manufacture, are abundant. The village is well supplied with pure spring water. The location is handsome, airy, and healthy, and commands a fine view of the rapids and the country around, of the Indian village Bokatink, and its ancient cultivated fields, mounds, and burial places on the other side of the river. It may be said to be one of the most flourishing and important villages of Michigan.

Lucius Lyon was elected to the Board of Trustees of the Village of Grand Rapids in 1843, one of the few instances in which he held a local office in the State of Michigan. On July 3, 1845 the village board met at his office. At this meeting the board approved a tavern license for Truman H. Lyon, among others, and both Lyon and Campau were requested to have the "original patents" of the lands on which the village was situated recorded, at the expense of the village.

Despite his interest in several Michigan communities, Grand Rapids was the only one where Lucius lived, for as much as a year, in a building he actually owned. In 1840 he brought his sister Lucretia from Vermont, and she took over care of his domestic arrangements in Grand Rapids, both living in the small building that had been built as an office for the Kent Co. and later the Grand River Bank. She lived in the city until her death in 1893.

On August 25, 1842, Lyon was elected president of a society to promote immigration to Grand Rapids. He also served as corresponding secretary. George Coggeshell and Darius Winsor were vice-presidents, S. M. Johnson acted as recording secretary, and E. B. Bostwick was treasurer.

The post office, when it was first opened on December 22, 1832, with Leonard Slater as postmaster, was called Grand Rapids. Lyon, with his political connections, had the name changed to Kent, September 1, 1836. The post office continued to be called Kent until February 6, 1844, even though the village had incorporated as Grand Rapids in 1838. Curiously it was Lucius Lyon himself, as the Congressional representative, who petitioned for the second name change. He wrote the post office department in January of 1844, "The office was established and received its name before the village of Grand Rapids began to grow much. The village now has upwards of 1,000 inhabitants, and persons abroad are often much puzzled to know how to direct their letters on account of the village bearing one name and the postoffice there another."

Prospects for the community were grim in the struggling economy following the panic of 1837, but some projects struggled on. It must have been poor consolation to William A. Richmond to find his predictions about the extravagances of the Grand Rapids project become reality. Everett later summed it up in a view of the progress made to 1846, echoing eerily the earlier remarks of Arthur Bronson, "Improvements -- and some of them great ones -- had been made, but in almost every case they had ruined those who had invested their capital. The fact was, at the start there was too much enterprise -- a throwing away of capital in works that should have awaited their demand. In attempting to do business where there was not the business to do, the capital was sunk. Abram S. Wadsworth had bankrupted himself in developing water-power; and Daniel Ball the same, by running good steamboats, when only the cheapest craft would pay. Lucius Lyon had sunk a fortune in developing various interests too soon. And the natural consequence of the whole was, a general abandonment of enterprises begun, and the beginning of no new ones. Discouraged, some of the leading spirits had withdrawn; and capital, seeking investment, was not to be found."

Because of financial difficulties Lyon was unable to pay off his $21,000 debt to Arthur Bronson. Bronson apparently held off foreclosure for several years hoping that Lyon would make enough money with the salt works, or other business, to redeem the land. In 1842 Lyon had written that he still held the Grand Rapids lands "at the mercy of the mortgagees." The question became more pressing in December of 1844, when Arthur Bronson, who actually held title to most of the

Grand Rapids property by 1840, died in New York. Lyon was especially eager to hold onto some of the Grand Rapids land and sacrificed most of his other holdings to do so. When even this was not enough, he must have written Frederick Bronson in an angry or threatening tone. Bronson responded in a letter dated, December 18, 1844: "There is intimation in your letter that if I should proceed to the foreclosure without examining the subject of your claims it might cause a very expensive and troublesome litigation which might last ten years. . . . I trust you know me too well and have a better opinion of my character than to suppose that I should be deterred from maintaining the rights of the . . . trusts for whom I act by the apprehension of trouble or expense." He adds, however, that he is "willing to negotiate on terms of friendship and equality."

After another period of waiting, Bronson began foreclosure proceedings in 1848. K. Woodward wrote November 29, 1848, that he feared "we are likely to have difficulty here in consequence of the Bronson mortgage." But on the surface all was business as usual, although Bronson's agent had to approve land sales, and the profit went directly east. After the initial uneasiness the Grand Rapids people seemed to become accustomed to the legal encumbrances on the property, and George Coggeshell wrote May 23, 1849, "The people here begin to think the Bronson mortgage is not so great a bugbear after all."

The first sale of significant size was held December 13, 1849. Even when the sheriff's hammer began to fall, the settlement on the Grand River remained one of Lyon's favorite achievements. As late as February of 1850 he was trying to redeem some of the land or buy it back at auction. He wrote H. Backus that month that he had attempted to bid on some land, "but it was sold all in a chunk. I have therefore lost my journey, and shall now have to try to get the sale set aside."

In 1856, five years after the death of Lucius Lyon, Frederick Bronson filed a claim in Michigan courts against Lyon's heirs for payment of the $21,000. There were 100 defendants listed in the suit including most of the Lyon relatives and various charitable institutions Lucius had donated land to. The court document also detailed 701 mortgaged parcels of land in the village plat of Kent.

Kent County

In addition to land in the City of Grand Rapids, Lyon owned at various times other lands in rural Kent County. In 1835 he purchased two parcels located where the Grand Rapids suburb of Kentwood would later be built.

Ann Arbor

August 7, 1835, Charles Thayer wrote to Lyon that he had been working on a deal to buy the Hale sawmill property in Ann Arbor, Washtenaw County, and had made a number of purchases of village property, concentrating his buying on lots near a proposed railroad. Six of the village lots that he had purchased were from W. S. Maynard, at $75 per lot, and of these six, two were situated "on Main Street south of the red house where you wished me to secure some lots. . . ." He noted that he had bought some in the name of Bronson and some in his own name which he would convey to Bronson "any time when it shall be thought advisable to have it known that Mr. Bronson is the purchaser." The following year George A. Robinson tried his hand at the purchase of lands in Ann Arbor but wrote July 31, 1836, "I could not do anything with Mr. Jewitt of Ann Arbor at all -- for he has within six months past sold property where those he sold it to have doubled their money in a few days, and it troubles him so that he is afraid to sell any thing."

Calhoun County

The first settlers arrived in the Marshall area of Calhoun County in 1830. On July 17, 1831, Lucius Lyon, Isaac N. Hurd, George Ketchum, H. H. Comstock, and John Bertram located 12 parcels in Marshall Township. It is not certain whether these lands were jointly owned or if each investor owned specific parcels. An early historian of the area noted, "The purchasers of land in this town were men who had their eye to the main chance . . . they bought expecting a large advance in a very short time, from the price paid." As late as 1845 David Burnett reminds Lyon that he had promised to pay the taxes on some land in section 21 of Springfield Township, near Battle Creek.

Hillsdale County

In a history of Hillsdale County Lucius Lyon is identified as one of 18 individuals who had located 10,280 acres in Moscow Township by 1833. Moscow Township is on the northern edge of Hillsdale County, the second township in from the eastern line.

City of Detroit

There are indications in his correspondence that Lyon owned several pieces of land in Detroit, including a house at one time. One parcel was Lot 5 of the Park lots, a five acre plot, bought in 1835 from E. A. Brush. In July of 1835 he sent James Watson a draft for $1,200 to pay for lots in Detroit and other Michigan lands.

In January of 1836 he purchased Lots 9, 10 and 11 of Block 12, and Lot 1, Block 13, on the Cass farm. These lots might have been purchased in association with fellow-senator John Norvell and Stevens T. Mason. Lewis Cass held the note on Lyon's purchase of at least one lot but he sent the canceled note to him in the summer of 1843 to satisfy a debt that Cass owed Lyon. The note was for $1940 and covered Lot 11, Block 12 on the Cass farm.

Wayne County

In addition to land in the City of Detroit, Lyon bought several parcels in rural Wayne County. At least one was just across the county line from Ypsilanti, along the old Chicago road. Two other parcels, were in Brownstown Township, south of Detroit. One, in section 5, was 160 acres. The second, in section 17, was 120 acres. The Brownstown Township land was purchased from Charles Cleland in September of 1836.

Allegan County

Lucius Lyon was one of the surveyors who set the township lines in eastern Allegan County in 1826, and the section lines 1830-32 in the townships of Otsego, Dorr, Gun Plain, Hopkins, Watson, Salem, and later Trowbridge. He liked what he saw. In an 1831 note he had called Otsego Township, "first-rate." There is a note in Gun Plain Township land records that Lucius Lyon owned a large plot of land in section 18 of that township that he sold to William Forbes, an early settler, in the spring of 1833. Two parcels of land in Gun Plains Township, in sections 5 and 21, were included in a list of lands transferred to George Washington Thayer in 1848. These lands were near a plank road connecting Kalamazoo and Grand Rapids. In addition early land records show that Arthur and Frederick Bronson of New York City, in 1834 and 1836, purchased extensive tracts in Otsego Township, as well as a large parcel in Saugatuck Township near the mouth of the Kalamazoo River, across from where the lighthouse was built in 1838.

A letter dated December 20, 1833, from early Allegan County settler William G. Butler, founder of the Village of Saugatuck, indicates that Lyon had expressed an interest in purchasing land near the mouth of the Kalamazoo River. Butler wrote in a letter from White Pigeon Prairie, ". . . it was no disappointment to me in you not furnishing me with the funds, as you expected . . . as I was able to enter the field much better fortifyed with Cash of my own, than I expected when I saw you. The Sand hills at the mouth of Kallamazoo went brisk at fair prices." Lyon apparently had a hand in the bidding on those sand hills, either at that time or later, for Truman H. Lyon, in his office as lighthouse superintendent in 1838 selected a site near the mouth of the Kalamazoo River for a new lighthouse, and wrote Lucius July 22, "The point which I thought most favorable and the one finally selected is on land owned by yourself and Hon. H. H. Comstock of our State Senate." Truman offered them $150 for one and a half acres on the north side of the river's mouth.

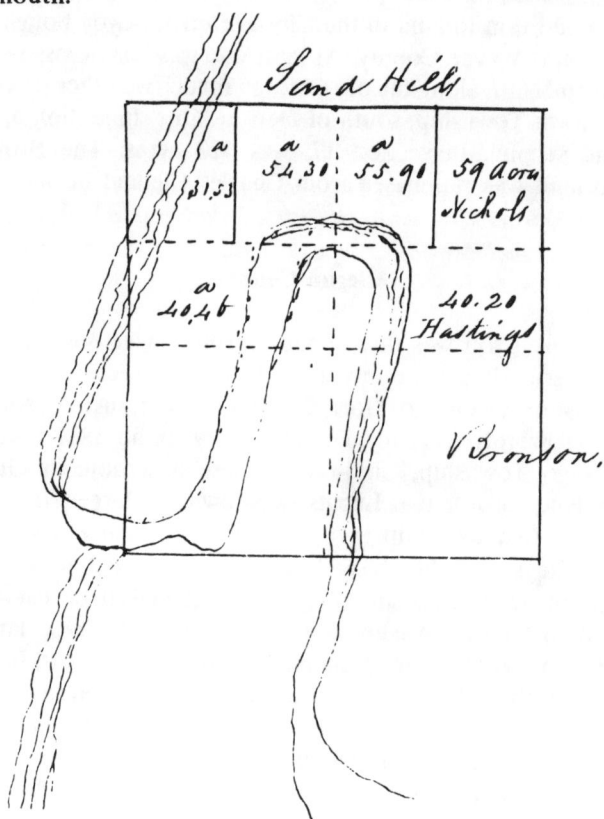

(Courtesy Burton Historical Collection)

An 1836 map of the Kalamazoo River mouth showing the site of the lighthouse, left, and land owned by Bronson, right.

In 1836 Oshea Wilder, manager of Singapore, a lumbering operation and settlement then just beginning near the mouth of the Kalamazoo River, and later one of Michigan's most famous ghost towns, wrote investors back east that he was negotiating with Lucius Lyon for 21,000 acres of pine land: "Mr. Lyon was for many years a Surveyor of the new lands in Michigan and from the knowledge then obtained he has been enabled to make some heavy and valuable purchases -- He has now given himself up to a political course of life and does not wish to take an active part in the sale or improvement of his lands. He owns about 21,000 acres of pine land of a quality and quantity . . . equal to or Superior to any pine land he ever saw in his life and he was brought up in a northern pine region. . . . I suppose and have no doubt of the fact that the money for the purchase of this land was advanced by some one, probably Bronson, altho' the title is in him." Wilder offered him $40,000 for the lands and a half interest in the project, but the deal was later postponed, then canceled.

In 1836 Lyon offered a quitclaim deed to William W. Corcoran which covered two parcels, one 80 acres, and one 160 acres, in Trowbridge Township, and another piece of unstated size in section 26, in the center of Saugatuck Township. As late as 1850 he retained some lands in the county including a 240 acre parcel on the eastern edge of Trowbridge Township and an 80 acre parcel near South Monterey.

St. Joseph

As a landowner on the west side of the state Lyon took an early interest in the harbor settlement of St. Joseph, Berrien County. He made the first survey of St. Joseph harbor at his own expense, and, while he was a territorial delegate, he tried to get funds for harbor survey and improvement. In 1843, writing to early settler and friend Thomas Fitzgerald he thanked him, "for doing justice to my efforts for the harbor of St. Joseph. I made the first survey and obtained from Congress the first appropriation for that work . . . and I think I obtained the second appropriation." In 1833 he purchased lands from E. Reid (probably Ebenezer Reid who died shortly thereafter), and, in 1834, land within the Village of St. Joseph from W. McKnobb and Louis March.

Fitzgerald, who had come to the settlement of St. Joseph by 1831 and was the harbor's first lighthouse keeper, was his frequent correspondent about St. Joseph matters and held power of attorney to enable him to sell lands while Lyon was off in Washington. Another good friend of Lyon's was Calvin Britain the first permanent settler who had come in 1827 and became postmaster in 1829. The settlement was incorporated as a village in 1834 during Lyon's first session as territorial delegate, and Fitzgerald wrote with some urgency that a new power of attorney was needed before deeds could be conveyed to some new settlers. "Some of the proprietors have sold lots, but can make no conveyance until these title deeds are completed -- 4 houses which had been commenced in that part of the village are suspended, causing a delay in the improvements going on here and to the inconvenience of the citizens."

The harbor was improved in 1834 and appropriations made for the digging of a new river mouth that would eliminate a sharp bend near the mouth in 1836. There were plans made for a canal which would link Paw Paw with Lake Michigan through St. Joseph, as well as a canal which would eliminate the portage and directly link the St. Joseph River with the Kankakee River near Elkhart, Indiana.

As late as January of 1840 Lyon still held some land in the Village of St. Joseph although most had been sold for taxes.

Berrien County

In addition to his interest in the village of St. Joseph, Lyon at various times owned land elsewhere in Berrien County. In 1835 he offered for sale parcels In Lincoln Township near where Stevensville was later located; in Sodus Township on Pipestone Creek; in Sodus Township on the Niles Road; in Watervliet Township where the City of Coloma now stands; and several pieces of land in Benton Township, just north of the present city of Benton Harbor. He owned property in the village plat of Niles that was sold for taxes in the early 1840s, but by 1842 he wrote his friend, Obed P. Lacey, asking what would be needed to clear the title. Lacey responded in a letter dated August 21, 1842, that it would take $300 and added, "I hope you are not poor -- I hope you are rich. I hope that 'salt works' will save you . . . But -- and here a thought strikes me -- if everything fails let us go to California." A note in an 1845 letter indicates that it was Lyon's intention to pay the taxes on two lots in the Village of Niles that year.

Van Buren County

At the same time that Lyon was interested in Berrien County lands he had in his real estate portfolio two parcels located in Van Buren County, east of Berrien County. The land was in sections 25 and 26 of Lawrence Township near Christie Lake.

Gratiot County

Gratiot County is located just west of Saginaw County and directly north of Clinton County where Lyon had done some survey work in 1826 and 1827. During the peak of his land speculating in the 1830s he purchased two pieces of land in Washington Township, Gratiot County, on the Maple River. One was bought in 1839 from F. F. Bell. An 1845 notice indicates that he was preparing to pay the taxes on land in section 28 of Fulton Township.

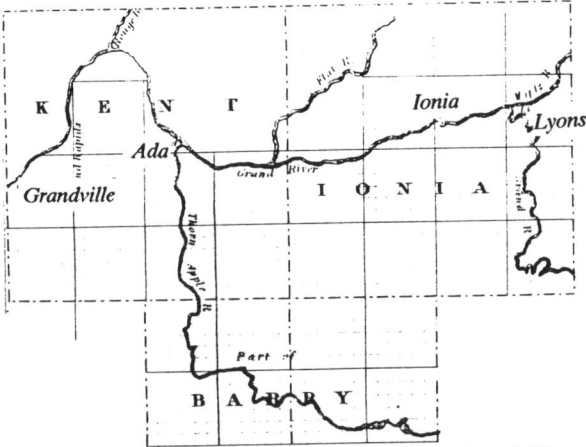

Lyon owned land at several places on the Grand and Thornapple Rivers including Ada, Lyons, and near the bend in Barry County.

Barry County

According to records of lands purchased kept by Lyon, he owned "over a hundred acres" of land in Irving Township in Barry County, near where the town of Irving later developed. Albert E. Bull of Schoolcraft was one of the first settlers in Irving and might have brought the land to Lyon's attention. The parcels near Irving were purchased with C. C. Trowbridge, from Joseph Miller. In 1832 he wrote to Thomas C. Sheldon that he had selected for purchase "several lots embracing a beautiful Prairie of two or three hundred acres on Apple River, near the center of Barry County and where the county seat will probably be located." This is probably the Thornapple River, and the future county seat, the Village of Hastings. The settlement had been named for Eurotas P. Hastings, who frequently joined with Lyon in business ventures. A list of lands transferred from Lucius Lyon to George W. Thayer in 1846 also lists two tracts of land, one 160 acres,

161

the second 80 acres, in Thornapple Township in the northwest corner of Barry County, south of the City of Grand Rapids, near where the settlement of Middleville was later established.

Sanilac and Huron Counties

In August of 1836 Jonathan R. White purchased 15 parcels of land in Sanilac County, and what would later be Huron County, in the Thumb area of Michigan for Lucius Lyon. The total price of the land purchased was $6,191.09.

Saginaw County

An 80 acre parcel of land in Saginaw County was in the list of lands signed over to George Washington Thayer in 1846. This land is now located in downtown Saginaw. During the internal improvements boom of the middle 1830s there was a plan to develop a canal that would connect the Saginaw River with the Grand River, thus effectively crossing the lower peninsula of Michigan. This plan was apparently supported by Stevens T. Mason, and Lyon wrote him September 9, 1838, "Your favor enclosing a map of Lower Saginaw was received a few days since and the reason you give why that place should be preferred over every other in that vicinity for a port of entry are certainly entitled to great weight. I am interested in Saginaw City, which I believe is much the largest town on the river, and I have no doubt the people generally in the neighborhood will expect a port of entry there." An 1846 list of lands includes two parcels in Thomas Township, near Shattuckville and two parcels on the eastern edge of what became the City of Saginaw.

Lyons

At the same time that he was fighting furiously for the admission of Michigan to the Union, Lucius Lyon was planning a new settlement near the intersection of the Maple and Grand Rivers in Ionia County in Maple (later Lyons) Township. He had first seen the site in 1826-7 during his survey of the Grand River and marked it as a likely place for a town. He purchased land as early as 1833, and in July of 1834 the Bronsons and Charles Butler offered him a one-quarter interest in the lands in return for his services as agent.

When the project was first conceived, the investors hoped that the settlement would be further enhanced by the establishment of the county seat for Ionia County. Arthur Bronson wrote in August of 1833,

"As to the county seats of Kent and Ionia Co., I know that you and Col. Daniels will neglect no measure calculated to secure them at the mouth of the Thorn Apple and the confluence of Maple and Grand Rivers." They sent petitions to Territorial Governor George B. Porter, and so did investors in what would become Ionia, being developed by Samuel Dexter and others. The governor appointed a three-man commission consisting of James Kingsley, an Ann Arbor lawyer, Stephen V. R. Trowbridge, and Charles J. L. Lanmon and sent them out to locate county seats for Clinton, Ionia and Kent Counties. They visited several places in each county by horseback and decided that the most suitable place in Ionia County was the Dexter property. After their recommendation was presented there were several letters of protest from residents who felt the selection was wrong, hinting that it had been unfairly chosen. While the protest was still going on Governor Porter died, July 6, 1834. The arguments continued until at least mid 1835 but the choice did not change.

Lyon described the site of Lyons in an 1836 letter as heavily timbered with no prairie except for four or five hundred acres of rich bottom land near the mouth of the Maple and some areas nearby that had been cleared off by the Indians to make corn fields. Many Indians remained in the area. Catherine Leonard, who arrived in 1837 with her father, a carpenter, wrote later, "I knew the Indians thoroughly, and can say they were always kind, honest and trustworthy."

The area had earlier been the site of a trading post run by William Hunt and two men named Belcher and Burgess. By 1833 H. V. Libhardt had built a sawmill just west of Lyons, so that lumber was available to the developers if they could get the builders. Lyons had three family members eager to come to Michigan. In January of 1834, James W. Tabor, who had married Esther Lyon, sent a note by way of Lucretia wondering "what the prospect is in Michigan for an active enterprising farmer." Some time later similar letters arrived from Truman H. and Edward Lyon (his stepmother's children by her first husband; Lucius sometimes referred to them as "cousins"). He sent letters recommending that all three settle in the new area. On February 24, 1836, he wrote Edward Lyon : "I think the best place for you to go will be to the mouth of the Maple river at the head of steamboat navigation on Grand river, about 95 miles from Lake Michigan. The place is called Arthursburg on the map which I send you, but we will change the name and call it, if you choose, Lyonsberg. I own the whole town site and a large tract of farming land of a most superior quality around it. It will be one of the most important towns in Michigan, though little or nothing has been there yet. I shall probably expend several thousand dollars there during the coming season in improvements." It was apparently Edward's plan to become a merchant, and Lucius recommends that he put in a small stock of goods "suitable to a new settlement" including 150 to 200 barrels of flour and 50 to 75 barrels of pork. "The country immediately around there will settle very fast next summer and you will probably in the course of the season be able to dispose of five or six thousand dollars worth of goods, besides selling a great quantity of all kinds of provisions which will command almost any price you choose to ask."

(Arthursburg, which Lyon describes in the letter above, is located at the confluence of the two rivers. There a high bluff, called Arthursburg Hill, was fortified by the Pottawatomi Indians. In 1785 the Chippewas and the Menominee Indians tried a coordinated attack on the defensive position, but owing to especially high water and a swift current, one tribe arrived the day before the other, the element of surprise was lost, and the Pottawatomies were victorious. There never was a white man's settlement named Arthursburg, and it is unclear how the hill acquired that name. The town of Lyons was located a little less than a mile upstream from the actual confluence of the rivers.)

James Tabor decided to go west and Lucius wrote him, "I am glad to hear you have decided on going to Michigan." and recommended that he too "had better stop at the mouth of the Maple and take charge of my business there." Then, Lucius, the experienced settler and woodsman, gave them detailed instructions. "You ought to take nothing with you but what you can box up and carry in a comparatively small compass with safety. Probably you had better carry your crockery, but no farming utensils except such as axes, hoes, chains, etc. Harrows, plows, carts and so forth are too cumbersome. You had also better dispose of your horses, oxen, calves, sheep, hogs, etc. The driving will cost you more trouble and delay than will balance the loss you will experience in consequent. Take nothing but your family and what you can put in boxes and travel conveniently with on board steam and canal boats to Detroit. At that place Giles S. Isham will meet you with my wagon and horses and convey yourself, family and baggage to the mouth of the Maple River, about 125 miles northwest by west from Detroit." He tells them that there are two log cabins already built on his land there. "one built by a man named Hunt three or four years ago without my permission, and the other built this winter by Isham and his family. You will have at first to go in with either Hunt or Isham unless Hunt can be removed and persuaded to go away."

In March of 1836 Edward wrote, "the offer you make me is a good one and I have no doubt but I could make more money in the place you recommend still I almost fear to take my family there . . . if there is no settlement at all, it will be verry unpleasant for some time until we could get some comforts around us. . . ." He made his coming contingent on the decision by his brother Truman. When Truman decided to go, Edward was nearly ready to begin packing, but wrote in some panic, March 21, "I find by reading a late history of Michigan that there are many Indians near the place you wish me to go, and Mrs. Lyon has never lived in a country where those animals are and fears to go there. Therefore shall be under the necessity of abandoning the idea." Edward, whose first wife had died in Ohio, had recently remarried, and apparently his new bride was unsure about the rigors of frontier life. Additional assurances were hastily sent eastward.

While the Lyon kin were back east debating the move former Vermonter Giles Isham was on site attempting to carve a new settlement out of the wilderness, desperate for help. He had written Lucius earlier that he had been forced to spend all of the money allocated to him. Lyon apparently was not pleased with this news, and Isham wrote in April of 1836, sending a detailed list of expenditures and explaining: "I came here late in the fall every thing high and I found that hands could not be boarded as there was not meat or flour to be had in this vicinity and I thought best to buy all the provisions or have you & I board the hands and I keep an account of the expenses and devote my whole time to your business. Had I undertook to have hired all the work done by the Job & had them boarded there would have been nothing done. I therefore purchased a good stock of provisions and am prepared to do something.

"Flint & Morse have given up their fence contract and we have the rails and logs strewed all around the prairie on the east side of G. River near the timbered land and also on the margin of the river of the Upper prairie and logs all cut and some split and strewed on to the Kookoosh prairie. Hunt gave up his Job a Day or two since we shall drive as fast as possible. I want Labourers. Newton we wish to hire: every Man that comes here will not stop all go to the rapids. I think we shall soon have help however. I wish to buy 150 bushels of potatoes to plant & we want two or three good yoke of Cattle. One of our oxen is dead, the other I sold to Baldwin for $55 to be paid in ploughing -- he wants I should assist him to money in advance to enable him to buy more team. I am not afraid to do it if I had the means & keep the cattle in our hands for security in case of any failure. I consider him a business Man and the only Man here that I can depend on.

"You say do what you think best but with what money I have of course. I must unless you advance more and we certainly need more immediately. This is a large farm & when improved . . . the receipts for one year will in my opinion amount to $5000 if we succeed in getting in wheat . . . I am sorry to have you say in your letter that 'nothing should have tempted me to use the whole amount of the cash you authorised me to draw.' I thought your interest required it and hope I have not injured your interest or feelings; yet I do not calculate to go contrary to my instructions. If I fail it is for want of Judgements not intentionally.

"I presume you will be satisfied if not let me be excused from doing business for you, for I have been up early and late in your business as well as my wife . . . I am pleased with the County & wish to continue in your business if I can gain satisfaction. . . . "

The Newton referred to was Isaac Newton Higbee, a Lyon cousin (and brother, or at least half-brother to George A. Robinson), who was trying to get work in the west as a surveyor but had determined to stop at Lyons while he was waiting for assignment. Lyon had written Isham that when the Congressional session was completed he planned to come to Ionia County and "take measures for building up a Town". That summer Lucius went to Ionia County and made plans including a canal to improve navigation, with a steamboat to connect it with Grand Rapids. The goal was to make Lyons a gathering place for goods on the way from Grand Rapids to settlers on farms in central Michigan, and for grain and other exports going from these farms to market. For a time hopes were also high for a canal that would form a cross-peninsula waterway by linking the Saginaw and the Grand Rivers. The project was actually begun in 1837 but was abandoned during the economic difficulties of 1838 despite crowds of Irish immigrants who paraded to protest the loss of work.

Lyon secured carpenters, including Henry A. Leonard and Andrew Hanse, to superintend the building of a store and a dwelling house or two. Back east, plans were in a state of flux. Edward Lyon, still worried about Indians, determined that instead of the wilderness he would prefer Detroit and made plans to open a store there with his sister Lenora's husband, David Irish, as a clerk. Edward wrote in May of 1836, "Brother Truman has concluded to remain in that mean place Parishville [New York]. I cannot persuade him to leave it." The Tabors went ahead with plans to move west and arrived in Michigan Territory near the end of May. Giles Isham did NOT meet them, and Esther wrote Lucius, who was still in Washington, in a letter dated June 1 that they had been delayed because of boat schedules on nearly every step of their journey. After their arrival in Detroit, "Mr. Tabor searched for a team to take us to Lyonsville . . . He found plenty . . . but none of the Teamsters were willing to go that route for any money, on account of the road being so very bad for the long rain we have had here for ten days in succession." Esther remained in Detroit, and Tabor went ahead on foot.

LYONS

LYONS TWP

Scale 300 feet to the inch

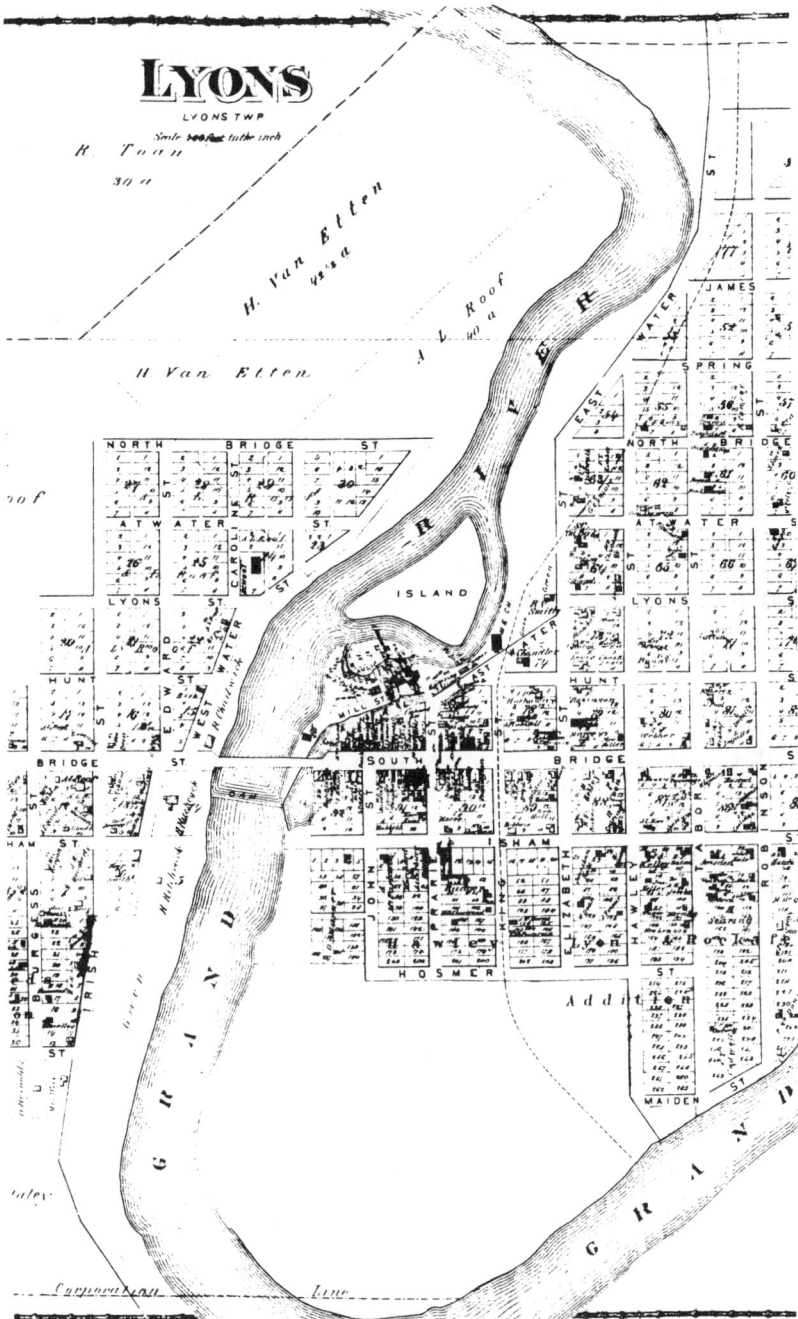

Lyons, from an old atlas, the intersection with the Maple
River is just off this map to the north.

167

Tabor was back in Detroit by June 12 and wrote Lyon that he had "been to Lyonsville and find that there is much to be done there." He discovered that the fencing had not been completed, there was no place to live, and "the crops that is on the ground are all late and don't look as promising as they might." He reports that "Isham has no friends there, they seem to be all against him . . . but I believe that he has tried to manage . . . so far as he was capable to."

Edward Lyon wrote in May that he had made arrangements to open a store in Detroit and had secured a house on Jefferson Avenue. He estimated that he had about $11,000 worth of goods and noted, "I have plenty of goods for a new place and think of locating a store in the country . . . if you have not made any arrangements for any one to take charge of your business at Arthursburg and should still be in favor of my going there I may conclude to do so."

The following month he wrote, "There is a great rush of emigration into the country this spring. Every boat is crammed to overflowing and every port is alive with people and business. All is life and animation." At some point during the summer or fall, his brother Truman and family arrived in Michigan, and both, along with David and Lenora Irish, decided to move on to Ionia County. They may have visited earlier, but all arrived ready to stay by October, 1836.

These additional workers eased the labor situation and things began to look up for the little settlement. There were minor problems. When Edward tried to claim the lots that he had picked out from the plat map, he discovered that "the little blacksmith" had already chosen to set up in that place. He wrote Lucius in November of 1836, that the blacksmith "made so much fuss I finally told him to take them."

Truman immediately set to work digging stones, sinking piers, and preparing to build a bridge over the Grand River. He worked through the winter of 1836-37 and by February 7, was able to write that six piers were built and filled, and the timber had been drawn for the framework of the bridge, although he felt it best not to complete the upper structure until after the thaw, lest it be swept away in a spring flood.

Edward had some problems with stock for his store. He had sent the merchandise around the lakes by boat to the mouth of the Grand River. Then, because of an unusually cold winter, ice had prevented him from bringing the goods upriver. Unable to get a boat owner to risk the water at that time of the year, in December of 1836 Edward bought a boat for $500. With seriously cold weather urging them to haste, Edward and crew went to the mouth of the river, loaded the goods aboard before daylight, and headed upriver. They reached Grand Rapids, removed the goods, "got the boat above the rapids," and the next day went on toward Lyons. In two days they reached the mouth of the Flat River (the future site of the Village of Lowell) where ice halted their progress. The goods finished the trip by sled.

There was continuing bitterness between Ionia and Lyons over the county seat selection. It was with a certain amount of glee that Edward wrote Lucius on December 29, 1836, that there had been a gradual increase of inhabitants at Lyons, and two men who had formerly lived in Ionia had recently joined them. "Ionia is fast going down," Edward wrote. "No one speaks in favor of it."

The establishment of the post office was another problem. From later correspondence it would appear that Lucius had told Giles Isham (when he was virtually the only settler in town) that when a post office was established he would be postmaster. After the application for the office was made, a lively rivalry developed between Isham and Truman Lyon for postmaster. Truman wrote in December of 1836, that he felt that Isham could not handle the job. "I do not feel that he is capable of making out the returns if he gets it." Isham for his part wrote a pleading letter, citing past promises, and sent Lucius a petition signed by many area residents. The office was established early in 1837 and Truman was named postmaster. Isham sent an angry letter to Lucius in Washington, "I can not but address you in relation to the manner in which I have been treated and abused. . . " He icily refers to Truman Lyon as "your connection."

Negotiations had gone on throughout the winter with a brick maker who had visited the settlement and declared that the clay would be excellent for brick-making, but he set his prices higher than Edward and Truman thought was proper. Another matter for wintertime speculation was a Mr. Burnett who had, in the fall of 1836, announced his intention to build a public house and had not been heard from since. By February 13, 1837, Edward was making alternative plans for building a small public house from the timber which had been cut the previous summer for a dwelling for David Irish. The plans were rendered unnecessary less than a week later when Mr. Burnett not only returned to the settlement, but also brought his own brick maker.

In the spring of 1837 there was a second contingent of Lyon relatives ready to enter into the business life of the settlement. Luman R. Atwater, a cousin, the son of Lucius's mother's brother, Thomas Atwater, wrote in March that he wanted "to get into a growing place." He accompanied Gaius S. and Mary (Lyon) Deane to Michigan. Mary was the sister of Edward and Truman Lyon and Lenora Irish. She was often called Maria, probably to distinguish her from her mother whose name was also Mary. A later biography of Atwater described their journey from Vermont ". . . amid tears and soul-rending leave-takings,

169

on the 10th of May, 1837, they embarked on Lake Champlain, his own new bandanna, as he waved it in last adieu, dripping with his briny tears. One day on the lake and six on the 'raging canawl' found them in Buffalo. There they were obliged to wait on account of ice in the lake. But they were soon in Detroit where each purchasing a yoke of oxen and a cow, they came in backwoods style, in ten days to Lyons, where the relations of Mrs. Dean were located." Both Deane and Atwater were all-around handymen who later worked in Grand Rapids in various capacities.

Another Lyon relative who arrived in 1837 was George A. Robinson, a cousin, who had been a partner in a store in Ypsilanti. When he got to Lyons he was seriously ill and moved in with the Tabors so that Esther could care for him. There were several worried letters that winter predicting that George would never see another spring. To their surprise he recovered and began work in Ada that summer.

When Lucius visited Lyons at the end of the Congressional session in 1837, he found a special celebration going on. He later wrote Lucretia, "I arrived here from Detroit on the 4th inst. and found a great number of persons had been assembled to celebrate the day. They had a procession, oration and dinner, at which about 80 persons sat down at table and in the evening they had a ball which I attended, at the house of Truman H. Lyon, where I found about thirty well dressed, respectable looking young ladies. All things through the day and evening were done in order and good taste. The ladies furnished several beautiful banners for the occasion and graced the dinner table with their presence. Several of the flags were flying at the tops of the houses when I arrived at sunset in the evening . . . "

The little Lyon family compound in the woods had some enjoyable times. In the summer of 1838, when Esther was trying to persuade Lucretia to join them she wrote, "Cousin Luman is our nearest neighbor, then near the bridge on South Bridge Street stands Truman's house and just across the bridge Edward and Gaius and David live all within a stones throw of each other. . . . The country abounds in strawberries and indeed berries of all kinds, cranberries we can have as many as we will buy of the Indians. Lucinda, Martha, Mary, Lenora and our cousin Ann and myself have had many good visits on the prairie this summer picking strawberries." She also mentions "pleasant horseback rides" and adds, Mary, Lenora and myself have been a great while talking about writing for our Mother's saddles." Mary (Hawley Lyon) Lyon had just died, leaving two saddles which she had used in Vermont. They were expecting visitors from the East that fall and Esther asked Lucretia if she thought the saddles could be boxed and sent with them.

The financial panic of 1837 put a serious crimp in most of

Lucius's carefully laid business plans, and he wrote Edward Lyon in January of 1838: "D. S. Baldwin wishes me to inform him whether I am going on with the construction of the canal across the bottom below the village of Lyons from the Grand river to the Maple. I have to state that I shall not go on with that work this year. I can begin it next year, and then have it done as soon as the Grand river and Saginaw canal will be finished. . . . In relation to a steamboat, I shall be able to buy as much of any boat that may be built as I shall want, after it is completed and when I can see how it suits me and what the cost is, and as the boat you speak of is to be built by others, I do not choose to subscribe for any stock at present. If the boat does not come to our place as much as we wish, I will build or buy one that shall come there. I have no fear on that head."

He likewise declined to participate in a scheme to institute a wildcat bank at Lyons, an opportunity offered by a temporary suspension of specie redemption passed by the Legislature. Edward, Truman and company, however, apparently went ahead with the scheme and wrote that the incorporators had met December 28, 1837, and made application for a charter for the Bank of Lyons with a proposed capital of $100,000. Another source of settlers and activity was to be brought about by a plan to divide the Grand River land office district into two portions putting one land office at Grand Rapids and one at Lyons. This plan was never realized and the office at Ionia continued to service the entire area.

One of the problems that made money so tight in Lyons was that, although the lots were selling at a fairly rapid pace, the money was mostly paper promises. Edward wrote in February of 1837 that he had made $17,200.50 worth of land sales and realized only $3,295.83 in cash. Although he served as land agent, Edward Lyon had come to Michigan expressly to enter into the mercantile business. According to local tradition because he lacked pioneer experience much of the stock he had purchased for his store was inappropriate for a new settlement in the wilderness. The bolts of silk were passed over by the pioneer ladies in favor of more substantial stuff, and he eventually gave away the champagne. However, a letter written by Edward, February 26, 1837, seems to say just the opposite. He recounted the progress in building a boat for their use and added, "Goods needed mostly are hardware and dry groceries. We have now on hand the largest stock of goods on the Grand River and the best assortment and our finest Goods sell the best."

However, less than three months later, on May 15, he sent an emergency message addressed to "Truman H. Lyon or Lucius Lyon at Detroit" that he wanted to let them know that the settlement was "entirely out of provision" and pleading that even if they couldn't afford a full restocking, to at least bring some flour and pork. He wrote Lucius the next day, "We all feel very anxious to see you here and we sincerely hope the time will not be long. I dare not agree to pay any money for any thing faster than we take it in at the store, and that is but little."

Still, everyone hoped the economic problems of 1837 would be just a minor setback and the settlement sounded very promising in a Gazetteer published in 1838, which stated:

> *Lyons.* This is a village in Ionia county, regularly laid out on both sides of the Grand river, at the site of an ancient Indian village, (Chi-gau-mish-kene,) 1 mile above the junction of the Maple river, with which it is to be connected by a canal, and at the head of steamboat navigation. It was commenced in the fall of '36. It has now 2 stores, several mechanics, 2 lawyers, and a physician. There is a fine hotel erected, and several elegant private dwellings, and between 20 and 30 more contracted to be built during the present season. The hydraulic advantages are important. It has been estimated by competent authority, that the head and fall in the Grand river here, is between 7 and 8 feet in the distance of half a mile, and that on the west side of the river, there are springs, issuing from a bluff, whose collected waters fall a distance of 46 feet, with sufficient power to propel 4 run of stone. The river is boatable above the village, for batteaux and flat bottomed boats, as far as Jackson. There is a State road from Pontiac, and one from Dexter, laid out, and terminating here. The location of the village is eligible, with about 700 acres of prairie land on the one hand, and on the other, a rolling country, with the richest soil. The elevated site of the village presents a varied and delightful scenery. It is 60 miles distant from the rapids of Grand river, and 100 from its mouth, 7 from Ionia, and 135 north-west Detroit.

It is not known why Lucius did not follow through on his plan to name the place Lyonsburgh, or Lyonsville, as it sometimes appears in correspondence. In a letter written March 10, 1836, Truman H. Lyon notes that he has received a letter from Edward who "invites me very strongly to go with him to this place Lyonsburgh. . . ." Yet, less than a year later when Truman became the first postmaster the post office was called Lyons. The "s" may have been added to the family name to separate it from the post office of Lyon (see below) established in Oakland County in 1834. However, it would seem that the name Lyonsburgh or Lyonsville would have performed the same service with even less opportunity for confusion.

The first homes and commercial establishments in Lyons were built on the west bank of the river. The Edward Lyon home, which an early history described as "a fine little cottage on the bluff of the river," was finished in late 1837 and stood until nearly 1980 when it was destroyed by fire. Edward's first store was on the west side of the river. The bridge across the Grand River, that Truman had worked on so hard during the winter of 1837-38, was nearly completed by March 9, 1838, when Edward wrote that the stringers were all on the bridge, it had been planked and Tabor was filling the piling with stone. David Burnett was engineer for the structure, but there is evidence that much of the work was done by Truman Lyon, Tabor, Higbee, Robinson, Atwater and Deane. After the bridge was finished the commercial center of Lyons shifted to the more level east bank of the Grand River where Truman built a tavern and served as the first postmaster.

The Edward Lyon home in Lyons from an old photograph.

In the fall of 1838 visitors arrived from Vermont, but it is not recorded whether they brought the saddles. The visitors were a trio of young men which included Homer Barstow, Lorain (Lyon) Barstow's 20-year-old son; the Lyon family's youngest brother, George H. Lyon, also 20; and Pamelia (Lyon) Thayer's son, Lucius A. Thayer, just 14. All had at least considered the possibility of remaining. George wrote his parents that they had arrived on September 25. "We were lucky enough at Detroit to find a man who was going directly to Pontiac with a team. We hired passage with him for $1.00 each." In Pontiac they found another man with a team who consented to carry their trunks, but the boys walked to Lyon, arriving, George wrote, with blistered feet. "There is about 900 acres of prairie here fit for ploughing, besides 80 or 100 acres of meadow. . . . There is no money here, only worthless wildcat and once in a while a slow straggling six pense which is given to the

Lyon Hotel for a glass of grog. . . . I have been at work for Gaius . . . thought of buying a farm. Brother Lucius has advised me to qualify myself for surveying." Lucius Thayer moved on to Grand Rapids to attend school. Barstow and young George returned to Vermont before the end of the year.

By 1839 there was a farm of considerable dimensions near Lyons which, in addition to other cash crops, served as an experimental station for the growing of sugar beets. Lucius, himself, was on hand in Lyons toward the end of May, 1839, at the planting of the first 30 acres. (Fifty years later the area became a large producer of sugar beets which were taken to a refinery in Lansing. See also chapter 10)

The settlers in Lyons felt the financial recession of 1837-8 more keenly than those in some places, because their settlement was at such an early stage of development. Many who had made down payments on land were forced to surrender it because of their inability to make second and third payments. Edward wrote Lucius August 11, 1837, "It makes me feel rather down to see our place running down, people giving up lots and the minds of people soured as they are towards it -- a people reporting stories of all kinds." By 1839 the recession had become a personal reality for Edward Lyon. He wrote in some frustration January 10, 1839, that he had just given one of their creditors $100 and "He was anxious to get more, but said he was not disposed to distress us but their want of money was very great." He explained that he had considered a suggestion to assign all of his property to pay off the debts but, "when I shall do that everything must be managed by someone else and that person must be paid for services. . . . The building of this house is what has cramped me, and I am not able to keep it. I shall be obliged to go to some other place and this I do not like to do, my mind was made up when I came here never to leave it. I found it a pleasant place as you recommended to me, and I still find it so and would like to remain here if I could make a living."

Edward and family held on through the summer of 1839, but by October he had decided to "take some public house and leave here until such time as I could get out of debt -- I would rather get some house in Detroit -- if I could, I believe I can keep a house as well as any . . . in Detroit, and could I get either the National, Exchange or American I think I could make money." Edward signed papers to run the National Hotel in Detroit, and concurrently he formally filed papers January 14, 1840, for the dissolution of the co-partnership of Lucius Lyon and Edward Lyon & Co. Shortly afterwards Samuel Dexter of Ionia had most of the company's remaining property (six oxen, seven heifers, a span of horses, harness and two wagons) levied on to be sold for debt.

As Edward Lyon left, the old plowman Baldwin was trying to

maneuver a lease on some area farmland. Truman H. Lyon wrote Lucius in some concern, August 27, 1840, "I hope . . . that he will not be able to obtain it, for I believe if he should come here with all his unruly herd of cattle and horses it would be the means of driving away what few people there are left here, for no person could have even a garden secure within two miles of him."

George Robinson had left Lyons earlier, to become part of the salt drilling crew in Grand Rapids. He wrote January 13, 1841, "Truman H. Lyon and Lady is now here to see what can be done in renting the Grand Rapids Exchange." Eventually a deal was struck and Truman took over the hotel the first of April. In a letter from Lyons dated February 21, Truman identifies the place as the Old Kent House, the hotel that Lucius and other investors had built in 1837. Truman notes, "I cannot tell how I shall prosper but hope that I shall be able to find more business than I do here."

Most of the farmland Lucius owned in Ionia County was lost in his settlement with the Isaac Bronson estate in 1840. By August of 1842, Lyon wrote a prospective settler who was a lawyer, "I know that the country around Lyons is but very thinly settled and that the village is consequently almost deserted, and I should think you would not be able to find business there to support you." By June of 1840 the Tabors had retired to a farm in Clinton County. In the late 1840s Lyon deeded to his nephew, George Washington Thayer, all of his land in Ionia County that had not been sold for taxes or lost as payment of debts. He still retained at least one lot, as late as December of 1845, when David Irish was advised by letter to "take care of business at Lyons," and received a quantity of grain as the annual rent on Lucius's log house in the settlement.

The settlement, while not exactly booming, continued to grow. In 1840 the population of the township was 485, in 1845 it was 634 and in 1850, 774. Lyons was incorporated as a village in 1859. The town very nearly scored a revival in 1847 when the Michigan Legislature finally got around to deciding on a permanent seat for state government. Busy with other problems when Michigan became a state in 1837 the Ligislature had put off the decision for ten years. In January of 1847 the first of many bills to locate a state capital was introduced. Many communities were in contention including Lyons, Ann Arbor, Marshall, Eaton Rapids, Charlotte, Caledonia, Owosso, Albion, Saginaw, Utica, Dexter, Detroit and Jackson. Communities in the hinderland of Michigan were so seriously considered that a Detroit area lawmaker wailed, "What! Shall we take the capitol from a large and beautiful city and stick it down in the woods and mud on the banks of the Grand River, amid choking miasma, where the howl of wolves and the hissing of massuagas and groans of bullfrogs resound to the hammer of the woodpecker and the solitary note of the nightingale!"

In the House representatives had voted, with only perfunctory debate, on a long string of losing proposals for a new capital when Lyons was approved by a vote of 30-28 on February 11, 1847. The lawmakers, apparently startled because something had passed in an otherwise negative session, promptly moved to call for a third reading of this motion. The approval for the third reading lost 29-32, with Jesse Seeley and Thomas McGraw of Oakland County, and Ebenezer C. Eaton of Wayne County tipping the scale for the nays. The motion was brought out again for reconsideration and this time it lost.

The Michigan Senate had gone through a similar string of losing proposals when, on March 6, the bill to create a new capital was approved by a vote of 14-7 with "Lyons in the County of Ionia" inserted in the blank. The Senate then recessed for the weekend. On March 8 there was a move for reconsideration, and, after several attempted amendments, the main question to insert Lyons lost 10-11. Nathaniel Balch of Kalamazoo County, Charles P. Bush of Livingston County, John P. Cook of Hillsdale County, Ephraim P. Danforth of Ingham County, and Samuel Denton of Washtenaw County, were vote changes that made the defeat possible. The traditional legend retold in a 1976 Lyons village history that Lucius Lyon had the deciding vote on this issue and sold his vote for a drink or a keg of whiskey; and another yarn, that Adam Roof, a Lyons lawyer and politician, sold his vote on the question for $500, are not only untrue but impossible. Neither man held an elective office in 1847 which was part of the decision making process on the state capital. Unable to agree lawmakers eventually chose a spot in the wilderness of Lansing Township, Ingham County, mainly because it was in the middle of the state and did not seem to favor anyone.

The oldest generation of Lyon-related settlers were gone from Lyons by 1845, although some of their descendants remained or returned. One relic of the Lyon family's sojourn in the town is a silver spoon in the Lyons-Muir Historical Museum in downtown Lyons. It was unearthed some years ago at the Staley farm on the west bank of the river and bears the name "L. C. Lyon" in fancy script on the handle. If Lucius had a middle initial, it is not recorded; the only other known family members bearing the name of Lyon and a given name beginning with an L, who lived in Ionia County were Lucretia (for whom no middle initial has ever been recorded either), who lived there with Esther for nearly a year after her arrival in Michigan in 1840, and Lucinda (Farnham) Lyon, the wife of Truman H. The most famous L. C. Lyon of Michigan history was LeRoy Churchill Lyon, who was born in Marshall in 1890 and was later a prominent lawyer in Detroit. This

L. C., however, had no direct link to the Lyons at Lyons.

Although his farms were gone Lyon held onto, or bought back some land in the village. The property that he retained included the site of the original houses built in 1837, and some lands that were signed over to Lyon and Calvin Britain by Allen Hutchins in 1839 to cover a debt. In early 1848, Lyon inquired about the title of a particular 77-acre parcel of land near the village, and P. R. Howe's answer was positive, by the yardstick of the era. "I had been impressed with the opinion and still am that yours and Maj. Britain's title is a perfect one. Save perhaps, and I think, that it has been sold 2 or 3 times for taxes."

The Lyon memorial (right) with the restored comfort station.

Today the only monument in Michigan erected to Lucius Lyon stands on the main street in downtown Lyons. It is a large boulder, with a bronze plaque which reads:

Memorial
LUCIUS LYON
Founder of the Village
LYONS
1836
Erected Research Club 1929

The boulder is near another historic Lyons site. In 1923 the village was the location of what was believed to be the state's first tourist camp. In 1976, the comfort station and an old pump which had been part of the tourist camp was restored and reopened, providing probably the oldest highway rest area in the state.

Ionia County

In addition to Lyons, Lucius owned several other pieces of land in Ionia County including a plot in section 5 of Portland Township on the Grand River, and in Sebawa Township, as well as some agricultural land in Lyons Township. He retained some of these lands as late as 1848. A tax bill from 1845 also indicates that he had some interest in land near Berlin Center. After Allen Hutchins defaulted on a bond that Lyon held on his performance as Ionia land office receiver, Hutchins signed over nearly 700 acres of land in 1841, most of it in Ionia County, to pay the judgement. This included land in the settlement of Ionia Centre, some farmland, and some land in Lyons. Because the Lyons land was only partially paid for, Lucius apparently redeemed it himself when the property was sold. He held some of these parcels as late as 1848.

Oakland County

Early in his land buying career Lyon purchased at least one parcel of land in Oakland County from M. Andrews. It is not certain if this is the same 80 acres he later owned on section 24 of Brandon Township. An 1835 purchase from Col. James Watson included land in Pontiac and near the Black River. In the middle 1840s Lyon also purchased some lots in and around the settlement of Birmingham in Oakland County as an investment for General John Neil of Boston.

Lapeer County

Lucius Lyon surveyed Lapeer County in 1824, but it was not until 1836 that he entered at least 13 full sections in Arcadia Township, in central Lapeer County, just northeast of the present city of Lapeer. One early Lapeer history indicated that he may have owned as many as 22 complete sections and parts of other sections and that this was one of his first major investments for Isaac Bronson. Because he was using money provided by Bronson, he had the cash needed to purchase land directly from the government.

In the Burton Historical Collection in Detroit there is a small memorandum book in the Isaac Bronson Papers which contains a copy of Lucius Lyon's original notes of Lapeer county taken during the survey in the winter and spring of 1824. The notes list the kinds of trees available on each parcel that was purchased or recommended for purchase. The notes also rate each section, first, second, or third, according to its desirability, but another note, added later, explains, "But a very small portion of the land in any country is ever put down as first rate where the surveys are made far in advance of settlement . . . these notes were taken in the winter of 1824 when there was not a white man living within 40 miles of where I then was."

From sketchy notes it would appear that the 21,000 acres of pine lands that he offered to the proprietors of Singapore in Allegan County in the summer of 1836 were located in Arcadia Township, Lapeer County. At that time there was a hesitation to purchase the property because it would be hard to get the logs to a mill.

An 1837 letter from A. N. Hart lists large land purchases including more than 600 acres in Arcadia Township, more than 3,000 acres in Goodland Township, and two parcels near Attica.

The area was generally not settled until the 1850s. By 1874 most of the northern portion of Arcadia Township was owned, still in large tracts, by the Moore family.

The Lucius Lyon that bought the tracts in 1836 was identified as "of Kalamazoo" and is undoubtedly the surveyor and future senator. It is interesting that a Lucius M. Lyon was elected justice of the peace, April 7, 1856, at the first township meeting of Burlington Township, Lapeer County, in the northeast corner of the county.

Ada

Lucius Lyon had met fur trader Rix Robinson as early as 1826 when he was surveying on the Grand River and had purchased goods from Robinson at a place he called "Forks". This was an early name for the area in what was later Kent County where the Thornapple River flows into the Grand River east of Grand Rapids.

In 1832 when he was attempting to get Thomas C. Sheldon to sell him some land near the Grand River rapids that adjoined some land he already owned, Lyon offered to give up his claim to some valuable lots "at the Forks of Grand River, near Robison's Trading House." It is not recorded whether or not Sheldon accepted the deal.

In 1833 Lyon purchased a number of parcels in sections 27 and 34 of what would later be Ada Township from Medast and Charles Beaubien as a good farming area and village investment site for Arthur

Bronson of New York City. Some time later he wrote Bronson, "You will recollect when I first saw you I was confident that lands at the Rapids, at the mouth of the Thorn Apple and at the mouth of the Maple river would some day be valuable. I have not changed my opinion in regard to any of these points. . . . All that is wanting is the settlement of the country around there and this will now shortly take place." In October of 1835 he sent another letter of gentle prodding, "I think it advisable to erect a saw mill as soon as practicable near the mouth of the Thorn Apple, where it is indicated on the map enclosed. The mill and dam will not cost over $2,000 and will bring us in clear of all expense at least $5,000 per annum, besides its effect on our other property. The reason why I would do this in preference to allowing some one else to erect a mill at present there is that the water power from its situation and advantages will increase in value quite as much as any of our property and can be sold to much greater advantage when the country around it shall be settled, as there is every probability it will be in two or three years."

Shortly afterward, on October 12, 1835, he tried again, "Something ought to be done immediately with our property at the mouth of the Thorn apple River. I could sell it now I suppose for $5,000 but we ought not to do so, for by building a good saw mill and a good public house there, we should commence a town and could then, I have not the least doubt, sell for $15,000 and keep the mill and house into the bargain both of which would be good property. Can we not by pledging the land raise the money to make these improvements? About $5,000 would be necessary."

On October 19, 1835, Lyon gave Hamilton S. Jackson written authority to purchase "such oxen, Horses, Waggon, harness, plough, chains, axes, hay and grain and such other articles as may be necessary to commencing and improving a farm belonging to myself and Arthur Bronson Esq. at the mouth of the Thorn Apple River in Kent County."

In a letter dated November 4, Jackson reports that he has been to the site, "And from what I saw of the river I don't think anything could be gained by moving the crossing place it is now in as good a situation for building a Dam as any place that I saw on the river. I have been inquiring about the land of Mr. Robinson and from what I can learn of him they mean to keep that valley for themselves. I did not say anything to them about what your intentions were with regard to that I should think that the best way to manage that business would be to say nothing to them what our intentions are till we can get the fence made from the crossing place and then have our rails ready and before they know any thing about it we will have complete possession and it will be a difficult matter to eject us. They have not made any improvements I can see. . . . I will raise a house Monday."

Within the month John Almy of Grand Rapids wrote Lyon that his agent at the Thornapple (apparently Jackson, although he is not referred to by name) was "unfit to manage the business committed to his charge," and later that month when Jackson came into town for supplies he found "I can get no goods at Grand Rapids . . . your friends are very much alarmed." He challenged Lyon to "appoint some person to come here that is not prejudiced against me and examine everything . . . if anything is not correct let me bear the blame to the fullest extent." However Lucius already had plans underway to replace him with a permanent agent.

Tory and Sidney Smith, sons of Lucius's second stepmother, Mary (Atwater Smith) Lyon, had expressed an interest in coming to Michigan. Their mother was the sister of Lucius's mother, Sarah (Atwater) Lyon, so in addition to being step-siblings, the Lyon and Smith children were first cousins. Tory and Sidney Smith were born in Burlington, Vermont, and later moved to Rochester, New York before moving to Michigan in 1836. Sidney Smith wrote September 11, 1836, that he was selling his business in New York and "am determined to leave for Michigan as soon as I can make it convenient -- I have been anxiously expecting to hear from you in relation to the Thorn Apple tract." He adds that he feels he can dispose of at least half of the lands in New York before he leaves and tells Lyon about a man who has expressed an interest in purchasing half of the settlement.

In a long letter on September 5, he reports that his brother has agreed to go with him in the fall and get enough rails cut and split to fence a farm in the spring. They plan to leave their families in New York through the winter. Sidney then gets around to the question of a name for the new settlement. "You propose 'Appleton' for the name of our Town. I do not know that I could furnish a better one. I will propose one, although I cannot say I have any choice and shall leave it to you. 'Ada' is a name conceived by the poetical mind of Byron and given to the 'sole daughter of his house and heart.' It is short and trite, and sounds very well. I do not know that it was ever applied to a town or village. 'The Village of Ada' would not sound bad." What he did not mention, but what Lucius Lyon surely knew, is that Mary Ada Smith was the name of his young daughter.

Sidney Smith wrote on October 5, 1836, that he had been delayed but that they planned to leave October 15 for the west. "I deem it very essential that some improvements should be started at our place this fall. Quite a number here have got the fever for emigration and want to go there in the spring -- I must be there and see to getting out timber &c for building a Tavern House this winter so that when

181

emigrants arrive there they may not find it quite a wilderness."

An 1836 map of Ada on the Thornapple River.

(Courtesy Grand Rapids Public Library)

On his arrival in Michigan Sidney spent some time trying to catch up with Lucius. He first waited in Detroit for his arrival, then went on to Kalamazoo, where he had heard Lucius was staying and missed him again. He wrote Lucius, November 8, 1836, from Kalamazoo that he was going to purchase a horse and ride back to Detroit; asked him to wait there for him if possible. He finally caught up with Lucius and received a power of attorney empowering him to sell property at Ada to incoming settlers.

Sidney Smith lived a short distance west of the Ada bridge. His brother, Tory (sometimes spelled Torrie or Torrey) bought land two miles above the bridge on the right bank of the river. Lucius Lyon had purchased a large claim that included about 1000 acres along the river, encompassing the area where the village was later constructed. Goods intended for the settlement had been left at the mouth of the river that first winter because of early ice. Smith reported that although they would have to be brought in by land, the sleighing was good.

The problems continued with the Robinson family. Rix Robinson was the undisputed first settler in the area, having built a trading post there as early as 1822. Although he had at first seemed in favor of development at that site, afterwards he seemed to resent the newcomers, and his suspicions were probably re-enforced by Jackson's behavior in 1835. Such shenanigans may not have been entirely Jackson's idea. A letter dated August 24, 1835, from Arthur Bronson advises, "You will recollect that suggestion was made to put a settler on a fraction 46.15 acres . . . giving lines with Robinsons two entries -- Do not let this escape your sensible attention -- connected as it is with the Beaubien purchase." In a letter dated February 13, 1837, Sidney Smith outlines some of the latest Robinson-related problems. "We have a new house just up and covered, windows in, &c, & Mr. Burnett & another joiner of his are at work finishing it. . . . Soon after Mr. Burnett came here he went over the River and made a claim on that fraction opposite the mouth of the Thorn Apple. He ran the lines around it and marked the trees & put his name on the corners. My Brother also took the quarter section below & marked it. They were about getting out a small frame of timber for a house to put on there when Robinson went over there the other day & hewed off the names of others & put his own on & has put up the body of a log house. Mr. Walker's project of a new pre-emption law has put the devil into people about here & there has been a general rush to the north side of Grand River. There is a legion of the Robinsons & they act as if they had the exclusive right to all the Government lands, north of Grand River. A man by the name of Bixford has located on the prairie at Flat River & I understand that the Indians have lately surrounded his house & threatened to pull it down. He was frightened & has called for assistance to protect himself. It is loudly asserted by everyone here, that the hand of Rix Robinson is in this thing. You know he has a brother who keeps a tavern at Flat River. Mr. Burnett is determined to put up a small building opposite here & live in it."

He adds that he is trying to get his own lot fenced, and has started the task of getting out timber for a bridge over the Thornapple River, but that he will probably not build it before the ice leaves the river. "I think a good strong bridge on the plan we propose, can be built for 3 or 4 hundred dollars. We propose to erect bents on mud sills, & not obstruct the stream with piers. I think such a bridge will stand the test, as I find that the River is not frozen after you get 3 miles from the mouth. Consequently there will be but little ice floating in the spring. The dam, I am convinced, ought to be built a little above the bridge, so that the ice when it comes down will break in pieces in passing over it & thus render the bridge more secure."

Lots sold fairly well in 1837, before the panic, and Sidney wrote in June of 1837 that he had been visiting in Grand Rapids and on his return home, "found the Tavern House filled (to overflowing) too uncomfortable for the family. Mary and I shall be obliged to put up a shanty. The crops all look well. . . . There is just beginning to be a great cry for money along the river here and I understand many are waiting very anxiously for the arrival of Mr. Carroll and yourself thinking I suppose that you will scatter the coin among them . . . . Burnett has contracted for the bridge and tavern house. . . . There is a wide rumor here that the village of Ada is to be sold at the Land office -- Please write soon."

The organizational meeting for Ada Township was held April 2, 1838, and Sidney Smith was elected township supervisor and justice of the peace. He was re-elected supervisor in 1839 and 1840. In 1837 he was asked to participate in organizing the Grand River Bank and bought 100 shares but wrote Lyon January 20, 1837, "I find that I occupy a rather too prominent stand in the community of Grand Rapids and am sure to be called upon to assist in building up and sustaining every institution . . . . Limited as my means are, it makes it rather unpleasant to be so dignified." He was elected treasurer of Kent County and moved to Grand Rapids in 1842, but he died in 1844. His widow and daughter later returned to Ada, and were living there as late as 1846.

At that first election in the township Tory Smith tied with Miniers Jipson for the office of Overseer of the Poor. It is recorded in an early Kent County history that Tory was the first, and for two years the only, Whig voter in the township. He owned an interest in the ferry which crossed the Thornapple River and ran it until the first bridge was built in late 1837. He was called upon later to run the ferry for a brief time after the bridge was seriously damaged by ice.

In an 1838 Gazetteer the settlement is described briefly and hopefully:

> *Ada*, a recent settlement at the mouth of the Thorn Apple river, in Kent county, contains a post office and a few inhabitants. It has a very handsome location, and possesses valuable water power on the Thorn Apple, which is about to be improved.

There was a delay in getting the first mill going, but in mid-winter 1838, Smith wrote that a man named Perkins, who had agreed to build the mill, was going forward with the project. "They are getting the mill irons &c to commence early in the spring."

The winter of 1838-39 was exceptionally intense. Sidney Smith wrote on December 28, 1838, "The severity of winter has been upon us for the last two months and yet continues with unabated vigor. Old Vermont is entirely outdone in this respect. . . . Some money might be expended here to good advantage if it can be obtained. Mr. Hodges has left the Tavern House, and I have rented it to the proprietor of the mail route for Kalamazoo to Grand Rapids and another person in connection with him." He also reports that Tory had left his house by the bridge and removed to the north side of the Grand River. Also that "my two younger brothers" have returned to Rochester. They may have visited about the same time as the Lyon-Barstow-Thayer contingent that fall.

Arthur Bronson seemed especially interested in farmland, and his correspondence reveals a good understanding of practical farming. During the economic maneuvering in 1840 following the death of his father, Isaac, Lyon's farms were the first property attached. In 1840 Lyon lost farm property in Kalamazoo, Kent and Ionia Counties to the estate. This left the trustees of the estate in control of a great deal of property in the town on the Thornapple River and brought progress in Ada to a standstill until titles could be cleared.

Clinton County

In 1838 Lyon purchased a large parcel of land in the southwest corner of Clinton County from E. B. Brown. In addition, in his collected papers there is a an undated notation of a purchase of land in Clinton County from J. W. Pierce. He also owned an 80 acre parcel in section 27 of Bath Township, in southeastern Clinton County and an interest in 80 acres in section 27 of DeWitt Township, north of Lansing. An 1845 listing of lands in which he had an interest included lots in the Village of DeWitt.

Branch County

Lyon owned a 160 acre parcel of land in the northeast corner of Branch County in Butler Township. Ira Dennis, who apparently owned land nearby, in a letter from Girard, Branch County, described Lyon's parcel as "100 acres of dry land and 60 acres of marsh. . . . The dry land is an excellent soil and as good a sugar bush as there is in Southern Michigan but it has been tapped by Indians and probably 5 or 6 years by the Whites." In a letter dated January 15, 1851, Dennis informed Lyon that someone had trespassed on his land and cut four whitewood trees and that it had been a poor year for swamp grapes. In October of 1851, in a letter written after Lyon's death, Silas Bogg offered to pay the county and road taxes on the land in return for the use of the marsh and the sugar bush for two years. He also asked for power of attorney, "so I could put those fellows strat through if they commenced their trespass this next winter." In addition an 1838 business paper mentions a mortgage to John Mullett on a quarter section of land on the southeast edge of Branch County, in Algansee Township. The parcel is near the intersection of two early roads not far from where the city of Coldwater was later built.

Shiawassee County

An 1846 list of lands includes seven parcels in Shiawassee County, between Clinton and Genessee County in central Michigan. These include two parcels in Middlebury Township on the western edge, near the Village of Ovid, and five parcels in Owosso Township, in and to the east of the settlement of Owosso.

Genessee County

A list of lands owned in Genessee County for which taxes had not been paid in 1846 includes three parcels in section 9, Vienna Township, in the north central area of the county near a major north-south road, not far from Farrandville and Clio.

There were two settlements in Michigan named for Lucius Lyon although he had no financial investment in them.

Lyon

In 1834 the Michigan Territorial Council approved a Lyon Township in Oakland County, named for Lucius Lyon. The choice was not overwhelmingly supported by the residents of the township. A county history reports that when it was decided in 1834 to detach Town 1 North Range 7 East, from Novi Township and give it a political entity of its own, "Considerable interest was manifested and some humor indulged over the naming of the township. The pioneers present seemed to think that they had found the best place in the world. . . . Thinking thus, they were anxious to bestow upon it a proper name. After several proposed names had been rejected by the meeting Chester Adams proposed the name 'Fruitland." The name was adopted and petitioned for, but the legislature gave the township the name of Lyon, in honor of Lucius Lyon, then a member of the Territorial legislature." [Actually he was territorial delegate to Congress.] A post office called Lyon was established in that township June 9, 1834, with Hiram Goodspeed as the first postmaster. The post office was renamed Kensington on September 5, 1836, and closed in 1902.

South Lyon

The city of South Lyon also received its name because of its location in Lyon Township, Oakland County. The first settlement there was called Thompson's Corners, but the first post office, established on July 13, 1848, with Zeri C. Colvin as postmaster, was called South Lyon. It was incorporated as a village in 1873 and as a city in 1930.

WISCONSIN INTERESTS

Lucius Lyon began surveying work west of Lake Michigan as early as 1828, and he was elected territorial delegate from Michigan Territory in 1833 when it included the entire area that later became the State of Wisconsin. His good friend, John P. Sheldon, former Detroit newspaper editor, was appointed receiver at the Dubuque land office in May of 1833 and in 1834 was put in charge of the new land office at Mineral Point in the middle of the lead mine district. Lucius introduced his brother, Orson Lyon, to the area in 1830, and together they surveyed the first townships. When Lucius left for Washington in 1833, Orson stayed on and completed the surveys of much of central Wisconsin.

Lucius is credited with discovering a new vein of lead there during his work on the northern Illinois border in 1831-32, and there is some intimation in correspondence that he held a government mining claim somewhere in Iowa County (the southwestern corner of Wisconsin) prior to 1835. In 1835 Isaac Bronson employed Lyon and Lyman J. Daniels to invest up to $24,000 in western lands and specified that he would prefer lands west of Lake Michigan. One estimate is that Lyon purchased, between 1834 and 1838, nearly 25,000 acres for the Bronsons, and another 25,000 acres in his own name. Some of the land deals turned out very well; one list of lands bought at Green Bay from the Wisconsin Land Co. in September of 1835 included 1082 acres in 16 separate parcels, mostly platted lots, and showed a paper profit in favor of Lyon of $1,470.88. Such lucrative deals, however, were rare. Most of the land Lyon purchased in Wisconsin was lost after the panic of 1837, much of it being relinquished to the Bronsons to cover debts.

Cassville

As early as January 4, 1829, when it was little more than a name, the town of Cassville was being considered as a place of political importance. On that date Lucius Lyon, who was visiting in Vermont, wrote A. E. Wing, then territorial delegate in Congress, sending him a map of the Fox and Wisconsin Rivers and the mining country of southwestern Wisconsin and added, "Cassville, in my opinion is decidedly the most eligible site for the seat of Government." He was referring to the capital of a new territory, then to be called Chippewa, west of Lake Michigan. At that time the majority of the region's population was still clearly centered on the Mississippi River where lead and other mining had drawn a considerable number of settlers beginning in the early 1820s. Both Green Bay and Milwaukee were a collection of small communities that had not yet united to give hint of the cities to come.

There was a deserted log cabin on the site of Cassville before 1820 indicating that there had been visitors earlier, but the town, named for Lewis Cass who had been governor of Michigan Territory 1813-1831, traces its beginning to about 1831 when Glendower Price settled there and opened a general store. It was located on the banks of the Mississippi about equidistant from Dubuque on the south, and Prairie du Chien on the north.

Lyon's large financial interest in Cassville began in the fall of 1834 when Garrett V. Denniston and Lyman J. Daniels, the latter acting as partner of Lucius Lyon and Isaac Bronson, purchased at auction a number of parcels in the area. Daniels wrote later that they had "entered into an arrangement to purchase all the property we could at Cassville." In addition to lands at the auction they purchased nearly a half of section 29 from Henry F. Lander and entered into another conditional contract with Richard Ray for part of section 20 "provided that Ray obtained the Pre-emption to said quarter section." The second sale was later seriously disputed.

The battle to make Cassville the seat of government for the new territory began in earnest in 1836 when statehood for Michigan was at least on the horizon, and a new Territory of Wisconsin was nearly a reality. When the Legislative Council of Michigan Territory passed a resolution supporting Michigan statehood in 1835, it adjourned after its last meeting in Detroit calling for the council to reconvene the following January in Green Bay. During the adjournment John S. Horner was named territorial secretary and acting governor to succeed Stevens T. Mason, who had been removed from office and then elected as governor of the new state. Horner was given no instructions by the President or

188

other Washington officials concerning the territorial council meeting or meeting site, apparently because they felt that to do so might be construed as giving official recognition to the State of Michigan. Lyon, who wanted both Michigan statehood and the capital of the new territory at Cassville, wrote Horner the day after his confirmation that he was of the opinion that Horner should proceed ". . . either to Green Bay or the mining country within the limits of the territory, as soon as convenient."

Horner, taking the advice of others, remained in Michigan, while the Legislative Council met at Green Bay. James D. Doty wrote Lyon. January 6, 1836, "The council is in session at this place but are unable to do much on account of the absence of Gov. Horner -- Judge Irwin is also absent, and on the whole, but few vestiges of a government remain." The assembled delegates petitioned President Jackson for the removal of Horner since he had not attended the session. On February 8, Lyon wrote that Horner should tell the Legislative Council that he had missed the meeting because of the lack of instructions on the matter, but "ought now to convene them at Cassville in Ioway county at some proper period, perhaps in April or May, and in the meantime visit different settlements in that region of the country and make yourself well acquainted with the people there. You will find them warm friends when you once get their good will. The legislative council have memorialized Congress, also, on the subject of a territorial government and the establishment of a seat of government at Cassville. I have no doubt that is the proper place for it."

At the same time Arthur Bronson, a major investor in Cassville, wrote Lyon on February 5, "Let me entreat you to see George W. Jones [the territorial delegate to Congress] and get him to insert immediately, a provision in the Wisconsin Territorial Bill now before Congress to locate the Seat of Government at Cassville until otherwise ordered by the people. We will expend $10,000 . . . to secure that object."

Lyon responded to Bronson, February 10, that the Legislative Council at Green Bay had approved Cassville as the seat of government, by a vote of seven to two, and that Jones "has said he would procure the insertion of a clause locating the seat of government there in the bill now before Congress. . . . There will no doubt be a strong remonstrance from the mines and other places and he will be censured."

However, by February 21, although the bill for the organization of the Wisconsin Territory was on course, Lyon wrote a friend in Chicago, "It is doubtful whether the seat of government will be fixed in the bill. The council have recommended Cassville, but private letters from Major Legate and some others say 'that place was fixed on, not to promote the interests of the people but to gratify foreign speculators,' and the people of Ioway and Dubuque counties are said to be strongly opposed to it. Before the receipt of such letters Gen. Jones had agreed to have the bill fix the seat of government as the council asked it."

The bill was passed with the question of capital left to the governor and council at their first session. Jones had received "many private letters" asking that it not be fixed and had also felt bound to carry out his election pledge that the people should have a voice in the location, so far as he could aid them. Lyon added in a March 28 letter, "I don't think he has any feeling against Cassville, but he must redeem his pledge to the people."

But Lyon had apparently convinced Territorial Secretary Horner, who wrote him April 7, "I am on my way to Cassville and shall set off in a canoe in the morning . . . write at once to Cassville that I am to be accommodated in a suitable manner in its plat of the town." He wrote two weeks later from Cassville, "I have now been a month or more in the Territory and have ascertained enough to satisfy me of the propriety of Cassville being the Seat of Government of the New Territory from its location, products, climate and other advantages but I am fully apprised that an attempt and a serious one is making to advance the claims of the English Prairie or Four Lakes. The Green Bay concern will go for the 4 Lakes and I hear Gov. Dodge and his interest will go for the English Prairie. A great, very great, oversight has been made by yourself and your friends not having the Seat of Government fixed by Congress on the recommendation of Council." He adds that he had been promised "as much land as I wanted" at Cassville and notes that he would like the plot designated "Graveyard Hill" on the map.

Arthur Bronson, never known as a patient man, was furious at the events that he could not control. He had arranged a meeting with L. J. Daniels in New York, then delayed the meeting, and Daniels, feeling that his presence in Wisconsin was sorely needed, had left the city. Bronson wrote Lyon, March 19, with dark slashing pen strokes, that he was very angry at Daniels for leaving New York without seeing him, ". . . however urgent his business, for it is our business if any body's that he goes on."

The new Territory of Wisconsin was formally inaugurated at Mineral Point on July 4, 1836, and Governor Dodge, instead of convening the next council at Cassville, chose the crossroads of Belmont in the mining district with the promise that the first order of business at the next session would be the question of designating a territorial capital. By doing this the governor was pointedly ignoring a great deal of hurried construction at Cassville including a four story brick hotel. To make the place more attractive Denniston made a proposal to the council that if Cassville was made the seat of government and $20,000 appropriated for public buildings, at the end of two years he would refund the sum expended, with interest. Other candidates for the honor of being territorial capital were Platteville, Belmont and Mineral Point (so close together that they tended to cancel each other out), and projected settlements in the four lakes region (see below). Dubuque, located in what is now the State of Iowa, wanted the capital there, but its advocates were discouraged by others on the basis that when Wisconsin applied for statehood its western boundary would probably be the Mississippi River. Some saw this as a favorable possibility that would allow the Wisconsin area another five or ten years to make a final capital decision. Horner wrote Lyon, November 5: "The contest is between Dubuque and the Four Lakes and I am pretty certain that neither place will get a majority. . . . Then I should not be surprised if Cassville should succeed by a majority of from five to 10. Cassville at this time certainly has the best chance."

Cassville lost to the four lakes region largely through the machinations of Judge Doty. Even after the unfavorable vote there was hope that legislators would become so discouraged at the wilderness that they would adjourn to the comforts of Cassville. Or that Cassville still had a chance for state honors at some date in the future. However, the immediate present looked bleak. On July 12, 1837, Lyon wrote from Lyons to G. V. Denniston, in response to a request for more investment capital and money for taxes, "If you can in any way raise it out of the property in Cassville it would relieve me very much. We must retrench our expenses there as much as possible for I greatly fear I shall not be able to meet my share of them this fall -- I am more and more pleased with my property here but can not sell a foot of it now to help myself."

As Wisconsin grew, Cassville was pushed aside. G. V. Denniston, who remained true, wrote February 22, 1841, "Times are dull here. . . . In 1837 we had a population of about 300, last spring 105. We are now down to 67 -- 27 of who intend removing from here in the Spring. . . . I still feel confidence in the ultimate prosperity of this place. We have a fine farming country around us, which is fast settling and the best natural situation on the River . . . but something must be done to give us a start, we want a grist mill, a furnace and several mechanical shops, and most of all we want to get rid of the Bronsons." Lyons remaining interest in Cassville had been lost to the Bronsons as a result of defaulted loans and debts.

When Iowa county was divided in 1836 Cassville was promised designation as county seat of Grant County, but even this honor was eventually lost to Lancaster. An 1853 gazetteer of the State of Wisconsin seemed to be rubbing it in a bit when it described Cassville as a post office and village, "formerly a place of considerable importance."

Four Lakes Region

The four lakes area was one of the major rivals with Cassville for the honor of being named capital. The region was the most centrally located of the claimants, being 100 miles east of Cassville, 80 miles west of Milwaukee, and 130 miles southwest of Green Bay. At that location there was a string of four lakes which gave the region its name.

James D. Doty

The area had been surveyed in 1834 by Orson Lyon. His elder brother had purchased land there as early as 1835, perhaps hedging his bets on the capital question. He bought entire sections between the first and the second lakes, had shares in four sections at the west end of the fourth lake, and other smaller scattered tracts. Some land was in his own name; some was purchased on a share basis with others. A large plot on the northwest shore of the fourth lake was held by Isaac Bronson. Most of this land was probably acquired when Lucius sent his brother Orson to the first major sale in the area, August 17, 1835.

One of the projected settlements in this area was the City of Four Lakes, located on the northwestern shore of the uppermost lake and owned mostly by Virginia investors, headed by William B. Slaughter of Culpepper, Virginia. Here a town was platted, including a large square reserved for the capitol. The settlement's chances to be chosen as capital were diminished when a lobbyist that investors had hired to represent them before the Legislative Council at Belmont failed to attend the session. Still a loyal council member made a motion to consider Four Lakes for the honor, and it lost by one vote, 6-7.

On the southern shore of the uppermost lake, on the isthmus between lakes four and three, was the proposed City of Madison, a land venture under the direction of Judge James D. Doty, former Detroit lawyer, judge, and member of the territorial council. After leaving government service he served as real estate advisor for John Jacob Astor of the American Fur Company, and others. Stevens T. Mason, governor-elect of Michigan, was a major investor in Madison. The incipient settlement was named for the former president who had died that summer. This settlement, which was still being feverishly platted while the council met at Belmont, was the eventual winner of the capital sweepstakes. Historians all agree that the choice of the four lakes region for the state capitol was the result of scheming by Judge Doty, and there has been speculation for more than a century, as to exactly how it was achieved. It is clear that free land went to council members, and there may have been other inducements as well. Although Doty's ability to get what he wanted was sometimes admired, he was personally disliked by many prominent men of the time, even by some who had not lost money in his projects. In an 1844 letter Henry Rowe Schoolcraft wrote that "Doty is not only an apostate politically," but noted he was also "a rascal in grain, & a bad fellow all round."

When the area was officially designated as the capital, it was said that the whole town consisted of but one log cabin. Following the vote there was an immediate rush on the land office at Milwaukee and all lands subject to entry in the vicinity and for many miles around all the four lakes were soon taken. A later history noted that the lands had been bought, "mostly by those who do not intend to occupy them for actual settlement and improvement. Hence the improvement of this county has not been as rapid as some others, where the 'speculators' have no opportunity or inducement to monopolize all the most valuable lands." Another description of the area was penned by George W. Featherstonhaugh, an English traveler, who was drawn to the area intending to inspect the burgeoning settlements of Madison City, the

City of Four Lakes, North Madison, East Madison, West Madison, South Madison, City of the First Lake, and the City of the Second Lake, all seven shown on his map. Instead of the bustling streets he had expected when he arrived in May of 1837, he found "one hastily patched up log hut . . . and this wretched contrivance had only been put up within the last few weeks."

In July of 1836, Lyon offered a large tract for sale for $36,188 to S. Page who replied, July 31, the day before his option was set to expire, "I am glad to learn that you have got hold of the choice lands in the vicinity of Four Lakes . . . I took my maps and examined your descriptions . . . and I find many of the lots such as I should like. . . " He declined, however, to take the whole property describing it as "too large for my purse."

An early plat map of the Madison area showing the city (right) and land entered by Lucius Lyon near left edge of the peninsula (center) and two quarter sections to the east. Land entered in 1835 for Isaac Bronson is at top left.

The Bronsons, who caught wind of the Four Lakes lands Lyon had offered Page, were not impressed. On April 27, 1836, Frederick wrote Arthur from Cincinnati, "I note the offer Lyon has received to sell

194

his lands in Rock River and the Four Lakes Country at an advance of 300 per %. I should not think the offer was a very large one -- as I am satisfied his selections have been good. . . ."

Even after Madison had been voted as site for the new capital, investors at the City of Four Lakes felt their settlement would grow because it was across the lake from the capital, near a contemplated canal that would connect the Rock and the Wisconsin Rivers, and by the military road between Prairie du Chien and Portage. Probably as a result of Lyon's maneuvering, there was a post office established at Four Lakes before the one at Madison, but it was closed August 9, 1837. In 1837-38 there was a bill introduced in the Legislative Council to establish a territorial university "at the City of Four Lakes" but before final passage the bill was amended to read, "in the vicinity of Madison." As late as 1841 Lyon recorded "a twentieth interest in the City of Four Lakes" among his assets. The fate of the settlement was sealed April 5, 1843, when the legislature voted to tax the former town plat as farmland. The City of Madison became a village in 1846, and a city in 1856.

View of Madison in 1836

It was lands in the vicinity of Madison that Lucius and Orson entered for their stepbrother, Dan Lyon, who had sent them money to invest. He still held these lands as late as 1846, when he wrote Lucius urging him to clear the titles and put them on the market.

Other Lands in Wisconsin

One listing of Wisconsin lands shows that Lyon was a major investor in the "townsite of Winnebago." The tiny settlement of

195

Winnebago is just north of the present-day City of Oshkosh, on a peninsula between Lake Winnebago and Lake Butte des Morts. An 1843 letter from A. G. Ellis mentions land that he seems to think that Lyon owns "in the neighborhood of Pipe Village, Winnebago Lake," near the southeast shore of the lake. Doty wrote to Lyon in 1844 about two lots that he wondered if Lyon still held title to "on the island in the outlet of Winnebago Lake."

Another highly valued area for investment was in the Rock River area, near Lake Koshkonong, about halfway between the Mississippi and Lake Michigan, at about the same latitude as Milwaukee. Arthur Bronson wrote April 27, 1836, "Williams says that he has been informed by one of the Surveyors that Lyon has got on Koshkonong Lake . . . a village site -- and that lands in that vicinity are quite valuable." An 1843 letter from Thomas W. Sutherland speaks of Lyon's interest in land near Koshkonong, and on the Rock River.

Lyon also owned at least a partial interest in six building lots in the Village of Green Bay. An 1841 listing of lands owned in Wisconsin included a parcel just north of the City of Milwaukee, several large lots on Hook Lake, Dunn Township, Dane County, south and west of the four lakes, and at least three parcels on the first lake, later named Lake Kegonsa, the southernmost of the four lakes.

In the frenzy of Wisconsin land-buying 1834-37, many deals of questionable legality were entered into -- even sought. One example is the Fort Howard military tract, across the river from Navarino and Astor, where Daniel Whitney had bought up settlers' claims that were located on the military reserve. Unable to sell the claims to the government, he divided the land and offered parcels to eager speculators. On July 30, 1836, Whitney sold a quarter of his total claim to Lucius Lyon who turned around that same day and sold the tract to Samuel Beall identifying it as the land "which Daniel Whitney is to convey to me." On June 2 Beall sold it to Seth Rees and James D. Doty for $19,000. When men began to straighten up their holdings partially as a result of the crash of 1837, Beall pressed Doty for payment, so that he could pay Lyon. Doty rebuked him, pointing out that the whole series of transactions could not become the basis of a legal contract because, "You must be aware that the sale by Whitney of land which belonged to the govt. of the U. S. and was then, and is now a Military Reservation, was void."

Lyon, with others, including John P. Arndt, E. Childs, G. V. Denniston, Morgan L. Martin, A. G. Ellis, Sylvester Sibley, Gurdon S. Hubbard, Joshua Hathaway, Daniel Wells Jr., W. B. Ogden, William Jones and George Smith in 1835 formed the Wiskonsin (later Wisconsin) Land Company. Lyon was treasurer and kept the books.

They were very busy for a few years, and bought and sold land from and to each other, as well as to other investors and settlers. The group had extensive holdings at Pipe Village on the southeastern side of Lake Winnebago and owned other parcels around the lake, including the northern tip and a large area along the northern shore.

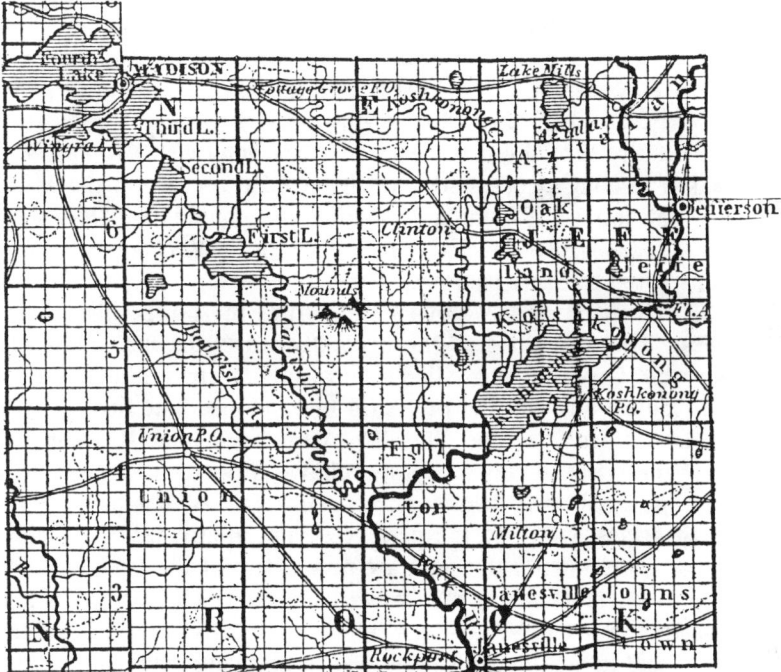

Central Wisconsin with Madison (upper left), and Lake Koshkonong (center right) flowing into the Rock River.

The Bank of Wisconsin had been incorporated January 23, 1835, when the area was still a part of Michigan Territory. Stock was offered for sale in August of 1835 and much of it was taken up by Judge Doty and investor John Jacob Astor. Others on the early board included Morgan L. Martin, his elder brother John Martin, still a resident of New York State, and several Michigan men including Lucius Lyon and Henry T. Stringham of Detroit who was named cashier. At this time Lyon had his hands full with efforts to have Michigan admitted to the Union and to oversee the just-beginning settlements at Grand Rapids, Lyons and Ada, consequently he transferred power of attorney to Daniel Whitney of Navarino (later part of Green Bay), giving Whitney control of 33 shares of bank stock.

The Bank of Mineral Point was chartered by the Wisconsin territorial council at its first meeting in Belmont and stock went on sale in the spring of 1837. After a slow start to the sales Judge Doty, on behalf of himself and several investors for whom he held power of attorney, purchased a controlling interest in the stock. Lyon also had an interest. Both banks issued notes considerably in excess of their specie reserve, and from the beginning their assets were illegally entangled. In 1839 the attorney general was authorized to commence suit against the Bank of Wisconsin for violation of the terms of its charter and apparent insolvency. On seizure of what few assets and records there were, the specie reserve turned out to be a keg in the vault which contained less than $90 in coin, paper assets which included a draft on the Mineral Point bank for $61,507, and a personal note against James Doty for just under $18,000. Both banks were closed by 1840, and disillusioned citizens voted to make chartered banks illegal.

The panic of 1837 put a serious crimp in land speculation in the midwest. To a large degree the overextended credit and inflated land prices were important ingredients in causing the panic, but there were earlier indications that the prices on undeveloped land had just about peaked. As early as June 30, 1836, Arthur and Isaac Bronson wrote Lyon, "The crisis in respect to speculative property it appears to me cannot be far distant; communities, self-organized companies, acting through agents, wild and inexperienced, and multitudes of individuals from the East, North and South are now swarming the west, presenting an opportunity for making sales which calm and prudent men should not permit to pass by unimproved. I hope you will feel the force of these remarks and in making sales require such payment and security as shall secure their fulfillment." In October of 1836 the Bronsons wrote that he had better "suspend purchases," suggesting that instead of investing new monies, he confine his purchases to the amount of the profits. But by then Lyon was too caught up to listen.

Lyon must have felt keenly the rebukes in a letter received in 1843 from David Page who had lent him $1134 in the fall of 1836. Page wrote, "As yet you have neglected and refused to refund me one copper . . . but urging as an excuse that you went into wild extravagant unwarrantable, speculations by which you lost the money -- as well the gambler might urge when called on to pay up. . . . I hold that no man has the moral right to borrow money of another and to risk it in the way you say you have mine." Page points out that Lyon is now serving in Congress and from his pay should "by common prudence and economy" be able to send him $350, or even $750 a year. In the Lyon letters there is no notation that the letter was answered.

10

Scientific Farmer

Lucius faced every task with enthusiasm, but he drew special pleasure from his farms. He wrote Major John Biddle in January of 1838, "You mention your farm. I wish you success with it. I feel proud of mine. If you make yours equal to any farm in eastern Michigan, I will try to make mine equal to any in the western part of the State, to be even with you."

As early as 1835 he was involved in farming on a scale that would have made him one of the largest farmers, in acreage, in the state. In October he wrote Arthur Bronson of New York that the expected expense of fencing, plowing and fitting 200 acres for a crop of oats, corn and potatoes would be about $1,500. The same winter he wrote Giles Isham who was taking over management of the farm at Lyons, near the confluence of the Maple and Grand Rivers, that he was hoping to have 400 acres plowed and ready for planting in the spring. "I wish to have as much of my prairie land at the mouth of the Maple plowed, planted and sowed next spring as possibly can be, for I am satisfied that everything we can raise will command a high price in cash on the ground as fast as we may wish to dispose of it."

Ira Lyon, a younger brother of Lucius's father Asa, had come to Michigan possibly as early as 1828 and tried farming near Pontiac. On October 9, 1835, Lucius wrote Lucretia that he had just set up Uncle Ira as manager of the Schoolcraft farm. "He is poor and has a large family of children, five girls and two boys," Lucius explained. Ira was commended in November of 1835 for "all your arrangements," although Lucius expressed concern that 31 cents per bushel for storing and transporting 400 bushels of seed oats down the Thornapple River and up the Grand River was a rather high price. He adds, ". . . but I presume you did the best you could in the matter and I am satisfied."

The Prairie Ronde, at Schoolcraft in southwestern Michigan, was considered prime wheat-growing land, and that was the principle crop Lyon tried there. He was always looking for better varieties of wheat and in January of 1838 sent Ira four barrels of Italian wheat for seed and a half barrel of Dutton lemma. Ira wrote January 28, thanking him for the seed and commenting, "Spring wheat done better here last season than the winter wheat. The eastern lemma does better than the Dent does here. I will endeavor to give this seed a fair trial."

In the late 1830s, when the depression and failure of the wildcat banks caused economic chaos in Michigan and throughout the north, Lucius hoped that his wheat would yet make him solvent. He wrote Thomas T. Whittlesey in Connecticut in October, 1839, "Our banks, all that remain of them, only three or four in number, are perfectly sound, because they have no paper in circulation, but we have very little money of any description among us. We have an immense crop of wheat, however, yet to be threshed out, and we have put in an immense number of acres into the ground this fall, so that we shall, I verily believe, within 18 months, be more out of debt and have more money in proportion to our population, than any people in the Union." He was shortly to discover that farm prices, too, were suffering.

Lucius Lyon was one of the first men in Michigan to experiment with the growing of sugar beets, prior to this time nearly all the sugar produced in the world was from sugar cane. In April of 1839 he forwarded a small package of seed "which was raised the summer before last in Pennsylvania" to James W. Tabor at Lyons. He gave Tabor detailed instructions for planting and added that he was hoping to get enough seed to plant 100 acres. The following month he bought additional seed which had been imported from France but wrote to Sherman McLean from Lyons May 26, 1839, "I am now engaged in planting it and intended to plant about 100 acres, but the spring continued so uncommonly dry that I fear all our crops will suffer, and I shall, therefore only risk the planting of about 20 or 25 acres this year. This, if it does well, will answer for this year and next year I can go on on a more extensive scale."

The sugar beet seeds were barely in the ground when he zipped off a series of letters to farms in the United States and abroad asking for advice on making sugar from the beet. Lyon was gone most of the summer in Wisconsin as commissioner to the Indians, and his experimental farmers back in Lyons puzzled over the proper methods of growing the beets. Edward Lyon wrote Lucius October 25, 1839, that if he was going to make sugar this season he had better do it soon since they were not certain how well the beets would keep. He reported that Tabor had not pulled all the sugar beets, but that the ones he had harvested, "look as green as they did in mid-summer and I think are still growing." When Lucius returned, he was still uncertain about the process of making sugar and in November of that year wrote a friend, "I raised a pretty fair crop of beets this year, but having been absent from the State I have done nothing toward manufacturing sugar from them. I shall make further enquiries on the subject, between this and next spring, and if I think the business can be gone into to advantage, now that I know I can raise the beets, I shall try it."

Sugar beets topped and ready for cooking.

In March of 1840 he reported to H. L. Ellsworth, Commissioner of Patents, that he was "fully satisfied that the beet will grow well on the soil of this State, for I raised last summer a crop of about 30 acres on my farm at Lyons, and though they were very much injured by the worms and grasshoppers when small, I still got about ten tons to the acre." He further reported that farmers on the White Pigeon prairie in St. Joseph county who were also experimenting with the beet had made a large quantity of molasses, but "have hitherto been unable to get from it much, if any, crystallized sugar." They were using a French method of rasping, first grating the beet pulp, which Lyon said he felt would be unprofitable, however, he also reported that the White Pigeon investors, including John S. Barry (later governor of Michigan) were preparing to send an agent to Europe to study and bring out workmen to teach them the process.

In April of 1840 while he was in the east for the wedding of his half-brother George H. Lyon, he visited David L. Childs in Massachusetts, who had recently written a book on the subject "and expresses the strongest confidence that the cultivation of the beet for making sugar will be more profitable than any other branch of farming." Childs was planning a course in the art of making sugar from beets which would begin in September, $100 per scholar.

Lucius was always on the lookout for new and better-yielding varieties of common fruits and vegetables. In April of 1839 he sent his Michigan farmers a packet of English beans received from the commissioner of patents and four seeds from a watermelon grown in

Pennsylvania. In 1841 he sent three seeds of the Billindean cabbage "which is said to have grown 11 feet high and 57 feet in circumference. The seeds are advertised as something extraordinary and I have paid sixpence a piece for 24 of them, though I think the chances are about 3 to 1 that I have been humbugged, and that the seeds are only the seeds of the common cabbage. They may, however, be seeds of a new variety and on that account I bought them. Please have them planted and see what they come to."

In September of 1840 his sister Lucretia was living in Lyons and reported that she had been to dinner at Gaius and Maria Deane's and "partook of some of the largest water melons that I ever saw, one weighed 24 and another 28 pounds." She said that the melons had been grown from some seeds that Lucius had sent from Washington.

Sending seeds got him into political trouble in 1839 and 1840 when he was accused of using the franking privilege of a U. S. Senator to send grain seeds to his farms in Lyons. His political enemies announced that they had affidavits from an individual who had seen packets of seeds at the home of J. W. Tabor which had been sent from Washington and franked, rather than mailed with proper postage. After a hurried correspondence it was decided that the packages that the individual had seen were some seeds sent by Henry Ellsworth from the Patent Office Department and had not been franked by Senator Lyon. James W. Tabor wrote out an affidavit to that effect, although he hinted in a later letter to Lucius that perhaps this was not strictly true, and that it could have been that the watermelon seeds had been sent from Washington under his frank.

(Even if Lyon's name may have been clear in this instance, he often abused the franking privilege. In the early days there was no postage paid on both mail bound to a government representative, and that mailed by him. When Lyon was in Washington, there were several instances where correspondents enclosed personal letters to others in their packets to him, asking that he frank the letters and send them on. Sarah McKnight, the wife of Detroit newspaperman Sheldon McKnight, often imposed in this way.)

Another kind of farming that Lyon at least considered at one time was the cultivation of silkworms. In a letter dated May 3, 1835, L. Crittenden of Albany, New York, sent him some books on silk culture with the note, "I most devoutly hope that all your anticipations in regard to the culture of silk may be fully realized, and I doubt not but they will be more than doubly so by your determined exertions." William A. Richmond, one of Lyon's colleagues in the Grand Rapids venture, was formerly employed in the silk houses of New York. Whether this had any bearing on Lyon's interest in silk culture or whether he ever attempted to establish silk worm cultivation in Michigan is not known.

Even as late as 1848, when he had very little farmland left, he received notice in a letter that a friend in Chicago was sending a new kind of grape, called the New Buffalo grape, to see how they would grow in various parts of Michigan.

He was an early advocate of machinery for farming and planned scientifically the most efficient methods of planting. In 1839 when the sugar beet experiment was just beginning, he first advocated planting the seeds 12 inches apart but later decided that the rows should be 24 inches from each other. He also devised a system for making rows in both planting directions in order to use the cultivator to do nearly all the work of weeding.

His most ambitious effort at mechanical farming was a fine idea but turned out to be a little ahead of the times. Lyon, along with pioneer fur trader, legislator, and town founder, Rix Robinson, was a major investor in the Moore-Hascall Harvesting Machine.

According to traditional accounts, the machine was the result of a dream. As Schoolcraft historian Henry Bishop recorded in the July 19, 1895, *Schoolcraft Express*, "The late John Hascall residing on the Genessee prairie was troubled to get help to harvest wheat and he claimed to have dreamt out such a machine, and told his dream to Moore, who was so impressed with its feasibility that he got Lucius Lyon and a Mr. Wood to assist him with the means to built it." The prototype of the harvesting machine was constructed by Hiram Moore, first of Comstock, later of Climax, Kalamazoo County. He built it in Rochester, New York, because this was the nearest place where the necessary gears could be obtained. Most accounts state that the machine was completed during the winter of 1837, but because of the financial crisis it took another two years for Lyon to muster the money to ship it around the lakes. In the spring of 1839, with great anticipation, Lyon went to Rochester to make arrangements to get the device to his farm near Schoolcraft, Kalamazoo County, where it could be put to a practical test. He loaded it aboard the brig *Virginia*, sending it on a journey around the Great Lakes, to the port of St. Joseph, on Lake Michigan. It is likely that Lyon had some problems getting all of the machinery to the dock and finding a boat willing to haul it, for he wrote the inventor in a somewhat gloomy vein:

"It consists of about 65 pieces of wood and board and two barrels containing the bars and bolts, belonging to them, so that the machine may be put together at St. Joseph and hauled to Prairie Ronde if you think it worth the expense and trouble of doing so. I leave it with you to decide that point. Nobody but you will be able to put it together and if it is to be prepared for use this season you will have to do it. . . . As to myself, I must say, I have very little expectation that it will ever be worked to any advantage anywhere, and I would be very glad to have my money back for my share in the invention. Not that I do not believe that grain may be harvested and threshed by machinery cheaper than it ever has been done by hand, for I do believe it, and furthermore I think the principle of your machine is correct and that it will lead to important results; but a machine to be useful on a farm must be far lighter and more manageable than the one I have been removing. It is too heavy and unwieldy for the average field, be it large or small, to be ever introduced into general use -- at least it so seems to me." Lucius had left behind the gathering cylinder and a cylinder which carried off the straw, bringing along the hardware, with the idea that the inventor could fabricate "something which will answer the purposes for which these cylinders were intended."

Moore rose to the challenge and had it ready for the harvest. When he returned to Michigan in the fall Lyon wrote Henry Ellsworth that there was no longer any doubt of the success of the Moore and Hascall harvesting machine. "Mr. Moore has had a machine in the field on Prairie Ronde in this county during the past summer which harvested and threshed 63 acres of wheat in very superior style and could have harvested 250 acres with the greatest ease, at the rate of 20 acres per day had it not been for one or two trifling accidents, the cause of which may be very easily guarded against in the construction of machines hereafter. Twenty of the 63 acres were harvested on my farm and every expense attending it does not exceed one dollar per acre. A great number of farmers witnessed its operation. All are entirely satisfied with its complete success and many, in sowing their wheat this fall, are calculating largely on the benefit to be derived from it next year." He went on to note that he had, in the last three or four years, advanced Moore between $3,000 and $4,000 to enable him to bring the machine as "near perfection as possible." He also asked what must be done to patent some of the improvements that had been added to the machine in Rochester during the winter of 1836-7.

There was little doubt that the machine greatly saved on manpower and total hours needed to harvest wheat. However, what was saved in manpower was expended in needed horsepower. It is recorded that the prototype machine that was tested in 1839 required 16 to 20 horses to provide the motive power. The animals were harnessed in pairs and pulled the heavy machine forward through the grain. As the harvester advanced, the blades entered the standing grain cutting off just the heads of the wheat plant. The heads passed into a receptacle where the kernels separated from the husks, continuing to into a fanning machine where the chaff was blown away. The grain dropped into a small bin and was raised by a screw elevator to an opening where a bag received it. Workers following with a wagon removed and replaced the bags as they filled.

The Moore-Hascall Harvesting Machine in action.

In the spring of 1840 Hiram Moore conveyed to investors Robinson and Lyon a percentage of ownership in all the improvements that may be made by Moore on the harvesting machine. In 1841 John Hascall (apparently in financial trouble) assigned his entire interest in the device to Lyon for $100 in cash, $200 in personal notes, and a promise of $5,000 of the profits from the sale of the machines.

At the same time Lyon wrote the commissioner of patents, "We have had our harvesting machines in the fields during the past harvest and mine has harvested 150 acres without much delay for alterations, and I have no doubt the invention will ultimately prove one of the most important labor saving inventions ever brought into use; but the operation of cutting, threshing and cleaning the grain in the field, all at one time, is so complex and the harvest season, which is the only season for experiments, is so short that it will require some years yet to perfect it so as to make it profitable."

Shortly afterwards Lyon wrote to Arthur Bronson asking him to take an interest in the harvesting machine. "Two of the machines were operated during the last harvest and worked most admirably and are now in as good or better condition than before they were used. When the machines are driven with an ordinary degree of care nearly every grain of wheat is saved, while under the old method fully one-fifth was lost. . . . The machines will work well on any ground that is free from large stones and stumps and may be operated by a man of ordinary common sense after two days' experience." Bronson replied shortly, declining the offer to take an interest in the project noting that his past experience with patent rights had been both unpleasant and unprofitable. Cyrus McCormick patented his sickle-bar reaper in 1834, using a principle similar to that employed by Moore and Hascall in their 1836 patent. Litigation concerning patent rights was inevitable. As a result of the legal problems Lyon advised Moore to patent each improvement that he had made to the machine, separately.

The harvester was run, with varying success, for several years on the Kalamazoo County prairie. Later, a portion of the stock was purchased by (or given to) Ira Lyon, and following his death in 1841 there was a question about ownership of the actual machine. In October of 1843 a correspondent reported to Lucius that it had been sold under a school tax warrant.

The Moore-Hascall Harvesting Machine ready for action.
Man in the top hat may be Hiram Moore.

In 1845 Lyon wrote a letter to the governor of Louisiana introducing Moore, who had gone south for his health. Lyons wrote, "He has done for the grain growing regions of the north what Whitney and his cotton gin have done for the south. . . . He has reduced the cost of harvesting and threshing and cleaning grain from more than three dollars to about one dollar per acre, and for this he is destined to be and deserves to be ranked in the first and noblest class of our country's benefactors."

According to one historical account use of the machine was short lived for two reasons. "It could not be used until the grain was ripe enough to thresh, and after it arrived at that stage it would remain but a few days before it would crinkle down and shell out, then it could only be used when the straw was dry . . . but when it was perfected and the wheat just right, it was one of the grandest sights ever seen in a harvest field and people came from a distance to witness its working." A similar machine was later used to much better advantage in California where the climate is drier.

There was another prominent early Michigan scientific farmer named Lyon. Theodatus Timothy Lyon was born in Livingston County, New York, January 23, 1813, and came to Michigan with his parents in 1828, settling first in the Plymouth area. He was later keeper of the Wayne County poorhouse before beginning farming in earnest in the South Haven area, Van Buren County. He was a founder of the Michigan Pomological Society in 1870, and served as its president from 1876 to 1893, continuing as honorary president until his death in 1900 at the age of 87. He was instrumental in setting up an agricultural experiment station at South Haven run by the Michigan Agricultural College (later Michigan State University). He donated a portion of his land to enlarge the project, serving as its director for more than 20 years. The station continued to function into the 1980s and the city grew up around it. A friend described T. T. (or Theo), "There was not a lazy thing about Mr. Lyon; he was continuously active, and while not a rapid worker was so continuous in his work that he accomplished a great deal." Lucius and T. T. were distant kin; it is likely that T. T. was part of the Timothy Lyon family, related more directly to Mary (Hawley Lyon) Lyon's first husband. Mary (Hawley Lyon) Lyon was Lucius Lyon's first stepmother. She was the mother of Truman, Edward, and Dan Lyon, Lorain Barstow, Maria Deane and Lenora Irish.

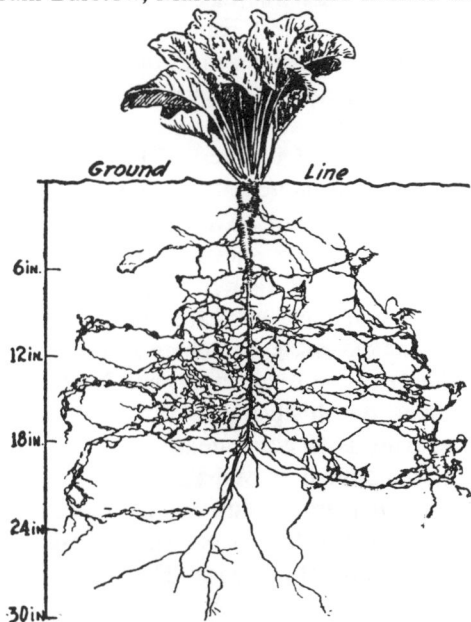

The sugar-beet has a very extensive root system.
207

11

Investor and Engineer

When Lucius Lyon left Vermont in 1822 his vocation was still very much undecided and he was open to whatever possibilities came his way for work, investment, speculation, or political service.

The Detroit Hydraulic Company

His first recorded investment opportunity came in February of 1825 when he associated with Rufous Wells of Detroit in the building of a pump house near the foot of Randolph street which would supply water for the growing settlement of Detroit. Using a horse-powered pump the water was forced into a 40 gallon cask on top of the pump house. From there it flowed through hollowed-out logs to a reservoir located on Randolph Street. The reservoir was sixteen feet square, built of white oak planks and caulked with oakum. Families paid $10 a year in quarterly installments for water.

On July 31, 1829, Lucius Lyon, along with Wells, Phineas Davis and A. E. Hathon, styling themselves The Hydraulic Company, applied to the Detroit Common Council and received, "sole and exclusive right of supplying the city of Detroit with water until 1860." Work began that summer on a well at the south end of Fort Street between Wayne and Shelby in Detroit. After reaching a depth of 260 feet, with expenditures totaling more than $6,000, they found no useable water and resolved to abandon the well in favor of a pumping site on the river. In June of 1830 Lyon brought before the common council a plan asking that the council repeal some of the restrictions they had placed on the project (the most important being the need to furnish service pipes and penstocks and a release from the obligation to turn over their works without compensation at the end of the franchise) and to extend the charter until 1865. After prolonged debate and seven separate sessions of the council, the plan was finally approved June 29, 1830. A charter was granted to The Detroit Hydraulic Co. by the legislative council, March 2, 1831, and the work continued.

The new reservoir on the Fort Street lot was built of brick and held 21,811 gallons. In 1831 capacity was expanded with an additional oak plank reservoir which held 119,680 gallons. According to a history of the waterworks written by Robert E. Roberts of Detroit: "The company continued to extend their works in the face of an increasing pecuniary loss on the striking of their yearly balances, and with the gloomy pleasure of hearing their customers declare, and reading the 'resolves' of the common council that the water they delivered came few and far between, and was by no means clear, pure and wholesome, and with the melancholy satisfaction of knowing it was all true."

In May of 1836, to everyone's relief, the city decided that the charter had been violated and forfeited. The city purchased the interest of the company by issuing city bonds, payable in 10 years, and took over the task of supplying water to its citizens.

Kalamazoo Riverboat

Lyon had been interested in navigation on the Kalamazoo River as early as 1831 when he did a great deal of survey work in Allegan County. The river begins in south-central Michigan and winds its way through Albion, Battle Creek and Kalamazoo before slicing through Allegan County and flowing into Lake Michigan. In the fall of 1834 he received a letter from Oshea Wilder of Eckford, Calhoun County, who also had considerable interest at the mouth of the Kalamazoo River, relating that Wilder had seen George Kitchener and asked him to accompany him on a river trip "to explore, survey and estimate the expense of rendering the Kalamazoo navigable from the mouth up to Marshall." Wilder continued that he felt it was probably too costly a project for the community, but that a careful estimate of what was needed might aid congress in granting land along the river to assist the work.

In 1836 a group of Kalamazoo businessmen including Lyon, Thomas C. Sheldon, Justus and Cyren Burdick, Hosea Huston and others formed a company to operate flatboats on the Kalamazoo River. They hoped eventually to have two vessels that would operate between the settlement of Kalamazoo and the mouth of the river, making various stops on the journey, and perhaps braving Lake Michigan as far north as Port Sheldon, near the northern boundary of Ottawa County.

A large craft was built and completed one successful round trip with Captain Albert Saxton in command, experiencing only minor difficulties with snags and low water. On the second journey the captain attempted to test the craft on Lake Michigan; however, it was wrecked between the mouth of the Kalamazoo River and the North Black River (where the settlement of Holland was later established).

There were two canal projects involving the Kalamazoo River which were heralded with much enthusiasm during the boom of the

1830s either of which would certainly have made river steamboating profitable. The first was the Clinton-Kalamazoo Canal, which would begin at Lake St. Clair near Mount Clemens, follow the Little Clinton River westward, pass through the lake district of Oakland County, coming, eventually, into the Kalamazoo River. This canal was actually begun in 1833 with a great deal of fanfare and completed as far as Rochester before railroads rendered it unprofitable. A second canal idea, which never got much beyond the planning stage, would have linked the Detroit River with the Kalamazoo River, traveling via the Grand River in Eaton and Ingham County, to the headwaters of the Huron and Rouge Rivers.

Grand River Bank

Although he had refused the offer to participate in the organization of a bank at Lyons, Lyon seems to have agreed readily when a similar establishment was organized in Grand Rapids in 1837. This was a "wildcat" bank. The Michigan Legislature had passed a general banking law in March of 1837 that permitted ten or more freeholders of any county to organize into a corporation for the transaction of banking business on furnishing an amount of specie, securities, or bonds, amounting to 30 per cent of the money issued. The general banking law required that paper money be redeemed in hard currency on demand, or within 30 days, or the bank was dissolved.

However, before any new banks had completed the chartering process, the panic of 1837 and the subsequent run on banks caused banks of New York, Philadelphia, Boston, and Baltimore to suspend specie payment and redemption of bank notes. Fearing that out of state depositors might flood the banks of Michigan with demands for note redemption, the Michigan Legislature, in a special session on June 12, 1837, suspended the specie redemption requirement, but they left the general banking law in force. Thus new banks could be organized and would be allowed to issue bills while the requirements to redeem the bills were still suspended. The 30 per cent capital requirement remained in force but was circumnavigated by a variety of ingenious ruses. It was common for several banks to pool their specie and send it from building to building as the bank inspector made his rounds. Citizens and companies often lent specie to the local bank for a few hours on inspection day.

Lucius Lyon recorded on August 14, 1837, that the Grand River Bank was to have a capital stock of $50,000. One-third interest in the establishment was to be owned by himself, one third interest by C.H.

and W. T. Carroll, and one third interest by the Kent Company. John Almy was named president of the bank, and William A. Richmond, cashier. (In some records Lyon is designated as cashier.) The bank was housed in the offices of the Kent Co. on the northwest corner of Kent and Bridge Streets. A statement of assets, dated December 7, 1838, makes the institution look quite respectable.

GRAND RIVER BANK, December 7, 1838.

ASSETS.		LIABILITIES.	
Overdrafts	$ 3,930	Capital, $50,000	$ 15,149
Disc. (under protest)	27,750	Deposits (27 Depositors)	8,860
" Not due	2,229	Circulation	16,949
Specie	4,403	Due to other Corpora-	
Bills of other Banks	4,021	tions	2,688
Personal and Real Prop-			
erty	1,313		
	$43,646		$43,646

Sidney Smith of Ada, who had a share of the bank, reported in a letter dated October 2, 1837, that there had been some delay in actually getting the bank open. He wrote that he feared that the establishment of the bank could not solve the economic problems of the area, "It is getting harder times here than ever before for Money. The people here, have raised but little with which to obtain money and the Bank can at present do but little to relieve them."

A rival company, headed by Louis Campau, Simeon Johnson and others, founded the People's Bank on the second floor of a Monroe Street store at about the same time. The bank folded almost before it was fairly begun, struggling to keep sufficient specie in the vaults. It is said that Rix Robinson lost $900 in silver that he had lent the cashier to make a show of assets for the bank inspector.

The Grand River Bank struggled on for about three years. After the general banking laws were changed, the bank ceased operation. On June 21, 1841, the final notice was published in the Grand Rapids newspaper.

RECEIVER'S NOTICE. — The under-signed, Receiver of the Grand River Bank, at Grand Rapids, Michigan, hereby notifies the creditors of said Bank, having their claims duly authenticated according to the provisions of law, that a meeting of such creditors will be held at his office, in this village, on Wednesday, the 25th day of August next, at 2 o'clock P. M., of that day, at which time the undersigned will lay before said meeting the details of his doings and ask the consideration of the said creditors thereon. Dated Grand Rapids, June 21, 1841. GEO. MARTIN, Receiver.

In a 1918 Kent County history Ernest Fisher reports that about 1851, when Louis Campau was building an observatory onto his house on the Fulton Street hill, he said, "I am pretty rich. I shall paper this room with money." He brought out a stack of bills from the People's Bank which served as wallpaper until the house was razed.

Grand Rapids Canal

The Grand Rapids Canal was begun in 1835. That October, Lyon wrote his sister, "I am constructing, or rather paying one-half the expense of construction, a canal 60 feet wide on the water line, 5 feet deep from the surface of the water to the bottom and about a mile and a quarter in length, around the rapids of the Grand river, where I own a part of the land. It is intended to furnish an excellent water power, and also to facilitate the passage of steamboats up and down the river, and will cost about $8,000." To get the plan under way Lyon and N. O. Sargeant had purchased $5,000 worth of land from those who had dammed the water above them, leaving only three feet of water in the route of the proposed canal.

Lyon pointed out to a New York investor that the proposed canal at the Grand Rapids was "the first ever made in Michigan and is turning public attention a good deal to that point." The canal called for a wing dam to direct the water away from the mainstream of the river and into the side canal. It would have a turning basin for boats and, eventually, a lock system that would open the river for navigation from its mouth to Lyons in Ionia County.

The project went on. By mid October 1835 Lyon reported "Mr. Sergeant has with him an excellent engineer and about 50 men who are prosecuting the work vigorously & will probably have the excavation nearly completed before winter sets in." The arrival of the workers, which Lyon related with such reserve, is a scene that various historians and others with a more dramatic bent, have made a colorful slice of Grand Rapids tradition. As Baxter tells it, "Nathaniel O. Sargeant was the contractor for digging the mill race. . . . He came here from Massachusetts, in 1835, with a company of men for that work. They marched in with their picks and shovels on their shoulders. At their head was Alanson Cramston, playing a bugle. . . . Hearing the noise and the music when the canal men came, Chief Noonday thought the company were enemies, meaning mischief to Louis Campau, and sent a message to the latter offering to drive the invaders away."

Lyon described the canal plan to Bronson in November, "The length of the canal as at present projected is something over a mile. It now is intended to terminate above the mill dam . . . but so soon as we can make satisfactory arrangement with Mr. Campau . . . we design to construct a dam across from the lower end of the Islands to his land. I allude to the foot of the two upper Islands. To this point Steam boats of light draught can at all times come up, and if we should not succeed in making an arrangement with him we shall excavate a channel between or around the Island to our work. The whole fall below the mill dam in low water is about 3 feet -- in high water nothing. This dam, with a saw mill and about a third of an acre of ground where the mill stands Mr. Sargeant & myself have lately purchased from Wadsworth, Frost & Junius H. Hatch of your city for $5,500. . . . We mean to excavate a 'tailrace' along the margin of the river above, so as to rise the water from the canal under a head of 12 feet all the way along the bank . . . down to the lower lock. . . . This will afford sites & power for a great many mills and as there are inexhaustible quantities of pine up the river on its north side, and an excellent grain growing Country on the south, a great many will be required."

The circumstances and project are outlined in the 1838 *Michigan Gazetteer*:

> *Grand Rapids.*—These consist of an obstruction in the Grand river, 40 miles from its mouth, " caused by a stratum of lime rock which shows itself in the bed of the river, and in both banks, for a distance of a mile and a half. Its inclination is remarkably uniform, causing the water of the river to descend with a velocity due to fifteen feet fall, without noise or commotion." Their length is about one mile. The banks at the head of the rapids are no more than four feet high above the surface of the water, and they keep a nearly horizontal level from thence to the foot of the falls where they are nearly 20 feet above the water. The width of the river is here about 60 rods. A canal is constructing by the Kent company, around the rapids, on the south side. Its dimensions are 81 feet wide and five feet deep. There are to be two locks constructed, each 40 feet wide and 150 feet in length, so that the largest steamboats that navigate the river above may pass. The estimated expense of a canal around these rapids, made by the engineer appointed to survey the Grand River, was $43,751. The rapids entirely obstruct the navigation of the river, except for boats descending in high water.

Part of the land above the mill and canal was owned by Sargeant, jointly with Janson Fairbanks of Boston, and others. As work progressed, the other riverbank owners asked for a joint contract with the owners of various pieces of the project so that all could "have a joint and equal interest in the whole." Lyon explained the plan to Arthur Bronson, his chief financial backer, in a letter in mid-October 1835. After several letters and two months of discussion, Bronson refused to agree to the arrangement and Lyons contracted to purchase his interest for $21,000.

In 1841 a $25,000 appropriation was set aside for the advancement of the Grand Rapids Canal. Lyon, however, felt the appropriation was still tied up in politics. He wrote C. H. Taylor September 8, "You will recollect that I expressed to yourself and Mr. Walker, the opinion that the board of internal improvement did not intend to give the Grand river country the benefit of the appropriation of $25,000 for a canal around the rapids and that their real object in all their movements was to throw the responsibility and odium of procrastinating and defeating the work on the shoulders of others." He goes on to cite a letter by William Foster in the Detroit newspaper. Lyon wrote, "Mr. Foster has omitted to state one of the objections and the most important one made by the acting commissioner to going on with the work, which was lack of funds. The commissioner evidently supposed the objection raised on account of the contract made by Judge Almy and myself with Granger & Ball would be fatal to the work and justify them in refusing to proceed with it, but when Mr. Foster returned and informed them, much to their surprise, and probably much to their annoyance, that he had made arrangements so as to completely obviate that difficulty, they found it necessary to start another. . . . The acting commission said it was impossible to do anything in the matter unless the contractor would take the warrants of the treasurer in payment. . . 'Very well,' said Mr. Foster, 'I will take the warrants of the treasurer at my own risk.' The judge then finding all his objections completely obviated was silenced and could say no more, excepting a suggestion that the work might possibly amount to more than the appropriation. This objection being disposed of by Mr. Foster offering to cut down his prices so as, in any event to come within the means at the disposal of the board, Mr. Germaine had to come to the relief of his colleague and to state positively that he could never agree to pay anything for the right of way and for the work that we proposed to surrender. 'Very well,' said Mr. Foster, "I will pay for it. Take the amount out of my pay.' . . . The commissioners then, after consulting together, told Mr. Foster that they had determined not to let the contract for the work unless the State could have the water power in addition to all that had been offered them. This modest requisition has not been mentioned to me, and I presume it will not be by them; but I understand it is now the only thing they want to enable them to decide on letting the contract. . . "

Work on the canal itself was eventually completed in mid-July 1842. The *Grand Rapids Enquirer* wrote, "By the enterprise of Messrs. Carroll and Lyon the Canal around the Rapids has been completed, and all that now remains to complete the navigation from the mouth to the head water of the Grand River is a lock from the basin into the river below. The Canal is over a mile in length, about five rods wide and as many feet deep with a basin at the foot a little over two hundred feet square. This work furnishes a portion of our immense water power. . . . It gives a fall of from six to twelve feet for three-quarters of a mile. . . . . The lock will probably not be built for some time yet, as it *ought* to be done by the state."

The lock was never completed. Using the wing dam to channel the water, several mills and other factories operated from the water power for at least two decades. Business along the canal mingled moments of prosperity with days of struggle. A broken culvert put portions of the canal out of business for a time in 1840 while it was still under construction, and in August of 1845, Stephen Hinsdill who was running the sawmill, reported that they were "suffering for want of water on several accounts, the wing being out of order, but most of all on account of Granger's pail factory whose planing machine -- runs most or all of the time." In a letter dated September 1, Gaius S. Deane, who was running the salt works, reported that Hinsdill wanted to extend his lease on the sawmill, that he could find no one who wanted to run the gristmill, and that Granger said he would sell the pail factory at a fair price, "but will shut his gate only when he pleases."

In the spring of 1847 the canal was seriously damaged by high water. Deane recorded under the date April 8, 1847, in the salt works record book, "Canal bank broke away this morning at sunrise on the river side at the upper culvert making a breach 23 feet wide and 12 feet deep before we could shut the water out of the canal as the River is very high and no Guard Gates. We commenced immediately at making a Dam at the Guard Gates with timber planks."

Later that year, with the wing dam seriously in need of repair and the canal banks crumbling, plans were begun for a new dam and a second canal in Grand Rapids. Both sides of the river vied for its location, working through the political process as well as in acquiring waivers for the right of way, a process complicated by the mortgaged titles on much of the former Kent Company land. Lucius Lyon felt that landowners should charge for the right-of-way since the canal would benefit all. Truman Lyon wrote June 10, 1847, that he felt the right-of-way should be offered at no charge and without the stalling tactics of negotiations because the new construction "would enhance the value of the property." By a single vote the Board of Supervisors decided in mid-July to approve construction on the west side of the river. Work was finally begun with a government appropriation in 1849 and by the first of October, 1849, J. W. Pierce wrote, "The dam across the river is a fine structure. The canal and waterpower now begins to look like business being done." In addition to the dam, which supplied water power for a large milling industry, the new canal was to have locks permitting the passage of boats around the rapids. Before 1850 the project ran out of money, and the locks were never completed.

Grand Rapids Steamboat

Early in his work with the Grand Rapids settlement, on October 9, 1835, Lucius Lyon wrote his sister Lucretia that he had engaged to pay $1,000 toward building a steamboat to run on the Grand River the following summer. Three days later he wrote a letter to investor Arthur Bronson with the news that a steamboat would be under construction during the winter months, to be ready in the spring. "I have agreed to take $500 and we hope you will subscribe that sum or more. The boat will cost about $6,000." He added that they hoped to have two boats which would connect with land transporation forming daily service from Detroit across the peninsula.

Although the boat was not finished, the outlook appeared even brighter in February of 1836 when Lyon received a letter from a Chicago man with the notice that he had made arrangements to run a vessel weekly from Chicago to the mouth of the Grand River at Grand Haven. Lyon and Bronson had disagreed over arrangements concerning the business end of the Grand Rapids canal and Lyon could not spare the cash to assist much with the boat. He wrote the Chicago shipper, "N. O. Sargeant and Richard Godfrey of the village of Kent (Grand Rapids) and some other gentlemen are now making provision for a steam boat to run regularly next summer from Kent to the mouth of the river."

A note in the Lyon papers dated October 27, 1836, indicates that he, and others, had researched the issue and determined that the total cost of the boat they felt they needed would be $7515.03.

The boat they built was named the *Gov. Mason*, and it was reported that Governor Stevens T. Mason presented the vessel with a set of colors. The new boat was fitted with the engine of the *Don Quixote* which had been wrecked bringing the first printing press to the settlement of Grand Rapids. On her first run down the Grand River to Grandville, July 4, 1837, the *Mason* was commanded by Captain William Stoddard. Later in 1837 with high water raising the shallow places and smoothing the rapids, the steamer went upriver as far as Lyons. With some wonder Edward Lyon described the scene. "Yesterday was a great day for the people of this part of Grand River -- the Steamer Gov.

Mason arrived at Lyons at 1 o'clock with a large company of Gentlemen and Ladies on board. It being the first time that ever a Steamboat descended [actually Lyons is upriver from Grand Rapids] the beautiful River to this part it was one of the most pleasing moments we have witnessed in a long time."

In 1838 when an early spring freshet flooded much of downtown Grand Rapids the *Gov. Mason* was forced inland and left aground near where the Union Depot was later built. At great effort and expense the boat was returned to the river and ran on a fairly regular basis between Grand Rapids and Grand Haven, but was never a success financially. In May of 1840 the *Gov. Mason* had completed the run to Grand Haven and had on board several passengers eager to pay passage onward to Muskegon. After an overnight stay in Grand Haven she set forth on Lake Michigan but encountered a severe storm and was washed onto a sandbar and dashed to pieces by the wind and waves. The passengers and crew escaped uninjured.

Grand River Steam Boat Co.

Upriver residents of Lyons, Ionia, and Ada met in February of 1837 and formed the Grand River Steam Boat Company. Members included Richard Godfrey, who would actually build the boat, Edward Lyon and John B. Guiteaux of the Lyons area, Samuel Dexter of Ionia, and Sidney Smith of Ada. This boat, when built, would travel between Grand Rapids and the towns upriver, and, after the planned canal at the rapids was completed, would be able to traverse the entire river below Lyons. From correspondence, they seemed to think that they had an agreement with Lucius Lyon to provide the engine. In a letter dated February 26, 1837, Edward Lyon wrote, "The boat is fast progressing and I think they have got some first-rate timber for her. . . " They were expecting to launch the vessel by the first of July.

In December of 1837 the steamer *Gov. Mason*, helped by high water, went upriver as far as Lyons and Edward Lyon wrote, "Now it can no longer be disputed that a steam boat cannot run to this place and it is high time there was one built to run from the Rapids regularly. I talked to Judge Almy and Mr. Richmond in relation to building one, they say there must be one built this winter and the people of Lyons should own considerable stock to always oblige her to run to Lyons."

Because of the multiplication of projects, and the shifting list of investors it is hard to tell which boat was truly the outgrowth of which meeting. Some of the men listed above contributed to a small steam vessel called the *John Almy* which was launched in 1838. The boat was named for the engineer of the city of Grand Rapids who may have provided the design. Her launch at Grand Rapids might be considered prophetic. As it was described later by Abel Page: "All eyes were eagerly watching to see the beautiful craft slide gracefully into its native element. At last the time came and the blocking was knocked out. The little steamer started, but just before it reached the water it stopped. An invitation was extended to the bystanders to give a lift. Everybody lifted, but she would not move. At this juncture, Samuel Baker appeared on the ground. He was a large man with powerful strength, seven feet tall, and weighed nearly 300 pounds. . . . He was called to give a 'boost,' which he did with a hearty good will. The steamer moved once more, and the huzzas of the citizens rang out on the clear air as she safely floated on the waters of the canal."

Everett, in his 1878 *Memorials of the Grand River Valley*, calls her "a miserable abortion of a steamboat." He relates that on her first trip upriver, "When she got as far as the mouth of the Flat River, it became evident that her builder had mistaken her element; and had not thought of fitting her for swimming in the water. She sunk, and the men waded ashore."

Grand Rapids Salt Works

It was probably during the preliminary survey of the Grand River in 1826 that Lucius Lyon first discovered salt springs on the banks of the river. Geologically, the brine is a product of old seabeds under the surface soils. The discovery furnished the seed of an idea for a salt making operation, to obtain useable salt by pumping up the brine, evaporating the water and drying the residue for use as ordinary table salt and in pickling and tanning. In 1828 the surveying business had been slow, and Lyon had visited the Kanawha salt operation, on the banks of the Kanawha River in what would later be West Virginia. Copious notes from that visit have been preserved, and show that the young businessman was concerned with the concentration of salt in the water necessary to make it worthwhile to extract it, as well as the engineering and mechanical means needed for pumping and evaporation.

While he was serving as territorial delegate in 1834, Lyon received a letter from Oshea Wilder of Calhoun County, asking his help in obtaining a lease from the government for the salt springs at or near the rapids of the Grand River. Wilder concluded the letter, "If a favorable lease can be obtained would you not like to be jointly interested in the project?" No further action on the project at that time can be documented.

218

As the land speculation business died out the Grand Rapids investors began looking about for another source of income. In 1840 Lyon wrote C. H. Carroll, a big investor in village lots, "We see pretty dull hard times here, though as we have enough to eat and drink we are not quite as badly off as we have been here for the last two years. I had hopes that before this time the State would have tested the salt springs in this vicinity, that the manufacture of salt would have been established so as to bring a little money into this part of the country. . . . The question is so important to the people of Grand Rapids and of this section of the State that I am determined to have it solved. I believe that good salt water may be obtained by boring deep enough, at almost any point on Grand River, as well as at the salt springs; and if you will send on to me or to Judge Almy one-half the necessary money I will furnish the other half immediately and we will try the experiment and see if salt cannot be procured and manufactured at this place. . . . It will not cost over $4,000 or $5,000 to sink a well on the rapids to the depth of 700 feet."

Work was begun in January of 1840. An undated item from the *Grand Rapids Times* that was pasted on the inside cover of the salt works account books reads in part: "We took a peep, as everybody else does, a few days since, into the building that covers the machinery now in operation in boring for salt. The machinery is driven by water taken from the canal. . . . The place selected for trial is at the foot of the Rapids, just on the margin of the river, and immediately below the foundation of the 'Mammoth Mill.'"

In the spring of 1841 Lyon visited Ohio near Zanesville where there were several salt wells near the mouth of Salt Creek. He found the business slow but steady, and that sinking the Ohio wells had cost about $1.50 a foot. He wrote to Sidney Smith, "The well that I am sinking at Grand Rapids will cost me at least $5 a foot unless Mr. Hulburt gets along faster than he has done so far. I am not at all disheartened, however, and I am more and more convinced that I shall succeed. . . . " Ansel Hulburt was an experienced well driller from Pennsylvania, who had come west with his two sons, Hijson and Henry.

George A. Robinson, a Lyon cousin, who had tried the mercantile business in Ypsilanti and worked in various capacities at Ada, had come to Grand Rapids to assist in the salt works venture. Ever resourceful, Lucius sent him directions for a homemade salometer to measure the strength of the brine. He relates in a letter dated September 18, 1840, that he had made a successful instrument with a straight piece of pine cut to the thickness of a pipe stem and a phial loaded with shot attached to the end. The weight, he explained, should be gauged to sink the upper end of the stick level with the surface in fresh water; how much it protruded from the salt water would be a rough measure of the strength of the brine.

Robinson kept a running narrative of letters between Grand Rapids and wherever Lucius Lyon was, sometimes sending out two or three copies to different places to give the missives a better chance at reaching him. Progress was discouraging for the first 75 feet, and there were several technical problems to overcome, but June 30 Robinson wrote, "Little did I think the last time I wrote you that I should so soon be able to give you the pleasing intelligence that Mr. Hulburt had almost got up (or down) "Salt River" -- On Saturday last at the depth of 81 feet Mr. H. produced me some of what he called Salt Rock & I think very appropriately named too, for it tastes quite strong of the article we are seeking for. . . . No one knows anything of our striking salt rock except Mr. H his two Boys and Myself and we have agreed to keep it to ourselves until we hear from you."

They continued to drill. By July 3 they were down to 100 feet and Robinson wrote, "I wish you would come. . . . Mr. Hulburt says it will be (in his opinion) difficult to keep the matter a secret long for he thinks when he strikes water it will be a large fountain and will rush up with such force that it can not be concealed." By the next week, when they were at 112 feet but had not reached a gusher, he feared his secret was out, "W. A. Richmond was at the works the other day when Mr. Hulburt was pumping and when the drill bar came up he put his finger on to it and tasted of the sediment, he said nothing but left the works immediately."

Drilling continued but the big gusher was not struck. There was some water at 198 feet, but when Lucius finally arrived in November they were down 276 feet without finding exactly what they were seeking. By the end of the year they had bored more than 310 feet and were once again bringing up salt rock.

Lyon was gone much of the winter in the east and sent back to Grand Rapids a device invented by Thomas Davenport to take broken drill bits, or any piece of iron or steel out of the well "without difficulty or delay." This device may have been designed by Lyon who added in a January 30, 1841 letter: "I believe I am the first person that has ever suggested this application of the electro magnetic power. The whole apparatus will weigh over 100 pounds and will cost $150." Shortly afterwards a drill bit dropped into the well in Grand Rapids and became jammed stopping the work, but the new device could not be used because of a lack of copper wiring in frontier Michigan.

By May of 1841 Lyon wrote his father that his drilling crew had bored to a depth of 550 feet "or within 50 feet of the level of the ocean" and that they had reached salt water "stronger than I expected to obtain when I began, and so strong that if it should prove to be sufficiently abundant salt can be manufactured from it with a good profit."

In March of 1841 Lyon and associates began a second salt well project near Grand Rapids. When Michigan was admitted to the Union, the Act provided that not more than twelve salt springs should be granted to the exclusive use of the state. In March of 1838 the legislature directed Douglass Houghton, the state geologist, to begin drilling operations at one or more of the state springs and appropriated $3,000 for the project. One of the springs he chose to try first was located about three miles below the village of Grand Rapids. When the money ran out, work was stopped, but a new appropriation of $5,000 for the Grand River well was made in 1840. Lucius Lyon got the contract for the work. Thus the drilling was under way at both wells at about the same time.

The Democratic newspaper of the settlement, the *Grand Rapids Enquirer*, was pulling for him. In August 2, 1841, S. M. Johnson editorialized, "We congratulate our fellow citizens of the Grand River Valley of Western Michigan upon the fortunate result of the undertaking of Mr. Lyon to obtain salt water at this place. His efforts are crowned with success co-equal with his wishes and in one particular exceed his imaginings."

Lucius spent a portion of the fall of 1841 in New York with the plan that he might be able "to prevail on some of the salt manufacturers at that place, Salina, or Liverpool, to transfer their kettles and capital to Grand Rapids. If I cannot do that on such terms as will be to our advantage I shall try to buy 68 of their kettles and we shall certainly have enough water from our well now sunk to keep them all in operation." He discovered that the saltmakers in New York were using a kettle of a new pattern, so he bought pig iron and coal and shipped them via the lakes so that his workers could make their own. He also found that the salt water in New York was twice the strength of that obtained in Michigan and that canal freight rates had just been lowered making it possible for the New York manufacturers to deliver salt at $1 a barrel in Chicago. "You will see by this that our well is worth very little if we do not get stronger water," he wrote Ansel Hulburt September 22, 1841.

In the meantime Hulburt had made a trial of the salt water that they were bringing up by boiling it down to yield about a bushel of pure salt. Truman H. Lyon wrote enthusiastically, September 2, 1841, that it was "of a very superior quality being as white as snow itself" and promising to send a sample.

221

Busy with other projects Lucius leased the salt works to step-brother Truman on December 27, 1841. Lucius was to receive 80 per cent of all net profits. Work continued on the salt works including the production of long flat cast iron evaporation pans. In January of 1842 the Grand Rapids newspaper announced that an evaporating house was being built at the salt works that would put them into full production "early in March." When production began, apparently on time, the editor wrote, "It is a matter of sincere gratulation that the undertaking of Mr. Lyon at great expense and risk and against the judgement of our own citizens, to obtain water from which to manufacture salt, has already passed into complete success. . . . That experiment which was denounced in its inception as a renewal of the halcyon days of '36 -- a mere delusion, which few pitied but many ridiculed and despised -- is now the sheet anchor of our hopes and expectations."

The press was a little more optimistic than the reality, but the first completed barrel of salt from the Grand Rapids works was sold to Lyon's friend, Charles Trowbridge of Detroit, May 5, 1842, for $2. The company continued operations for less than a month, finding that it took 192 gallons to make 56 pounds of salt, much more water, and less salt than Lucius had expected. He wrote July 2, 1842, ". . . either the brine is very weak or fresh water flowed in. Manufacturing has been stopped for the present until stronger brine can be procured, either by rimming out the well and putting the bag down to a greater depth or by some other means."

Douglass Houghton replied July 25, "In your raising Salt water by pumps you have encountered the very difficulty which I most feared viz. the descent of the upper fresh water through the porous sandstone, a difficulty which it will, I imagine, be impossible to overcome." Houghton suggests that Lyon try a graduation house, common in France and Germany but "heretofore wholly unknown in our country."

With little delay the company started construction. They built a "brush house," a large structure with bundles of brush tied together forming a tall wall. Using the water power of the river the brine was pumped to the top of the wall and allowed to trickle down to a pan at the bottom. Evaporation of water into the air from the many surfaces of the brush strengthened the brine and made it less expensive to boil down in the finishing kettles. This worked fine in dry weather, but as Lyon wrote Douglass Houghton in September of 1844, was of little use in wet weather.

Work continued on the state salt well until 1843 when it had reached a depth of nearly 900 feet. Shortly afterwards the boring hole became seriously obstructed. Douglass Houghton wrote, October 26, 1843, "Your letter gives a sorry picture of the accident which has befallen us at the state well and I fear from the tenor of your letter that it will effectively prevent our sinking any deeper." At the time there were rumors that the workers at the Lyon mill saw the state operation as a threat to their own business and either purposely sabotaged the mill or at least made only ineffectual efforts to solve the problem.

Douglass Houghton wrote Lyon, September 4, 1844, that he had learned of reports being circulated "that the State Salt works have been abandoned and are a total failure and that you have also abandoned your works which are also a total failure." He suggests that Lyon prepare a "strong article" for the paper refuting these reports. Houghton adds, "The report is evidently circulated with the intention of producing injury and for ulterior objects."

Salt Exchanged for Wood!

THE undersigned having rented the Grand Rapids Salt Works, now erecting, will give for good hard WOOD, well corded up at said works in quantities of not less than five cords, one hundred and thirty pounds of salt per cord, to be paid at any time when called for after the expiration of three months from the date of the delivery of the wood. The wood must be four feet long, and well split into suitable size for salt boiling, and delivered before the first day of June next.

Farmers will do well to embrace this offer, as they cannot now get more than ninety pounds of salt for a cord of wood.   T. H. LYON

Grand Rapids, Jan. 10, 1842.

The salt works often traded salt for goods and services.

Although the project was certainly not a total failure, financial problems haunted the salt works. Iron seemed to arrive just when there were no funds available for payment. And others were watching closely. In February of 1842, George A. Robinson reported that two men had come by the state salt well drilling site and were "very inquisitive." He described them to Lucius. "The elderly man was tall and slim with a very large nose . . . the other a man approximately about 30 years of age, short and thick." A year later when things seemed to be going best much of the equipment was attached for taxes. The sale of four tubes, 400 barrels, 20 cords of wood, a cutter, and all of the salt, was set for March 2. The equipment was rescued and the work went on.

The year 1844 was one of the best years for the Grand Rapids Saltworks. In January S. M. Johnson wrote, "The salt works are doing first rate -- the people have yielded and many feel that they are indebted for that dollar they saved in buying a barrel of salt, to you."

Robinson reported that the brine seemed stronger than it had been the previous year and "when we pump the fastest for any considerable length of time, our brine is the best." For a time in early 1845 they tried pumping 24 hours a day, with workers on six hour shifts. This yielded about 50 bushels a day. Even then Lucretia reported that most of the salt was traded for equipment they needed, or food and other personal supplies, and little money was received. A note from the firm of Strong & Avery in March of 1844 indicated that they could no longer accept salt in payment for debts because it had become, "a drag on the market."

In 1844 the workers tried a new system of using steam to provide the heat in the evaporation process. In this way the heat provided by the burning of wood could be used more efficiently. In a letter dated December 22, 1844, William B. Hill reported that it had not worked as well as anticipated because some of the steam condensed on the upper floors of the salt house and dripped back into the pans.

When Lucius was named surveyor general and moved to Detroit in 1845 he leased the saltworks to James Allen and Carlton Neal, and later Joseph Cordes and Michael Thome. They ran the works for only a short time and the job as manager seems to have landed on the shoulders of Gaius S. Deane, husband of stepsister Maria (Lyon) Dean. He wrote Lyon in September of 1845 that the salt works had at least been successful in stemming the flow of salt imported from the east. "There has been but a few barrels of Eastern salt boated up the river to this place." He also complained that he could not get barrels for the salt as fast as it was produced.

In the spring of 1846 B. A. Parnell made a survey of the saltworks and reported, "Decay is going on everywhere. You will make money by saying to any honest man 'go and make salt -- I will charge you nothing' only require him to keep the works in thorough repair." Deane, busy with other activities, did not put the works into operation that year and wrote Lyon, May 2, 1846, "This community are beginning to say they are sorry that no salt is to be made here this season, even the merchants who were not willing last year to pay you a fair price for your salt (and even that they wanted to pay in goods) say that they will sustain an injury if the salt works are not kept up. There is salt enough now in Grand Rapids to last until the middle of July."

At the end of 1845 Lyon had offered to lease the works to his nephew, Lucius A. Thayer, for $1500 a year. Young Lucius had gone back to Vermont the previous summer but was itching to return to Michigan. He arrived early in 1846 but was immediately sent to the Upper Peninsula to tend to mining prospects and did not get around to the salt works until the fall of 1847. The following spring there was high water, and he was busy boring pipes for use in the water system. In October, Lucius Thayer wrote his uncle in Detroit, "I have not got the

224

salt works in operation yet. I have been taking up the tubes. I found in the pump chamber a piece of file which I think must have been put in by some one. The tubes are now fast. I can neither get them up or down. The well is full of stone."

The Grand Rapids Salt Works had gradually taken over the local market for salt, and in December the price was up to $2 a barrel, higher than it had been in years. Still young Lucius could not free up the tube; he only succeeded in breaking it in several places and further caving in the sides of the well. He worked through the winter but wrote sadly March 21, 1849, that his already ineffectual efforts had been thwarted by a very high river that broke up the salt arches, dissolved the salt from the brush wall, and shattered the building. He wrote that the situation was "unforeseen and unexpected to me and I am unable to meet it. . . . I have laid out all ready now for the salt works $1000 and it is more than I am able to do. I have exerted myself in every shape that I possibly could but every thing seems to be against me . . . unless something is done immediately I shall have to leave this place . . . I cannot support the family any longer." The operation was quickly broken up. In August a man from Marshall asked to lease the dwelling house at the works and a portion of the water power for a pail factory. In September G. S. Deane purchased the least battered of the salt pans to melt down in his foundry operation. When D. F. Tower in November of 1849 inquired about purchasing the salt works, it was already too late. The Lyon salt manufacturing dream was dead. Instead of being the instrument for raising him out of debt, the salt works had only increased his indebtedness by more than $20,000.

Patents

In addition to being a heavy investor in the Moore-Hascall Harvesting Machine, a very early wheat combine, Lyon occasionally invested in other potentially useful machines. An 1836 paper conveys to Lucius Lyon "for value received" a one half interest in an invention by fellow surveyor William A. Burt described as "a new and useful improvement in the instrument for determining the variation of the needle, the true meridian and the apparent time."

He also held at least an interest in the patent on Burt's solar compass, the surveying invention that he had tested on the Illinois-Wisconsin border in 1832-33. The instrument, designed to accurately survey areas where the presence of minerals made it impossible to use a magnetic compass, had been improved and was in limited production. In 1844 Burt wrote that a man in Washington was manufacturing a solar compass that was inferior in quality, "I think he is a good workman and

225

could be instructed, to make them right. Probably you had better see him and make some arrangement to have him manufacturing solar compasses in a proper manner and allow you what is right for the privilege."

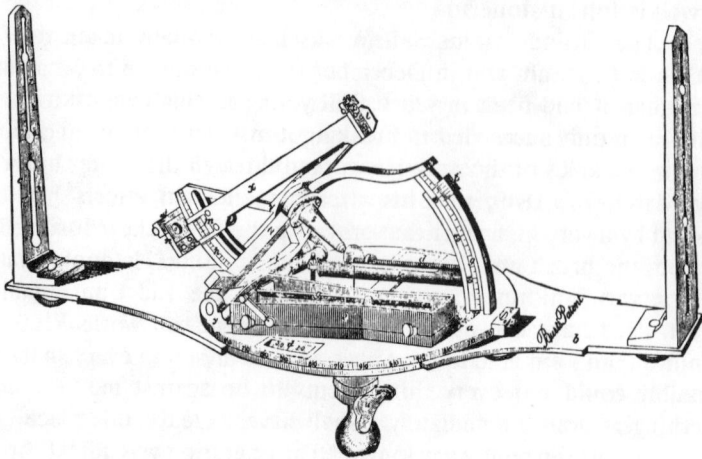

Burt's Solar Compass

In 1841 during the development of the saltworks in Grand Rapids Lyon was the recipient of a patent from Henry Smith for "a machine for saving of heat in arches applicable to boiling salt pot ash &c &c". An account of his assets about 1850 lists a one-quarter interest in a "seeding machine" and a one-quarter interest in a "water pump."

Surety Bonds

While standing surety is not a good way to earn money, it can sometimes be a quite effective way to lose money. Lyon had two unfortunate circumstances, and one caused him serious financial distress for a while.

While Lyon was serving as Territorial Delegate to the U. S. Congress, Allen Hutchins, formerly of Ontario, appeared in Washington one day bearing a letter of introduction from Charles Butler, one of Lyon's investor friends, which read in part: "He is a gentleman of excellent and amicable character, of good talents and sound political principles."

Hutchins apparently had inquired about a government post, but on his return to Michigan wrote Lyon: "Since I parted with you I have thought much of the matter of my application, and have come to the conclusion to withdraw it altogether unless when the appointments come to be made, you should find yourself at liberty to give me your support. This sir, is not an indirect request for your aid, your ultimate action upon the subject will be, I have not the least doubt, in pursuance of your convictions of duty, and otherwise, the Lord knows I would not ask or desire you to act, though it should be to the advancement of my interests. . . . I am poor, and my pecuniary embarrassments may be traced to the part, humble as it may have been, which I was compelled to take in the political contests of the past seven years. . . ." He lists several questions which he actively supported, including Indian treaties, resisting the encroachments of antimasonry, and of course, his personal support of the candidacy of Lucius Lyon in the recent election. "If you shall see any place in which my services can be useful to the public, and at the same time afford a humble competence to my family, your aid in procuring such a place will not be forgotten either by me or them. If you can not recommend me for a situation in the new Land offices, it may be you can in some other department of the Territory, during your term . . . And here let me request that, if you shall feel bound to lend your name to some one else, when the appointments in the Land offices come to be made, you will in such case inform the President that my name is withdrawn from the list of applicants."

In 1836 Hutchins made a serious effort to be named receiver of lands in the office in Ionia. He gathered signatures from Michigan legislators who favored his appointment, and, when the assignment did not come quickly enough, sent a second petition February 23, 1836, with the signatures of legislators "who did not sign the earlier petition because they were not solicited." Lyon not only recommended Hutchins for the appointment, but, with Calvin Britain of St. Joseph, stood bond for him, making a legal promise that if Hutchins did not perform the task properly, they would be responsible for any deficiencies in accounts.

The first herald of trouble that Lyon received was probably a letter from Edward Lyon dated January 2, 1838. At that time Edward was in charge of the settlement at Lyons and reported weekly to Lucius in Washington. Edward wrote, "Mr. A. Hutchins left Lyons on the first for Detroit. He had with him his wife and four boxes specie. . . . "

On February 7, 1838, Lyon wrote Hutchins from Washington (addressing the letter to the land office in Ionia) that evidence had been received which indicated that he was in default to the government in the amount of $9,000, and that the Michigan delegates to Congress were to visit the Treasury Department on the following day to see the papers. "I think there must be some mistake in this statement," Lyon wrote. "I do not believe it, and shall not believe it till I hear from you. Pray write instantly on the receipt of this and explain everything. If you do not, your character must suffer, of course. I repeat, I do not believe it, but if it should be true, I hope you will at least save me from harm as one of your bondsmen. I shall wait with great impatience to hear from you."

A confidential letter to Hutchins two days later gave a more detailed description of the charges, a complicated scheme that occurred when the funds in the land office accounts came up short. Hutchins had apparently claimed that there were funds due him from another bank account. Then he borrowed the gold in the land office safe, which had already been counted, and tried to pass it off as the funds recently paid out by the other bank. Lyon urged him to prove he was not a defaulter by paying the government drafts as they came to him. He added that Hutchins must send "full proof that you are able to account for all the money in your hands. In the meantime, I shall take care to guard your character and interests here and elsewhere if occasion requires."

By March 8 Hutchins had been removed from office and Lyon wrote Sheldon McKnight, "Nothing could save him any longer, and what I want you to do now is to see him as soon as you can and have him turn over to his successor all the money he has or can get and then to convey all his property to you or to Maj. Britain and myself, or to me alone, in trust, for the purpose of securing us and the government against loss or damage. I feel confident he will do so. I have been his friend and stood by him at all times and on all occasions and I am sure he is honorable enough to secure me now against loss in consequence of such friendship. . . ."

But nothing had been heard from Hutchins himself since his New Year's Day flight from Ionia County. He had left his ill wife in Detroit, with no information concerning his whereabouts, and was rumored to be in New York, and then, it was feared, in Texas. Lyon wrote Edward Lyon at Lyons asking him to have all houses and lands that were owned by Hutchins, even a costly set of mahogany furniture, seized by the deputy marshal to assist in covering the shortage in the accounts. Lucius wrote on March 10, ". . . he appears to be a defaulter to a considerable amount. I have the misfortune to be one of his sureties and Major Calvin Britain of St. Joseph is the other. We shall, I fear, lose some ten or fifteen thousand dollars, perhaps more. But that is enough to nearly or quite ruin me as the times are at present."

Edward replied that deeds had been received that placed the title of most of Hutchins's property at Ionia in the hands of his infant child. "He is a great fool and deprived of the least spark of honor," Edward declared.

After nearly a half a year of silence Hutchins wrote Lucius Lyon, still in Washington. An outer letter, dated June 22, 1838, enclosed a four-page, tightly written confession, and said in part, "The enclosed letter is long and tedious; I beg you, however to read it at your leisure and with all the charity of your benevolent nature. . . . I shall receive your chidings or your advice with equal acquiescence and consideration." The letter began, "To you this communication will be as a voice from the dead." It went on to explain in detail the business and personal problems, and the temptations which led up to his disappearance with the money and ended, "All the property I possess shall be cheerfully surrendered to satisfy the claims of the Government so far as it will go, and if my body be called for it shall not shrink from the demands of justice." After a further stay at a New York mineral spa, to improve his health, Hutchins wrote to Lyon asking for the details of the charges and enclosing the deed for some property near Ionia. Lyon replied, "I thank you for the deed of the Ionia farm and hope now to make your property pay the government all you owe it." Hutchins later relinquished the deed to land at the mouth of the St. Joseph River. When the accounts were audited the amount in default and due the government was $13,056; with costs and interests the total debt was nearly $20,000. Lyon wrote co-surety Britain in July of 1841 that he had succeeded in having all of Hutchins's suspended accounts allowed and deducted from the judgment "so that we have got off quite as well as could be expected." Some records indicate that their personal loss was less than $1000 apiece.

Hutchins's position as receiver in the Grand River land office at Ionia was taken over by William A. Richmond of Grand Rapids, one of Lucius Lyon's closest friends. Richmond would later be a state senator, 1844-5, superintendent of Indian affairs, 1845-51, and in 1851 was the Democratic candidate for lieutenant governor.

Appointing close friends was no guarantee. A second surety bond caused Lyon great anxiety for a while. This bond was held jointly with Oliver Newberry on their good friend Henry Rowe Schoolcraft as Indian agent.

Irregularities in Schoolcraft's accounts had come to light in 1843. He was accused of finagling a special grant of $8,200 for Mrs. Susan Johnston, an Indian woman, who was also the mother of Schoolcraft's wife, Jane, and, furthermore, not paying the money to Mrs. Johnston. When this incident brought his books into question, additional investigation revealed other shortages and a verdict was issued against Lyon and Newberry, as sureties for Schoolcraft, in the U. S. District Court in Detroit in the fall of 1844.

With the Hutchins experience still fresh in his mind Lyon wrote Schoolcraft, in a letter dated October 23, 1844: "A verdict has been rendered in favor of the United States against O. Newberry and me as your surety for the sum of $9,965.23 including interest. The verdict is by $2,000 the most favorable that we can hope to obtain, and I have learned that you have made no provision to save Mr. Newberry and myself from having our property levied on and sold to pay the debt as soon as judgment shall be entered up against us. Under these circumstances I feel no little anxiety to hear from you and to know certainly whether you will save me or not. If you do not I must of course be utterly ruined beyond all hope of recovery."

Schoolcraft promptly replied, reiterating his innocence, but noting that he had "abundant resources in Michigan and Wisconsin" to more than cover the debt. Two weeks later he turned over to Lyon and Newberry various properties that covered the shortages and his sureties were relieved of financial embarrassment.

During these problems Lyon wrote a letter of advice to a young relative, "When you have made it (money) I hope you will take care and see that it does not get into the hands of any other person, even the best friend you have on earth, without the very best security. Another thing I must caution you against and that is endorsing or becoming surety for others. Never do it in any case whatever, unless you have property put into your hands enough under any circumstance to indemnify you for any loss you may suffer. If I had observed this rule it would have saved me from ruin."

Mining Interests

The last enterprise which Lyon hoped would put his lifetime on a firm financial footing concerned mining interests in both the Upper Peninsula of Michigan and in Canada. When he ran for territorial delegate in 1833 a resident of the mining district of the upper Mississippi had noted that the candidate was a "digger of the first order" indicating that he had actually tried his hand at the business of lead mining. A surveyor in the field is duty bound to make some observations of the geology of the area surveyed, and Lyon's interest in the life of the Galena area probably made this an enjoyable task.

In early 1836, Lyon wrote Morgan L. Martin, a Wisconsin lawyer and land speculator, that he was eager to become part of a mining company that Martin and "Genl. Jones" (probably George W. Jones) were forming. "I wrote to you," Lyon said, "that I should like to be concerned with you, and that I would take as much stock as you might be disposed to assign to me, but I have not heard from you, and am left somewhat as a loss as to what to do." He also recommends to Martin the addition of Henry Ledyard of Detroit, noting, "He is an excellent business man and his high standing and general acquaintance among the capitalists of New York and in Europe are strong reasons for preferring him to any other man here."

After Michigan attained statehood with the mineral resources of the Upper Peninsula attached, Lyon and friends were interested in some of the profits to be gained in the mining business. The last barrier to the exploitation of the northern mineral resources was removed with the Indian treaty of La Pointe in 1842. A trip that Lyon went on in 1845 shortly after taking office as surveyor g eneral continued after the official portions of the journey were over. Mr. Broadhead of New York, described as "a friend of Mr. Ledyard" one of his mining partners, had gone north with Lyon, Dr. John H. Bagg, and the two Thayer boys. They had left Detroit in early August, taking provisions, tools and outfit enough to last ten men two months. At Sault Ste. Marie they were joined by Ledyard, and purchased a boat and sails. Lyon, with a party of seven men, coasted up Lake Superior to Eagle River on the northwest coast of the Keweenaw Peninsula. From there they sent J. Stacy of Maine to look over locations on the Montreal River and in the Porcupine Mountains. The rest of the party went around the peninsula, stopping briefly at Fort Wilkins near the tip, and personally inspected three locations southwest of the mouth of the Dead River and west of the mouth of the Chocolay River. Lyons wrote on his return in October that they had found these locations "to cover one of the most extensive and valuable deposits of micaceous or specular iron ore that have ever been found in the world. I doubt if such a deposit can be found elsewhere, either in Europe or America, for richness and abundance and the facility with which it may be quarried and worked."

At this time they sent representatives into Canada and made preliminary contacts with the Canadian government concerning the possibility of mineral rights there. In 1848 they joined the throng of mineral speculators who had been drawn by evidence of old Indian mines on Isle Royale in Lake Superior.

By the spring of 1846 the Douglass Houghton Mining Co. and the New York and Michigan Mining Co. had been organized with directors Lucius Lyon, J. Coe, E. K. Collins, C. G. Hammond and H. Ledyard. Some papers also mention a U. S. Mining Company with many of the same investors, and there was also the American Exploring Mining and Manufacturing Company. They headed out to sell shares of stock to provide working capital. Levi S. Humphrey, who was trying to interest Vermonters in the project, reported in July that sales were lagging. In a letter dated November 26, 1846, their Boston representative was optimistic and wrote, "Interest in copper is beginning to revive and I have strong hopes of selling at least 2000 shares in each of the five mines." In September the stockholders of the New York and Michigan Mining Co. met in the U. S. Court Room in Detroit to discuss reorganizing under a new law.

In addition Lucius Lyon bought 20 shares in the British North American Mining Co. of Montreal, in September of 1847.

In the summer of 1846 Lucius A. Thayer, who had been to the Upper Peninsula briefly in 1845, was sent north again. He wrote from Sault Ste. Marie June 4, that he had failed to make contact with the person that he was supposed to meet who would conduct him to the mining claim on the Dead River, west and slightly north of where the settlement of Marquette was just beginning. He had been advised by one of his uncle's Detroit friends to leave the area. The young man had remained, writing that he hoped his uncle would come soon, "I am getting very tired of this place. Time seems very long here to me." He went on to report that "Mr. Parks up near Fondulack . . . made some good locations there and found a silver bowlder large as a two quart basin of pure silver."

Shortly afterwards Henry D. Rogers of the Franklin Mining Company hired young Lucius and his companion, Peter Thome of Grand Rapids, to go out to his company's claim and build a log house. To speed them on their way he gave them a bark canoe. Back in Detroit Lucius Lyon played host to Edward Verniel, president of the Geological Society of France, who had been given a tour of the mining district by Jacob Houghton, younger brother of Douglass Houghton.

The following summer Lucius Thayer was back on the claim although he had discovered that there was a boundary dispute between two companies and the rival claimants had pulled down his house and set fire to it. "They found I was not easily frightened," he reported in a letter dated Dead River, June 23, 1847. He added that he had put two or three blasts in to open vein No. 1 and "got out some very beautiful and rich specimens better than any I have seen yet," and that in exploring the claim of the Douglass Houghton Mining Co. he had found "one very rich vein of the yellow sulfurous copper." Specimens were brought back for analysis and in March the following year the shareholders received word that analysis of a potential mining site near Eagle River showed some silver.

The early days of Upper Peninsula mining were confusing and rowdy. When the boom began, there were no specific laws to deal with copper mining and claims, and attempts to apply federal rules designed for lead mining only added to the muddled situation. To make it less fathomable to those with historical perspective there was only a limited demand for copper worldwide. It was used mainly for fancy cookware and to sheath the keels of wooden boats in an effort to discourage marine growth. Electicity would create a demand for copper wire and eventually make copper mining a paying proposition, but this was still a half century away. Lyon and friends at least seemed to understand the second point, and concentrated their efforts on finding silver, a mineral which often occurred with copper deposits.

Not all of Lyon's business associates were pleased with his preoccupation, beginning in 1846, with mining. Thomas Whittlesey wrote with some impatience in the summer of 1846, "And now my dear sir, I beg you divert from your copper visions -- I tell you, though you are in the heart of the copper speculation, that it will all explode. . . . I entreat you to give your attention to the redemption of your interest in Grand Rapids. . . . Your interest near Hook Lake which is now forfeited for taxes. . . . I wonder that you should neglect present interests for future and visionary wealth . . . nothing but honest industry is rewarded."

The frenzy of activity that took place in the 1830s and 1840s could not mask a fact that was becoming increasingly evident. Lucius Lyon, instead of growing rich as he had envisioned, was getting deeper and deeper in debt.

On a balance sheet dated March 1, 1840, he lists liabilities of $100,400, including $64,000 owed to the Bronsons. On the asset side were lands worth $75,000, a figure that was probably optimistic. Even after the lands were gone, the debts were enormous by 1840 standards.

He wrote William Woodbridge from Grand Rapids, January 6, 1842, "I have been struggling against increasing debt and embarrassments for the last five years, while my property has been growing every day less valuable, till at last it will not sell for enough to pay the mortgages with which it is encumbered. My Prairie Ronde farm in Kalamazoo County - - My farm of 1,000 acres at the mouth of the Thorn Apple River in this County, and my farm of 1,200 acres (the best and most beautiful farm in this State) at the confluence of the Grand and Maple Rivers in Ionia County -- all had to be given up last year, together with 25,000 acres of wild land, the best in the North western States; and all my property here has got to go soon, unless I should meet with success in the salt manufacture sufficient to enable me to pay off the mortgages upon it, which I do not now expect. When that takes place (and I now hold it at the mercy of the mortgagees) my property will all be gone, and I shall be left in consequence of the expansion and contraction of the currency, just as poor as when I began in the world nineteen years ago, when you first saw me in Detroit. I am willing and anxious to do all I can to pay the United States, but when I have given up for that purpose, all the property that I have . . . I want a discharge, and I want it, too, without submitting to the humiliation of applying for the benefit of the bankrupt act."

He tried to borrow more money to pay past debts or at least to keep the noisiest creditors at bay. In March of 1842 A. E. Bull wrote him from Boston that the had put Lyon's case up to a Boston bank and that the bank was "not loaning money." To a man of Lyon's integrity, the mail was sometimes painful. One letter from W. Truesdail, dated May 20, 1842, said, "I am sorry to learn . . . that you cannot pay your note for five hundred dollars due at this office on the 15th Instant. Such things are extremely discouraging to us. I had hoped you would not forget your assurances to me when the money was obtained. . . . We have no disposition to pay ourselves out of the securities in our hands to your loss. . . " They were also aware that the securities would bring little in a depressed market. On the back of the letter the weary Lyon had noted the date of delivery and penned the brief description, "Dunning letter for $500."

He wrote Thomas Fitzgerald of St. Joseph and explained, "All the property in St. Joseph which you purchased for me and I paid for with money obtained from Isaac Bronson, I reconveyed or rather conveyed to his executors, and they have, besides, my farms in Kalamazoo county, this county and at Lyons to pay the balance that I was owing them on account of investments made for Isaac Bronson. These investments and my guarantee to refund the money invested and interest, over and above all costs and taxes, ruined me. I have to be sure been helped down the hill a good deal by being endorser and surety for my friends, but my dealings with the Bronsons injured me more than anything else. It will require ten years of diligent attention to business and the strictest economy on my part to enable me to pay my debts. I have been hard at work since 1839 to effect this object, but make slow progress."

He was to continue this task for the rest of his life, trying all manner of schemes and plans. One possibility that was considered but never tried, was a letter of introduction to showman Phineas T. Barnum of New York, written in 1847 by Thomas T. Whittlesey, who was apparently acquainted with Barnum and knew Lyon because of some land dealings. Whittlesey recommends Lyon as an honest businessman who had met with some reverses and could make good use of a small subsidy to get back on his feet. The letter remains in the Lyon Papers at the Clements library, but nothing indicates that he ever attempted to contact Barnum.

12

U. S. House of Representatives

By 1843 Lucius Lyon had lost his farms and much of his other property. What little land he had retained was not selling very quickly, and the fortune that he had expected as a manufacturer of salt had not materialized. When the suggestion was made to return him to Washington as a public official, it must have been tempting. Still, he responded cautiously and explained in a letter, dated June 11, 1843, to Samuel J. Bayard, "I live in the second Congressional district in this State and am informed that I can have the nomination for Congress if I desire it. My business affairs are in such condition that I shall make no effort to obtain it and shall not allow my name to be used as a candidate before the convention. . . . I am struggling under the pressure of the heavy load of debt contracted under an inflated currency and shall probably lose every dollar's worth of property that I have in the world. The pay of a member of Congress is not enough to afford me much assistance."

When Michigan was admitted to the Union in 1837, the state was allotted one member in the U. S. House of Representatives. After the 1840 census was fully tabulated it was discovered that the population of the state was 212,267, sufficient to qualify for two additional members in the House. Thus, in 1843 there were two Congressional seats with no incumbents. Lyon was offered a chance to be the Democratic candidate for one of these.

The idea had been broached with hesitation because his place of residence was somewhat unclear. In November of 1838 he had written Edward Lyon that when he returned from the Senate and his stint as Indian commissioner, he had determined to make Grand Rapids his place of permanent residence. Edward responded from Lyons, ". . . we shall live in hopes you do as you say you may do, change your mind. . . . Everyone in this section of the country knows very well you have many houses which no one but yourself has any business to claim." However, when he returned from La Pointe, he did not go to Grand Rapids but settled instead in Detroit. He had been in Grand Rapids for only brief periods in 1840 and 1841. In March of 1840 a friend wrote with some sarcasm, "The people say . . . that *de facto* you belong to Detroit and of course are not interested in the affairs of Grand Rapids." He traveled frequently and, when in Michigan, usually lived at the National Hotel in Detroit, run by Edward, who still owed him money as a result of the Lyons venture. Perhaps the debt had been reduced, or, perhaps after the closing of the bank at Grand Rapids there was a residence available to him for no charge, but he left Detroit and remained in the area of the Grand River most of 1842. In 1843 Lucius Lyon was elected a trustee of the Village of Grand Rapids, perhaps to settle the residence question before it arose in a broader arena.

When the seat in the House of Representatives was offered to him, he continued in the stance he usually used when proposed for public office, that he would not actively seek office, but he would accept the nominattion if it were offered. Obed P. Lacey of Niles wrote August 14, 1843, "Our county convention meets on the 26th instant. It has been said that you would, and again that you would not, consent to be brought before the district convention as a candidate. . . . I desire specific information on this point." The reply was not very specific. Lyon wrote, "The nomination I consider in many respects desirable and I should be glad to receive it if a clear majority of the Democratic party of the district prefer me to any other person, but I have not sought and do not intend to seek it. I take it for granted that whenever the party to which we belong wants my services they will let me know."

He sent delegates William A. Richmond and H. P. Yale off to the Democratic convention in Battle Creek with a letter of instruction, "As you are the delegates from this county to the Congressional convention . . . and understand my views and feelings in relation to the presentation of my name to the convention for a nomination, I hereby give you full authority to act for me as my friend in reference to that matter, and shall consider myself bound by your action whatever it may be."

At the convention on September 12 there were seven candidates for the office, including his friend Thomas Fitzgerald of St. Joseph, and several ballots gave no one a majority. Eventually Lyon emerged with 23 votes to 20 scattered among six others, and the delegates voted to make Lucius Lyon their unanimous choice. By resolution they noted that in their candidate they recognized "a tried, high-minded democrat, with the ability and experience which peculiarly fit him to advocate and sustain the principles of republicanism and the cause of his constituents. . . . "

The Democrats in two of the Second District cities he had founded gave him strong support. The *Grand Rapids Enquirer* editorialized, September 20, 1843, "We are persuaded that a more unexceptionable selection could not have been made. . . . A *long tried* and *faithful* public servant, he has ere this received the approval of *well done*, from a grateful constituency, and his return to public service will be hailed as a favorable omen to the best interests of our young and enterprising state."

The editor of the *Kalamazoo Gazette*, who first notes that the people were disappointed not to have a candidate from their own county, continued, "Depriving this county, however, of that benefit no nomination could have been made more acceptable to us than that of Mr. Lyon. Of Mr. Lyon it is unnecessary to speak. Indeed it would appear to any person who has resided any time in Michigan as unwise as, 'To hold a candle in the noon-day sun.'"

GRAND RAPIDS ENQUIRER.

GRAND RAPIDS : OCTOBER 11, 1843.

R. D. WARR, EDITOR

FOR PRESIDENT
JOHN C. CALHOUN,
Subject to the decision of a Democratic National Convention.

DEMOCRATIC TICKET,

FOR GOVERNOR,
JOHN S. BARRY,
FOR LIEUT. GOVERNOR,
ORIGEN D. RICHARDSON,
FOR CONGRESS—SECOND DISTRICT,
LUCIUS LYON,

In 1843 the Grand Rapids paper was advancing the candidacy of Lucius Lyon and his former arch-rival John C. Calhoun.

The Detroit Democratic newspaper pointed out to readers that the nomination of Lyon to this office should be a lesson to other politicians. The reporter noted that after leaving the Senate Lyon had gone straight back to Grand Rapids and tended to his business with no attempt to use his former political position to control or direct state politics for gain. They called him "a common soldier in the democratic cause" and concluded that "the result of this laudable course of action is his present voluntary and unsolicited nomination for Congress by the Democrats of his district."

As could be expected the Whig papers were less pleased. The *Marshall Statesman* grumbled, "Mr. Lyon's abilities are rather below mediocrity, and fit him to move only in the subordinate walks of life."

In the campaign one of the claims leveled against Lyon was that as a senator he had been author or mover of a provision in the preemption law which removed all lands located by the state for educational purposes from the general law, removing these choice parcels of land from those available for settlement. Lyon replied to O. P. Lacey, October 27, 1843, that he did not recall that he was involved in that law and added, "But if it were true that I had introduced this provision into the laws, it seems to me that the pre-emption claimants ought not to oppose me on that account, for I presume it will be readily admitted that a member of the United States Senate should prefer the interests of his whole State to the interest of any man or set of men in it in all cases where the two come in conflict." Lacey, after further research on the question, concluded that it was Norvell who had introduced the pre-emption law in question.

Lyon's Whig opponent was Joseph R. Williams of Constantine, St. Joseph County, who had been educated in the east and once played foot ball (in the early days it was written as two words) for Harvard. When the Whig campaigners emphasized Williams's sports record the *Democratic Free Press* responded in the October 12 issue: "The Democratic opponent of Mr. Williams, Lucius Lyon, is a plain farmerlike character, whose strong arms, in early life, were employed in felling the heavy forest. And though we doubt whether he has ever been at college or had the honor of kicking a foot ball upon a college green, yet we believe the hard working farmers of Michigan are sufficiently keensighted to repose more confidence in the *practical* characters of a man who has been thus bred, than in the interesting accomplishments of this Whig Candidate." Williams became the first president of Michigan Agricultural College near Lansing in 1857 and later served in the state senate.

Lyon's fears that his part of the state was too sparsely populated to make much difference in the election were unfounded and he did better in western Michigan than he had expected. He wrote to Allen Goodrich, on November 14, as results of the balloting began to arrive, "My majority as reported in the counties of Ottawa, Kent, Ionia, Allegan and Barry is 450, and in all the counties in the district, excepting Cass and Eaton, which I have not yet heard from, is about 2,200, which is at least three times as great as I expected. . . . Gov. Barry's majority must be not far from 6,000 in the State, and so far as I have heard there is not a Whig Senator [in the state legislature] elected. We have glory enough for one election. Our forces are everywhere victorious. But we must follow up the advantage we have gained and prepare at once for the great battle of 1844."

All three Representatives from Michigan, Lyon, James B. Hunt, and Robert McClelland, were Democrats, although they had to contend with two Whig senators, William Woodbridge and Augustus S. Porter.

Lyon was late arriving in Washington at least partially because of mechanical problems at the Grand Rapids salt works. The Congressional session opened on December 4, but by December 22 he had only gotten as far as Buffalo where he wrote Lucretia that he had left Grand Rapids on Monday the 11th, reached Kalamazoo on Tuesday, Battle Creek on Wednesday, Jackson on Thursday, and Detroit on Friday. The following Monday he took the stage through Canada and found the "roads muddy and the traveling hard." He had arrived at Buffalo finally Friday, December 22, and was preparing to take the train to Washington via New York, hoping to arrive by December 27.

It was not until January 4, 1844, that the rookie representative from Michigan introduced his first bill in the House of Representatives as a voting delegate. It was the by-now familiar one calling for construction of a harbor at the mouth of the Kalamazoo, at the mouth of the Grand River, and at New Buffalo at the mouth of the Galien River, all on the eastern shore of Lake Michigan.

At least partly in response to claims during the election that he was not effective in obtaining federal funds for western Michigan projects, he worked diligently for the passage of these and similar bills during the session. On January 10 he presented a petition from 303 Indiana citizens from LaPorte asking for the harbor at the mouth of the Galien River; also a similar resolution from a public meeting held at New Buffalo. On January 24 he added a petition from 94 citizens of Milwaukee asking for the new harbor, and February 20 a new petition with 69 signatures from St. Joseph County, Indiana. Nothing seemed to help.

Other measures introduced by Lyon included a bill to give the consent of Congress to sell or otherwise dispose of various salt springs that had been granted to the State of Michigan in its charter and a request that Congress pass a resolution that disapproved the Wisconsin legislature's move repudiating the bonds which they had sold to obtain funds for a canal and direct the legislature to pay out funds derived from the sale of these bonds.

Citizens of Branch County, perhaps with the leadership of H. H. Riley of Constantine, petitioned twice asking for a reduction of postage costs and for the abolishment of the franking privilege for federal officials. At a time when the mailing of a letter often cost 18 to 20 cents, correspondence was a luxury that some people could not afford, and they felt that the free postage extended to government officials under the franking act was an expense that kept the cost of postage high for the ordinary citizen.

When the first attempt at getting monies for the construction of a harbor at the mouth of the Kalamazoo River failed, Lyon on March 25, introduced a bill "for improvements of the entries of the Kalamazoo and Grand River." When this also was struck down in committee he attempted to amend the river and canal bill on April 8, 1844, adding $12,500 each for work on the Kalamazoo and Grand Rivers. This too was rejected.

Lighting the chandelier for a night session in the old House chamber in Washington.

Angered over federal lands that had been given to the State of Ohio, Lyon gave notice on February 19 that he would at a future date introduce a bill "to grant to each of the States in which public lands are situated, a quantity of land equal to that which has been granted to the State of Ohio."

The big questions of the year, which tied up the legislative process for many weeks, were the tariff and the National Bank. Lyon attended most sessions and is listed in the voting tallies, but he rarely spoke on issues other than those pertaining strictly to Michigan and the midwest. One exception occurred in March, 1843, when he called for reconsideration of a bill to pave Pennsylvania Avenue in Washington, D. C.

A major focus of all Washington during the Congressional session of 1843-4 was the nomination of a presidential candidate to run for office in the general election to be held in November of 1844. Lyon was in the thick of this; he was one of the major movers in favor of Michigan's Lewis Cass as a presidential candidate on the Democratic ticket. Even by Washington standards the presidential prospects were disorganized in 1844. John Tyler, who had succeeded to the Presidency on the death of William Henry Harrison only a month after the latter's inauguration, had so thoroughly alienated the Whigs, his own party, over the National Bank issue, that many felt he was hoping for the Democratic nomination in 1844. It was obvious that Democratic front-runner Martin Van Buren, who had been defeated by Harrison in 1840, would have trouble fielding the two-thirds majority of the convention needed for nomination.

Lyon started out in January of 1844 feeling that "it is almost certain that Van Buren will be nominated next May for the presidency." He added in a letter later that month, "one-half of our Democrats here are predicting that Van Buren will be defeated, and the other half are dull and lifeless. I wish the nomination was over." By February the Whigs were beginning to spring to life and Lyon was seeing some fear of a Democratic loss at the polls. He wrote February 29, "If Van Buren and Clay would be the candidates of their respective parties the Whigs have two chances to one in their favor. . . . Either Cass or Johnson would be stronger than Van Buren. . . . There is no state in which Cass would not run as well as Van Buren. He can be elected, but Van Buren, I am sorry to say, I fear cannot."

In March he wrote Thomas C. Sheldon back in Detroit that he had presented his view that Cass was the stronger candidate to many of his Democratic friends in Washington. "They generally agree with me, but they think that Mr. Van Buren is the choice of so large a majority of the party that it is too late now to change and concentrate public opinion on another candidate." In a confidential letter to Lewis Cass, April 6, he asked for a list of men that Cass considered friends in the Senate and House "with whom Mr. McClelland and myself can confer confidentially on the subject of your nomination by the Baltimore convention. We have long entertained the opinion that you would be the strongest candidate that could be brought before the people in opposition to Mr. Clay and we are disposed to do what we can to effect that object."

As the convention approached Lyon wrote that he felt Cass could have the votes of at least 50 percent of the delegates. A hope that Van Buren would withdraw from the race was dashed when he presented a letter on the annexation of Texas which Lyon felt would "drive from him the whole south, while it gains him no friends in the north."

Lyon's advice to Cass, as the convention neared, was that "it will be necessary for you to come out at once boldly for the annexation of Texas to the Union. . . . Write a short, forcible, patriotic, anti-British letter (such as you know how to write) in favor of annexation at the earliest practicable moment . . . allude to the fact that Texas extends almost as far north as the city of Detroit; treat it as a northern and western as well as a southern question and above all as a great national question. Say not a word about slavery and you will occupy a position in which you will be sustained by the feelings and judgement of a large majority of the people of the United States, a position which will in all probability secure your nomination by the Baltimore convention, harmonize the jawing sections of our party and place you in the presidential chair on the 4th of March next."

Cass wrote the letter, although apparently he did so before the receipt of Lyon's letter, for the presidential prospect replied from Detroit, May 9, "I am obliged to you for your intended in my behalf. Before this reaches you you will have seen my letter on the subject of Texas. I hope it meets with your approbation. Had I received all your suggestions before I wrote it, it would no doubt have been better. But it must go as it is."

Two days later, Cass, clearly anticipating that his nomination was likely, wrote again, complaining that Colonel Richard Johnson of Kentucky was being openly advanced as a vice presidential candidate in a way that made it look as if the idea was coming from Cass himself. He wrote that he thought it was "indelicate and improper" but said that Johnson would be an acceptable vice presidential candidate, "so would Gov. Woodbury, Col. Polk, or any of our prominent men."

Lyon was a delegate to the convention in Baltimore and arrived early "for the purpose of seeing the delegates from the different states as they come in, and giving them such information as I possess."

Cass remained in Detroit but wrote Lyon a long letter on May 12. "I am so distant from the scene of action, that I do not know what circumstances may arise at the last moment to render it necessary to have my sentiments upon these topics in the hands of a friend, ready for production." There followed nine topics of national interest and a brief statement of his stand. He was opposed to a national bank, favored a one-term presidency, and advocated the "economical administration of government."

The convention was deadlocked through seven ballots. On the eighth ballot delegates began changing their votes and the Michigan men were looking forward to receiving the 21 delegates that had previously gone to former vice-president Richard M. "Tecumseh" Johnson of Kentucky which would nearly give Cass the nomination. Lyon wrote Cass later, "Up to that hour the name of Gen. Polk had never been

242

mentioned as a candidate for the presidency by any one -- certainly not in my presence. . . . At 9 o'clock the convention met . . . when the eighth ballot was taken the Tennessee delegation and some few other delegates who had previously voted for you gave their votes for Polk. Cave Johnson and Maj. Donelson were there very active in going around the hall among the delegates from Maine, New Hampshire, New York, Pennsylvania and Ohio, and immediately afterwards the delegations from New York, Pennsylvania, Ohio and Virginia retired separately for consultation. After being out a few minutes they began to return one after the other, and as they came in each on the ninth ballot voted for Polk. . . . When so many changes had taken place that it was certain Gov. Polk would be nominated, Mr. Bradley, chairman of the Michigan delegation, rose, and after a very appropriate and sensible speech, which did him and you much credit, asked leave to have the vote of Michigan changed and recorded for the man who seemed to be the choice of the convention. . . . This result was brought about by a sudden, secret and dexterous movement on the part of Van Buren's friends. . . . Some of the secret means used were exceedingly unfair, and the movement would not have been successful if they had been known. You were the first choice of more than one-third (and I think one-half) and the second choice of more than two-thirds of the convention, and now, when the Democratic party here have had time to reflect on what has been done, the regret that you were not nominated is almost universal. Your friends here feel that you have been wronged, and they are determined that you shall be the candidate of the party in 1848, whether Mr. Polk be elected or not. We must give him the vote of Michigan this time if we can, and then claim the support of his friends for you at the next convention."

Ballots:	1	2	3	4	5	6	7	8	9
Van Buren (N.Y.)	146	127	121	111	103	101	99	104	0
Cass (Mich.)	83	94	92	105	107	116	123	114	0
Johnson (Ky.)	24	33	38	32	29	23	21		
Buchanan (Pa.)	4	9	11	17	26	25	22		
Polk (Tenn.)								44	272

Cass responded from Michigan with "thanks for all you have done for me. I shall be in the remembrance of it till my dying day. As to the result, I regret it only for the sake of others. For myself, I never had set my heart upon success, and I am as well contented as it is possible to be."

To James K. Polk, Democratic candidate, Lyon wrote, June 7, "Among the thousands of congratulatory letters which are pouring in upon you from all parts of the Union, permit me to send mine. . . . I believe that you will get many more votes than Mr. Van Buren could even in the northern states, and in the south we expect that you will sweep all before you. But let other states go as they may, we shall endeavor to give you the vote of Michigan, and I beg you to present my compliments to Mrs. Polk and tell her that I expect to have the gratification and honor of paying my respects to her at the 'White House' from and after the 4th of March next."

Lyon knew the Polks socially from his earlier days in Congress when Polk was Speaker of the House. In an 1838 letter he had described them to Lucretia, "Col. Polk is the speaker of the House of Representatives and a man of talent. His wife is not handsome but her kind manners have made her one of the most popular ladies in Washington. They are from Tennessee."

An 1892 biography of Mrs. Polk records an incident that occurred as the Polks were returning to Tennessee following a Congressional session, "On one occasion, while travelling in the Virginia mountains, the stage was overturned and several gentlemen injured. Mr. Lyon, a senator, who was one of the passengers, said to her [Mrs. Polk], 'Put your foot in my hand, Madame, and I will help you out.' She did so, and came out of the wreck unhurt, not understanding how it could be, but still thankful for the deliverance."

Polk was the hand-picked candidate of former president Andrew Jackson; the two men were known as Old Hickory and Young Hickory and lived not far from each other in the hills of Tennessee. Contributing to Cass's inability to garner the handful of votes that would have resulted in his nomination was the reluctance of the Ohio delegation to vote for a candidate from Michigan. The political relations of the two states were strained for many years following the bitter fight for Michigan statehood. The nomination of Polk turned out to be a fairly popular one to Michigan Democrats. Simeon M. Johnson of Grand Rapids wrote that the Democrats in his area were "full of enthusiasm. Never did the mercury of public opinion rise so quick to fever heat." Thomas Fitzgerald wrote Lyon from St. Joseph that the nomination was "entirely satisfactory on a compromise ticket, and I have no doubt the Democracy of this State will unite in its support with cordiality and zeal."

The Congressional session of 1843-4 stretched out into the heat of a Washington summer adjourning finally in very late June. On June 25, as he prepared to leave Washington, Lyon wrote a friend that the town was "miserable, lonely and deserted" and that the only news of note was that President John Tyler, who had not been nominated as candidate for another term, walked down to the train, unknown to anybody, and went north to New York City, where he married Julia Gardiner.

While he was working so hard for the nomination of Cass for

244

the presidency, Lyon kept putting off consideration of running for re-election to his seat in the House of Representatives. He took his usual modest stance, "that I did not intend to do anything myself or to make any interest through my friends to procure a renomination, but if it should be offered to me I should accept. I have never sought an electoral office and do not intend to begin now, though I presume I value such favors as highly and feel as grateful for them as any other man."

He became even less eager about the House seat as the nominating convention drew nearer and wrote James Hunt in August of 1844 that he hoped that his name would not come before the convention unless they were absolutely unable to agree on anyone else. Following the nominating convention Lyon wrote, in some anger, to Thomas Fitzgerald, that there had been a plot to bring him forward as a candidate on the first ballot "for the double purpose of injuring me before the convention then assembled and also with reference to any other occasion that I might be a candidate for hereafter."

The lame duck representative from Michigan was on time for the Congressional session of 1844-45 although a later letter from Edward indicated that Lucius had been ill when he left Michigan. In the opening days he announced his intention to introduce a bill to apply certain alternate sections of the public domain toward the completion of works of internal improvement in Michigan and a bill to give the consent of Congress to sell or otherwise dispose of the salt springs that had been granted to the State of Michigan.

Near the end of the previous Congressional session, Lyon, along with fellow representatives Hunt and McClelland, had submitted a proposal to President Tyler to remove the office of the Surveyor General of the United States for Ohio, Indiana and Michigan from Cincinnati to Detroit "making it easier to supervise the field work since most of the unsurveyed lands are in Michigan." If Lyon had designs on the office he does not betray them in the letter.

On February 21, 1845, the bill to move the office came up in the House. As the *Congressional Globe* reported the debate, "Mr. Lyon observed that a good many amendments have been offered to take money out of the treasury, but this one was intended to prevent it from being taken out." He pointed out that the lands of Ohio are all surveyed, and the principal part of the surveying work is going on in Michigan. Because of the distance from Cincinnati "it was impossible for the Surveyor General to superintend the surveys and consequently they were frequently inaccurate and sometimes fraudulently made. This involved the necessity of having new surveys made and an additional and unnecessary expense to the government." He added that the bill calling for the move was in accordance with the advice of the General Land Office and the Chairman of the Ways and Means Committee. After a brief attempt by a representative from Indiana to get his state, instead of Michigan, inserted in the proposal as the site of the new office, the bill was passed.

A few minutes after this bill was approved, Lyon spoke for the first and only time in his Congressional career on a bill concerned with international affairs. The next order of business was an appropriations bill to outfit foreign ministries. After the vote was taken there was a complaint from the floor that the ministry in Brazil had been left off the reading of the bill, and that there had been some irregularity in the taking of the vote. Lyon, who was probably still on his feet, called for another count.

On the most important issue of the session, the annexation of Texas, Lyon voted in favor of the question, although both of his colleagues were opposed. It was probably some comfort several days later when he learned that the Michigan Legislature had adopted a resolution supporting annexation.

There is some indication that one of the reasons Lyon was reluctant to work very hard for re-election to the House is that he had his eye on moving up to the Senate. Or, if Cass was nominated and then elected President, of serving the administration in some other way. The term of office of Senator Augustus S. Porter, a Whig who had replaced Lyon in 1840, expired in 1845, and the Democratic state legislature was prepared to replace him with one of their own. Some of the same people who were trying to get Lyon to declare whether he intended to run for re-election to the House were hinting at the possibility that the Senate seat might be available. In reply to one of them Lyon wrote, March 30, 1844, "I thank you for your two letters . . . on the subject of the next election of United States Senator. . . . I have received intimations from other quarters that if our party should continue in the ascendant I might be brought forward for Governor or United States Senator, but I place very little reliance on some of the persons who have written me. The course that I am disposed to take in regard to the matter is to leave it to my friends and to make as many friends as I can."

From correspondence it would appear that Lyon truly wanted the Senate seat, but he felt that Cass had first choice if he did not go into Polk's cabinet. Others had similar views: H. H. Comstock wrote, December 20, 1844, "I do not think that Genl Cass will be chosen U. S. Senator. . . . In the first place I do not think that he would take it under the present circumstances" but adds that he is in favor of giving it to Cass "if he insists upon it." Comstock then adds a post script, "I have this morning received a letter from a friend of yours and mine urging my little small influence to elect the Hon. L. Lyon. I shall try!"

Cass was not helping matters with his indecision. He wrote Lyon, in a letter dated December 26, 1844, "It is a terrible thing to be in a state of betweency." He adds that it is "probable from appearance, that if I were a candidate, I might be elected -- I am looking every day and hoping for something which will convert my indecision into resolution. But it does not come -- Tell me your feelings, I have equal confidence in your judgment and friendship."

To add to all of the intrigue and uncertainty, there is a copy of a letter in the Lyon Papers that is dated December 28, 1844 with a note that the copy was made January 5, 1845, the day the letter was received by the addressee. The letter is from "the Hon. C. G. Hammond" and addressed to "Genl. John Stockton." It reads in part: "Since writing you last I have received some letters from Washington and seen more. You are sufficiently backed up in your letters to the Genl. & Doct. Houghton, even, should not Col. Ledyard agree with you. On the other hand those who oppose these counsels and advise the General to go to the Senate are equally strong and urgent in pressing their opinion. Mr. Lyon is of this number, while he admits that there may be a doubt, he expresses his opinion clearly and decidedly that Cass should be elected, thinking probably that where there is so much difference of opinion it is best to take that course that will result most certainly in benefitting Michigan and our friends generally. Do not understand me as saying that Mr. Lyon does not present both sides; he does; but as time advances his letters come more and more strongly to the conclusion above. I have seen his letters of 16, 17 & 18th, Dec. and yours of the 19th -- now when Doctors of acknowledged ability disagree what shall be done? I again repeat to you that I have all along felt that Lyon unprovided for, it would be perhaps difficult for me to succeed in procuring a seat at Washington, but then how is it to be done? If Cass should withdraw Mr. Lyon can not now be elected to the Senate as I have advised you. My plan is this, to make myself so necessary to Cass that he will desire my location there, as others do, that he will see either in the Surveyor Generalship or the succession to the U. S. Senate, as heretofore advised, a place for his friend. . . ." In the margin is a note, "Don't let a bird see this."

While assuring Cass that the seat was his if he wanted it, and urging him gently to make up his mind, on January 2, 1845, Lyon wrote to W. A. Richmond who was serving in the Michigan legislature, that if Cass declined to serve in the Senate, "You may procure my election to the Senate if you choose and find you can do so without injury to our party if successful or injury to myself if defeated." The suspense was shortly ended by a letter from Lewis Cass himself with the news that he would accept the position if it was offered.

Lyon replied, "I have all along thought that you ought to go into the Senate for reasons alluded to by you, and am glad to see that you are coming to the same conclusion. . . . Those who oppose the idea of you going into the Senate think your standing is so high now that nothing that you can do can add to it, while an unlucky combination of circumstances or a false step might injure you. . . . It appears to me they do not consider that in the onward progress of men and things standing still is about the same as going backward."

Shortly afterwards Lyon received a letter from Richmond indicating that the election was not wrapped up yet although Cass "is generally considered as the man for that post yet few in their hearts approve it and the various candidates and their friends appeal to his friends with the hopes that he will be withdrawn from the field and they receive his influence and the support of his friends. The various candidates would doubtless rather have the Genl elected than either of their competitors." But he went even further, "Now I am fully satisfied that you can be elected to the U. S. Senate without said influence, and in direct . . . opposition to it. . . . You stated to me before last leaving Grand Rapids that you would leave the matter to my judgment and decision, suggesting that you did not wish to be considered a candidate and spoke favorable of Genl. Cass &c. . . . But the time is fast approaching when rejecting the crown may lose us its possession."

Lyon replied to Richmond in a letter dated January 15 and marked private, that the idea "takes me by surprise; and were it not for the knowledge that I have of your sagacity and caution I should doubt the correctness of your opinion. . . . The prize is almost too tempting to be rejected," but he reiterated that he would only be a candidate for office if Cass chose not to run, or to accept the position.

After Cass's appointment Richmond was disappointed and wrote from the floor of the Michigan Senate in a letter dated, March 7, "I came here as your friend for the object when the time arrived of securing your election to the United States Senate. . . . All was arranged as I thought with perfect safety, to such a result, and but for your letter to me which I felt bound to regard you would now be holding the seat of U. S. Senator."

Another disappointed state legislator, Adam L. Roof of Lyons, wrote March 7, 1845, "The legislature is grateful of the course you took on the Texas resolution. Should you not accept of an appointment, I am determined as well as many others to bring you forward for Governor next fall unless it should meet with your decided disapprobation."

As Lyon finished up his duties in Washington, his last official act was to recommend to the incoming president Michigan men who were good enough Democrats to be named to government posts including foreign ministries. He also wanted to secure the post of Superintendent of Indian Affairs for his good friend William A. Richmond of Grand Rapids. However, Cass, the new senator, and Representative Robert McClelland united in recommending Elon Farnsworth for the office, and Lyon wrote Richmond March 7, 1845, that his name had been withdrawn along with the applications of "Major Edwards, R. A. Forsyth, Gen. Schwartz and T. C. Sheldon, all of whom were urging their claims for the appointment, and share the same fate as you."

William A. Richmond

However, less than a month later Lyon wrote again in some triumph, "Permit me to congratulate you on your appointment this day as Indian Agent and Superintendent of Indian Affairs in the State of Michigan. The order has been given by the President to have your commission for his signature, and I saw the clerk in the office of the Commissioner of Indian Affairs writing it about two hours ago. It is by this time, I presume, signed by the President and sealed with the great seal of the War Department. . . . Your success will occasion much disappointment to Gen. Cass, Chancellor Farnsworth. . . and several other warm personal and political friends of mine." Lyon explained the next day in a letter that he had supposed that the Indian Affairs position was settled and Farnsworth would be appointed, but, after Cass left Washington, President Polk had asked him to recommend a man to succeed Robert Stuart, and, seeing his chance, he had recommended Richmond. After an unsuccessful attempt by the opposition to accuse Richmond of irregularities in his books as land office receiver, the office was secured.

Both Lyon and Richmond were concerned about the reaction of Cass and some of the others, but Richmond wrote with some relief the first week in May, "I have seen Gen. Cass and he has nobly and manfully declared himself my friend and, as completely satisfied with your conduct in the promise. . . . Farnsworth is reconciled to the result."

With someone else nominated for his seat in the House, and Cass filling the Senate vacancy, Lyon was casting about for direction. He had earlier rejected the idea that he become a foreign minister. On December 25, 1844, he wrote S. M. Johnson, "I observe what you say about my employment as a minister at some foreign court, but do not think it worth while to move in the matter because there are so many more prominent men that are looking for such stations. Besides this, I speak no language but the English, and every man appointed to a foreign mission ought to be able to speak and write the language of the country to which he is accredited. I had formerly some knowledge of the French language, but that is nearly forgotten now. . . . "

Richmond had ideas for Lyon's future as well, and it could also be that he had spoken to Cass and had advance information. He wrote to Lyon in January, "The Genl will be with you about the 15th February in the capacity of U. S. Senator and from indications your chance for the succession will be good -- altho should you secure a post abroad or at Washington or the Gen. L. O. [General Land Office] or as Surveyor Genl, accept would be my council. . ."

Being named to the post of surveyor general could not have been a totally unexpected idea to Lyon. In March of 1844 he had received a letter from Edward Brooks of Detroit relating the news that there were two aspirants for surveyor general, Douglass Houghton, who was a Democrat, and John Mullett, who was a Whig. Brooks said that Mullett "asked me to sign his petition -- bearing the names of numerous Clay Whigs. I politely informed him I didn't train in that company and declined. Now on this subject, I wish you distinctly to understand, your friends have long since selected this place for you, if you desire it, and a change takes place."

In the letter from C. G. Hammond to General Stockton, quoted above, the idea is alluded to, and, even urged, to get Lyon out of the way and make room for Hammond's political ambitions. It is not known if Lewis Cass was thinking along the same lines or if others mentioned it to him, but it was apparently Cass who suggested to incoming President James K. Polk that Lyon be appointed to the office of surveyor general under a reorganization of that department. Lyon wrote W. A. Richmond, March 7, 1845: "I have just been informed that the office of Surveyor General will be offered to me by the president, unsolicited on my part, and I shall probably visit Cincinnati for the purpose of removing it to Michigan before returning home."

Lyon was pleased with the idea but had a scare later that month and wrote Cass, March 31: "I have not yet received my appointment, but for an accidental allusion to it the other evening when conversing with the President I should have lost it, and a man from Ohio would have been appointed. The President had forgotten that he made you any promise in my behalf."

The promise secured, Lyon headed back to Michigan.

An old ambrotype of Lucius Lyon, probably shortly after his return to Michigan in the mid-1840s.

13

Surveyor General

Lyon left Washington after the close of the Congressional session in 1845 and returned to Michigan. He traveled by way of the east coast and Vermont to transact some business and see his father and other family members. In Vermont he also picked up his nephew, George Washington Thayer, then 17 years old, who was to join Douglass Houghton, state geologist for Michigan, who had a contract from the federal government for linear and topographical surveys of the unexplored portion of the upper peninsula of Michigan. Washington was to be apprenticed to Houghton and learn the surveyor's trade.

This was a second choice for Washington. In 1844 Lucius wrote his sister Pamelia, and Washington himself, with a view to nominating his nephew to the United States Military Academy at West Point. Dan Lyon visited the family and discussed the possibility with Pamelia and wrote, February 15, 1845, that Washington was "bright and active in his appearance, good looking and will make a commanding, dignified man. His mother says he always had a particular liking for a military life."

Washington wrote that he may be "too young to go," he feared that he was "not as qualified as I should be," and "had not the means to go." But added, quickly, "Take away all these objections and I should be perfectly willing to go. Yes more than willing, I should be glad to go."

Another outlook on the subject was penned by Jason F. Walke, one of Washington's teachers, who wrote Lyon that the boy was "possessing of good faculties" but, by his own admission, "had never laid out <u>half</u> his strength in his studies yet." He concluded, "He is probably a full blooded <u>Yankee, ripe for speculation</u>." It was shortly discovered that Washington lacked a few months of being the correct age for the appointment, and it was decided he should study surveying in Michigan.

Uncle and nephew left Burlington, Vermont, May 17, 1845, and traveled by steamer up Lake Champlain to St. Johns, Canada, where they boarded a train headed for Montreal. They crossed the river by steam ferry where they spent two days transacting business, then continued by boat up the St. Lawrence for the 200-mile journey to Lake Ontario, taking a series of stage coaches around the rapids. At Kingston they boarded a lake steamer for the trip to the Niagara River, went up the Genesee River for a quick stop at Rochester, and back to the Niagara River, landing at Lewiston, and then by train to Buffalo.

Finishing business at Buffalo they took the steamer *London* to Detroit. When they arrived in Detroit, they discovered that Washington had missed the Houghton expedition which had already left for the north. They went on to Grand Rapids, where Washington worked for several weeks with his older brother, Lucius A. Thayer, hauling wood for the Grand Rapids salt works, while his Uncle Lucius waited for his official commission as surveyor general to arrive from Washington.

Spring turned into summer, and still the coveted paper had not arrived. Finally on June 30, 1845, William A. Richmond, who was working in Detroit, wrote, "I learned with unfeigned joy by the Boat of this morning that your appointment has been announced in Washington and forwarded to you. I had been quite anxious (secretly no man knew it or saw it) and I now feel that all is safe." Richmond said that he had been to see Lewis Cass that morning and that Cass also had been worried about the delay and now was "relieved from some anxiety." Richmond had also been to see outgoing Surveyor General William Johnston, who advised him to tell Lyon to come to Detroit and meet with him to transfer the responsibilities of the office even if the official paper had not yet been received. "I think you ought not to tarry on the road," Richmond concluded.

Official notification of his appointment to the office of surveyor general was dated May 26, 1845, and his commission arrived finally in Grand Rapids on July 1. He left for Detroit and was sworn into office and commenced official duties on July 11.

Lyon had been gone from Grand Rapids less than a month when Lucretia wrote in some despair July 22, 1845, "Lucius and Washington have occupied your room since you left it. . . . I wish you would give Washington an opportunity of going out on a survey as soon as possible . . . . He is discontented unhappy and constantly fretting because he is not doing as well as he expected to do." At about the same time Lyon determined that it would be useful for the new surveyor general to travel to Lake Superior "to fix upon the best plan for carrying on the surveys there." He sent a message and carfare to his two nephews and they joined him in Detroit. The three of them left in August to meet Houghton in the north country. The Houghton party was full, and Washington was told that the only possible position was in the physically demanding job as pack carrier and camp handyman for Houghton's brother, Jacob. Washington's story of the trip, told years later at an Old Resident's Association meeting, gives a rare glimpse of Lucius Lyon as the stern father-figure. Washington had been offered the position, but had been discouraged by Jake who didn't want him to accept it, and left to think it over.

"At the end of an hour my uncle came to know of my decision. He would think I had no grit, that I expected to be a parasite of his if I declined. I would go if I died in the woods, but I felt humiliated and disappointed, but gave no expression of it. When I said in as cheerful a manner as I could, I have decided to go, he said: 'Don't undertake this and then back out.'" Washington endured the hardships and completed the task. Their work was finished early and Houghton saw the young man aboard a boat back to Detroit. The vessel encountered a terrible storm but rode it out. He wrote later, "I reached Detroit, found my uncle, who as soon as I entered the room, greeted me with the query, 'Have you been discharged?' I said I had. He looked glum. I handed him Dr. Houghton's letter. I thought I could guess what was in it, as I saw his countenance change with reading it. He only remarked that 'the doctor has written some very pleasant things about you.'" Before his own return south Lyon had received the news that Houghton had drowned off Eagle River, October 13, 1845, in the same storm that Washington's boat had encountered. The sad task of reporting the death of Douglass Houghton and trying to find someone to complete his task in the Upper Peninsula was one of Lyon's first acts as surveyor general.

The frenzy of surveying in the middle west had died down although there remained much to be done, and Lyon was to soon be involved in having areas resurveyed that were done poorly the first time. However, in April of 1844, in answer to a letter from O. Hungerford, who was apparently looking for work as a surveyor, Lyon wrote, "There will be very little surveying done this year for the appropriation reported by the Ways and Means Committee is only about one third as large as usual."

The history of surveying in the Northwest Territory dates back to November 5, 1795, when Rufus Putnam was named Surveyor General of the Northwest Territory and opened an office in Marietta, Ohio. He was succeeded in 1803 by Jared Mansfield who moved the office to Cincinnati, and by Josiah Meigs in 1812. Lyon's first work was done under Edward Tiffin, appointed in 1824, who moved the office to Chillicothe, Ohio, followed by William Lytle, appointed in 1829 who moved it back to Cincinnati. Others filling the post were Micajah T. Williams, 1831-5; Robert T. Lytle, 1835-8; Ezekial S. Haines, 1838-42; and William Johnston who took office in 1842 and served even after the office was officially moved to Detroit. At this time the work was split up among several individuals and Lyon became Surveyor General of Ohio, Indiana and Michigan. On May 12, 1845, George W. Jones had been notified of his appointment as Surveyor General of Wisconsin and Iowa with an office at Dubuque, Iowa and on May 13, Frederick R. Conway received his appointment as Surveyor General of Illinois and Missouri.

On July 24, 1845, shortly after Lyon had officially taken office, the records of Ohio surveys were ordered to be transferred to the State of Ohio if all the public lands, including islands, in that state had been surveyed. Samuel Williams, chief clerk, had been working for some time to get the records ready for the transfer, and, although they were not fully complete the records were turned over to the State of Ohio, August 11, 1845, partially to avoid the physical task of hauling them to Michigan, then taking them back to Ohio. This had the effect of reducing Lyon's title to Surveyor General of Michigan and Indiana.

In the organization of the new office he was careful to consider the opinions of his political friends. Shortly after the office opened he wrote Thomas S. Atlee of Detroit, who had apparently sought a position: "I have appointed Geo. S. Frost, selected by Gen. Cass: Hiram Burnham of Saline, selected by Mr. McClelland; and Joseph E. Hyde of Pontiac, selected by Mr. Hunt, as clerks in the Surveyor General's office. I have also appointed John Almy, of Kent, to be one of the two draughtsmen employed in the office. Mr. Morrison, the other draughtsman, and Mr. Williams the chief clerk, having long been in the office and intimately acquainted with its business, cannot well be spared. The arrangements of the clerkships in the office may therefore be considered as completed."

Samuel Williams, who had been chief clerk for more than 30 years, moved to Michigan at Lyon's request but found that he and his family could not live in the state's climate. Therefore he returned to Ohio but continued on the payroll until early 1848, organizing, codifying and binding together records of the surveys in Ohio. He and Lyon had been acquainted since the deputy surveyor days of the latter beginning in 1823, and Lyon's signature is on a petition circulated in 1837 among the deputy surveyors to recommend nomination of Williams to the post of surveyor general. The attempt was not successful.

Later, Lyon took his nephew George Washington Thayer into the office as clerk, and made a place for his cousin Isaac Newton Higbee, who had been surveying in Wisconsin and Iowa territories since 1837. However after a couple of years Lyon reported later that Higbee "got unsteady and left us", headed for California. Orson Lyon also left off his surveying and farming in Iowa Territory and was assigned several Michigan townships each season to resurvey. According to official records the annual salary for the surveyor general was $2,000. The chief clerk was paid $1,500 and two draftsmen received $1,000 to $1,100. There were also clerks paid at the rate of $3 a day, and two records clerks paid at the rate of 7 cents per 100 words.

When Lyon first went to Detroit to serve as surveyor general, he lived at the National Hotel, still run by Edward Lyon. After he returned from the Upper Peninsula he rented the former home of Colonel Henry Whiting, who, in addition to his military duties had served as Detroit's first historiographer and was a poet of considerable reputation. When Whiting was transferred during the Mexican War his house on Fort Street became available. It was here that Lyon asked Joseph P. Taylor to deliver a load of firewood in a letter dated October 22.

National Hotel

In April of 1849 Lieutenant U. S. Grant was ordered to Detroit where he served as quartermaster to a portion of the 4th Infantry of the United States Army. Grant and his young bride lived first at the National Hotel and later moved to a two story house on Fort Street between Rivard and Russell. Mrs. Grant loved dancing and is credited by some Detroit historians with giving the first masked ball ever held in the city. Grant sold his old gray horse Nellie that he had ridden in the Mexican War and bought a fast little French pony from Jim Cicotte for $250 (according to a traditional story) on the condition that the pony could pace a mile at 2:55 or under with two men in a buggy. The test occurred on Jefferson Avenue and the pony exceeded expectations. Grant was said to be an active participant in the traditional Christmas Day horserace. Julia Grant left Detroit to have her first child at her parents' home in May of 1850, and, when she returned, the couple moved into a home on Jefferson Avenue which they shared with another officer and his wife. Silas Farmer wrote in his 1890 history that during the Civil War he was in Washington and met Grant at the War Department. He identified himself as from Detroit and Grant smiled, "I used to live there once. Have you seen Charley Trowbridge lately?" Since Trowbridge was one of Lyon's closest friends, and Lyon and Grant lived only blocks apart on Fort Street, it is likely that they were well acquainted, although no existing correspondence confirms this. Grant was promoted to captain during his stay in Detroit and he left in early June of 1851. His old Fort Street home has been preserved, and in 1936 it was moved to the Michigan State Fair Grounds in Detroit.

During his term as surveyor general Lyon promoted to his colleagues the use of the solar compass invented by William A. Burt, a Michigan surveyor. The design had been tested during the survey of the northern Illinois boundary in the middle 1830s, and in 1837 Burt had received a medal and a cash award from the Franklin Institute in Philadelphia. He was too busy to pick up the award and wrote Lyon to stop for it next time he was in Pennsylvania on his way to New York, or on his way home from Washington. In a special report written in November of 1845 Surveyor General Lyon noted that "the solar compass has been used with great satisfaction in all of the surveys of public lands in this State (Michigan) for some years past and its introduction into general use would unquestionably promote the accuracy of the public surveys in all parts of the United States." The instrument permitted accurate readings where local mineral deposits interfered with magnetic compasses by using sun and star sightings.

The appointment that Lyon received in the summer of 1845 was an interim appointment only. His name was presented for confirmation for a regular four-year term in January of 1846 and Michigan Senator Lewis Cass wrote a short note dated January 5, "Your nomination . . . came into the Senate yesterday. There will of course, be no question of your confirmation." Another note from Cass the following day, "You have this moment been confirmed by the Senate without opposition," promised an appointment until January 6, 1850.

With Polk determined to serve only a single term as President, Lewis Cass was the obvious Democratic presidential nominee in 1848. As a federal appointee based in Detroit, Lyon's role in the 1848 election was far less active than it had been in 1844 when Cass had narrowly missed the nomination. There is no record that he made any attempt to be a delegate to the national convention, held that year again in Baltimore, but a letter to him dated, May 15, 1848, and signed "D. E. Whitewood, delegate; Francis Cicott, alternate" states, "Unforeseen events which we deeply regret, and which it is not necessary for us to state, render it impossible for either of us to attend the Democratic National Convention at Baltimore. . . . Having full confidence in your

257

ability and integrity to carry out the options and wishes of the Democracy of this State, as expressed in the State Conventions, we hereby appoint you as our substitute."

He attended the convention and was present when Lewis Cass of Michigan received the nomination on the fourth ballot. Zachary Taylor, something of a war hero in the Mexican War, was nominated by the Whigs, and opted not to campaign at all. He wrote that he "believed that if the people wanted him to be chief magistrate they would vote for him; if not they would vote for someone else. In either case, he would serve in whatever post they assigned."

The election of 1848 probably would have swept Cass into office in a two-way contest. However, a number of northerners, many of them Democrats, felt that Cass was not sufficiently anti-slavery (he had always maintained that it was a question not within the jurisdiction of the federal government) and they organized and backed Martin Van Buren on the Free Soil ticket. As early as July 20, Frederick Hall wrote Lyon from Ionia that there had been a meeting of "barnburners" in Ionia and that he felt "immediate action necessary. You perhaps may think that I am alarmed unnecessarily in regard to the Election, but it is my candid opinion that unless immediate and vigilant action takes place and every friend of General Cass and his <u>country</u> puts his shoulder to the Wheel, the State will go against him."

Michigan held for Cass but the anti-slavery forces proved the crucial factor and lured enough votes from the Democratic ticket to elect Taylor. The final popular vote was Taylor, 1,360, 099; Cass, 1,220,544; and Van Buren, 291,263.

Lyon's hope for higher office, or at least for continuing in his present office, was dashed by the results of the presidential election. His term of office as surveyor general as stated in the commission expired January 6, 1850. However, after Zachary Taylor's ascension to the presidency in March of 1849, all Democratic appointees began watching the mail nervously. Before the end of the month Lyon received a letter from his former chief clerk, Samuel Williams, "A change in the Administration of the Government, you know, in these latter days is expected to give a practical illustration of the detestable political doctrine -- 'To the victor belong the spoils'. . . <u>Your</u> office is sought for by some of these <u>cormorants</u>." Efforts to remove Lyon from office began almost immediately by a man named Morrison. In April of 1849, Samuel Williams recommended to Lyon a plan of action to end Morrison's efforts to discredit him, "To estop Mr. Morrison in his efforts to supplant you, it seems to me, you would do well to enlighten Mr. Secretary Ewing, as to his true character and total unfitness for office. For you can easily satisfy Mr. E. that he is wholly deficient in at least the first two of the three good old Jeffersonian 'prerequisites for office' to wit: Honesty and capacity . . . if you do not succeed I should be exceedingly grateful to have our friend Mullett."

The work of surveying was winding down in Michigan, and Lyon apparently felt that there was a chance that he could get an appointment to finish up the task. He wrote Williams, April 7, 1849, "I have endeavored to discharge my duties faithfully, so far, and if continued in my present position expect to close up all the business of the office, so that it may be abolished within four years from this date." He was concerned with collecting, arranging and binding letters, surveys, contracts and other papers generated by the surveyor general since 1797, and in the spring of 1849, he received an appropriation from Congress for $10,000 to examine erroneous and defective surveys.

In October Lyon wrote Williams that he had recently, "on the advice of leading Whigs here" appointed one of their party to fill a clerk vacancy in his office. He reported in the same letter that Ewing had concluded "to allow me to remain until my commission expires on the 6th of January next."

In November Lyon began action against the bond holders of several deputy surveyors whose work had been found unsatisfactory. He explained to Williams in a letter dated November 22, 1849: "About two weeks ago I enclosed to the United States District Attorney of this State copies of Eleven bonds and contracts on which I requested him to commence suits immediately, on account of false and fraudulent returns to which they relate, and I mean to pursue a similar course, in every case where fraud can be discovered, for the short period that I have got to remain in office. The frauds brought to light by the examination of the past season are of the most astounding character, and require adoption of the most vigorous measures to secure the Government faultless as far as practicable and to operate a check on those who may be disposed to commit fraud in the future."

In the same letter he notes that he would like to remain in office. "I shall probably write to Mr. Ewing in a few days expressing my willingness to continue . . . if the President should see fit to reappoint me . . . some personal friends who are supporters of the Administration have, without consulting me, united in an effort in my favor. . . . I do not believe there is much prospect of success."

Lewis Cass, who was back in the U. S. Senate, put in a word for Lyon's reappointment with President Taylor, but nothing seemed to help. Former Governor Alpheus Felch, Michigan's second senator, wrote, December 29, 1849, "I need not say to you how much I should be gratified by having you retain the office, but I suppose I cannot expect to be gratified by any such result. Democrats seem all destined to walk

259

<u>the plank</u> under the present powers. We may as well submit with good grace."

No reappointment appeared and Lyon wrote Williams in May of 1850 that "all efforts for me were useless" but thanking him for a letter Williams had written in his favor.

John Mullett had been a friend of Lyon's since his earliest days in Detroit. It was with Mullett that Lyon learned about surveying in 1822-23, and for several years they would take care of one another's mail and business when the other was off in the field. Mullett was a Whig and both Lyon and Williams had hoped that he would be named to succeed Lyon in the surveyor general's office, but Mullett held the bond for several of the surveyors charged with fraud including his own son. When he did not receive the appointment, Mullett was angry at Lyon for mentioning the fraudulent surveys and the names of the bondholders in his official reports. The favor fell instead on Charles Noble of Monroe. The new surveyor general was a Whig, a former judge, and the first president of the Southern Railroad.

Noble, who took office January 14, 1850, used the Detroit office. He was succeeded April 1, 1853, by Leander Chapman, and the Detroit office was closed May 11, 1857. Records were turned over to the State of Michigan between May 1857 and May 1858.

It was during his years as surveyor general, with an office in Detroit, that Lyon became interested in religion. He had been raised Episcopalian, and there were at least two clergymen among his mother's family. He had given land in his various settlement enterprises to any denomination that applied and promised to build a house of worship and a parsonage, but he seldom attended any kind of services himself although there is some evidence that he toyed with some of the popular spiritual-philosophical ideas of the time. Among the collected papers of Lucius and Lucretia Lyon are a number of relics that show interest in popular religious ideas of the day. There is a bound numerology chart and references to phrenology (the idea that certain traits in a person are controlled, or at least revealed by the shape of the skull). He also had a copy of the *Book of Mormon* and may have been related distantly to Joseph Smith. Temperance (Bond) Mack, wife of Stephen Mack, was Smith's aunt.

The first contact in his new found religious interest appears to be a letter from Abiel Silver of Marshall dated May 24, 1846, that stated "Since our last brief acquaintance you have been often much in my thoughts . . . " and enclosed a number of magazines from the Church of the New Jerusalem with a request that they be returned to him with Lyon's comments. Silver, a former judge and land registrar from

Marshall, is considered a prime mover in the organization of the Michigan and Indiana New Church Association in 1843. Silver had been converted to the faith following the amputation of an arm. The fact that he continued to feel the presence of the arm convinced him of the reality of the spiritual body as Swedenborg had described it.

If the May 24 letter was one of the first contacts, it did not take Silver long to bring Lyon into the fold. In a letter dated June 3, 1846, Lyon wrote his sister, Lucretia, in Grand Rapids, "You know that for many years past I have been a skeptic. I did not believe the Bible to be the word of God, nor the Savior to be God himself. I now most fully believe both. I have not time now to tell you all the steps in the process of the change of my belief, which has taken place, mainly, within the last month, but I can truly say the perusal of Swedenborg's writings has completed a revolution in my sentiments so effectually that I have not one single solitary doubt remaining. His writings contain such internal evidences of truth that no unprejudiced mind sincerely desiring to know the truth and willing to receive it can resist the conclusion that his spiritual sight was opened and that he actually saw and heard the things the he describes." He also included a biography of Swedenborg and his book *Heaven and Hell*.

In her response, addressed to "My Dear,-- My Very Dear Brother," Lucretia thanked him for the letter and books and commented, "Nothing could have given me greater pleasure and satisfaction than to hear of the change of your sentiments with regard to the Bible and the religion it teaches. You may readily suppose I should have preferred that you should become a good Episcopalian, rather than anything else; and so I should, with my present limited knowledge, but when I shall have become fully acquainted with the faith and doctrine you have adopted, I may think it is best as it is."

Emanuel Swedenborg was a Swedish scientist who lived 1688 to 1772 and regarded himself as a prophet and herald of the world's final religion, although the Church of the New Jerusalem was not organized until after his death. The doctrines of Swedenborgianism are a complicated blend of science, philosophy and religion with a great deal of emphasis placed on conditions in the afterlife. The liturgy of the General Convention sets forth as it primary doctrines: "That there is one God, in who there is a Divine Trinity; and that He is the Lord Jesus Christ; That saving faith is to believe on Him; That evils are to be shunned, because they are of the devil and from the devil; That good actions are to be done, because they are of God and from God; That there are to be done by a man as from himself; but that it ought to be believed that they are done from the Lord with Him and by Him."

Swedenborg wrote that man, on earth, has both a physical body and a spiritual body, and only the spiritual one will survive and begin the progression through the various levels of heaven provided that the individual had begun his regeneration before his physical death. Swedenborg wrote that reading of the Bible should be practiced daily but divided the Scriptures into two parts. He considered as inspired the historical and prophetical books and some of the Psalms in the Old Testament, and the Gospels and Revelations in the New Testament. Other books he felt were "doctrinal writing." His followers tended to put great emphasis on reading the works of Swedenborg.

A later book Lucius sent Lucretia, *A Dictionary of Correspondences, Representatives and Significatives Derived From the Word of the Lord Extracted From the Writings of Emanuel Swedenborg* by Otis Clapp, is a sort of encyclopedia of New Church beliefs and begins with A, which it describes as "in the angelic language . . . one of the vowels used in the third heaven, to express a sound corresponding with affection," to Zuzims, "A race of people who signify persuasions of the false, or those who through a persuasion of their own height and preeminance made light of all things holy and true and who infused falsities into evil lusts."

Court Room at Griswold and Congress

The resurgence of interest in Swedenborgianism that struck Detroit in 1845-6 had begun in the United States in Philadelphia in 1817 and gradually spread westward. Swedenborg's theological ideas, as embodied in the Church of the New Jerusalem were spread by the Rev.

George Field who became a popular lecturer in southern Michigan beginning about 1844. Lyon was part of an active congregation under Field's leadership which met in Detroit, and included John Allen, founder of Ann Arbor and a state senator; Digby V. Bell, auditor general; H. P. Bush, state senator; and Amos T. Hall, deputy state treasurer. Field wrote later that in Michigan the Church of the New Jerusalem was called the "state church" because so many people holding office were receivers of New Church doctrines. When the legislature was casting about for a new name for the capital city in 1848, Swedenborg, was one of many proposed. For at least one full session Field was chaplain of the Michigan Senate. The small congregation of New Church believers met in the second story of a building opposite the Michigan Exchange Hotel in downtown Detroit beginning in 1844. On January 13, 1846, Field rented a store underneath the old hall, and in May they moved to an upper room in the Republican Block. The following spring Lyon and Digby Bell petitioned for use of the U. S. Court Room when the court was not in session and this use was approved in a letter dated April 30, 1847 from A. E. Wing, of the U. S. Marshall's office, although use of the room was specifically limited to "day time on the sabbath." In September they moved to the County Court Room, on the corner of Griswold and Congress Streets.

A number of the believers lived in community, probably at the National Hotel, although Lyon also had sleeping quarters set up in one part of his office. They took to signing their letters, "Yours in the bonds of Christian Affection." In the fall of 1846 John Allen, who was staying in Detroit during his service as a state senator from Ann Arbor, wrote Lyon, "I feel grateful to you for the trouble you have taken to fit up my room . . . . I fear that you are giving yourself more trouble than my small friendship will ever be able fully to repay. We will be so comfortable and happy in our little circle, that I fear that the time of separation will be one of pain. How little the world appreciates the feelings which bind those together, who love the Lord and the neighbor."

A friend wrote later to another friend of the noticeable change that was brought about by Lyon's conversion to the Swedenborgian view of Christianity. The writer, while assuring his friend that Lyon displayed a "sound mind", said that he also "exhibited the greatest sincerity, and in all his actions and intercourse with others he evinced a purely Christian spirit. He seemed void of selfishness, which is the great enemy of righteousness, and was humble and childlike, selfsacrificing and charitable, so that no one could possibly doubt his entire change of heart."

The New Church doctrines also forcefully struck Lucretia and started a religious revolution in Grand Rapids. On December 15 she gave up her pew in the Methodist church, which the pastor noted had been paid for in salt, and began lending books to everyone who showed an interest. She wrote in March of 1847, "A little spark has kindled a flame which, -- judging by present appearance -- will, by and by, become a great fire. The good they have done and the happiness they are producing in the hearts of some, is incalculably great." She added, however, that she was also receiving the "reproof of the <u>Spiritual guides</u> of the church to which I am professedly attached."

The following month interest was growing so rapidly that one of the converts, Charles Shepherd, wrote Lucius in Detroit, "Mr. Taylor, the Dutch Reformed minister, cannot bear to hear the name of Swedenborg mentioned, Mr. Parker, the Methodist minister, says he will investigate matters, but seems so well entrenched in his preconceived notions that I think a casual reading will not do him much good." Shepherd notes that the people in Grand Rapids are "anxious to have lectures."

His newfound religious assurance meant a great deal to the debt-ridden and beleaguered Lyon who wrote Samuel Williams in the spring of 1849 ". . . though I have lost all my property and am very poor, I enjoy more peace of mind and real happiness than I have ever before experienced; for I know the Divine Providence gives me as much of what is generally called wealth as is good for me, and more I do not desire. I read the Word every morning and evening and endeavor to live according to its teachings, looking to the Lord Jesus Christ, as the sole and only God of heaven and earth, to give me strength to resist all evil as sins against Him, and to guide me and lead me in all that I do, and finally to regenerate and fit me for heaven. You have been a follower of the Lord for many years, and have doubtless made much more progress in the regenerate life than I have. I have often thought of you since I began to shun and fight against evils as sins, and have bitterly regretted that I did not sooner follow your example."

Lyon became an eager evangelist for the cause although his dislike of public speaking made him look to other avenues to spread the message. In January of 1848, he wrote to John Allen, congratulating him on a series of lectures and adding, "<u>My</u> way of doing good is to lay out all the means that I can spare in the purchase of New Church books to lend to such persons as will read them -- and if I were able I would place a full set of New Church writings in every Township and School District library in this State, so that they would be accessible to all.

"The expense of doing so would amount to only a few thousand dollars, and the good they would be the means of doing, if only two or three good lecturers or preachers were to go through the state and call attention to them, would, it seems to me, be very great. The people would soon call upon the old church clergy to modify their doctrines in several important particulars, so that the change which, even now, is every where perceptible in them, would then progress with far greater rapidity and the true relation of the Spiritual and Natural worlds being generally so much better understood, its effect would be visible in the lives of thousands, who now hardly even think of another state of existence."

One of the ideas expounded by Swedenborg was the theory that marriages persist in heaven, along with conjugal love, but without the issue of children. At a time when sexual love was not spoken of aloud in polite society, it was considered outrageous to do so in church and in religious writings. Because of this and other doctrines and practices, the Church of the New Jerusalem was looked at with some fear and disdain by most of the mainline denominations of Detroit. The little New Church congregation was incensed by an editorial which appeared in the January 17, 1847, edition of the *Christian Herald*, headlined "Attempts to foist Swedenborgianism into notice." Field, Lyon and his associates wrote a rebuttal which the *Christian Herald* would not publish, but it was run in the newspaper owned by John Allen, and later as a paid advertisement in the *Detroit Daily Advertiser* and elsewhere.

Lyon is listed as a delegate to the fifth annual meeting of the Michigan and Northern Indiana Association of the Church of the New Jerusalem, held in Detroit February 5, 1847, and an 1848 list indicated that he was a baptized member of the faith. In July of 1850 he was elected vice-president of the American Swedenborg Printing and Publishing Society.

Although not an official part of the New Church doctrine, mesmerism or animal magnetism, often called hypnotism, was sometimes associated with the faith. Many adherents saw it as a special help in understanding the complex ideas of the afterlife that Swedenborg espoused since with the use of hypnosis it was believed possible to speak directly with the spirit world. Lyon felt that mesmerism was an important part of his conversion and wrote, "I do not see how I could ever have been brought to recognize and acknowledge the psychological truths given to the world by Swedenborg, but for the confirmation afforded by the phenomenon of Mesmerism." There are several pages of notes in his papers in the Clements Library dated February 24, 1846, outlining a method of casting trances by eye contact, stroking, and the use of certain signs. He had learned this method from Charles W. Hopkins who told him that he had been commanded by a man who lived three thousand years ago to impart it to Lyon. According to the notes, Hopkins had told him that it would "help his mind though it would injure his body." On the same pages that outlined this method of mesmerism, Lyon later appended a note, dated April 8, 1850, "I was thereby led to know that there is a spiritual world, of which I was previously ignorant, and consequently to examine and receive the truths of the New Church; though my bodily health has apparently been injured by it ever since."

John Allen, whose personal fortunes in Michigan land paralleled most of Lyon's successes and eventually financial ruin, was a fellow convert to the New Church, and wrote Lyon December 19, 1849, thanking him for a letter which helped him to understand the uses of spiritualism in the church, "Your extracts and your remarks have thrown great light up on the subject of Magnetism, or Clairvoyance, as a means for the acquisition of truth. I had not see the subject in as clear a light . . . until I received your letter."

Lucius was acquainted with several clairvoyants who professed to be able to diagnosis health problems by touching a part of the ailing person's body. In the fall of 1846, Lucretia, who suffered severe head-aches, sent Lucius a lock of hair "clipped from the back part of my head. You may do as you think proper about sending it to the clairvoyant you mentioned. It is impossible to foresee what may be the result of either attending to, or of neglecting it. But I should be glad to know that it is nothing seriously dangerous." The clairvoyant prescribed several sessions of magnetizing and in this Lucretia was assisted by Lucius Thayer who had recently returned from the Upper Peninsula and fell right in with the spiritualism practiced by his friends and family in Grand Rapids.

In September of 1847 Lucretia reported that Lucius Thayer had become "a general favorite in this place. . . . He magnetizes Mr. Calder twice every day and keeps him sleepy enough to be subject to his will for about an hour and a half at a time. . . . One evening being down in the Village at 9 o'clock, the usual time for his visits to Mr. Calder, he was engaged so that he could not come till fifteen minutes after, but at the precise hour of nine willed him to go to sleep, and at the same time, for some reason, unaccountable to him, Mr. C. began to feel very sleepy and said he believed Lucius was trying to magnetize him, and was not a little amused when he found that such was the fact."

There was dissension in the Detroit congregation concerning who was to be permitted to preach the Word, and the disagreement also may have been related to conflicting ideas concerning the need and importance of spiritualism, and Rev. George Field resigned suddenly in 1849. Lyon wrote Rev. Jabez Fox of Marshall asking if he would serve the Detroit congregation, "There is little or no compensation," he wrote, "but it is supposed that you might publish the Medium here as well as at Marshall, and perhaps, be quite as useful here." *The Medium* was a magazine associated loosely with the New Church which centered on the spiritualist side of study and worship. Fox arrived in Detroit just before the start of 1850 and served until 1855 when Field returned.

Lyon's enthusiasm carried much of his own family into the embrace of the New Jerusalem fellowship. Nephew George W. Thayer was a member of the Detroit group and in 1849 Lyon was the primary mover in the establishment of a New Church Association in Grand Rapids. In 1850, while still residing in Detroit, he donated a church site, 169 by 50 feet, in Grand Rapids at the corner of Lyon and North Division Streets, and he contributed toward the erection of a church edifice. The building was completed and opened for services April 4, 1852. The Grand Rapids congregation had a number of members who were particularly bound up in mesmerism, spiritualism and communication with the spirit world, including the Coffinberry family that Lucretia resided with, and Henry Weller, an Englishman who had become pastor of the congregation April 30, 1850.

Weller was apparently sent, or recommended, to the organizing Grand Rapids congregation by Lucius Lyon. Lucretia wrote him March 27, 1848, "I thank you sincerely for having introduced to this Place, the Good Mr. Weller, and you will be glad to know I am not alone in this sentiment. . . . The interest manifested . . . is truly astonishing."

His ministry rapidly produced converts including Lyon stepbrother Sidney Smith's widow, and Truman H. Lyon and his wife. Lucretia wrote that Truman and Lucinda's interest was "aided by information they received respecting their relations in the Spiritual World from the clairvoyant Alverson of Ann Arbor who was here in early spring, soon after Mr. Weller's first course of lectures. He told them many things respecting their deceased friends some of which they know to be true."

Not all the family was as accepting. Sister Pamelia Thayer wrote a long letter from Vermont, February 14, 1848, thanking Lucius for some books and tracts that he had sent her, but continuing, "You say that Swedenborg teaches that no person that does not strive to live a good life and keep the commandments of the Decalogue and look to the Lord as the author of all good can ever come in to Heaven. . . . Now this is precisely the instruction that I have ever received from the Episcopal Church." She also wrote that her parents had read some of the books but were not fully convinced, and she had given material to their younger brother George and his wife, Phoebe, and that "Phoebe says her parents have advised her not on any account to read them."

The last chapter of Lucius Lyon's participation in the Swedenborgian communities occurred after his death. According to Rev. Field in his *Memoirs, Incidents and Reminiscences of the Early History of the New Church*:

"In the beginning of the year 1852, several of the Ministers of the New Church and leading and influential laymen received each a communication from Rev. Henry Weller, then of Grand Rapids, Michigan, notifying them that they were to attend a meeting he had appointed, to be held in that city about the middle of February, that same year, to commence and lay the foundations of the New Church, under his direction and supervision. That he received authority for doing this from Swedenborg; and that he was chosen as the Lord's High Priest on earth, with authority to appoint all those who were to officiate in the Ministerial office. This meeting was appointed to be held in Grand Rapids on the same days that the Tenth Annual meeting of the Michigan and N. I. Association was to be held in Detroit.

"The letter which I received at St. Louis, requiring me to attend, Mr. Weller informed me, 'was written by direction of Lucius Lyon, your [my] old friend in Detroit; but now as you will know the Lord's instrument for establishing true order in the Church.' Mr. Lyon was then living in the Spiritual world. The letter was as follows: -- 'To George Field. -- You are hereby informed that a meeting of the brethren called to lay the foundation of the Lord's Church on earth, will be held at Grand Rapids on the 13th, 14th, and 15th of next month; at which meeting you are requested to attend. Moreover it is the Lord's will that you be then, and there present, if it be possible, to receive such instructions as may be given you by me, through the Lord's High Priest, who is already known to thee; and within whose jurisdiction thou hast been placed in vision, by the Lord's servant, Emanuel Swedenborg, who hast given thee a testimony in the Latin language, a language thou canst not write; and which few can write at the present day. Wherefore it is the Lord's will that you bring that testimonial with you, to be produced, how, and when, and where, the Lord pleaseth:

Lucius Lyon,

through the hand of the Lord's High Priest

Henry ----'

"This was dated January 22nd, 1852.

"I was as much bewildered as I was surprized, to receive such a communication. It was inexplicable, and yet it was absurd and presumptuous.

"I had received no such document, either in Latin, or any other language, as he said I had; and so of course I could not bring it; and if I had, I should not. Of course I did not attend the meeting; nor did I answer, or pay any attention to the summons. A *few*, (a very small few), did attend, and inaugurated a sort of spiritualistic fraternity, seeking open intercourse with the spiritual world; and a kind of spiritual wife system, together with other peculiarities and assumptions, and follies, which led to much discord and unhappiness."

According to the Baxter history, the Weller incident "alarmed and dispersed the congregation." But the remnants of the church reported Weller to the next annual convocation and there a resolution was passed removing him as a pastor since "letters and communication received by Henry Weller of Grand Rapids . . . do most conclusively demonstrate in him, a state of mind eminently unfitting him for the useful discharge of a pastor, or minister" and a committee of three was appointed, "to endeavor to draw him, as a misguided brother, from the lamentable delusion into which he has fallen."

After Weller finally left Grand Rapids the congregation was in disarray and about 1859 several of the former New Church members formed an association of Spiritualists under the name Religio-Philosophical Society. The Rev. George N. Smith, Jr. gathered what was left of the New Church and conducted services in 1858-9, and sporadically afterwards, since the group was too small to support a full-time minister. Smith was the son of the Rev. George N. Smith, a Congregationalist missionary to the Indians of western Michigan, in Allegan and Ottawa Counties, and, later, in the Northport area. Both father and son arrived in the area of Otsego in Allegan County in 1833 and, according to preserved correspondence, were acquainted with Lucius Lyon. The younger Smith lived in Grand Rapids from 1859 to 1867, and in 1863-4 was president of the New Church Association of Michigan. The Grand Rapids congregation scarcely met from 1860 until 1889 when the society was reactivated in the same building. Both

Lucretia Lyon and George W. Thayer were members at the time of the resumption of worship. During the twenty-plus years that the society was inactive the little church building witnessed the birth of five congregations, the Second Congregational Church, the Westminster Presbyterian Church, a Christian Reformed congregation, a Free Will Baptist assembly, and one affiliated with the Disciples.

In the Baxter history of Grand Rapids there is an incident related in a biography of George Washington Thayer which would have made his Uncle Lucius proud:

"Years ago, soon after making his acquaintance, the writer said to him: 'Mr. Thayer, what is your religion?' A rare smile lit up his usually grave face as he replied, as a Yankee may, with another question: 'How do you know that I have any religion, as you call it?' The answer made was this, 'Because you live it. You have never talked about it to me, but it is perfectly apparent that positive religious convictions control your action and life.' That was true then, and the many years that have since elapsed have intensified the feeling then expressed. He embraced the religious views expressed in the teachings and doctrine of Emmanuel Swedenborg while yet a young man, and has devoted his life since to a study of them and an exemplification of his faith."

George Washington Thayer in later years.

14

Back to the Woods

Charles Noble of Monroe was named the new surveyor general and Lyon, still deeply in debt, started searching for a new occupation. He had been in ill health most of the early part of 1850, but as he explained to Samuel Williams, "believing, from former experience, that a life in the woods would tend to improve my health" he applied for a position as deputy surveyor and prepared to go back into the field.

There is some evidence that Lyon looked back on his former days in the woods with less than a rosy view. In 1835 in reply to a letter from Moses M. Strong of Rutland, Vermont, later a prominent Wisconsin businessman and politician, who had inquired about the possibility of a position as deputy surveyor, Lyon wrote that to become a deputy surveyor it was necessary to make application to a surveyor general stating your qualifications and then "all the political and other influence that you can bring to bear will be requisite to ensure a favorable consideration of your claims for there are thousands of applicants and many of them highly talented and of the first respectability." He goes on to tell Strong, "I have surveyed about 11,000 miles . . . in Ohio, Indiana and Michigan -- and while in the woods have usually averaged 6 to 8 miles per day, and my expenses per day for chainmen, axemen, cook, packman, horses, provisions, and the entire outfit, which is always furnished by the Deputy himself, have averaged between 5 and 6 dollars, leaving a net profit . . . of about $15 per day. This may seem high wages but it is not quite enough to compensate for the exposure in all weather, at all seasons, and for the severe labor and exertion necessary in order to prosecute the business to advantage." Now a decade older than when he wrote these words there is no doubt that, despite his brave words to Williams, he was entering the woods of necessity and with reluctance.

On January 9, 1850, Lewis Cass, still in the U. S. Senate, wrote Lyon a sympathetic letter, "Noble's name has just come in as Surveyor General. I suppose he will be confirmed without debate. If we must have a Whig, we could not expect a more favorable one. I only regret, my friend, that you could not retain an office, which you have so well filled honorably and acceptably." The letter is signed, "Ever your friend, Lewis Cass."

Lyon's term of office as surveyor general expired January 6, but because Charles Noble did not arrive immediately to take over, Lyon continued in the post until January 24, 1850, carefully signing papers and correspondence "Acting Surveyor General."

Shortly after he turned over the office, its responsibilities and contents, Lyon wrote a long letter to Alpheus Felch, former Michigan governor, now a U. S. Senator, "Having turned the Surveyor General's office and all that belongs to it, to my successor with the understanding that the River Raisin surveys are to be finished by me, and being now poor and out of employment, I find myself under the necessity of returning to my old business which I followed for ten years previous to entering into public office in 1833; Provided, the present Surveyor General will appoint me one of his deputies which, I presume, he will not object to, as political opinions have never been regarded heretofore, in making such appointments in this office. About half of my deputies and half of my clerks were Whigs . . . I assume therefore, that I can have employ-ment as a Deputy Surveyor, if I choose to ask it; and have concluded that under the circumstances in which I find myself placed, I ought not to allow pride to prevent my engaging in any employment in which I can be useful, even though it may be as humble as the one here referred to. . . ." He expresses concern that he is 17 years older than when he was last in the field and may not be able to endure the hardships. To make the physical task easier on himself he asks Felch what would be the possibility of changing a rule established in 1845 before he took office as surveyor general, which prohibited the formation of partnerships in receiving surveying contracts. Lyon writes that he can see no difficulties to allowing partnerships if both partners are experienced surveyors. He continued that this would allow him to supervise the work in the field without requiring that he personally run every line.

In a letter dated February 8, 1850, Felch wrote that he had talked to a friend at the surveyor general's office who had promised to do anything he could to aid Lyon and had immediately proposed that he write a letter to Noble to encourage the acceptance of Lyon's application and take up his concerns. Felch added,"I wish, My Dear Sir, something better could be done, still I hope you may be able to turn this to good account. I trust the time will come when you will be placed in a position more in accordance with your tastes and your merits."

Financially things were improving slightly for Lyon. By living with utmost frugality and managing what little money he had, his years as surveyor general had shown him that there was some hope. In May of 1848, Frances H. Williamson wrote him concerning a project he was planning, and added, "I have seen General Cass, he gave me your address and said you were getting through all your difficulties, and had paid off mostly for property which had been in difficulty and were paying. . . "

It took the economy of the west several years to recover from the effects of the wildcat banks and the inflated land values of 1835-37 and get money flowing again in a responsible manner. The struggles to pay off debts extended from the big land owners down to the ordinary consumer. In the summer of 1849 Lucretia had asked Lucius to purchase some toiletries for her that were only available in Detroit with the promise that she would send him the money later. After several months, and three letters apologizing for her tardiness in paying the debt, she finally sent him the $25.06 that she owed him on November 15 and noted that the payment included State Bank of Ohio notes for $1, $2 and $3; a Wisconsin Marine & Fire Insurance Company $2 note; a $2 note drawn on the Michigan State Bank, two $5 gold pieces, one $4.84 gold piece, and 22 cents in silver coin.

Lyon's second oath as a deputy surveyor, dated 1850.

If he finished the Raisin River survey, it was quickly done. By March, Lyon had been promised a contract for an examination and, if necessary, a resurvey of several townships in the vicinity of Grand Traverse Bay, on the east shore of Lake Michigan near the tip of the

Lower Peninsula, the distance not to exceed 1,020 miles. He apparently wrote S. S. Shaw, who had previously worked in the region, for advice and must have been relieved when he received a letter dated March 29 that Shaw believed that it was possible to use horses in the region "if you do not start too early."

On April 23, 1850, Lyon appeared before an officer of the circuit court in Detroit and renewed his deputy surveyor's oath. He also wrote out the oath for his partner, Leonidas S. Scranton of Grattan, Kent County, to sign. The two began collecting a crew and, after some haggling about price and benefits, the men signed on and were ready to leave. Robert Hunt went north early and sent a letter April 26, 1850, to Lyon who was still in Detroit, with the news that he had arrived at his destination but with some trouble as the captain was very much opposed to going down into Grand Traverse Bay any further than the mission where he had left 22 barrels of provisions with the government farmer, W. B. Fair. Hunt advised Lyon that the only way to receive mail in the unsettled region was through Mackinac Island.

Lyon's start from Detroit was delayed by illness. He wrote Samuel Williams, in a letter dated May 11, 1850, that the state of his health had been such "for a long time past as to render me almost entirely unfit to attend to business of any kind." Lyon had suffered from lung disorders in the past and was frequently laid low by "infection of the lungs." At this time his main physician seemed to be W. N. Choate of Jackson who specialized in homeopathic medicine and frequently prescribed herbs and mineral powders. In an 1850 letter Choate recommended the application to the chest of fresh animal skins or fresh fish bladders "to draw off all the rum and exilation", with a fresh application every six hours. In a letter the following month he advised that 12 juniper berries be taken internally each day.

By the second week in May Lyon had reached the straits of Mackinac on the way to join his crew. He brought some extra woolen hats for the workers who had failed to take sufficient warm clothing. The 1850 census taker found them working in the field in what was officially designated Michilimackinac County which then covered much of the upper portion of the Lower Peninsula. Workers on the project included Robert Hunt, Joseph Hunt, Marcellus Faxon, Andrew Jackson Edmunds, Parmenio Long, Jolin Winfield, Francois Cicotti, Leonidas Scranton, Nicholas C. Ganin, George Beaubien, Peter Beaucillo, and F. Chovin.

In addition to tools and provisions Lyon took a multi-volume set of the writings of Swedenborg to Grand Traverse Bay. He explained later that he had left the bulk of the books at the base camp and when men went back for additional supplies they would trade the completed book for a new one. By this method he read seven volumes during the course of the survey.

The work involved finding the old stakes and corners, testing their validity, and making corrections. Areas covered included parts of what would later be Grand Traverse County, Benzie County, Leelanau County, Kalkaska County and Antrim County. The part of Antrim County that was included in the survey covered what was later Helena Township, where Lyon's nephews Lucius A. Thayer and Henry E. Lyon (son of his half-brother George) were early settlers. Probably their surveyor uncle brought back news of a particularly beautiful and fertile section of the country. It could also be that he had visitors during his work and they were especially taken with the area.

In the account book that includes daily expenditures of the Traverse Bay expedition there is a sworn statement from Lyon that when the work was carried out, "I was myself personally with them, either at camp or on the lines, during the whole time they were engaged." This could not have been strictly true since there are several letters to Lyon in Detroit relating how the work was progressing after his departure.

He still showed a lively interest in state politics and business. In the September 6, 1850, issue of the *Daily Free Press* there is a long letter from Lucius Lyon, datelined, "August 12, 1850, Grand Traverse Bay." The discussion centers on a proposal for the state to purchase unsold federal lands, make improvements, and sell to incoming settlers at a profit. Lyon answers critics who fear the state would wind up in debt (like many of the land speculators, including Lyon, had in recent years) by claiming that the income from the sale of the lands would pay for the improvements, and that the profits would be so vast that it would take a major show of mismanagement to cause a negative balance in the accounts. He then concludes:

"But to bring the matter to a practical test and try the sincerity of those who assert to the contrary, I pledge myself, that if the constitution shall leave such purchase optional with the Legislature, and that body, for the purpose of guarding the state from loss, shall think proper to favor the arrangement, a company of not less than one hundred efficient and responsible business men, residing in the several counties of the State, shall be organized and enter into a contract with such person or persons as may be appointed by the State for that purpose, and shall give satisfactory security to double the amount of the purchase money, that if such purchase be made from the United States they will take the bargain off the hands of the State -- pay punctually, when due, all the payments to be made to the general government -- bring in, or cause to be brought into the State, an average of at least ten thousand emigrants a year to settle the lands so purchased -- open through these lands at least one hundred miles of new roads every year, for the next fifteen years, making fifteen hundred miles in all, (five hundred miles of which shall be made plank roads, or railroads, as soon as the country may be sufficiently settled to reasonably require them) -- and pay into the state treasury, after the first five years, the sum of twenty thousand dollars a year, forever. . . . The question is one which concerns every citizen, and especially every tax payer to look into; and with them I leave it."

An engraving of Lucius Lyon made from an 1850 portrait.

Lyon had left power-of-attorney with his nephew, Washington Thayer, so the young man could carry on some of the land business during his uncle's absence. Washington had continued as a clerk in the surveyor general's office after Noble took office. On the side he cared for Lyon's property and sent many letters north with news and questions. In one of the letters he invited his uncle to live with him in Detroit on his return from the woods. Washington's mother, Lucius's sister, Pamelia, had just recently removed from Grand Rapids to Detroit. During a previous prolonged stay in Michigan, following his service in the U. S. Senate, Lucius had lived with his sister Lucretia, in Grand Rapids, but she had recently begun living with a family from their church. When Lyon returned from the woods, he apparently accepted the invitation and moved in with the Thayer family.

The surveys of the Grand Traverse Bay area were certified in January and February of 1851, and, shortly afterwards, Lyon left for Vermont to assist with the settling of his father's estate. Few letters and papers exist from Lucius Lyon's last year; it is not certain whether few were written, or if they have just not survived. One letter, written to Ross Wilkins of Detroit in February, accompanied a carpetbag full of New Church tracts and books, says that Lyon was about to leave on a long trip, and would call on Wilkins to pick up and discuss the reading material when he returned.

There is nothing to indicate that he made any effort to get a surveying contract in 1851. He apparently returned to Detroit and concerned himself with the activities of the church. Twenty-two-year old Edward Wilmot Barber, a Vermonter by birth, who had moved to Detroit with Jabez Fox in 1850 to assist in the production of *The Medium*, was a frequent visitor. Barber wrote later, "Mr. Lyon was a man worth knowing. His mind was a storehouse of accurate information. In all his acts he was deliberate and calm. My acquaintance with him was during the last years of his life, when it was my good fortune to meet him often." Barber later went into politics and served as clerk of the Michigan House of Representatives in 1861 and 1863, and later as a supervisor of internal revenue. He was appointed by President U. S. Grant as third assistant postmaster general. In 1880 he became editor of the *Jackson Daily Patriot*.

There are no letters or recorded memories that Lucius Lyon was dangerously ill for a long period. Nathan B. Haswell of Vermont, who visited him on September 5, just three weeks prior to his death, does not mention a life-threatening sickness but notes that he "was grateful to see the simplicity and earnestness which he enjoyed in improving the moral truths which he had embraced."

277

The Democrats of Michigan were preparing for their annual meeting to convene September 24, at the Fair Grounds, near the corner of Third Street and Grand River, Detroit. The *Detroit Daily Free Press* carried a small story in the lower left hand column of the front page, Tuesday morning, September 23:

Alarming Illness of Hon. Lucius Lyon

We are greatly pained to announce the alarming illness of Ex. Senator Lyon. He was suddenly attacked with paralysis on Sunday evening, and now lies in an insensible state.

Lucius Lyon died at his nephew Washington's home in Detroit on Wednesday, September 24, 1851, at half past one o'clock in the morning. Edward W. Barber wrote later, "I was in company with young Dr. Burpee, a watcher by the bedside, and witnessed the closing scene of an honorable and eventful earthly career." (This was apparently Martin W. Burpee, a fellow New Church member.) The newspaper wrote of a four-day illness. A later biography-obituary in the *Michigan Tradesman* listed the cause of death as apoplexy.

Services were held September 29 at the First Presbyterian Church at the corner of Woodward Avenue and Larned Street in Detroit. The church seated 1000 people, and the funeral was attended by many of Lyon's friends. At this time the New Church congregation to which he had belonged was still meeting in the court room. George S. Frost, who was chief clerk when Lyon was surveyor general, wrote later to Alpheus Felch that a violent rain storm "added greatly to the gloominess of the occasion. The sermon was delivered in the Presbyterian Church by the Swedenborgian clergyman, and he dwelt somewhat at length upon the peculiar views of their church; concluding by a short sketch of Mr. Lyon's religious experience in their connexion."

Burial was in Elmwood Cemetery which had only recently opened on what was then the east edge of the city. Several years after his uncle's death George Washington Thayer had a tall pylon of white marble from Vermont placed in the center of the plot. Affixed to the marble is a bronze depiction of the Great Seal of the State of Michigan which is said to have once been part of a chandelier that hung in the House of Representatives chamber in Washington. The lighting fixture was made up of seals from the States of the Union, but proved too heavy for its intended use and fell. The Michigan seal was removed and given to Lucius Lyon who played such a large part in creating both the seal and the state it symbolized.

The Lyon monument in Elmwood Cemetery
with bronze seal in center of pylon.

The *Detroit Free Press* carried an obituary which called Lyon, "a well-known, much beloved and most intelligent citizen." And continued, "It has been a singular feature in the official career of Mr. Lyon, embracing within its range some of the highest offices in the country, that he has never been charged at any period with a forgetfulness of the obligation of his position or a neglect of the duties entrusted to his hands. The intellect of Mr. Lyon was of the highest order; he was qualified to fill and adorn any position under the government. In him was united to great modesty and diffidence, the most eminent qualifications in politics and in the sciences a personal demeanor which won the confidence of all; a christian life of undoubted purity. He has left behind him an example worthy of all praise and imitation.

"Peace to his ashes."

Lyon's own ideas on death were written in December of 1844,

279

following the death of cousin/step-brother Sidney Smith. Lucius wrote his sister that he himself expected to die within the next ten years and probably within five years, and that he did not see death, the severance of earthly ties, as a sad or dreadful change. "If we are to exist hereafter, as I believe we shall, there is good reason, from analogy, to believe that we shall occupy a higher rank in the scale of created beings than we now do . . . and it is not improbable that if we could know or have any just conception of the enlarged faculties and powers that our friend now possesses, instead of grieving for him, we should rejoice on his account and be impatient to follow him."

Base of the Lyon monument in Elmwood Cemetery.
This is the only stone on the plot, inscriptions for
other family members continue around the base.

15

Home and Family

There is no house in Michigan that bears a historical marker describing it as the "Home of Lucius Lyon". It is even difficult to say that he was "of Grand Rapids," or Detroit, or Kalamazoo. He lived many places, in hotels, rooming houses, and in the homes of friends and family. As a surveyor he spent many nights in temporary shelters or under the stars. As a member of Congress he attended elegant balls and slept in feather beds in Washington.

Lucius Lyon remained unmarried his entire life, although he appears to have been a favorite with the ladies and apparently considered marriage on at least two occasions. He was linked romantically with Lewis Cass's daughter Elizabeth and following her death in July of 1832 he wrote Lucretia: "I know not when I shall marry I have no one in view at present, nor have I ever had. The story you mention about Miss Cass and myself is one of the thousand every day circulated by the gossips who have nothing else to talk about and was without foundation. I write frankly and in confidence when I say this. She was a fine girl. I knew her well, but the vision of beauty and loveliness has not passed -- the spirit that was too angelic for this world has fled to a better, and if there lie in Heaven a place more pure, more holy and more exalted than another, it is there to rest forever."

Lyon may also have had some romantic understandings with Mary, another Cass daughter. While he was serving as territorial delegate in Washington, she is mentioned in a letter from Stevens T. Mason, secretary of Michigan Territory, another eligible bachelor. The friendly banter makes the reader realize that despite his exalted political position Mason, at that time, was still a young man of 22. He wrote: "I have neglected giving you an account of passing events in this part of the world till now, under the expectation that I should hear from you, as to the state of affairs since I left Washington. But to my regret I have not heard from you; and as you seem disposed to stand upon ceremony I most cheerfully and promptly make the first attack, and this too with the express purpose of provoking retaliation. . . . " He goes on to relate the political events of Detroit, even offering to embarrass Lyon's enemies, "Tell me when and where to strike and I'll give the blow." He closes with, "Remember me to Dr. Phileo. . . . Also remember me, if you have an opportunity to the powers that be. Last, though not least, remember me to Mary Cass, if it does not interfere with No. 1. To tell the truth Lyon I'm a wounded pigeon."

In March of 1834 Lucretia wrote Lucius, "By the bye we heard a rumor' the other day that you were recently married. If it is a fact, I offer you my most hearty congratulations on the joyful and interesting occasion of your happy matrimonial alliance with -- I cannot tell whom."

In Washington Lucius Lyon stayed in a boarding house where several other bachelor lawmakers made their quarters. He writes in 1835 that he was boarding at "Mrs. Pittman's in Third street, a few doors above Polk's." In the Lyon Papers in the Burton Historical Collection there is a curious letter dated April 3, 1834, from W. L. Newberry to Lyon in Washington which reads in part: "As all your messmates have left you, I presume you have taken Miss Keyser into your parlour in order to assuage your grief. If so I hope you will treat the dear little fairy tenderly. Don't forget in your next letter to tell me about your domestic arrangements."

According to a reply written by Lucretia on May 10, 1834, Lucius had written to her April 27 with the news that he was considering marriage, apparently to a Mrs. Royal, and asking what his sisters thought of the idea. Her reply, addressed to, "My Dear, Dear Brother" was swift and to the point. "Whatever may be her standing and character at the South, my esteem for you prompts me to say it is black enough here . . . the veil that conceals her real character must be removed, or, I fear very much, that your reputation and happiness will sink far below those who are doomed ever to remain in the humble station where you were when you first began to rise. . . . Everybody who knows you -- & there are few who do not -- speaks with wonder & praise of your beneficence, your talents & the rapid advances you have made from the little ignorant ploughboy to a respectable seat among the rulers of the Nation! . . . But how different will be the opinions of the people towards you . . . should you unite your destiny with one so utterly lost to all sense of moral virtue. . . . Brother, cast aside, I entreat you the false garb, by which that 'little amiable creature' has allured you, & forget not the confidence of your friends -- verify the truth of Dr. Young's assertion that 'with the talents of an Angel a man be a fool.' I hope before you take the irrevocable step, that you will investigate the subject fully."

He apparently assured her by return mail that his previous letter had been written as a joke to see how they would respond. His sisters were the ones most interested in seeing him married. In 1838 Esther (Lyon) Tabor wrote Lucretia that it appeared that their brother Orson was following the same path, "He keeps bachellor's hall and I guess always will, as is the case with brother Lucius, he will never take time

282

and set about getting a wife."

In February of 1838, Lucius was making no definite plans, but not ruling out the possibility. He wrote Col. D. Goodwin of Detroit denying news of an impending marriage, "There is not the slightest truth to any such report and there never has been and probably never will be, though of that I may think better hereafter. I like the society of intelligent and interesting ladies, but I can't say that I particularly admire those who fancy that every man who looks at or speaks to them civilly half a dozen times wishes to marry them, and there are a great many such, who give rise to all sorts of ridiculous reports and surmises about every gentleman who happens to be thrown into their company."

At least one serious possibility of marriage occurred in 1838 when he was in Detroit following a trip to Boston, New York and other eastern cities. He wrote Lucretia in August: "I became acquainted with all the most distinguished belles and had two or three flirtations, some one of which may become serious hereafter, if I should find time to go to New York and renew it; and should not in the meantime fall in love with some one else, against which I shall not promise, for I feel that I am in some danger from a certain pair of black eyes that you are acquainted with, which are near me at the National Hotel where I am now staying."

The lady with the dark eyes was probably a Miss Prescott who was at that time in Michigan with her mother and grandmother, visiting her uncle, a bachelor, who lived in the National Hotel in Detroit. The Prescotts were friends of the Lyon family in Vermont. "Miss Prescott is just such a belle as I am proud to see from my native state," Lucius wrote.

Lucretia was not impressed. She responded, "You have carried the joke so far as to avow that you are in danger from those black eyes from Vermont. I know they are bright and glance most bewitchingly but am sorry to say that they are the index of a mind which has failed to be sufficiently impressed with that solidity of principle and strict regard to veracity, which should be the foundation of character. . . "

In July, he had written brother-in-law James Tabor at Lyons from Washington, that he had a date to dine at the home of Philip Kearney. "He has an unmarried daughter worth $300,000 in her own right, left by her grandfather and is therefore an object of special admiration with all the fortune hunting beaux. I am not one of them though I certainly should not object very strong to a lady on that account. I have already a negotiation half completed with a lady of considerable fortune, but I am not certain I can love her well enough to marry her. . . "

One possible identification for this romantic reference is a Miss

Blair, who was a daughter of the editor of the *Washington Globe*. In the spring of 1838 Lucius sent some invitations and calling cards he had collected to his sister, Lucretia, and noted, "I have added to each invitation a short account of the person who gave it. They will afford you amusement for an hour or two and will at the same time give you a better idea of the forms of society here than you can get from any other source." By Miss Blair he wrote, "She is the most sprightly and popular young lady in Washington and a confidential friend of mine." Farther down the list a Miss Kane is described as "one of the finest girls in the world" and a "good friend." But later he observed, specifically about Miss Blair, that "The climate of Michigan would be, I fear, too cold for a Washington belle. . . ."

He wrote in 1839 that he was "on excellent terms" with Emily Virginia Mason, younger sister of Governor Stevens T. Mason. They had met in Detroit probably soon after the arrival of the Mason family in 1830 when Emily was only 15. She matured rapidly and at some stage in their relationship Lucius made her a gift of a thimble, and in an undated letter signed E.V.M., she wrote, "If Mr. L-- had thought Miss M-- at all deficient in industry he could not better have tempted her with the exercise of that admirable quality -- for who would not sew with such a thimble? and there is no doubt but the quality will be improved as well as the quantity of work increased for every one must be sensitive that smaller stitches may be made with a gold than with an Iron thimble!" She promises to try it out on a handkerchief for him and "successfully show what a gold thimble can do!"

Although in letters back home Lucius always tried to appear the accomplished man-of-the-world, on a face to face basis sometimes his romantic efforts went less smoothly. In 1835 when he was a would-be senator fighting for the admission of his state to the Union, Emily Mason was visiting her aunt and uncle in Washington. In a letter dated January 26, 1835, she wrote her sister Kate back in Detroit:

"Capt. Howard called to see me the other day with John Sprague and Nathan Rice -- "Lucius,, (of course) bringing up the rear. Indeed I begin to find "Lucius,, quite troublesome -- under pretence of bringing me news he comes very often & then stays such a terrible while. I would not mind it if he only made visits like other folks but when he does come I promise you he sticks it out -- I have endeavored to get rid of him by introducing him to Mary Osterhout. I had promised to take him to see her & he came every day for three days previous to see about it. Spent two evenings in succession, which was too much for human nature to stand, particularly as each time he stayed till 11 o'clock. You would have been amused to see Aunt C. -- she would fidget about & get behind him & make the most awful faces imaginable at him. It was with the greatest difficulty I could keep my countenance."

Emily spent a good deal of time in the south, in Kentucky and Louisiana, and was wooed by others, but never quite got to the altar. She and Lucius Lyon remained friends and their relationship was a matter of some speculation by others. In a letter dated February 23, 1837, when Emily was 21 and Lucius 37, Sarah McKnight, wife of Detroit newspaperman Sheldon McKnight, added a postscript to her husband's letter to Lyon, "Emily Mason has decided not to marry Mr. Center -- quite a disappointment for the poor fellow . . . this I tell you in confidence, as I had it from an intimate friend. So you see there is still a chance for you." The following year John B. Murray who was in Detroit on a visit wrote Lyon in Washington, "Miss Emily talked very much about you and I think her a very fine girl." He asks if perhaps she ought to become a "Lyoness" and adds, "You have excellent taste in most matters."

In 1838 Lucius had written Lucretia that he felt it unlikely that he would ever marry and she responded, November 13, 1838, "You cannot imagine how much I was surprised at the declaration in the latter part of your letter viz. that you doubted whether you should ever marry. Has not Miss Mason charms enough to fill your eye? If I could believe that dreams foretell the truth; I should have no occasion of asking you this question, for I was shown some two years ago, in a vision of Monsieur Morpheus that you were finally married to her, in all the pomp due to one of the most exalted rank which a republican government confers . . . I have half indulged the hope that that vision would one day prove to be reality; but now it is gone with the wind."

Lucius's response to Lucretia, after some delay, was that he had considered the possibility of a marriage between them and that he still thought that Emily Virginia Mason was "one of the finest girls in the United States; but we have known each other too long and too well to let such a violent, rowdy fellow as young Cupid sometimes proves himself to come in to interrupt our friendship."

After the marriage of her brother in 1839, Emily lived with various relatives and frequently visited Washington. She was in town on New Year's Day, 1844, when, by tradition, society spent the day calling on each other. Lyon wrote Lucretia that he had joined Emily and Laura Mason, and "Mrs. Bonnycastle, a rich widow and cousin of theirs, to call on the ex-president J. Q. Adams and his lady, on Mrs. Madison and her nieces, the Misses Cutts, on James Larned and his family; on C. A. Wickliffe, Postmaster General and family . . . and at many other places too numerous to mention." Both Emily and Laura wrote about the events of New Year's Day to their sister Kate, now Mrs. Isaac Rowland, back in Detroit. Neither mentions the presence of Lucius Lyon.

Emily Virginia Mason as a mature woman.

Sarah McKnight, who did not give up easily, wrote Lyon in December of 1844, "Miss Mason is very beautiful. I should think you would try and <u>catch</u> her for she seems to me to be on the <u>lookout</u>."

There were other suitors courting the young sister of the governor; at least one old Detroit resident claims that Major Lewis Cass, son of General Cass, was in love with and proposed to her. Friend Palmer in his book of reminiscences, *Early Days in Detroit*, passes on the rumor and remarks, "Well, he no doubt might have admired the young lady, as all the young and old bachelors of that day did." However, like

Lucius Lyon, Emily Mason, 15 years his junior, never married. Because of her Confederate sympathies during the Civil War (she was described as a "dear friend" of General Robert E. Lee, and Jefferson Davis had stayed with the Mason family during a visit to Detroit in 1832) Emily lived for a time in Europe following the close of hostilities. Several years later she returned to the United States. In 1905 the body of her brother was brought back to Michigan with honors, and Emily, then nearly 90, participated in the ceremonies on June 4, when the coffin was interred below the memorial in Capitol Park, Detroit.

Lyon must have become used to his friends' attempts at matchmaking, but, in 1836, he faced another approach. He received a letter which stated, "You deserve your happiness" and recommending that he take a wife. The anonymous writer goes on to tout the qualities of a particular lady in some detail and finally reveals that this sterling example of unmarried womanhood was named Williamson, and that she was boarding with Mrs. McKnight. It would seem unlikely to be a coincidence that shortly afterwards he received a letter from Frances H. Williamson, who had some money that he wanted invested in western lands in the name of his daughter, Abigail Janet Williamson. Lyon apparently took the money and did as he was asked, but the ruse was unsuccessful in its matrimonial object. Williamson wrote May 28, 1838, sending his daughter's thanks for Lyon's kindness in becoming her agent, "and she hopes you will make her fortune as she expects to be an old maid; she would like very much to be rich, as old maids need something to recommend them to the world."

By 1839, with his 40th birthday fast approaching, Lucius had pretty much given up the idea of marriage although he still found a certain appeal to it. He was being proposed as a candidate for governor and felt he would be more popular if he had a wife. "I look upon a woman as the connecting link in the scale of creation between man and the angels, and I begin to regret that I have not secured some one of these celestial beings to lead me to heaven. There are few men in the United States whose acquaintance with the most beautiful, interesting and distinguished ladies of this continent has been more extensive or more intimate than mine has been for the last eight or ten years; and there are very few who have been more flattered or who have had better opportunities to make an advantageous selection. But I have never thought seriously on the subject and now I find myself growing rather too old to please and quite too fastidious to be pleased myself, so that I doubt very much whether I shall not remain a bachelor, notwithstanding my resolve to the contrary."

Toward the end of his life there was another romantic interlude. In 1849 he began receiving letters in a spidery feminine handwriting, proclaiming "I must have one friend to love and sympathize with." The letters were obviously from an articulate and educated person and were signed "Mignonette." The first contact that has been preserved is dated December 25, 1849 and enclosed a bookmark for his Bible as a Christmas present and a poem which reads in part:

> Thy beauty consists not
> in thy sparkling eyes,
> thy damask cheeks,
> or forehead high;
> not in thy form
> or glistening hair,
> or melody of voice!
> Ah no not there
> But in the <u>soul</u> . . .

The letters continued for at least two months and at this time one of the letters ended with the revelation that they were from a "L. A. Northrup" and that she would like to have him call. "It is well known to both Mr. Lyon and myself that our spirits are congenial . . . it is no crime to be attached to our friends." Lyon called on the lady several times although not, apparently, with the result that she had hoped.

A valentine, which arrived in February of 1850, carries words that would seem to be written by another suitor, but the handwriting looks a lot like that of Mignonette. Within a lacy oval it says in part":

> Pray pardon my candor
> and call it not slander
> But 'tis said sir that you have done wrong
> In flirting with her
> Whom you do not prefer
> And with whom you have trifled so long. . .

> I sincerely do hope
> The fair one will elope
> Before you again do deceive her.
> You have played the coquet
> Without any regret
> And now it is time you should leave her.

The letters continued, and in one dated April 10, 1850, she pouted, "You have forbidden me to love you, and I try to obey you, but cannot." An invitation to call was attached, and, when he did, she "told my feelings" with such fervor and emotion that she described in a letter April 20 how her heart fell "as I saw your proud countenance beam upon me with disapprobation." Even after he left for a surveying job up north she continued the correspondence. She wrote in June, "How insipid is society when not helped by your presence." Finally, September 10, 1850, Lyon addressed her from Grand Traverse Bay, in what he apparently hoped was a final letter. He wrote, "The difference in our ages and situations in life must always prevent our being more to each other than friends. For conjugal love cannot long exist where there is great disparity in these respects, but friendship may, and I hope always will exist between us. On my part I am sure it will. On yours it will be more difficult and you will have to struggle against your natural feelings to prevent your love from being changed into hatred. You must not, however, allow this to take place, for I have not intentionally done anything to mislead, deceive or injure you. I was pleased with your personal appearance and doubtless showed it in my manners and expression towards you, but this had as its origin 'the love of the sex' which is a general love implanted in every man, and not in 'conjugal love' which is a love of one of the sex. If in anything, you think I have done wrong, I hope you will forgive me, for I assure you I would not have done so knowingly, on any account whatever." This final letter in the Lyon collection is not in the hand of Lucius, even as a first draft, but a typed copy. This indicates that perhaps before his papers were presented to the library, the original was removed. There is no indication, however, that the copy omits or alters any of the words in the original.

Although Lucius Lyon had no offspring to carry on the work he had begun, many family members remained in Michigan. Baxter wrote in his 1881 history of Grand Rapids, "The Lyons are an important family in that State [Vermont] and representatives of the family who have made Michigan their home of whom a large number have been among the most respected and useful members of the communities of which they were a part in Grand Rapids, Detroit, and other portions of the state."

The oldest sister of Lucius, Pamelia (Lyon) Thayer, was divorced from her husband in 1831 and was ill for many years, living sometimes with her parents and Lucretia, or the family of her sister, Esther, in Vermont, and sometimes in places where the family was forced to pay for her care. She moved to Michigan about 1848 and lived with Lucretia in Grand Rapids until 1850 when she moved to Detroit. Pamelia is described in one of her son's biographies as, "a woman of strong sense and equable temperament; and although quiet and retiring in disposition, exhibited a lively interest in the temporal and spiritual welfare of her family and friends." She died January 10, 1857, and is buried in the Lyon family plot in Elmwood Cemetery, Detroit.

The two sons of Pamelia were special charges of their Uncle Lucius. George Washington Thayer, usually called Washington, travelled to Michigan in May of 1845 with the plan that he would participate in the survey trip led by Douglass Houghton and then study under Houghton to outfit himself for the profession of surveyor and engineer. Houghton and his two boatmen died in a storm October 13, 1845, shortly after he parted from Washington, and the young man returned to Detroit and worked in the office of his Uncle Lucius who was then surveyor general. He remained in the office even after his uncle was succeeded by a Whig, and was working there in 1851 when Lucius died at Washington's home in Detroit. Washington married an English girl, Anna Grace Cubley, and moved to Flushing Township, Genessee County, where he farmed. He served as a State Representative from Genessee County in 1863-4, and again in 1865-6, running as a Republican. He moved to Grand Rapids before 1870 and was a jobber and retailer of groceries located in a building on the southeast corner of Monroe and Michigan until his retirement in 1888. He was clerk of the City of Grand Rapids, and mayor of the city, 1877-78. A Grand Rapids history notes that the first ordinance prohibiting chickens, pigs and cows from roaming the streets was passed during his term of office. Washington served nine years as a member of the Board of Public Works beginning in 1879. On September 9, 1885, as the president of the Board of Public Works, he delivered an address at the laying of the cornerstone of the Grand Rapids City Hall. He was for several years manager of the first street railroad in Grand Rapids and served as president of the North Park Street Railway, one of the early suburban lines. He was the first president of the Western Michigan Agricultural and Industrial Society when that association was organized in 1879. Anna (Cubley) Thayer died in 1877, and Washington took as his second wife the widow Marshall, daughter of Amos Sherwood of New York State. Washington died September 2, 1916. He and Anna are buried in the Lyon family plot in Elmwood Cemetery, Detroit. They had at least four children, Walter Lyon Thayer was born January 16, 1850, and would have been acquainted with his Great-uncle Lucius who lived with them in Detroit. Walter died in 1888 and is buried with the rest of the Lyon family in Elmwood Cemetery. Edward Pierson Thayer, born June 4, 1855, died prior to the death of Washington in 1916. Two other sons, Cassius T. Thayer and George Washington Thayer Jr., were still living in Grand Rapids at the time of their father's death. Also buried in the Lyon plot in Elmwood Cemetery is Walton Cubley, born in Burlington, Vermont, died May 13, 1860 in

Detroit at the age of 22 years.

Lucius Alexander Thayer finished his schooling in Grand Rapids where he lived with his Aunt Lucretia, and, later, his mother. He was involved in some of his uncle's Grand Rapids projects. He hauled wood for the brush wall at the salt works before he left for the Upper Peninsula to catch the Houghton expedition. Because there was no place for him in the expedition he decided to return to Vermont, but, shortly after his arrival, he must have received a letter from his Uncle Lucius asking him to take over the salt works. He responded, "I think I would not like the surveying business at all. I should prefer the salt business to any other. . . . I do not like Vermont as well as I supposed I should. I had rather live in Michigan." He was the moving force of his uncle's Upper Peninsula mining interest before returning to Grand Rapids and the salt works. The first election for Marquette Township was held in his house near the Dead River claims in Marquette County in 1847. According to a Kent County history it was Lucius Thayer who bored the wooden pipes for the first Grand Rapids public water system in the fall of 1848. The work was done with an auger especially fitted for the purpose, using the water power in one of the factories above Bridge street between the canal and the river. Lucius Thayer married Helen Maria Donley (or Donnelley, sometimes recorded as Douley, and Lucretia, writing to tell her brother of the midnight elopement which culminated in a wedding ceremony at her house, calls the bride Helen Marie Stanford) in Grand Rapids on August 30, 1849. It may be that the bride's family objected to her marriage with Lucius because of his religious views and reputation as a hypnotist. In the summer of 1850 Lucius Thayer became seriously ill and Washington wrote his Uncle Lucius that his "life was despaired of for several days." The family was living in Grand Rapids in the 1850 census, when Lucius Thayer's occupation is listed as laborer. In the fall of that year he was again trying to get someone to lease the water power at the old salt works. Shortly afterwards Lucius Thayer and family moved north, settling in Antrim County, near Traverse City. According to a newspaper article written by grandson, Charles H. Coy, January 2, 1913, in the *Bellaire Independent*, the area was so sparsely settled that for the first 11 months of her residence in the township Helen Thayer saw no white woman, only squaws and Indians. The township of Helena was named for her in 1865, and there is a Thayer Lake. The first township meeting of Helena Township was held at the home of Truman Hawley, probably a relative and Lucius Thayer was the first supervisor of the township. Helen and Lucius Thayer had eight children: George, Helen, Anna, Hattie, Fred, Abbie, Carrie and Edward. Anna Thayer was married August 20, 1876, to Henry E. Lyon. Lucius Thayer died September 3, 1876, and is buried with the rest of the family in Detroit. Helen later married Andrew F. Anderson, and died in Helena, December 22, 1912.

George H. Lyon, a half-brother to Lucius, was the only offspring of Asa Lyon and his second wife, Mary (Hawley Lyon) Lyon. George had visited Michigan in 1838 but returned east and was married in 1840 to Phoebe Russel. They moved to New York, where he was a music teacher; he made a living conducting singing schools and teaching in the common schools. George and Phoebe had five children, Phoebe M., Horace Hawley, Homer Russell, Henry Edward and Ellen Matilda. Horace and Homer were twins, and both died in the Union Army during the Civil War. George H. came to Michigan before 1857, stopping first in Genessee County. After the death of his wife in 1862 he moved to Antrim County with his son Henry E. Lyon. They settled first at Clam Lake and cleared the land. According to an old history "after bringing it up to a high state of cultivation" it was sold and they purchased a new 94-acre farm in Helena Township. Henry was described as an "uncompromising and earnest Republican" and served the community in several capacities including township clerk, supervisor, and a member of the local school board. He was married August 20, 1876, to Anna L. Thayer, the daughter of Lucius A. and Helen (Donley) Thayer. Lucius A. Thayer was the son of Pamelia (Lyon) Thayer, Lucius Lyon's oldest sister. Asa Lyon was Anna Thayer's great-grandfather and her husband's grandfather, although different wives were involved in the two family lines.

Truman H. Lyon

292

Truman Hawley Lyon was the son of Timothy and Mary (Hawley) Lyon. Mary was the second wife of Asa, father of Lucius. Mary had several children with the last name of Lyon by her first husband. Truman was one of these. Lucius, in a letter in 1838 referred to him as a "cousin." This may be an honorary title, the relationship of Mary Lyon's two husbands named Lyon is uncertain. Truman moved to Michigan late in 1836 and settled at Lyons in Ionia County. There he kept a hotel, was justice of the peace, postmaster, and judge. In 1838 he was appointed superintendent of lighthouses on Lake Michigan. Shortly after Truman's appointment Lucius wrote a friend in Wisconsin that Truman was "a man of highly respectable character, excellent good sense and practical, thorough business habits, which qualify him well for the station . . . and will, I know, push forward the building of the new lighthouses as rapidly as practicable. He has no inducement to delay for his only compensation is his actual traveling expenses and two and a half percent of the disbursements he may make in payment for the buildings when completed." In 1840 Truman moved to Grand Rapids where he kept the Bridge Street House for two years, and afterwards the Rathbun Hotel. When a Temperance Society was founded in Grand Rapids in 1842 with Lucius Lyon as president, Truman banished liquor from his bar and kept a temperance house. It was not successful and he applied again for a tavern license in May of 1844. He also carried on business as a cloth dresser, and, on a small scale, as a woolen manufacturer, and was an officer in the Grand Rapids Chair Co. He was postmaster of Grand Rapids whenever a Democrat held the presidency, serving from 1844-49 and from 1853-58. Truman was a member of the Kent County Board of Supervisors from Grand Rapids Township in 1845, and from the City of Grand Rapids at Large in 1851-2. In 1853-4 he served in the State Senate from the 24th District. An advocate of education, he was elected school trustee for the Grand Rapids Union School, September 24, 1848, and also served on the Board of Education, District No. 1. He was on the board of the Grand Rapids Academy organized in 1844 which had the first "high school" classes in the city. The school was located first in a small building on Prospect Hill and moved later to a structure near the Court House Square. It was dissolved after the founding of the Union School. Truman was married in 1823 to Lucinda Farnham, and they had a family of six sons and one daughter. His Grand Rapids home was a brick cottage-style house he built in 1845 at 280 E. Fulton Street. In 1991 the building, with a large addition in back, but little changed in the front, was in use as a doctor's office. The modern address is 222 Fulton Street. Truman H. Lyon Sr. died September 14, 1872. An 1878 biography concluded, "The character of Mr. Lyon is easily summed up. With no strikingly brilliant qualities, his plain good sense, his business capacity, his clear judgement, and personal integrity gave him a marked position among the leading men." Lucinda lived to be 98 years old and died in Grand Rapids, February 9, 1899.

The Truman Lyon home on Fulton Street.

Several of Truman's sons also figured prominently in the history of early Michigan. Truman Hawley Lyon Jr., who was named for his father, was always called Hawley, and many Grand Rapids records try to separate the two by calling the younger man T. Hawley Lyon. In the 1850s he had an interest in a stage line that traveled from Grand Rapids to Kalamazoo along the old Plank Road. This business was largely halted with the coming of the railroad. Following in his father's occupation Hawley ran the Rathbun House for most of the years between 1861 and 1870, and, later, Sweet's Hotel 1870-78. He was manager in 1872 when the building was seriously damaged by fire, and also in 1874 when the entire four-story structure was raised four feet to bring it up to a new street grade. Hawley was a director of the First National Bank when it commenced operation in December of 1861, and one of the original incorporators of the Kent County Soldier's Monument Association, which was organized February 13, 1864, and in 1885 erected the Soldier's Monument in downtown Grand Rapids.

Hawley's brother Farnham was another Lyon hotelier. He was clerk for his Uncle Edward at the Michigan Exchange in Detroit until the outbreak of the Civil War when he was an early enlistee and given the rank of lieutenant on the quartermaster's staff of the 7th Michigan Infantry. He later served on the personal staff of General George A. Custer, and, according to a Kent County history, "established a splendid record for gallantry and fidelity." Farnham was discharged after the war with the rank of major. Following service he returned to Grand Rapids and ran the Rathbun House with his brother Charles, then in 1874 joined into partnership with A. V. Pantlind to lease and run the Morton House, a predecessor of the Pantlind Hotel which served Grand Rapids for more than a century, and, in the 1980s, was refurbished and incorporated as part of the Amway Grand Plaza, a hotel and convention complex. In 1876 Farnham moved to Saginaw and ran the Bancroft House, also serving as director on several bank boards. He was married to Carrie Merchant, the daughter of Joel Merchant, an early Grand Rapids baker and merchant. Farnham was a Democrat and served as a delegate to the national convention in 1892. He died February 14, 1911.

Farnham Lyon

James D. Lyon, a son of Truman H. Lyon Sr., was an early bookseller in Grand Rapids, opening a shop in 1848 at the east corner of Canal and Pearl. Having been brought up in post offices (his father was postmaster first at Lyons, then at Grand Rapids) he became a clerk in the Grand Rapids post office under his brother-in-law Harvey P. Yale. He was deputy postmaster under N. L. Avery, 1861-5, and also worked under postmaster Blair. In 1852 he was named constable for the City of Grand Rapids, was assessor in 1856, and marshal in 1872. He was treasurer of the city in 1869. He was a partner with Charles W.

Hathaway in the Edge Tool Making Co., which manufactured axes, also tools for coopers, carpenters and shingle makers, in a factory on the canal bank of Grand Rapids near the site of the old Lyon sawmill. In 1870 they were turning out 240 axes a day. In addition to his other enterprises he tried his hand at the hotel business and took over the Michigan Exchange in 1881 on the occasion of Edward's retirement. He also was landlord at the Lansing House in Lansing for a time.

Charles D. Lyon, another son of Truman H. Sr., served in the Third Michigan Infantry during the Civil War, rising to the rank of captain. He became involved with the book business joining Henry M. and Chester B. Hinsdill at 22 Canal Street, in Hinsdill Brothers, Inc. In 1870 when the Hinsdills were bought out by Charles W. Eaton the firm was known as Eaton & Lyon. (Several of the Michigan Eaton family were related to the Lyon family by marriage.) They adopted as their trademark a depiction of an owl based on a stuffed owl which sat in their shop. In 1881 the store was moved to 20-22 Monroe Street, and the partners were C. W. Eaton, C. D. Lyon, H. W. Beecher and J. L. Kymer. In 1881 the firm of Eaton, Lyon & Allen Printing Co. was doing $225,000 business annually. Charles D. was married to a daughter of William Sears.

EATON & LYON,

(Successors to H. M. Hinsdill,)

22 Canal Street,

BOOKSELLERS & STATIONERS

And Dealers in

PAPER HANGINGS.

A grandson of Truman H. Lyon Sr., Fred D. Lyon, son of Darwin B. Lyon, who had died of illness contracted during the Civil War, was a Western Union messenger early in life, and after some time in Detroit he returned to Grand Rapids and became chief operator of the telephone company. His widowed mother married Carlos Burchand, a tailor, and Fred learned the tailoring trade from his step father, likely with some assistance from his Grandfather Lyon who had been a cloth dresser. Fred took over the Burchand tailoring business in 1877. He was married in 1876 to May Graham.

Edward Lyon

Edward Lyon, a brother of Truman H., was an early sailor on Lake Champlain, serving ten years on the steam packet *Franklin* which plied between Whitehall, New York, and St. Johns, Canada. He visited Michigan in 1828-9, but invested instead, about 1833, in the Franklin Hotel, Cleveland, Ohio. He sold his interest in the hotel to Benjamin Harrington in 1836, and, while visiting relatives in New York, wrote Lucius, in a letter dated February 12, 1836, that he and his wife had $4000 and "wish to invest $3000 in some kind of business and apply to you for advice what to do." Lucius recommended that he go to Lyons, in Ionia County and become a merchant. When they were nearly packed ready to leave for Lyons Edward read about the number of Indians that he would encounter in the wilderness of Michigan and became increasingly concerned about primitive conditions. When his brother Truman balked at leaving New York, Edward and his wife went only as far as Detroit, where he opened a store and acquired a house on Jefferson Avenue. Within a year Truman and family arrived in Michigan and went on to Lyons, and Edward and family joined them and opened a second store there. They grew to like the place very much, but struggled financially. He wrote in January of 1839 that unless economic matters improved "I should be obliged to go to some other place. This I do not like to do. My mind was made up when I came here never to leave it. I found it a pleasant place as you recommended to me, and I still find it to be so and would like to remain here if I could make a living." He struggled on for another year, but eventually he assigned his property and house to settle debts and moved to Detroit. He ran the National Hotel, beginning in April 1840, but had problems because the people he was buying it from wanted it back, and tried to foreclose whenever he fell behind on payments, which, in the tight economy of the times, happened often. Edward had refurnished the hotel in 1840 and each time he missed a payment they would put a lien on some of the furniture. First they took the public room furniture, then the bedding, carpets and cookstoves. Edward had friends in the East who were willing to help and they put new furniture into the hotel so it could remain open. The antagonists filled a warehouse with furniture they had confiscated in payment of debt, but they could not get their hotel back, "which made them so mad they hardly know what to do with themselves," Edward wrote Lucius, April 17, 1842. Anti-saloon sentiment was growing, and May 26, 1842, Edward wrote, "I have taken the Liquors out of my bar and do not sell any more. . . . I think perhaps it will be a good thing for me in relation to business . . . as the Temperance people have said they will do all they can for me and to sustain the house." He hung on at the National until January 1, 1847, when he bought the Michigan Exchange on Shelby and Woodbridge Streets near the river in downtown Detroit. He ran the hotel until his retirement in May of 1881 associated with various other individuals, including nephews Farnham and James D. Lyon, sons of his brother Truman; George W. Thayer, son of his step-sister Pamelia; and Homer Barstow, son of his sister Lorain. A 1918 biography called him "for nearly half a century one of the best known hotel proprietors in Michigan," and notes that, "He was peculiarly adapted by nature for his business, possessing urbanity of manner, energy, and the tact so essential to highest success." Edward served as alderman from the Fourth Ward in 1853 and 1854. He was appointed by the citizens of Detroit in 1862 to a committee charged with raising money to pay bounties to encourage young men of the city to enlist in the Union Army. He and his wife Martha contributed bell number 8 in a nine bell chime erected in October of 1864 at Christ Church, an Episcopal church on Jefferson Avenue in Detroit. He was appointed in 1881 a lifetime trustee for St. Luke's Hospital, Church Home, and Orphanage on Fort Street in Detroit. Edward became a wealthy and influential citizen in Detroit and in addition to his quarters at the hotel had a large home on Jefferson Avenue. In 1865 he built a grand summer home on Grosse Ile, an island in the Detroit River, and later became a legal resident of the island. On an 1876 plat map he owns 160 acres about in the middle of the west shore of the island, just south of the old schoolhouse. He was interested in grape culture and the *Free Press* of June 14, 1874 speaks of his "extensive vineyard of Delawares, Ionias, and Concords." When his grape house was not busy with the pressing of grapes it was frequently used by local residents as an opera house. Using local people the productions were elaborately done, with scenery, costumes and printed programs, and drew audiences from the mainland.

A program from Lyon's Opera House

An epilogue for one of the plays notes:

> We view this Lyon Opera House with pride,
> Which draws the people from the other side;
> From Trenton, from Detroit and Wyandotte,
> And e'en from Malden, where a queen they've got.

They all are drawn to this most charming spot. . .

Edward had also made a number of investments in Florida real estate and before retirement built a summer home in Crescent City, Florida. He died at his home in Florida, February 29, 1884.

Homer Augustus Barstow, born August 18, 1817, was the eldest son and second child of Heman and Lorain (Lyon) Barstow. His mother was the firstborn of Timothy and Mary (Hawley) Lyon. Lorain (sometimes called Laura) resided in Vermont her entire life and died in Shelburne, January 27, 1857. Homer visited Lyons in the fall of 1838 when he was about 20 but stayed only a short time. In January of 1839, Edward wrote, "Homer has left for Buffalo and will return to Vermont where I think he will always remain, for he is a home boy." Despite the prediction Barstow returned at least as far as Detroit about 1840 and worked for a time in Edward's hotel although he was back in Vermont by 1846. He returned again by 1848 and was associated with Edward in the hotel business at the Michigan Exchange. On July 26, 1849, Homer was married in Detroit to 15-year-old Julia Elizabeth Estep of Cincinnati, Ohio. She died January 24, 1852, in their rooms at the Michigan Exchange and the funeral was held at the home of his uncle, Edward Lyon, on Jefferson Avenue. Homer purchased land on Grosse Ile prior to the Civil War and built a home there. When the old hotel on the island was destroyed by fire he offered "his large experience in hotel management" to a local group who proposed to build a new structure. Shortly afterwards he was seriously injured when a gun accidentally discharged while he was hunting on Canard Creek, Canada. During the Civil War he was part of the island militia and rumored to be enamored of the local schoolteacher. Shortly after the war he sold his land on Grosse Ile to his Uncle Edward.

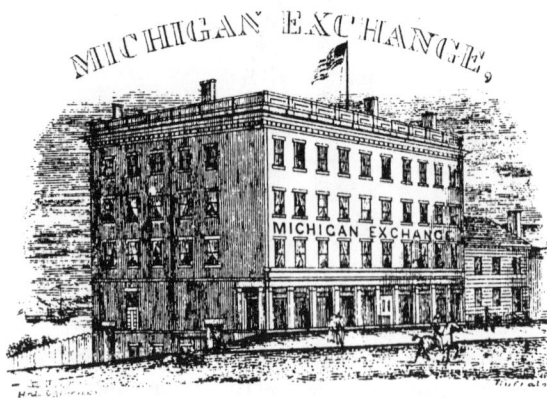

Detroit

Three sisters of Homer also moved to Michigan. Laura Barstow, born August 12, 1819, was married to William Brown Nash, and died in Detroit, January 22, 1892. Three of her sons, William Brown Nash, George R. Nash and Homer W. Nash were later active in southern Michigan. Miranda Levina Barstow, born September 7, 1827, was married to Martin A. Nash, later moved to Michigan and died in Belding. Marietta Esther Barstow was married to Solon Hinsdill Finney and lived for a time in Grand Rapids before moving to Easton, Michigan.

David Irish married Lenora Lyon and moved to Michigan in 1836. He was a clerk in Edward Lyon's store in Detroit and then Lyons, and afterward a storekeeper in his own establishment at Lyons. He bought a half section of land in Clinton County in 1836 next door to land owned by James W. Tabor, but had sold it to Tabor by 1840. David was the last of the first-generation Lyon family to reside at Lyons. He was later postmaster of Ionia. Irish was clerk of Ionia County in 1844 when he was recommended by Lucius Lyon to fill a vacancy in the Ionia land office after his first recommendation, Frederick Hall, had been rejected "for no other reason than because he is a Democrat." Lyon wrote to the president that although Irish is "in politics a Democrat of the State rights school, he is mild and conciliatory in his intercourse with men and commands the respect and esteem of all parties." The nomination of Irish was also rejected. Eventually Thomas Fitzgerald of St. Joseph filled the post.

Dan Lyon was a boat captain and plied the waters of Lake Champlain for many years before working for a short time on the Great Lakes. In the 1840s he gave his stepbrother Lucius money to purchase land in Wisconsin for him, and a letter dated December 26, 1845 indicates that he was expecting to move there in the spring of 1846. In September of 1850 when Asa Lyon, Dan's stepfather, died in Rochester, New York, one of his last requests was to be buried in Vermont. Dan made arrangements to pick up the body by boat in New York and convey it to the landing at Burlington, Vermont, where it was met by wagon and taken to the cemetery.

Gaius S. Deane and his wife Maria (Lyon) Deane, arrived in Michigan in 1837 and lived first in Lyons, and perhaps Ada. Shortly after 1840 they moved to Grand Rapids where Deane assisted with the salt works and other Lyon projects. He wrote Lucius October 18, 1845, that he would continue to care for his business in Grand Rapids until Lucius came to town, but "I have made my calculations for other business as soon as we can have a settlement." He later ran a small foundry and was a manufacturer and dealer in castings. Deane served on the board of education of District No. 1, was a trustee of the Division Street M. E. Church in 1844 and an early officer in the Bible Society.

He was treasurer of the Kent County Agricultural Society in 1864. The Baxter history of Grand Rapids notes, "He was a thoroughly upright man who enjoyed the highest respect and most implicit confidence of his fellow citizens." The Deane home in Grand Rapids was located at 158 Washington Street.

G. S. DEANE & SON,
Manufacturers and Dealers in all kinds of
☞Agricultural Implements and Machinery.
Ware Rooms, Corner Canal and Bridge Sts.   Foundry on Canal, (East side,)
Grand Rapids, -   -   - Michigan.

Tory and Sidney Smith, who arrived in 1837 and settled at Ada, were sons of Lucius's mother's sister Mary (Atwater) Smith who was later his second stepmother, his father's third wife. Sidney was the first supervisor of Ada Township and served on the County Board of Supervisors from that township 1838-9, and again in 1843. When the settlement at Ada folded, Sidney moved to Grand Rapids where he was elected treasurer of Kent County in 1843. He died in Grand Rapids on December 3, 1844. His daughter, Mary Ada, married Grand Rapids lawyer James Miller and the couple was later active in the Grand Rapids Swedenborgian Church. Tory Smith moved near the end of 1838 from his home near the bridge in Ada to the north side of the Grand River. He remained in Ionia County until his death October 6, 1870.

Ira Lyon, a younger brother (or at least half-brother) of Lucius's father Asa, was working at a cooper shop in Pike County, New York, alongside his nephew, Orson Lyon, in 1827. In a Kalamazoo County history it is recorded that Ira and family, "came to Michigan in 1828 in a wagon drawn by oxen." He wrote his nephew, Lucius, in April of 1834, that he had moved to Michigan and had purchased a small place "on the Saganaw turnpik thirteen miles west of north from Pontiac village." He continued, that he regretted that "I had not moved when you requested me to, you recommended the Country to be a verry fine for farming and likewis for my trade I did not think as much of it as I ought to have done." Lucius must have written or visited him shortly after receiving the letter. Correspondence shows that he was working on the Lyon farms in Ionia County by 1835, and was installed as manager of Lucius's property in the Schoolcraft area of Kalamazoo County by 1836. Ira, his wife, Anna (Lewis) Lyon, and seven children are recorded in the 1840 census in Brady Township, Kalamazoo County. This family may have been the occupants of the "large house" that Lucius was building in 1835 in Schoolcraft. In Schoolcraft there is a traditional story that Lucius Lyon built a home there for his mother. The story may have risen around the house that he built for his aunt and uncle although actually his Uncle Ira was a year younger than Lucius. Ira was a delegate from Kalamazoo

302

County to the "frostbitten convention" in Ann Arbor, December 14 and 15, 1836, which finally ratified the Congressional proposal for Michigan statehood. After Lucius lost the farms near Schoolcraft, Ira was hired by the Bronsons in June of 1841 to be their farm manager and agent in that portion of Kalamazoo County, but he died October 11, 1841, following a two-week illness.

One of Ira and Anna Lyon's nine children, son Lucius V. Lyon, was one of the first white children born in Schoolcraft, March 6, 1837. He attended the local schools and then went on to Baptist Seminary working his way through as a janitor. Although he had recently married, he enlisted in the Union Army during the Civil War serving first in Company C of the 6th Michigan Infantry, a unit he was mustered into August 20, 1861. "On the results of a rigid examination" he was discharged in October of 1863 from the 6th Infantry to accept a commission as Second Lieutenant of the 73rd Colored Regiment of New Orleans, the Twelfth Corps d'Afrique. His regiment patrolled the Alabama River, blockading cotton shipments out of the south, always on the lookout for Confederate infiltrators. For a period during the war he was also sent north as a recruiter. During service he rose to the rank of first lieutenant and it is recorded that Lucius V. "handled the colored troops with great tact and wisdom." On his return from the war he bought a farm in Brady Township, Kalamazoo County, and he served as justice of the peace, pension claims agent, and in several other local offices. One county history states, "In politics he is a Republican, active and vigilant in the councils of his party, and received as one of its valued leaders."

George A. Robinson, a cousin, first ran a store in Ypsilanti. He was seriously ill in 1837 and went to Lyons to live with the Tabors. Throughout the winter several letters written to various family members mentioned that they did not expect George to see another spring. He surprised them by recovering and moved to Ada for a short time. When those lands were lost he went on to Grand Rapids where he was one of the Lyons who worked hard in the business of salt manufacture. He had serious eye trouble and lost his vision for a time. In 1845 he and his wife Julia (Withey) Robinson returned to Vermont to stay with other members of his family while his eye problems mended. He returned to Michigan in 1848.

Isaac Newton Higbee came to Michigan in 1836 and hung around Schoolcraft and Lyons until January of 1838 waiting for appointment as a deputy surveyor. He worked in Wisconsin and Iowa territories, in the beginning as an assistant to Orson Lyon, later, on his own. He returned to Detroit in 1845 to work with Lucius in the surveyor general's office but after two years "got unsteady" and left. In 1849 he was doing a little surveying and causing political trouble for some of Lucius's friends in Wisconsin and Iowa Territory. It was rumored that he later headed for California although he eventually returned to the lead mine district.

Luman R. Atwater

Luman R. Atwater arrived at the settlement of Lyons in 1837 with Gaius and Maria (Lyon) Deane and worked as a carpenter. He was son of Thomas Atwater, brother of Lucius's mother. A biography lists Luman Atwater's occupation as mechanic, but adds that he "has followed a variety of occupations and professions always with strictest honesty and propriety." He moved to Grand Rapids in 1843 and worked as a machinist and plow maker for Stone, Deane & Co. He was a devout Methodist and was active in the first Methodist church in Grand Rapids and instrumental in organizing the second. He was one of the organizers and vice-president of the Kent County Bible Society, established in 1846 to study Scripture and distribute Bibles. An "unswerving prohibitionist," he was an organizer of the Lodge of Good Templars (a temperance imitation of the popular Knights Templars) in the 1860s. He held several minor political offices including Director of the Poor in 1855 for the City of Grand Rapids; Collector for the 2nd Ward of Grand Rapids, 1888; charter board member of the Fulton Street Cemetery Association, and member of the Board of Education for District No. 1, Grand Rapids. In the early 1870s he was an organizer and officer of the Old Settler's Association. Luman Atwater died July 23, 1892.

L. R. ATWATER,

NOTARY PUBLIC,

Represents the following Reliable Companies:

Great Western—Grand Rapids Branch	Capital	$1,000,000
Lamar—Grand Rapids Branch	"	1,000,000
Sun, Cleveland, O.	"	200,000
Buffalo German, Buffalo	"	200,000
Lumberman's, Chicago	"	200,000

27 CANAL STREET,

GRAND RAPIDS, - - MICHIGAN.

James W. Tabor, the husband of Lucius's sister, Esther, was a farmer in Vermont. In a letter dated February 28, 1834, Lucretia wrote Lucius that Tabor "has the western fever, as the phrase is, most violently." On behalf of Tabor she asked Lucius where an enterprising farmer might make a living and he advised Tabor to move to Lyons, in Ionia Township. On February 23, 1836, Tabor wrote that he had sold his farm and most of his household goods and would start as soon as navigation was open, "though Esther is afraid that she shall get a little homesick." In the 1840 census he is listed in Ionia County with two females under five, one male child between five and ten, one female child between 10 and 15, and with two males 15-20, two males 20-30, two females 20-30, and one male 30-40. It is clear that Tabor had brought his own work force. The home they built in Lyons must have been one of considerable proportions. Esther wrote Lucretia in 1838 that they had selected a large sunny room in the front of the new house for her when she arrived from Vermont and were outfitting another room for Lucius to use when he came to Lyons. Tabor was a good worker and may have been one of the best businessmen in the family, but was treated with a certain distance. The family, including Esther, always called him "Mr. Tabor" in their letters. George Robinson, who spent most of the winter of 1837-8 at their house, near death, wrote Lucius, "Mr. Tabor is a Whig in principle and I believe he voted the Whig ticket throughout at the last election." Tabor ran the Lyon farms in Ionia County until the land was lost in the Bronson settlement. Shortly after his arrival in Michigan he had purchased the eastern half of section 18, Lebanon Township, in the northwest corner of Clinton County near Hubbardston, a settlement which straddles the Ionia-

Clinton County line which was begun by former Vermonter James R. Langdon in 1836. On September 26, 1836, the same day that Tabor purchased his land, David Irish, husband of Esther's step-sister Maria, purchased the west half of section 18. Tabor entered the parcel at the land office paid for it with cash apparently from the proceeds of the sale of his Vermont farm. By June of 1840 Tabor owned the entire section. Most probably he traded his home, or other land in Lyons, to David Irish who remained in Lyons for at least another five years. By the 1850 census, James and Esther were living in Lebanon Township, Clinton County, with children, Walter J., 15; Martha, 13; Evelyn, 11; Julia A., 8; and John A., 1. He records his occupation as farmer, with real estate valued at $3,500. Tabor was elected supervisor of Lebanon Township, 1844 and 1848-50; clerk in 1851 and 1853, and justice of the peace 1842, 1845, 1847, 1849 and 1855. The couple eventually had seven daughters and five sons. James died in 1859 at the age of 52 years, and Esther and the remaining children at home moved to a house on Pleasant Street, Hubbardston. Esther died July 19, 1889 and was buried by her husband in the Hubbardston East Cemetery. Also in the Tabor plot are daughters, Sarah L., 1833-1843; Martha M. (Tabor) Walker, 1836-1915; Julia A. (Tabor) Homan, 1841-1926; Jane K., 1845-1848; Hellen C., 1850-55; and Ellen A., 1850-55. In the Hubbardston West Cemetery are sons Walter J., 1835-1896; Roderick D., 1828-1891; and John A., 1848-1912.

Orson Lyon began his working career at a barrel factory in New York State when he was about 20. In the fall of 1828 Lucius wrote Lucretia that Orson had quit barrel-making and hired out for four months as a farm laborer and adds, "I am afraid that for want of energy and a higher ambition, he will pursue groveling objects all his days -- This is a fault with many persons of good intellectual powers; for the want of energy to seek proper channels for their exercise, their talents lie dormant or are bestowed on unworthy objects." Lucius persuaded Orson to become qualified as a surveyor, and, in 1830 Orson arrived in Michigan Territory to assist his elder brother, first on the western side of Michigan and then west of Lake Michigan. When Lucius left for Congress in 1833, Orson continued work in southwest Wisconsin, and, later, in Iowa Territory. In 1838 Isaac Newton Higbee, a cousin, went west to assist Orson with the surveying. In a letter to Lucretia in 1838 Esther Tabor mentions that Orson had purchased a farm about 30 miles from Galena and it was his intention to go into farming. By April of 1845 he was married to Malinda Kimbrel and living on a small farm near Dubuque, Iowa. Later correspondence indicates that Orson was considering a move to California.

Lucius Lyon's sister, Lucretia, who was seven years his junior, seems always to have been a special friend. Lucius left Vermont when she was 15 and corresponded frequently with her giving advice on education, proper decorum for a young lady, and any other subject that she seemed to need. One letter, written in 1827 when she was nearly 20, notes that he had just received a letter from sister Merab saying that Lucretia was "dressing tight" (probably wearing snug fitting corsets) and not eating. He admonished, "'Dressing tight' may, and undoubtedly does much to impair health; going without eating will destroy life altogether. Why! I have known -- No! I have not known, but I have read of persons who died in consequences of such <u>foolishness</u>. And that not of choice, but of necessity. Now if in this land of <u>Milk</u> <u>and</u> <u>Honey</u> -- <u>Bread</u> and <u>Butter</u> -- <u>Pork</u> and <u>Potatoes</u> -- and all this, you should voluntarily and foolishly starve yourself to death; what a crime twould be!! Think! -- Reflect! -- Consider!" She was with him for at least a short time in Washington as there were several invitations, place cards, and letters in her papers addressed to "Miss Lyon" in Washington. Both she and Esther Tabor received invitations to an "Inauguration Ball to be held February 25, 1837 at Carusi's Saloon" in Washington to celebrate the inauguration of Martin Van Buren. One obituary of Lucretia Lyon stated, "Miss Lyon in her early life was accomplished and is described by those who remember her as rarely beautiful. She spent a season with her brother in Washington and was a popular belle."

There was talk and correspondence about Lucretia moving to Michigan at the time of the third marriage of her father in 1837, but she wrote in February that she would like to put off the trip until the next spring to give her a chance for further schooling, "I am too ignorant to go so soon." She eventually moved to Michigan in 1840 and spent most of a year at Lyons, then lived with various friends and family members in Kalamazoo and Detroit before moving to Grand Rapids. In Grand Rapids she lived in a small building at the corner of Kent and Bridge Streets which had been built in 1835 as a land office. When the land office was opened instead in Ionia the building became the business office for the Kent Co., and from 1837 to 1841 the home of the Grand River Bank. Her brother Lucius usually lived with her when he was in the city. She provided a home and laundry service for Lucius Thayer when he arrived in the early 1840s to attend the Grand Rapids Academy although both of them took their meals at the Deanes. Even after her move to Grand Rapids she frequently visited Edward and family at the hotel in Detroit, sister Esther in Clinton County, and others, especially when she was needed to help out in times of illness or birth confinements.

When Lucius left for Detroit in 1845 after his appointment as surveyor general, Lucretia remained in Grand Rapids. At this time money was very tight. After receiving a letter from her detailing a number of parties she had attended Lucius chided her for her high living while he was pinching pennies in Detroit. This elicited a six-page epistle from her detailing her frugal ways. She said that she was "here yet in your old office." She had given up boarding at the Deane's because they had other obligations and in order to save the money, and she was cooking for herself on the old box stove in the office. Because there was no pump or running water within the building, she had to haul water for cooking, washing, and laundry. Since there was no back door she was forced to bring the water by the pailful through the front door, a task she did before dawn so she would not be seen. She wrote February 17, 1846, that she had sold some of the clothes he had left behind and had lived quite well for several months on the $6.39 that she had received for them. Lucretia was fond of parties and the trappings of high society, and she wrote Lucius during a stay at Edward's hotel in Detroit that she spent most of her time keeping her party dress in repair.

Former office used as residence in Grand Rapids

Pamelia Thayer lived with Lucretia in Grand Rapids for at least a year after her arrival in Michigan, and after Pamelia moved to Detroit to be with her son, Washington, in 1850, Lucretia traded houses with Lucius Thayer, and the Coffinberry family, friends from church, lived with her "or rather I with them" in the second of the two houses that were owned by Lucius. Her concern at the time was the furnishing of the parlor. She wrote her brother, March 31, 1850, "Mr. Coffinberry has not the means of furnishing the parlor for the comfortable reception of company; and as the greater number of <u>fashionable</u> people that visit the house, will probably come on my account, they will think I <u>ought</u> to do it, and I think myself that I <u>ought</u> but cannot without getting myself in debt." She asks Lucius for a carpet and perhaps a card table that he no longer needs in Detroit and adds, "I will get a carpenter to make some cheap lounges which I will cushion with cotton and cover with chintz." Before heading north for his last surveying trip he sent her a number of pieces of unneeded furniture, much to her delight. At least two houses in Grand Rapids were deeded to Lucretia before the death of Lucius, and the rent from the buildings seems to have been her sole source of income. She kept careful records, detailing the rooms each renter had leased and payments made. Cash was not always necessary; her records show that on March 20, 1854, Benjamin Eaton paid his rent with "a half pound of butter, a half pound of dried raisins, and a partial making of one calico dress." In addition to the former office, she served as landlord for the "Pannell House" and the "Old Brewery House." John Pannell was the first brewer in the city, arriving in Grand Rapids in 1836 and setting up a small brewery on the east side of Kent Street, north of Lyon Street, at the base of Prospect Hill. In her rent book Lucretia also kept a written account of books borrowed by others.

An 1875 Grand Rapids City Directory lists her as "Miss Lucretia Lyon, scientist." Her address is given as 96 Kent Street. One possible explanation for the occupation named in the directory is the historical record that Wright L. Coffinberry was, during that period, engaged in excavating some Indian mounds near the Grand River under the auspices of the Kent Scientific Institute. It is likely that Lucretia was assisting in the work. Grand Rapids attorney Dwight Goss wrote later that she lived alone for nearly 40 years in a little house on Kent Street between Crescent Avenue and East Bridge Street, "always ready to discuss in an entertaining way, the old days when Grand Rapids was a frontier village and she was a belle in Washington society."

In the 1880 census Lucretia is recorded as an "inmate" at the United Benevolent Association home, an institution designed as a charity home "for the friendless and destitute" at the corner of Lyon and College. Her short obituary in the Grand Rapids paper at the time of her death December 16, 1893, indicates that she had lived the last year of her life at Butterworth Hospital "that in her old age she might receive the best and tenderest of care." The funeral was held from the house of her nephew, George W. Thayer, at the corner of North Ionia and Hastings, a site that would be directly under the present interstate highway in downtown Grand Rapids. She was buried in the Lyon plot in Elmwood Cemetery, Detroit.

One of the strangest stories about Lucretia that was retold at her death concerns a note that was given to her in 1857 by George M. Pullman, the well-known railroad car manufacturer, for rent on one of her houses when he ran a furniture store in Grand Rapids. After she moved to the U.B.A. house she showed it to Grand Rapids attorney Dwight Goss and asked him to see if he could collect on it as she needed the money. He wrote Pullman and eventually called on him in his office in Chicago where he headed one of the biggest companies in America. Goss reported later that at first Pullman shrugged off the note and told Goss he could not legally collect it in Illinois. Goss became angry and, faced with this reaction, Pullman "turned pleasant." He agreed that it was his signature on the note although he could not recall anything about the circumstances nor could he remember ever having met Lucretia Lyon. Pullman said he would honor the note if Goss would write him the full particulars about how the debt was incurred. Goss did this, but no reply was received and Lucretia died a year or two afterwards. The uncollected note is still in her papers in the Bentley Library, Ann Arbor.

According to a story in the *Michigan Tradesman* of November 18, 1894, her nephew, George W. Thayer, had gone through Lucretia's house shortly before her death and saved some old letters, but he had sold 800 pounds of other miscellaneous papers to a junk dealer for a penny a pound. A friend hearing of the sale "immediately raided the junk shop to look things over. Many extremely rare and interesting documents were found relating to the early history of Michigan." Most of the papers were reclaimed from the junk dealer at two cents a pound.

A second story of the means by which many of the Lyon papers were saved involves Caroline P. Campbell, wife of Michigan lawyer James H. Campbell. Mrs. Campbell saw a State of Michigan seal on a flag which she felt was not a true representation. The flag-maker told her that the design "was not stable," and she then began writing to various state agencies to determine what kind of seal they were using on official stationery. This led to a search for the original design. Aware that Lucius Lyon had headed the committee at the constitutional convention of 1835 which had moved for the adoption of the official state seal, she contacted George W. Thayer who was then living in Grand Rapids, seeking the original drawing. He invited her to peruse the thousands of documents left by his Uncle Lucius which were housed in his barn. Mrs. Campbell found the answer to her state seal question elsewhere, but she remained interested in the documents that Thayer was saving and sent a representative of the Kent Scientific Institute to look at the collection. "He returned at once saying that there were thousands of letters and documents. They were in barrels, carpet bags, desks and on the floor. Many had been nibbled at by rats and mice," she wrote later. She made a date in August of 1914 to visit Washington's barn, dressed in old clothes, to go through the collection.

She later wrote, "Pending that date I was out of the city for a few days. The afternoon of my return when attending a reception, I learned that Mr. Thayer's barn had burned August 8, 1914. Later that afternoon I met Mr. Thayer at the home of Mr. Thomas Hefferan. After my expression of distress to him over the fire he said, 'There, there, my child! There are enough left to occupy you for the rest of your life.'" He explained that when the fire began Mr. Sargent, the man from the Kent Institute who had evaluated the collection for her, rushed over and had the papers shoveled into barrels to preserve them although a few were lost, and others were burned around the edges.

Thayer gave the barrels to Mrs. Campbell, to "look them over at your leisure." She spent many years working with the letters, organizing and cleaning off the worst of the mice-nibbled edges and burned places. Most of them were eventually given to the William L. Clements Library in Ann Arbor where they form part of their collection on the Northwest Territory and early Michigan.

* * * * *

During his financial difficulties, in 1843, Lucius Lyon had written his father:

"I have known what it is to be rich as well as poor, and with reference to happiness, do not think there is so much difference as most people imagine between the two states of poverty and riches. I have lived long enough and had experience enough to know that, constituted as I am, all the real happiness that I can ever enjoy in the present life must arise from the consciousness of having done good in the world, either to my friends, my country or mankind at large so that the world may be improved in some way and to some extent at least by my agency and exertion. I desire to know when I die, and before I die, that I have not lived in vain; and in all that I do, I keep this object constantly in view. I am therefore, less desirous to be rich than to be useful; and it does not grieve me to be poor so long as I know that my labor is not lost to the world."

311

Source Notes

Major repositories for Lucius Lyon papers include the William L. Clements Library, University of Michigan, Ann Arbor; Michigan Historical Collection, Bentley Historical Library, Ann Arbor; and Burton Historical Collection, Detroit Public Library, Detroit. There are also letters in two published sources, "Letters of Lucius Lyon," edited by L. G. Stuart in Michigan Pioneer and Historical Collections, XXVII, p. 412-606, and Territorial Papers, edited by Clarence E. Carter. All of these sources are hereafter given abbreviated citations. Newspaper articles fully identified in the text are not noted here.

Pg. 6 "My motto is. . ." LL in article about saltmaking, written in 1838, copy in Lyon Papers, Clements.

1 "An Eminently Useful Citizen"

Pg. 7 "No man in Michigan. . ." Charles Moore, *History of Michigan*, I, p. 341.
"Fifty years. . ." George W. Thayer, "Life of Senator Lucius Lyon" MPHC XXVII, p. 404.

Pg. 9 "Mr. Lyon was . . ." *History of Kent County*, p. 196-7.
"Soon will. . ." LL to Lucretia Lyon, Aug. 21, 1825(?), Stuart, p. 439.

2 New England Roots

Family history of the Lyon family is drawn from papers left by Lucretia Lyon, now in the Michigan Historical Collection, Bentley Historical Library, and a typescript of the family records in the Asa Lyon 2nd Bible, recorded in published Antrim County Records.

Pg. 11 "a robust. . ." Thayer, op. cit., p. 405.
"from an excellent. . ." ibid.

Pg. 14 "Tell me. . ." LL to Lucretia Lyon, Oct. 19, 1833, Stuart p. 449.
"You need not. . ." Lucretia Lyon to LL, Sept. 14, 1836, Lyon Papers, Clements.
"It is yet. . ." Lucretia Lyon to LL, Aug. 19, 1836, Lyon Papers, Clements.
"I notice what. . ." LL to Lucretia Lyon, Sept. 5, 1836, Lyon Family Papers, Bentley.
"I mentioned. . ." Mary Smith to Asa Lyon, Nov. 5, 1836, Lyon Papers, Clements.

Pg. 16 "He was 5 feet. . " Bert Klopfer in Charles Fuller's *Historic Michigan*, I, p. 337.
"nearly perfect" Thayer, "From Vermont to Lake Superior in 1845," MPHC XXX, p. 551.
"He was a man. . ." Thayer, "Life of Senator Lucius Lyon," MPHC XXVII, p. 411.

Pg. 17 "quick, active. . ." Klopfer, op. cit., p. 336.
"Dear Sir. Allow me. . ." Ezra Mack to Solomon Sibley, April 24, 1822, Solomon Sibley Papers, Burton.

Pg. 18 "He could only. . ." Thayer, op. cit., p. 410.

3 Educator

Pg. 21 "quite short. . ." George C. Bates, "By-Gones of Detroit," MPHC XXII, p. 324.

"It should be borne. . ." Silas Farmer, *History of Detroit and Early Michigan,* p. 186.

Pg. 23 Bill from Mansion House, Lyon Papers, Burton.
"So here I am. . ." LL to Lucretia Lyon, Aug. 21, 1825(?), Stuart, p. 439.
"author of. . ." LL to Lucretia Lyon, July 4, 1828, Stuart, p. 442.

Pg. 24 "Reading, Writing. . ." Sister Mary Rosalita, *Education in Detroit Prior to 1850,* p. 185.

Pg. 25 "Any boy. . ." Lancaster as quoted in Rosalita, p. 189
"This school had. . ." B. O. Williams, "My Recollections of the Early Schools of Detroit," MPHC V, p. 549-50.

Pg. 27 "Finding it impossible. . ." LL to Stevens T. Mason, July 10, 1839, Stuart, p. 524.
"And now my dear. . ." LL to Lucretia, Sept. 25, 1826, Stuart, p. 441.

Pg. 28 "to prevent. . ." LL to Lucretia, Nov. 24, 1830, Stuart, p. 444.
The story of Lyon's first meeting with Douglass Houghton is related in Moore, p. 441, as well as numerous Houghton biographies.

Pg. 29 LL to Samuel Williams seeking material for lyceum speech, Jan. 27, 1831, Samuel Williams Papers, Clements.
"No duty. . ." Schoolcraft, *Personal Memoirs of a Residence of Thirty Years with the Indian Tribes on the American Frontier,* p. 341.

Pg. 30 Lyon's manuscript description of Jonathan Kearsley's service in the War of 1812, apparently as related by Kearsley, is in the Lyon Papers, Clements.

4 Deputy Surveyor

This account of the surveying done by Lucius Lyon and associates between 1823 and 1833 is drawn from copies of surveying contracts in the Lyon Papers, Clements; summaries published in various county histories; and field notes of the surveys, now in the possession of the State Archives of Michigan, Lansing.

Pg. 31 "I am employed. . ." LL to Solomon Sibley, Jan. 16, 1823, Solomon Sibley Papers, Burton.

Pg. 32 "I accompanied. . ." LL to George Graham, April 25, 1828, Lyon Papers, Clements.
"The Territory. . ." LL to Garrad Burritt, Nov. 10, 1822, Stuart, p. 438.

Pg. 33 "If I can. . ." Cadwallader Washburn, quoted in the Galena (Illinois) Museum.

Pg. 34 "to faithfully. . ." LL's oath as surveyor, July 2, 1823, State of Michigan Archives, Lansing.
"the meander. . ." LL to William Woodbridge, July 8, 1823, William Woodbridge Papers, Burton.
"further employment. . ." Solomon Sibley to Edward Tiffin, Nov. 24, 1823, Carter, XI, p. 420.

Pg. 36 "disinterested person" Petition is printed, MPHC XII, 553, (where date is wrongly

given as 1814).
"designing men" Edward Tiffin to George Graham, Feb. 11, 1826, Carter, XI p. 950-1.
"Forks, Grand River" Bill LL to Rix Robinson, April 10, 1826, Lyon Papers, Burton.

Pg. 37 "As I have not. . ." LL to Edward Tiffin, Dec. 21, 1826, Carter, XI, p. 1019.
"bilious fever" LL to Samuel Williams, Sept. 27, 1826, Samuel Williams Papers, Clements.
"where three or four. . ." LL to Lucretia Lyon, September 25, 1826, Lyon Family Papers, Bentley.
"almost impervious. . ." LL to Edward Tiffin, Sept. 8, 1827, Carter, XI, p. 1117.

Pg. 39 "Having understood. . ." LL to Edward Tiffin, Feb. 7, 1828, Lyon Papers, Clements.
"$2 a mile" Edward Tiffin to LL, Feb. 16, 1828, Lyon Papers, Clements.
"The inevitable. . ." LL to Lewis Cass, Feb. 27, 1828, Lyon Papers, Clements.

Pg. 40 "Looking on. . ." LL to S. W. Dexter, April 14, 1828, Lyon Papers, Clements.
"Yesterday. . ." LL to Samuel Williams, May 11, 1828, Samuel Williams Papers, Clements.
"as I am now. . ." LL to Lucretia Lyon, June 8, 1828, Lyon Family Papers, Bentley.
"shall proceed. . ." LL to Edward Tiffin, June 12, 1828, Carter, XI, p. 1187
"go up the Fox River. . ." LL to Lucretia Lyon, July 4, 1828, Stuart, p. 442.
"as formation. . ." LL to A. E. Wing, Jan. 4, 1829, Carter, XI, p. 1236.

Pg. 41 "a primitive sort. . ." Morgan L. Martin, "Narrative of Morgan L. Martin," Collections of the State Historical Society of Wisconsin XI, p. 397.

Pg. 43 " to the western. . ." LL to Lucretia Lyon, July 4, 1828, Stuart, p. 442.
"scarcity of provisions. . ." LL to Edward Tiffin, April 25 1829, Carter, XII, p. 37.
"Wilderness of the St. Joseph. . ." LL to Samuel Bayard Oct. 10, 1829, Lyon Papers, Clements.
Contract and correspondence concerning Fort Gratiot Lighthouse in Lyon Papers, Clements.

Pg. 45 "the whole. . ." LL to John Johnson, April 27, 1829, John Johnson Papers, Bentley.
"The truth is. . ." LL to Lucretia Lyon, Feb. 4, 1830, Lyon Family Papers, Bentley.

Pg. 46 "my young professor. . ." LL to Lucretia Lyon, Nov. 24, 1830, Stuart, p. 444.
"Sir, at a time. . ." LL to M. T. Williams, July 26, 1831, Carter, XII, p. 313.
"the shortest passage. . ." LL to John Johnson, Aug. 7, 1831, John Johnson Papers, Bentley.

Pg. 47 Notes on trees. . . LL to William Lytle, Dec. 6, 1830, Carter, XII, p. 217.
"The township of. . ." *Allegan and Barry County History,* p. 293.

Pg. 49 "in whose fidelity. . ." Elijah Hayward to M. T. Williams, Aug. 18, 1831, Carter, XII, p. 340.

Pg. 50 "Foot of the Illinois. . ." LL to M. T. Williams, Oct. 16, 1831, Carter, XII, p. 357.
"this is the first. . ." LL to M. T. Williams, Nov. 5, 1831, Carter, XII, p. 376.
"It is almost. . ." LL to M. T. Williams, Dec. 3, 1831, Carter, XII, p. 390.

Pg. 51 "and leave. . ." LL to M. T. Williams, March 28, 1832, Carter, XII, p. 459.

Pg. 52 "Our work. . ." Edwin Jerome, "Incidents in the Black Hawk War," MPHC I, p. 48-51.
"the State boundary. . ." LL to M. T. Williams, May 18, 1832, Carter, XII, p. 477-8.

Pg. 53 "My health. . ." LL to Lucretia Lyon, Oct. 13, 1832, Stuart, p. 445.

Pg. 54 Letter to Gov. Reynold quoted in *The Galenian*, Dec. 5, 1832.
"if my interest. . ." LL to Lucretia Lyon, May 24, 1833, Stuart, p. 446.

5 Territorial Delegate to Congress

Pg. 57 The account of the Democratic Convention of 1833 was recorded in a newspaper article LL sent to his father, and reprinted in Stuart, p. 448.
"I am about. . ." LL to Lucretia Lyon, May 24, 1833, Stuart, p. 447.

Pg. 58 "the office should. . ." White, op. cit., p. 329.

Pg. 59 "the writer witnessed. . ." Jerome, op. cit., p. 51.

Pg. 60 "nearly all. . ." Addison Philleo to LL, Aug. 26, 1833, Lyon Papers, Clements.

Pg. 61 "there is no act. . ." Democratic Free Press, July 3, 1833.

Pg. 62 "This result. . ." Reprinted from the Schnectady Whig in the Democratic Free Press, Aug. 7, 1833.
"We are delighted. . ." Reprinted from the Cincinnati Republic in the Democratic Free Press, Aug. 14, 1833.
"With the promise. . ." Democratic Free Press, Sept. 4, 1833.
"I can well imagine. . ." John P. Sheldon to LL, Oct. 7, 1833, Lyon Papers, Clements.

Pg. 63 "I suppose you. . ." Samuel Williams to LL, Dec. 14, 1833, Lyon Papers, Clements.

The listing of bills introduced by Lyon during his service as Territorial Delegate is gleaned from the Congressional Globe, a predecessor of the Congressional Record, which recorded the transactions of Congress and some of the debates; from petitions and other correspondence, and from letters printed in Carter's collection of Territorial Papers. Unless otherwise noted quotations from the Congressional Globe are contained in the record of proceedings for the day cited.

Pg. 65 "It will be. . ." LL to Joel Sutherland, Feb. 19, 1834, Carter, XII, p. 737-8.
"If lighthouses. . ." LL to J. Sutherland, Feb. 19, 1834, Carter, XII, p. 736.

Pg. 66 "Your valued. . ." LL to John P. Shelton, May 19, 1834, John P. Sheldon Papers, Burton.

Pg. 67 "I am now. . ." LL to William Woodbridge, May 14, 1834, William Woodbridge Papers, Burton.
"The committee. . ." LL to John P. Sheldon, May 19, 1834, John P. Sheldon Papers, Burton.
Several apparently unused copies of the form letter are in the Lyon Papers, Clements, a copy of the pamphlet is in the Library of Michigan, Lansing.

Pg. 69 "I need not recur. . ." Utley, *Michigan as a Province, Territory and State,* p. 301.

"Mr. Lyon objected. . ." Congressional Globe record for June 11, 1834, and more debate on the following day.

Pg. 70 "necessary and. . ." LL to Lewis Williams, March 17, 1834, Carter, XII, p.753.

Pg. 71 "The bill for. . ." LL to John P. Sheldon, July 5, 1834, John P. Sheldon Papers, Burton.

Pg. 72 "I look for. . ." LL to John Johnson, Sept. 15, 1834, John Johnson Papers, Bentley.
"I doubt whether. . ." *Correspondence of Andrew Jackson,* p. 284.
"I shall consider. . ." Stevens T. Mason to LL, Nov. 24, 1834, Lyon Papers, Clements.

Pg. 73 "as the time. . ." LL to Andrew Jackson, Feb. 12, 1835, Carter, XII, p. 855, also undated copy in the Lyon Papers, Clements.
"a bill was. . ." Stevens T. Mason to LL, Dec. 5, 1834, Lyon Papers, Clements.
"confines the selection. . ." Stevens T. Mason to LL, Dec. 28, 1834, Lyon Papers, Clements.
"I beg leave. . ." LL to John M. Clayton, Dec. 12, 1834, Lyon Papers, Clements.
"Notice will. . ." John M. Clayton to LL, Dec. 17, 1834, Lyon Papers, Clements.
"I was deputed. . ." Letter from S. F. Vinton, quoted in a letter to the editor of the Menoninee Enterprise written by Lewis S. Patrick, published Feb., 1895, copy in the L. S. Patrick Papers, State Historical Society of Wisconsin Archives, Madison.

Pg.. 74 "The case. . ." LL to Democratic Free Press, Dec. 19, 1833, Lyon Papers, Clements.
"Understanding that. . ." Petition to Senate, Jan. 7, 1835, Lyon Papers, Clements.

Pg. 75 "I can inform. . ." Anthony McKey to LL, Dec. 22, 1834, Lyon Papers, Clements.
"The western. . ." L. J. Daniels to LL, Dec. 24, 1834, Lyon Papers, Clements.
"the result. . ." Capt. A. Talcott to LL, Jan. 31, 1835, Lyon Papers, Clements.

Pg. 76 "he understood. . ." Congressional Globe report for Feb. 20, 1835.
"though in pecuniary. . ." John S. Barry to LL, Feb. 6, 1835, Lyon Papers, Clements.

Pg. 77 "Messrs. J. Q. Adams. . ." LL to William Woodbridge, Feb. 5, 1835, William Woodbridge Papers, Burton.
"March 18. . ." *The Diary of John Quincy Adams, 1794-1845,* p. 457.

6 Constitutional Convention

Pg. 79 "Not knowing. . ." Thomas C. Sheldon to LL, March 15, 1835, Lyon Papers, Clements.
"by allmost. . ." Thomas C. Sheldon to LL, April 15, 1835, Lyon Papers, Clements.
"I am highly. . ." P. R. Toll to LL, April 21, 1835, Lyon Papers, Clements.

Pg. 80 "the approbation. . ." Petition to LL, May 7, 1835, Lyon Papers, Clements.
"As to any. . ." Lewis Cass to LL, April 29, 1835, Lyon Papers, Clements.

Pg. 81 "Lyon's influence. . ." Harold Dorr, *Michigan Constitutional Convention,* p. 21-2.
Proceedings, debates, and rules of the Constitutional Convention of Michigan, 1835, are taken from the published proceedings of the convention unless otherwise noted.

Pg. 82 "to inquire. . ." Democratic Free Press, June 3, 1835.

Pg. 83 Introduction of State Seal, in Journals of Convention, also "Old Seals and the State Seal of Michigan," by Mrs. Marie B. Ferrey, p. 305-338, MPHC XXX, and "The Great Seal and Coat of Arms of Michigan," by W. J. Beal, p. 339-343, MPHC XXX.

Pg. 85 Debate about vote for Indians, Democratic Free Press, June 3, 1835.
"The whole subject. . ." LL to Col. Geo. Wm. Boyd, Dec. 29, 1835, Stuart, p. 468.

Pg. 88 "Within a week. . ." LL to Lucretia Lyon, Oct. 9, 1835, Stuart, p. 450.
"I am happy. . ." J. Jay Langdon to LL, May 15, 1835, Lyon Papers, Clements.
"I saw. . ." Mrs. Josiah F. Polk to LL, Nov. 4, 1835, Lyon Papers, Clements.

Pg. 89 "John Norvell. . ." LL to H. D. Gilpin, Nov. 16, 1835, Lyon Papers, Burton.

7 Senator from Michigan

Pg. 90 Letters written before leaving Detroit, Stuart, p. 463.
"I shall leave. . ." LL to Edwin Crosswill, Nov. 15, 1835, Stuart, p. 462.
"The Legislature. . ." LL to H. D. Gilpin, Nov. 16, 1835, Lyon Papers, Clements.

Pg. 91 "a fatiguing. . ." LL to John S. Horner, Nov. 29, 1835, Stuart, p. 464.

Pg. 92 "I find. . ." LL to E. D. Ellis, Dec. 6, 1835, Stuart, p. 464 [where name is wrongly given as John T. Mason. The two men, John T. Mason, father of Stevens T. Mason, and John Y. Mason, representative from Virginia, were distantly related.]

Pg. 95 "I need not. . ." LL to C. K. Green, Dec. 27, 1835, Stuart, p. 467.

Pg. 96 "Situated as. . ." LL to A. E. Wing, Dec. 27, 1835, Stuart, p. 468.
"The committees. . ." LL to O. D. Richardson, Jan. 3, 1835, Stuart, p. 470.

Pg. 97 "Never in. . ." John Quincy Adams quoted in Utley and Cutcheon, op. cit., II, p. 358.
"communicate this. . ." Stevens T. Mason to Lewis Cass, Aug. 16, 1835, Stevens T. Mason Papers, Bentley.
"That letter. . ." Stevens T. Mason to LL, Jan. 4, 1835, Lyon Papers, Clements.

Pg. 98 "there is a bad. . ." Stevens T. Mason to LL, Jan. 25, 1836, Lyon Papers, Clements.
"Things look. . ." LL to Charles W. Whipple, Jan. 3, 1836, Stuart, p. 470.
"Will you write. . ." LL to David White, Jan. 17, 1836, Stuart, p. 473.
"post master of. . ." PM Gen. William J. Barry to LL, Apr. 9, 1835, Lyon Papers, Clements.

Pg. 99 "Tommorrow I. . ." LL to Charles W. Whipple, Jan. 31, 1836, Stuart, p. 474.
"The essence. . ." Copy of speech in the Stevens T. Mason Papers, Bentley.
"I fear. . ." LL to Stevens T. Mason, Feb. 28, 1836, Stuart, p. 482.
"If Michigan be. . ." Letter written by S. F. Vinton, quoted in a letter to the editory of the Menominee Enterprise by Lewis S. Patrick, published February, 1896, copy in the Patrick Papers, State Historical Society of Wisconsin Archives, Madison.

Pg. 100 "I thank you. . ." LL to Col. D. Goodwin, Feb. 4, 1836, Stuart, p. 475.

Pg. 101 "The corruption. . ." LL to Dr. A. Phileo, Feb. 18, 1836, Stuart, p. 477-8.
"If you can. . ." E. D. Ellis to LL, March 15, 1836, Lyon Papers, Clements.
"remonstrating. . ." Letter written by S. F. Vinton, quoted in a letter to the editor of the Menominee Enterprise by Lewis S. Patrick, published February, 1896, copy in the L. S. Patrick Papers, State Historical Society of Wisconsin Archives, Madison.

Pg. 102 "it seems to me. . ." LL to Andrew Mack, Feb. 21, 1836, Stuart, p. 478-9.
"My course. . ." LL to C. K. Green, Feb. 25, 1836, Stuart, p. 481.
"Reports have. . ." LL to James Kingsley, March 2, 1836, Stuart, p. 483.
"I send. . ." LL to Z. Pitcher, March 12, 1836, Stuart, p. 485.
"It is now. . ." LL to D. Goodwin, March 27, 1836, Stuart, p. 490.
"Humiliating. . ." LL to Thomas C. Sheldon, April 3, 1836, Stuart, p. 494-5.

Pg. 103 "We can chose. . .: E. D. Ellis to LL, May 15, 1836, Lyon Papers, Clements.
"the anomalous. . ." John Garland to LL, Nov. 13, 1836, Lyon Papers, Clements.

Pg. 104 "We have as. . ." LL to Alpheus Felch, Dec. 23, 1836, Felch Papers, Bentley.
President Jackson's message to Congress, Congressional Globe proceedings for Dec. 27, 1836, with debate following.

Pg. 105 "The legislature. . ." John Almy to LL, Jan. 9, 1837, Lyon Papers, Clements.
"is not admitted. . ." Mark Norris to LL, Jan. 30, 1837, Norris Family Papers, Bentley.

Pg. 106 "Permit me. . ." M. Sterling to LL, Jan. 30, 1837, Lyon Papers, Clements.

Pg. 107 "We have just. . ." Sidney Smith to LL, Feb. 13, 1837, Lyon Papers, Clements.

Pg. 107-9, the debate with Clay and Calhoun is reported in the Congressional Globe, Appendix for the 1836-7 session, p. 138-9.

Pg. 109 "The state. . ." LL to William Woodbridge, Apr. 25, 1838, William Woodbridge Papers, Burton.
"I am well. . ." LL to Nathan M. Thomas, Jan. 7, 1838, Nathan M. Thomas Papers,Bentley.

Pg. 110 "What slaves. . ." LL to Mary Tott, Jan. 19, 1839, Stuart, p. 516.

Pg. 111 "I arrived. . ." LL to Stevens T. Mason, Oct. 20, 1838, copy in Lyon Papers, Clements.

Pg. 112 "I would not. . ." William A. Richmond to LL, Sept. 3, 1838, Lyon Papers, Clements.
"Mr. Norvell. . ." LL to T. C. Sheldon, Jan. 28, 1839, Stuart, p. 516.
"There are many. . ." E. F. Cook to LL, Jan. 30, 1839, Lyon Papers, Clements.
"If you fail. . ." W. A. Richmond to LL, Dec. 2, 1838, Lyon Papers, Clements.
"You seemed to be. . ." LL to Sheldon McKnight, Feb. 4, 1839, Stuart, p. 517.
"There is still. . ." Isaac Q. Adams to LL, Feb. 4, 1839, Lyon Papers, Clements.

Pg. 113 "No result. . ." Joseph Vickery to LL, Feb 12, 1839, Lyon Papers, Clements.
"Goodwin is. . ." Sheldon McKnight to LL, Jan. 9, 1839, Lyon Papers, Clements.
"If you are. . ." Thomas Fitzgerald to LL, Feb. 12, 1839, Lyon Papers, Clements.

"The result. . ." LL to S. H. Webb, Feb. 24, 1839, Stuart, p. 518.
Pg. 114 "without agreeing. . ." LL to Charles C. Hascall, March 7, 1839, Stuart, p. 519.
"I arrived. . ." LL to Edward Lyon, Jan. 24, 1840, Stuart, p. 529.
"my whole time. . ." LL to John P. Richardson, Nov. 29, 1839, Stuart, p. 528.

Pg. 115 Copies of letters sent by George Templeman concerning the Lafayette painting, May 26, 1837, Lyon Papers, Clements.
"When I was. . ." LL to George Templeman, June 30, 1840, Stuart, p. 536.
Henry H. Holt wrote an article in 1894, "History of Michigan's Portrait of General Lafayette," MPHC XXIX, p. 298-301.

Pg. 117 "Uncle Lucius. . ." Quoted in papers of Caroline Campbell (largely concerned with the preservation of Lucius Lyon correspondence), filed with Lyon Papers, Clements.

8 Indian Commissioner

Pg. 118 "Mr. Schoolcraft. . ." LL to Rix Robinson, Dec. 25, 1835, Stuart, p. 466.

Pg. 120 "On their way. . ." George H. White, "Sketch of the Life of Hon. Rix Robinson," MPHC XI, p. 186-202.
"Mr. Schoolcraft is. . ." LL to A. E. Wing, March 19, 1836, Stuart, p. 486.

Pg. 121 The Free Press article is reprinted in Stuart, p. 494.

Pg. 122 "he had no authority. . ." LL to C. C. Trowbridge, March 27, 1836, Stuart, p. 490.
"I have consulted. . ." LL to Leonard Slater, March 14, 1836, Stuart, p. 520.

Pg. 123 Contract as Indian commissioner dated April 9, 1839, in Lyon Papers, Clements.

Pg. 124 "an Indian killed. . ." T. Hartley Crawford to Henry Dodge, April 12, 1839, copy in Lyon Papers, Clements.
"I have had. . ." LL to T. Hartley Crawford, July 16, 1839, Lyon Papers, Clements.

Pg. 125 "I have nearly. . ." LL to Henry R. Schoolcraft, Aug. 18, 1839, Indian Agency Letters, State Archives of Michigan, Lansing.
"After the half. . ." LL to Robert Stuart, Nov. 17, 1839, Stuart, p. 526.

Pg. 126 "in the event. . ." LL to R. D. Turner, Feb. 17, 1840, Lucius Lyon Papers, State Historical Society of Wisconsin archives, Madison.
Account of Michigan-Wisconsin border disputes, Franklin R. Van Zandt, *Boundaries of the United States and the Several States,* p. 209-11.

9 Land Speculator

Land transactions not otherwise annotated are from land records, early county histories, and tax records of the areas being described, or from lists and comments in various Lyon correspondence.

Pg. 127 "This section. . ." LL to Garrad Burrit, Nov. 10, 1822, Stuart, p. 437-8.
Profitable deal of June-July, 1836, recorded in LL notebooks, Lyon Papers, Clements.
"without the necessity. . ." LL to Lucretia Lyon, Sept. 5, 1836, Lyon Family Papers,

Bentley.

Pg. 129 "The new Surveyor. . ." LL to John Johnson, Apr. 27, 1830, John Johnson Papers, Bentley.
"There are few. . ." Arthur Bronson to LL, Aug. 24, 1833, Lyon Papers, Clements.
Contract with Isaac Bronson, Oct. 24, 1834, in Lyon Papers, Clements.
"Do not mention. . ." Arthur Bronson to LL, Dec. 13, 1834, Lyon Papers, Clements.

Pg. 130 "I had met. . ." C. C. Trowbridge Memoirs, p. 33.
"the closest. . ." George C. Bates, op. cit., p. 379.
"I hope. . ." Charles Butler to LL, July 2, 1835, Lyon Papers, Clements.

Pg. 131 "at that small. . ." Orson Lyon to LL, Jan. 12, 1836, Lyon Papers, Clements.
"You will hardly. . ." Thomas C. Sheldon to LL, April 7, 1836, Lyon Papers, Clements.
"So great. . ." Isaac Barnes to LL, Feb. 28, 1836, Lyon Papers, Clements.

Pg. 132 "Judge Woodward. . ." LL to Asa Lyon, Sept. 25, 1826, Stuart, p. 441-2.
"I shall probably. . ." LL to Lucretia Lyon, Apr. 16, 1827, Lyon Family Papers, Bentley.
Account of meeting with Daniel B. Brown in History of Washtenaw, p. 969.
"in Ypsilanti. . ." George A. Robinson to LL, March 29, 1834, Lyon Papers, Clements.

Pg. 133 "A railroad. . ." Mark Norris to LL, Dec. 2, 1833, Norris Family Papers, Bentley.

Pg. 134 "If we are. . ." Mark Norris to LL, Sept. 30, 1835, Norris Family Papers, Bentley.
"I have surveyed. . ." Mark Norris to LL, Feb. 23, 1836, Norris Family Papers, Bentley.
"The engineer. . ." Mark Norris to LL, Dec. 22, 1837, Norris Family Papers, Bentley.
"The commissioners. . ." Mark Norris to LL, Dec. 24, 1837, Norris Family Papers, Bentley.
"Can I have. . ." Mark Norris to LL, Nov. 21, 1837, Lyon Papers, Clements.

Pg. 135 "Your offer. . ." LL to Mark Norris, Dec. 11, 1837, Norris Family Papers, Bentley.
"lend or procure. . ." Arthur Bronson to LL, Aug. 24, 1833, Lyon Papers, Clements.

Pg. 136 "The result of. . ." Arthur Bronson to LL, Aug. 24, 1833, Lyon Papers, Clements.
"though this is low. . ." LL to Arthur Bronson, Jan. 8, 1836, Stuart, p. 132.

Pg. 137 Purchase of lands near Saline, Orange Risdon to LL, Jan. 10, 1836, Lyon Papers, Clements.
Battle Creek transaction, MPHC V, p. 262, also V, p. 256.

Pg. 138 " I also own. . ." LL to Lucretia Lyon, Oct. 19, 1833, Stuart, p. 449.

Pg. 139 "I saddled. . ." E. Lakin Brown, "Autobiographical Notes," MPHC XXX, p. 454-5.

Pg. 140 "I found. . ." Letter from James Smith Jr. in Democratic Free Press, July 3, 1833.

Pg. 141 "In 1831. . ." Copy of the 1840 affadavit in Lyon Papers, Clements.
Power of attorney to Ira Lyon, Oct. 17, 1835, Lyon Papers, Clements.
Ira Lyon's letter about rails, Nov. 7, 1835, Lyon Papers, Clements.

Pg. 142 Letter with details of Bronson mortgage, from Hezekiah G. Wells to LL, Oct. 20, 1842, Lyon Papers, Clements.

Papers concerning early Kalamazoo land purchases in business file, Lyon Papers, Clements.

Pg. 143 "which was Saturday. . ." *History of Kalamazoo County, Michigan,* p. 254.
"Bronson. . ." LL to Lucretia Lyon, Oct. 19, 1833, Stuart, p. 448-9.

Pg. 144 "he asserts. . ." Cyren Burdick to LL, Dec. 23, 1833, Lyon Papers, Clements.
"This village. . ." Col. A. Edwards to LL, May 15, 1834, Lyon Papers, Clements.
"Mr. Sheldon. . ." Arthur Bronson to LL, June, 1835, Lyon Papers, Clements.
"neatest and. . ." T. C. Sheldon to LL, April 1836, Lyon Papers, Clements.
"The importance. . ." Epaphroditus Ransom to LL, March 25, 1836, Lyon Papers, Clements.

Pg. 145 "There is no. . ." Thomas C. Sheldon to LL, March 11, 1846, Lyon Papers, Clements.
The 1833 accusations and answers were published in the Detroit Democratic Free Press, July 3, 1833.

Pg. 146 Affadavit by A. S. Cotton dated Oct. 8, 1835, in Lyon Papers, Clements.

Pg. 147 "A large. . ." Arthur Bronson to LL, Aug. 24, 1833, Lyon Papers, Clements.
"I am afraid. . ." C. C. Trowbridge to LL, Dec. 3, 1833, Lyon Papers, Clements.

Pg. 148 "a jealous, selfish. . ." LL to Arthur Bronson, Oct. 12, 1835, Stuart, p. 459
"I ought to also. . ." LL to Arthur Bronson, Oct. 12, 1835, Stuart, p. 459.

Pg. 150 "Mr. Sargeant. . ." LL to Arthur Bronson, Oct. 12, 1835, Lyon Papers, Clements.
"Arthur Bronson. . .: LL to N. O. Sargeant, Dec. 5, 1835, Stuart, p. 464.
"Almy says. . ." George A. Robinson to LL, July 31, 1836, Lyon Papers, Clements.
"a large. . ." John Almy to LL, Oct. 15, 1835, Lyon Papers, Clements.
"Upon an examination. . ." William A. Richmond to LL, Nov. 24, 1836, Lyon Papers, Clements.

Pg. 151 "I hope you. . ." John Almy to LL, Dec. 4, 1836, Lyon Papers, Clements.

Pg. 152 "say at Washington. . ." John Almy to LL, Dec. 14, 1836, Lyon Papers, Clements.
"The extravagant. . ." William A. Richmond to LL, Mar. 1, 1837, Lyon Papers, Clements.
Description of Grand Rapids, John T. Blois, *Gazetteer for Michigan, 1838,* p. 292-3.

Pg. 154 "The office. . ." LL to J. W. Tyson, Jan. 21, 1844, Stuart, p. 567.
"Improvements. . ." Franklin Everett, *Memorials of the Grand River Valley,* p. 374.
"at the mercy. . ." LL to William Woodbridge, Apr. 4, 1842, William Woodbridge Papers, Burton.

Pg. 155 "There is intimation. . ." Frederic Bronson to LL, Dec. 18, 1844, Lyon Papers, Clements.
"we are likely. . ." K. Woodward to LL, Nov. 29, 1848, Lyon Papers, Clements.
"The people. . ." George Coggeshell to LL, May 23, 1849, Lyon Papers, Clements.
"but it was sold. . ." LL to H. Backus, Feb. 13, 1850, Lyon Papers, Clements.
Bronson vs. Orson Lyon et. al., copy in the Grand Rapids Library.

Pg. 156 "on Main. . ." Charles Thayer to LL, Aug. 7, 1835, Lyon Papers, Clements.
"I could not. . ." George A. Robinson to LL, July 31, 1836, Lyon Papers, Clements.
Purchase in Marshall area mentioned in MPHC I, p. 130.
"The purchasers. . ." MPHC II, p. 234.
Hillsdale County land, F. M. Holloway, "Hillsdale County from 1829 to 1836 Inclusive,"
MPHC I, p. 171-180.

Pg. 157 Land on Cass farm in Detroit, Lewis Cass to LL, July 10, 1843, Lyon Papers,
Clements.

Pg. 158 "it was no. . ." William G. Butler to LL, Dec. 20, 1833, Lyon Papers, Clements.
"The point. . ." Truman H. Lyon to LL, July 22, 1838, Lyon Papers, Clements.

Pg. 159 "Mr. Lyon was. . ." Oshea Wilder to Knowles Taylor, July 22, 1836, copy in Taylor
Letterbook, Burton.
"for doing justice. . ." LL to Thomas Fitzgerald, Sept. 26, 1843, Stuart, p. 562.

Pg. 160 "Some of the. . ." Thomas Fitzgerald to LL, Apr. 16, 1834, Lyon Papers, Clements.
"I hope. . ." Obed P. Lacy to LL, Aug. 21, 1842, Lyon Papers, Clements.

Pg. 161 "several lots. . ." LL to Thomas C. Sheldon, Sept. 6, 1832, Lyon Papers, Clements.

Pg. 162 "Your favor. . ." LL to Stevens T. Mason, Sept. 9, 1838, Lyon Papers, Clements.

Pg. 163 "As to the county. . ." Arthur Bronson to LL, Aug. 24, 1833, Lyon Papers,
Clements.
"I knew. . ." Catherine Leonard, "Early History of Lyons," copy in Library of Michigan.
"what the prospect. . ." Lucretia Lyon to LL, Jan. 13, 1834, Lyon Papers, Clements.
"I think. . ." LL to Edward Lyon, Feb. 24, 1836, Stuart, p. 481.

Pg. 164 "I am glad. . ." LL to James W. Tabor, Mar. 2, 1836, Stuart, p. 483.
"the offer. . ." Edward Lyon to LL, March 7, 1836, Lyon Papers, Clements.

Pg. 165 "I find by. . ." Edward Lyon to LL, March 21, 1836, Lyon Papers, Clements.
"I came here. . ." Giles Isham to LL, Apr. 8, 1836, Lyon Papers, Clements.

Pg. 166 "take measures for. . ." LL as quoted in a letter from Giles Isham, Apr. 8, 1836,
Lyon Papers, Clements.
"Brother Truman. . ." Edward Lyon to LL, May 15, 1836, Lyon Papers, Clements.
"Mr. Tabor searched. . ." Esther Tabor to LL, June 1, 1836, Lyon Papers, Clements.

Pg. 168 "been to Lyonsville. . ." J. W. Tabor to LL, June 12, 1836, Lyon Papers, Clements.
"I have. . ." Edward Lyon to LL, May 15, 1836, Lyon Papers, Clements.
"There is a great. . ." Edward Lyon to LL, June 4, 1836, Lyon Papers Clements.
"made so much. . ." Edward Lyon to LL, Nov. 14, 1836, Lyon Papers, Clements.
"got the boat. . ." Edward Lyon to LL, Dec. 18, 1835, Lyon Papers, Clements,

Pg. 169 "No one speaks. . ." Edward Lyon to LL, Dec. 29, 1836, Lyon Papers, Clements.
"I do not feel. . ." Truman Lyon to LL, Dec. 12, 1836, Lyon Papers, Clements.
"I can not. . ." Giles Isham to LL, Jan. 29, 1837, Lyon Papers, Clements.
"to a get into. . ." Luman R. Atwater to LL, March 13, 1837, Lyon Papers, Clements.

"amid tears. . ." Everett, op. cit., biographical sketches, p. 3.

Pg. 170 "I arrived. . ." LL to Lucretia Lyon, July 12, 1837, Stuart, p. 450.
"Cousin Luman. . ." Esther Tabor to Lucretia Lyon, July 13, 1838, Lyon Family Papers, Bentley.

Pg. 171 "D. S. Baldwin. . ." LL to Edward Lyon, Jan. 17, 1838, Stuart, p. 499.
"Goods needed. . ." Edward Lyon to LL, Feb. 26, 1837, Lyon Papers, Clements.
"entirely out. . ." Edward Lyon to LL, May 15, 1837, Lyon Papers, Clements.

Pg. 172 "We all feel. . ." Edward Lyon to LL, May 16, 1837, Lyon Papers, Clements.
Description of Lyons in John T. Blois, *Gazetteer for Michigan, 1838,* p. 315.
"invites me. . ." Truman Lyon to LL, March 10, 1836, Lyon Papers, Clements.
"a fine little cottage. . ." Everett, op. cit., p. 35.

Pg. 173 "We were lucky. . ." George H. Lyon to Asa Lyon, Sept. 25, 1838, Lyon Papers, Clements.

Pg. 174 "It makes me. . ." Edward Lyon to LL, Aug. 11, 1837, Lyon Papers, Clements.
"He was anxious. . ." Edward Lyon to LL, Jan. 10, 1839, Lyon Papers, Clements.
"take some public. . ." Edward Lyon to LL, Oct. 27, 1839, Lyon Papers, Clements.

Pg. 175 "I hope. . ." Truman Lyon to LL, Aug. 27, 1840, Lyon Papers, Clements.
"Truman H. Lyon. . .: George A. Robinson to LL, Jan. 13, 1841, Lyon Papaers Clements.
"I cannot. . ." Truman Lyon to LL, Feb. 21, 1841, Lyon Papers, Clements.
"I know. . ." LL to S. Yorke, Aug. 5, 1842, Stuart, p. 556.
"What!" Levi Bishop, "Recollections," MPHC I, p. 515, quoted in *Lyons-Muir, Michigan,* 1976, p. 5.

Pg. 176 Review of the voting on Lyons as state capital in 1847 is compiled from the proceedings as recorded in the House and Senate journals.

Pg. 177 "I had been. . ." P. R. Howe to LL, Feb., 1848, Lyon Papers, Clements.

Pg. 179 "But a very small. . ." Memorandum Book, Isaac Bronson Papers, Burton.
"at the Forks. . ." LL to Thomas C. Sheldon, Sept. 6, 1832, Lyon Papers, Clements.

Pg. 180 "You will recollect. . ." LL to Arthur Bronson, not dated, Stuart, p. 461.
"I think. . ." LL to Arthur Bronson, Oct. 15, 1835, Stuart, p. 460.
"Something ought. . ." LL to Arthur Bronson, Oct. 12, 1835, Lyon Papers, Clements.
Written authority to Hamilton S. Jackson, Oct. 19, 1835, Lyon Papers, Clements.
"And from what. . ." Hamilton S. Jackson to LL, Nov. 4, 1835, Lyon Papers, Clements.

Pg. 181 "unfit to manage. . ." John Almy to LL, Nov. 22, 1835, Lyon Papers, Clements.
"I can get no. . ." Hamilton S. Jackson to LL, Nov. 26, 1835, Lyon Papers, Clements.
"am determined. . ." Sidney Smith to LL, Sept. 11, 1835, Lyon Papers, Clements.
"You propose. . ." Sidney Smith to LL, Sept. 5, 1835, Lyon Papers, Clements.
"I deem. . ." Sidney Smith to LL, Oct. 5, 1836, Lyon Papers, Clements.

Pg. 183 "You will recollect. . ." Arthur Bronson to LL, Aug. 24, 1835, Lyon Papers, Clements.

"We have a new. . ." Sidney Smith to LL, Feb. 13, 1837, Lyon Papers, Clements.

Pg. 184 "found the tavern. . ." Sidney Smith to LL, June 15, 1837, Lyon Papers, Clements.
"I find. . ." Sidney Smith to LL, Jan. 20, 1837, Lyon Papers, Clements.
Description of Ada, Blois, op. cit., p. 21.

Pg. 185 "The severity. . ." Sidney Smith to LL, Dec. 28, 1838, Lyon Papers, Clements.
"100 acres of . . ." Ira Dennis to LL, May 29, 1847, Lyon Papers, Clements.

Pg. 186 "so I could. . ." Silas Bogg to LL, Oct. 4, 1851, Lyon Papers, Clements.
Naming of Lyon, *History of Oakland County,* 1877.

Pg. 187 Accounting of the 1835 Wisconsin land deal in Lyon Papers, business file,
Clements.

Pg. 188 "Cassville, in my. . ." LL to A. E. Wing, Jan. 4, 1829, Carter, XI, p. 1236.
"entered into. . ." Letter of L. J. Daniels, giving an account of the his proceedings in
relation to the purchase of lands at Cassville, April 4, 1836. Lyon Papers, Clements.

Pg. 189 "either to Green. . ." LL to John S. Horner, Jan. 17, 1836, Stuart, p. 473.
"The council is. . ." J. D. Doty to LL, Jan. 6, 1836, Lyon Papers, Clements.
"Let me entreat. . ." Arthur Bronson to LL, Feb. 5, 1836, Lyon Papers, Clements.
"has said he. . ." LL to Arthur Bronson, Feb. 10, 1836, Stuart, p. 477.
"It is doubtful. . ." LL to W. L. Newberry, Feb. 21, 1836, Stuart, p. 478.

Pg. 190 "I don't think. . ." LL to W. L. Newberry, March 28, 1836, Stuart, p. 491.
"I am on. . ." John S. Horner to LL, Apr. 7, 1836, Lyon Papers, Clements.
"I have now. . ." John S. Horner to LL, Apr. 24, 1836, Lyon Papers, Clements.
"however urgent. . ." Arthur Bronson to LL, Mar. 19, 1836, Lyon Papers, Clements.

Pg. 191 "The contest. . ." John S. Horner to LL, Nov. 5, 1838, Lyon Papers, Clements.
"If you can. . ." LL to G. V. Denniston, July 12, 1837, Lyon Papers, Clements.
"Times are dull. . ." G. V. Denniston, Feb. 22, 1841, Lyon Papers, Clements.
"formerly. . ." John Warren Hunt, *Wisconsin Gazetteer,* 1853.

Pg. 193 "Doty is not. . ." Henry R. Schoolcraft to LL, Apr. 18, 1844, Lyon Papers,
Clements.
"Mostly by. . ." I. A. Lapham, *Wisconsin: Its Geography, and Topography, History, Geology
and Mineralogy,* p. 174.

Pg. 194 "one hastily. . " From "A Canoe Voyage up the Minney-sotor, with an Account of
the Lead and Copper Regions of Wisconsin," written by Featherstonhaugh in 1847, and
quoted in David V. Mollenhoff, *Madison: A History of the Formative Years,* p. 60-1.
"I am glad. . ." S. Page to LL, July 31, 1836, Lyon Papers, Clements.
"I note. . ." Frederick Bronson to Arthur Bronson, Apr. 27, 1836, copy in Lyon Papers,
Clements.

Pg. 196 "in the neighborhood. . ." A. G. Ellis to LL, Dec. 11, 1843, Lyon Papers, Clements.
"on the island. . ." J. D. Doty to LL, Dec. 28, 1844, Lyon Papers, Clements.
"Williams says. . ." Arthur Bronson to LL, Apr. 27, 1836, Lyon Papers, Clements.
Letter from Thomas W. Sutherland concerning Koshkonong, Feb. 23, 1843, Lyon Papers,

Clements.

Six building lots in Green Bay, listed in Lyon's account book, Grand Rapids Museum archives.

The 1841 list of lands is in Lyon Papers, business file, Clements.

Fort Howard deal is described in Smith, p. 169-70.

Books of the Wisconsin Land Co. are in Grand Rapids Museum archives.

Pg. 198 "The crisis. . ." Arthur and Isaac Bronson to LL, June 30, 1836, Lyon Papers, Clements.

"suspend purchases" Arthur Bronson to LL, Oct. 17, 1836, Lyon Papers, Clements.

"As yet you. . ." David Page to LL, Dec. 28, 1843, Lyon Papers, Clements.

10 Scientific Farmer

Pg. 199 "You mention. . ." LL to Maj. John Biddle, Jan. 13, 1838, Stuart, p. 496.

Cost of fencing, plowing. . . Ll to Arthur Bronson, Oct. 15, 1835, Stuart, p. 460.

"I wish to. . ." LL to Giles Isham, Nov. 3, 1835, Stuart, p. 461.

"He is poor. . ." LL to Lucretia Lyon, Oct. 9, 1835, Lyon Family Papers, Bentley.

"all your arrangements. . ." LL to Ira Lyon, Nov. 16, 1835, Stuart, p. 463.

"Spring wheat. . ." Ira Lyon to LL, Jan. 28, 1838, Lyon Papers, Clements.

Pg. 200 "Our banks. . ." LL to Thomas T. Whittlesey, Oct. 25, 1839, Stuart, p. 525.

"which was. . ." LL to James W. Tabor, April 4, 1839, Stuart, p. 521.

"I am now. . ." LL to Sherman McLean, May 26, 1839, Stuart, p. 523.

"look as green. . ." Edward Lyon to LL, Oct. 25, 1839, Lyon Papers, Clements.

"I raised. . ." LL to John P. Richardson, Nov. 29, 1839, Stuart, p. 528.

Pg. 201 "fully satisfied. .." LL to H. L. Ellsworth, March 19, 1840, Stuart, p. 533.

"and expresses. . ." LL to T. H. Lyon, April 28, 1840, Stuart, p. 534-4.

Pg. 202 "which is said. . ." LL to Sidney Smith, Feb. 1, 1841, Stuart, p. 541.

"partook of some. . ." Lucretia Lyon to LL, Sept. 7, 1840, Lyon Papers, Clements.

Affadavit concerning mailing charges, J. W. Tabor, Oct. 15, 1840, Lyon Papers, Clements.

"I most devoutly. . ." L. Crittenden to LL, May 3, 1835, Lyon Papers, Clements.

Pg. 203 "It consists. . ." LL to Hiram Moore, May 4, 1839, Stuart, p. 523.

Pg. 204 "Mr. Moore has. . ." LL to Henry Ellsworth, Nov. 17, 1839, Stuart, p. 527.

Pg. 205 Contract with John Hascall, Aug. 6, 1841, Stuart, p. 543.

"We have had. . ." LL to Commissioner of Patents, Aug. 7, 1841, Stuart, p. 543.

"Two of the. . ." LL to Arthur Bronson, Aug. 15, 1841, Stuart, p. 544.

Pg. 206 Harvester stock lost under warrant, Isaac B. Lewis to LL, Oct. 11, 1843, Lyon Papers, Clements.

Letter to Gov. Mocton of Louisana, Oct. 31, 1845, Stuart, p. 604

"It could not. . ." Henry Bishop, "The Reason so Many Men are Out of Employment," MPHC XXIX, p. 219.

Pg. 207 Biography of T. T. Lyon from Charles W. Garfield, MPHC XXIX, p. 481-91.

11 Investor and Engineer

Pg. 208 History of the Detroit Hydraulic Company is largely from the account in Silas Farmer, *History of Detroit and Early Michigan,* p. 64-5, and a history of the waterworks by Robert E. Roberts, MPHC IV, p. 468-9.
"The company. . ." Roberts, op. cit., p. 468-9.

Pg. 209 "to explore. . ." Oshea Wilder to LL, Sept. 12, 1831, Lyon Papers, Clements.

Pg. 210 Account of Grand River Bank, Aug. 14, 1837, business file, Lyon Papers, Clements.

Pg. 211 "It is getting. . ." Sidney Smith to LL, Oct. 2, 1837, Lyon Papers, Clements.
"I am pretty. . ." Ernest B. Fisher, *Grand Rapids and Kent County History,* p. 477.

Pg. 212 "I am constructing. . ." LL to Lucretia Lyon, Oct. 9, 1835, Stuart, p. 449.
"the first ever. . ." LL to Arthur Bronson, Oct., 1835, Stuart, p. 461.
"Mr. Sergeant. . ." LL to Arthur Bronson, Oct. 12, 1835, Lyon Papers, Clements.
"Nathaniel. . ." Baxter, op. cit., p. 102.
"The length. . ." LL to Arthur Bronson, Oct 12, 1835, copy in the Lyon Papers, Clements.

Pg. 213 Description of Grand River and canals, Blois, op. cit., p. 292.

Pg. 214 "You will recollect. . ." LL to C. H. Taylor, Sept. 8, 1841, Stuart, p. 545-6.

Pg. 215 "suffering. . ." Stephen Hinsdill to LL, Aug. 24, 1845, Lyon Papers, Clements.
"but will shut. . ." Gaius S. Deane to LL, Sept. 1, 1845, Lyon Papers, Clements.
"Canal bank. . ." Note in saltworks record book, Grand Rapid Museum archives.
"would enhance. . ." Truman Lyon to LL, June 10, 1847, Lyon Papers, Clements.

Pg. 216 "The dam. . ." J. W. Pierce to LL, Oct. 1, 1849, Lyon Papers, Clements.
To pay $1,000 toward steamboat, LL to Lucretia Lyon, Oct. 9, 1835, Stuart, p. 449.
"N. O. Sargeant. . ." LL to David Carter, Feb. 28 1836, Stuart, p. 483.
Cost of boat, Oct. 27, 1836, Lyon Papers, business file, Clements.
"Yesterday. . ." Edward Lyon to LL, Dec. 8, 1837, Lyon Papers, Clements.

Pg. 217 "The boat. . ." Edward Lyon to LL, Feb. 26, 1837, Lyon Papers, Clements.
"Now it can no. . ." Edward Lyon to LL, Dec. 8, 1837, Lyon Papers, Clements.

Pg. 218 "All eyes. . ." Account of launch, dated Dec. 19, 1897, in scrapbook in Grand Rapids Library.
"a miserable. . ." Everett, op. cit., p. 10.
Notes from the Kanawha River visit in Lyon Papers, Clements.
"If a favorable. . ." O. Wilder to LL, Dec. 18, 1834, Lyon Papers, Clements.

Pg. 219 "We see pretty. . ." LL to C. H. Carroll, Jan. 7, 1840, Stuart, p. 529
Undated account in saltworks account book, Grand Rapids Museum archives.
"The well. . ." LL to Sidney Smith, Apr. 3, 1840, Stuart, p. 534.
Instructions for making salometer, LL to George A. Robinson, Sept. 18, 1840, Stuart, p. 537.

Pg. 220 "Little did. . ." George A. Robinson to LL, June 30, 1840, Lyon Papers, Clements.
"I wish. . ." George A. Robinson to LL, July 3, 1840, Lyon Papers, Clements.
"W. A. Richmond. . ." George A. Robinson to LL, July 11, 1840, Lyon Papers, Clements.
"I believe. . ." LL to George A. Robinson, Jan. 30, 1841, Stuart, p. 540.
"or within. . ." LL to Asa Lyon, May 12, 1841, Stuart, p. 542.

Pg. 221 "to prevail. . ." LL to Ansel Hulburt, Sept 12, 1841, Stuart, p. 546.
"You will see. . ." LL to Ansel Hulburt, Sept. 22, 1841, Stuart, p. 547.
"of a very. . ." Truman H. Lyon to LL, Sept. 2, 1841, Lyon Papers, Clements.

Pg. 222 "either the brine. . ." LL to Douglass Houghton, July 2, 1842, Stuart, p. 555.
"In your raising. . ." Douglass Houghton to LL, July 25, 1842, Lyon Papers, Clements.
"Your letter. . ." Douglass Houghton to LL, Oct. 26, 1843, Lyon Papers, Clements.

Pg. 223 "that the State. . ." Douglass Houghton to LL, Sept. 4, 1844, Lyon Papers, Clements.
"very inquisitive" George A. Robinson to LL, Feb. 4, 1842, Lyon Papers, Clements.
"The salt works. . ." Grand Rapids newspaper, Jan. 19, 1844.
"when we pump. . ." George A. Robinson to LL, Feb. 4, 1844, Lyon Papers, Clements.

Pg. 224 Report of earnings at saltworks, Lucretia Lyon to LL, Jan. 18, 1844, Lyon Papers, Clements.
"a drag. . ." Strong & Avery to LL, March, 1844, Lyon Papers, Clements.
"There has been. . ." Gaius S. Deane to LL, Sept. 1, 1845, Lyon Papers, Clements.
"Decay is going. . ." B. A. Parnell to LL, May 25, 1846, Lyon Papers, Clements.
"This community. . ." Gaius S. Deane to LL, May 2, 1846, Lyon Papers, Clements.
"I have not. . ." Lucius Thayer to LL, Oct. 23, 1848, Lyon Papers, Clements.

Pg. 225 "unforeseen. . ." Lucius Thayer to LL, March 21, 1849, Lyon Papers, Clements.
"a new and. . ." William A. Burt to LL, Sept. 10, 1836, Lyon Papers, Clements.
"I think. . ." William A. Burt to LL, Feb. 29, 1844, Lyon Papers, Clements.

Pg. 225 Account of assets, 1850, Lyon Papers, business file, Clements.
"He is a gentleman. . ." Charles Butler to LL, Dec. 13, 1833, Lyon Papers, Clements.
"Since I parted. . ." Allen Hutchins to LL, Jan. 20, 1833 [wrongly dated, should be 1834], Lyon Papers, Clements.

Pg. 227 "who did not. . ." Allen Hutchins to LL, Feb. 23, 1836, Lyon Papers, Clements.
"Mr. A. Hutchins. . ." Edward Lyon to LL, Jan. 2, 1838, Lyon Papers, Clements.
"I think. . ." LL to Allen Hutchins, Feb. 7, 1838, Stuart, p. 503.

Pg. 228 "full proof" LL to Allen Hutchins, Feb. 9, 1838, Stuart, p. 503-4.
"Nothing could. . ." LL to Sheldon McKnight, Mar. 9, 1838, Stuart, p. 504.
"he appears. . ." LL to D. Goodwin, Mar. 10, 1838, Stuart, p. 504-5.
"He is a great fool. . ." Edward Lyon to LL, Mar. 16, 1839, Lyon Papers, Clements.
"The enclosed. . ." Allen Hutchins to LL, June 22, 1838, Lyon Papers, Clements.

Pg. 229 "I thank you. . ." LL to Allen Hutchins, Mar. 16, 1839, Stuart, p. 521.
William A. Richmond appointed, LL to Ross Wilkins, Mar. 6, 1838, Ross Wilkins Papers, Burton.
"A verdict. . ." LL to Henry R. Schoolcraft, Oct. 22, 1844, Stuart, p. 592.

Pg. 230 "abundant resources. . ." H. R. Schoolcraft to LL, Nov. 7, 1844, Lyon Papers, Clements.

"When you have. . ." LL to I. N. Higbee, Oct. 11, 1840, Stuart, p. 538.
"I wrote to you. . ." LL to Morgan L. Martin, Jan. 24, 1836, Morgan L. Martin Papers, Neville Museum, Green Bay, Wisconsin, microfilm copy in State Historical Society of Wisconsin, Madison.

Pg. 231 "to cover. . ." LL to S. M. Johnson, Oct. 17, 1845, Stuart, p. 604.
"Interest in copper. . ." F. E. Phelps to LL, Nov. 26, 1846, Lyon Papers, Clements.

Pg. 232 "I am getting. . ." Lucius Thayer to LL, June 4, 1846, Lyon Papers, Clements.
"They found I. . ." Lucius Thayer to LL, June 23, 1847, Lyon Papers, Clements.
Analysis of ore showing some silver, March 12, 1848, Lyon Papers, Clements.

Pg. 233 "And now my dear. . ." Thomas Whittlesey to LL, June 13, 1846, Lyon Papers, Clements.
Balance sheet dated Mar. 1, 1840, Lyon Papers, business file, Clements.
"I have been. . ." LL to William Woodbridge, Jan. 6, 1842, William Woodbridge Papers, Burton.

Pg. 234 "Not loaning. . ." A. E. Bull to LL, March, 1842, Lyon Papers, Clements.
"I am sorry. . ." W. Truesdail, May 20, 1842, Lyon Papers, Clements.
"All the property. . ." LL to Thomas Fitzgerald, Sept.26, 1843, Stuart, p. 563.
Letter of introduction from Thomas T. Whittlesey to Phineas T. Barnum in Lyon Papers, Clements.

12 U. S. House of Representatives

Pg. 235 "I live. . ." Ll to Samuel J. Bayard, June 11, 1843, Stuart, p. 230.
"we shall live. . ." Edward Lyon to LL, Nov. 19, 1838, Lyon Papers, Clements.
"The people say. . ." S. M. Johnson to LL, Mar. 11, 1840, Lyon Papers, Clements.

Pg. 236 "Our county. . ." O. P. Lacey to LL, Aug. 14, 1843, Lyon Papers, Clements.
"The nomination. . ." LL to O. P. Lacey, Aug. 2, 1843, Stuart, p. 561.
"As you are. . ." LL to W. A. Richmond and H. P. Yale, Sept. 10, 1843, Stuart, p. 562.
"a tried. . ." Proceedings reported in the Democratic Free Press, Sept. 19, 1843.

Pg. 237 "Depriving this. . ." The Kalamazoo Gazette as quoted in the Grand Rapids Enquirer, Sept. 20, 1843.
"a common soldier . . ." Democratic Free Press.
"Mr. Lyon's. . ." Marshall Statesman as quoted in the Grand Rapids Enquirer, Sept. 20, 1843.

Pg. 238 "But if it were. . ." LL to O. P. Lacey, Oct. 27, 1843, Stuart, p. 563.
"My majority. . ." LL to Allen Goodrich, Nov. 14, 1843, Stuart, p. 564.

Pg. 239 "roads muddy. . ." LL to Lucretia Lyon, Dec. 22, 1843, Stuart, p. 565.
The account of debate and bills introduced by Representative Lyon is gleaned from the Congressional Globe account of proceedings and debate. Petition from citizens of Branch County are located in the petitions file, Lyon Papers, Clements.

Pg. 241 "it is almost. . ." LL to S. M. Johnson, Jan. 20, 1844, Stuart, p. 567.
"one-half of. . ." Ll to Samuel Yorke, Jan. 24, 1844, Stuart, p. 567.
"If Van Buren. . ." LL to W. S. Sherwood, Feb. 29, 1844, Stuart, p. 570.
"They generally. . ." LL to Thomas C. Sheldon, March 13, 1844, Stuart, p. 571.
"with whom. . ." LL to Lewis Cass, Apr. 6, 1844, Stuart, p. 574.
"drive from him. . ." LL to Lewis Cass, Apr. 29, 1844, Stuart, p. 577.
"it will be necessary. . ." LL to Lewis Cass, May 21, 1844, Stuart, p. 578.

Pg. 242 "I am obliged. . ." Lewis Cass to LL, May 9, 1844, Lyon Papers, Burton.
"indelicate. . ." Lewis Cass to LL, May 11, 1844, Lyon Papers, Burton.
"for the purpose. . . " Ll to Lewis Cass, May 19, 1844, Stuart, p. 582.
"I am so distant. . ." Lewis Cass to LL, May 12, 1844, Lyon Papers, Clements.
"Up to that. . ." LL to Lewis Cass, May 31, 1844, Stuart, p. 582-3.

Pg. 243 "thanks for. . ." Lewis Cass to LL, June 8, 1844, Lyon Papers, Clements.
"Among the. . ." LL to James K. Polk, June 7, 1844, Stuart, p. 584.

Pg. 244 "Col. Polk. . ." LL to Lucretia Lyon, Apr. 8, 1838, Stuart, p. 451.
"On one occasion. . ." Amos and Fanny Nelson, *Memorial of Sarah Childress Polk*, p. 33.
"full of enthusiasm. . ." S. M. Johnson to LL, June 8, 1844, Lyon Papers, Clements.
"entirely satisfactory. . ." Thomas Fitzgerald to LL, June 6, 1844, Lyon Papers, Clements.
"miserable, lonely. . ." LL to R. S. Wilson, June 25, 1844, Stuart, p. 586.

Pg. 245 "that I did. . ." LL to H. H. Comstock, Aug. 4, 1844, Stuart, p. 587.
"for the double. . ." LL to James B. Hunt, Aug. 23, 1844, Stuart, p. 591.
"Making it easier. . ." Proposal to President Tyler, Stuart, p. 585.

Pg. 246 "I thank you. . ." LL to N. Dunham, Mar. 30, 1844, Stuart, p. 573.
"I do not think. . ." H. H. Comstock to LL, Dec. 20, 1844, Lyon Papers, Clements.

Pg. 247 "It is a terrible. . ." Lewis Cass to LL, Dec. 26, 1844, Lyon Papers, Clements.
"Since writing. . ." C. G. Hammond to Gen. John Stockton, Dec. 28, 1844, copy in Lyon
     Papers, Clements.
"You may procure. . ." LL to W. A. Richmond, Jan. 2, 1845, Stuart, p. 595.

Pg. 248 "I have all along. . ." LL to Lewis Cass, Jan. 6, 1845, Stuart, p. 595-6.
"is generally. . ." W. A. Richmond to LL, Jan. 10, 1845, Lyon Papers, Clements.
"takes me. . ." LL to W. A. Richmond, Jan. 15, 1845, Stuart, p. 596.
"I came here. . ." W. A. Richmond to LL, Mar. 7, 1845, Lyon Papers, Clements.
"The legislature. . ." Adam L. Roof to LL, Mar. 7, 1845, Lyon Papers, Clements.

Pg. 249 "Major Edwards. . ." LL to W. A. Richmond, Mar. 7, 1845, Stuart, p. 598.
"Permit me. . ." LL to W. A. Richmond, Apr. 14, 1845, Stuart, p. 600.

Pg. 250 "I have seen. . ." W. A. Richmond to LL, May 6, 1845, Lyon Papers, Clements.
"I observe. . ." LL to S. M. Johnson, Dec. 25, 1844, Stuart, p. 595.
"The Genl. . ." W. A. Richmond to LL, Jan. 30, 1845, Lyon Papers, Clements.
"asked me. . ." Edward Brooks to LL, Mar. 21, 1844, Lyon Papers, Clements.

Pg. 251 "I have just. . ." LL to W. A. Richmond, Mar. 7, 1845, Stuart, p. 598.
"I have not. . ." LL to Lewis Cass, Mar. 31, 1845, Stuart, p. 598.

13 Surveyor General

Pg. 252 "bright and. . ." Dan Lyon to LL, Feb. 15, 1845, Lyon Papers, Clements.
"too young" G. W. Thayer to LL, Feb. 12, 1845, Lyon Papers, Clements.
"possessing. . ." Jason F. Walke to LL, Feb. 18, 1845, Lyon Papers, Clements.

Pg. 253 "I learned. . ." W. A. Richmond to LL, June 30, 1845, Lyon Papers, Clements.
"Lucius and. . ." Lucretia Lyon to LL, July 22, 1845, Lyon Papers, Clements.
"to fix upon. . ." LL to Hiram Burnham, July, 1845, Stuart, p. 602.

Pg. 254 "At the end. . ." George W. Thayer, "From Vermont to Lake Superior in 1845,"
    MPHC XXX, p. 550.
"There will be. . ." LL to O. Hungerford, April 1, 1844, Lyon Family Papers, Bentley.

Pg. 255 "I have appointed. . ." LL to Thomas S. Atlee, July-August(?), 1845, Stuart, p. 603.
Petition for Samuel Williams as Surveyor General in 1837, Samuel Williams Papers,
    Clements.
"got unsteady. . ." LL to Samuel Williams, Oct. 18, 1849, Samuel Williams Papers,
    Clements.

Pg. 256 Firewood order to Joseph P. Taylor, Oct. 11, 1845, Stuart, p. 604.
Farmer's encounter with Grant during Civil War, Farmer, op. cit., p. 106.

Pg. 257 "the solar compass. . ." LL to James Shields, Nov. 10, 1845, quoted in Albert C.
    White, *A History of the Rectangular Survey System,* p. 102.
"Your nomination. . ." Lewis Cass to LL, Jan. 5, 1846, Lyon Papers, Clements.
"You have. . ." Lewis Cass to LL, Jan. 6, 1846, Lyon Papers, Clements.
"Unforeseen. . ." May 15, 1848, Lyon Papers, Clements.

Pg. 258 "believed that. . ." Taylor quoted by K. Jack Bauer, *Zachary Taylor,* p. 238.
"immediate action. . ." Frederick Hall to LL, July 20, 1848, Lyon Papers, Clements.
"A change. . ." Samuel Williams to LL, Mar. 26, 1849, Lyon Papers, Clements.
"To estop. . ." Samuel Williams to LL, Apr,. 28, 1848, Samuel Williams Papers, Clements.

Pg. 259 "I have endeavored. . ." LL to Samuel Williams, Apr. 7, 1849, Samuel Williams
    Papers, Clements.
"on the advice. . ." LL to Samuel Williams, Oct. 18, 1849, Samuel Williams Papers,
    Clements.
"About two. . ." LL to Samuel Williams, Nov. 22, 1849, Samuel Williams Papers, Clements.
"I need not. . ." Alpheus Felch to LL, Dec. 29, 1849, Lyon Papers, Clements.

Pg. 260 "all efforts. . ." LL to Samuel Williams, May 11, 1850, Samuel Williams Papers,
    Clements.
The numerology chart and phrenology notes are in the Lyon Papers, Clements, which also
    has a listing of books Lyon owned including a copy of the *Book of the Mormons.*
"Since our. . ." Abiel Silver to LL, May 24, 1846, Lyon Papers, Clements.

Pg. 261 "You know. . ." LL to Lucretia Lyon, June 3, 1846, Stuart, p. 458.
"Nothing could. . ." Lucretia Lyon to LL, Aug. 2, 1846, Lyon Papers, Clements.
"That there is. . ." Arthur Carl Piepkorn, *Profiles in Belief,* p. 657-8.

Pg. 262 The Swedenborg dictionary that Lucius sent Lucretia, with his name on the flyleaf, is in the Lyon Family Papers, Bentley.

Pg. 263 "day time on. . ." A. E. Wing to LL, Apr. 30, 1847, Lyon Papers, Clements.
"I feel grateful. . ." John Allen to LL, Nov. 27, 1846, Lyon Papers, Clements.
"sound mind" George S. Frost to Alpheus Felch, Sept. 29, 1851, Felch Papers, Bentley.

Pg. 264 "A little spark. . ." Lucretia Lyon to LL, Mar. 7, 1847, Lyon Papers, Clements.
"Mr. Taylor. . ." Charles Shepherd to LL, Apr. 18, 1847, Lyon Papers, Clements.
"though I have. . ." LL to Samuel Williams, Apr. 7, 1849, Samuel Williams Papers, Clements.
"My way. . ." LL to John Allen, Jan. 24, 1848, John Allen Papers, Burton.

Pg. 265 List of meeting attendees at various New Church functions, George Field, *Memoirs, Incidents and Reminiscences of the Early History of the New Church.*
"I do not see. . ." Marguerite Beck Block, *The New Church in the New World*, p. 132.
"help his mind. . ." Charles W. Hopkins to LL, Feb. 24, 1846, with note dated Apr. 8, 1850, Lyon Papers, Clements.

Pg. 266 "Your extracts. . ." John Allen to LL, Dec. 19, 1849, Lyon Papers, Clements.
"clipped from. . ." Lucretia Lyon to LL, Oct. 29, 1846, Lyon Papers, Clements.
"a general favorite. . ." Lucretia Lyon to LL, Sept. 21, 1847, Lyon Papers, Clements.
"There is little. . ." LL to Jabez Fox, July 23, 1849, copy in Lyon Papers, Clements.

Pg. 267 "I thank you. . ." Lucretia Lyon to LL, Mar. 27, 1848, Lyon Papers, Clements.
"You say. . ." Pamelia Thayer to LL, Feb. 14, 1848, Lyon Papers, Clements.
"Phoebe says. . ." Pamelia Thayer to LL, Dec. 26, 1846, Lyon Papers, Clements.

Pg. 268 "In the beginning. . ." Field, op. cit., p. 216-7.

Pg. 269 "Alarmed and. . ." Baxter, op. cit., p. 346.
"Letters and. . ." Field, op. cit., p. 218.

Pg. 270 "Years ago. . ." Baxter, op. cit., p. 381.

14 Back to the Woods

Pg. 271 "believing. . ." LL to Samuel Williams, May 11, 1850, Samuel Williams Papers, Clements.
"all the political. . ." LL to Moses M. Strong, Dec. 5, 1835, Moses M. Strong Papers, State Historical Society of Wisconsin archives, Madison.
"Noble's name. . ." Lewis Cass to LL, Jan. 9, 1850, Lyon Papers, Clements.

Pg. 272 "Having turned. . ." LL to Alpheus Felch, Jan. 28, 1850, Alpheus Felch Papers, Burton.
"I wish. . ." Alpheus Felch to LL, Feb. 8, 1850, Lyon Papers, Clements.
"I have seen. . ." Frances H. Williamson to LL, May 10, 1848, Lyon Papers, Clements.

Pg. 273 Lucretia's debt repayment is described in a letter, Nov. 15, 1849, Lyon Papers, Clements.

Pg. 274 "if you do. . ." S. S. Shaw to LL, Mar. 29, 1850, Lyon Papers, Clements.

Lyon's second surveyor's oath is in the DNR file of the State Archives of Michigan, Lansing.

Letter from Robert H. Hunt, Apr. 26, 1850, Lyon Papers, Clements.

"for a long. . ." LL to Samuel Williams, May 11, 1850, Samuel Williams Papers, Clements.

"to draw off. . ." In 1850 there are several letters from W. N. Choate to LL, with herbal prescriptions, Lyon Papers, Clements.

Pg. 275 Field notebooks for the resurvey work done in 1850-1 are in the DNR collection, State Archives of Michigan.

"I was myself. . ." Account book, notebook file, Lyon Papers, Clements.

Pg. 277 Letter to Ross Wilkins, Feb. 9, 1851, Ross Wilkins Papers, Burton.

"Mr. Lyon. . ." Edward W. Barber, "Michigan Men in Congress from 1819 to 1861," MPHC XXXV, p. 455.

"was grateful. . ." Nathan B. Haswell, remarks at the Washington Lodge, Oct. 1, 1851, printed in the Burlington [Vermont] Courier, copy in Lyon Family Papers, Bentley.

Pg. 278 "I was in the company. . ." Barber, op. cit, p. 455.

"added greatly. . ." George S. Frost to Alpheus Felch, Sept. 29, 1851, Felch Papers, Bentley.

Pg. 280 "If we are. . ." LL to Lucretia Lyon, Dec. 22, 1844, Stuart, p. 458.

15 Home and Family

Pg. 281 "I know not. . ." LL to Lucretia Lyon, Oct. 13, 1832, Stuart, p. 445.

"I have neglected. . ." Stevens T. Mason to LL, Feb. 10, 1834, Lyon Papers, Clements.

Pg. 282 "By the bye. . ." Lucretia Lyon to LL, Mar. 23, 1834, Lyon Papers, Clements.

"As all. . ." W. L. Newberry to LL, Apr. 3, 1834, Lyon Papers, Burton.

"My Dear, Dear. . ." Lucretia Lyon to LL, May 10, 1834, Lyon Papers, Clements.

"He keeps. . ." Esther Tabor to Lucretia Lyon, Apr. 13, 1838, Lyon Family Papers, Bentley.

Pg. 283 "There is not. . ." LL to D. Goodwin, Feb. 25, 1838, Stuart, p. 506.

"I became. . ." LL to Lucretia Lyon, Aug. 22, 1838, Stuart, p. 454-5.

"You have carried. . ." Lucretia Lyon to LL, Sept. 14, 1838, Lyon Family Papers, Bentley.

"He has an. . ." LL to James Tabor, July 17, 1838, Lyon Family Papers, Clements.

Pg. 284 "I have added. . ." LL to Lucretia Lyon, Apr. 8, 1838, Stuart, p. 452.

"If Mr. L. . ." Emily V. Mason to LL, undated, Lyon Papers, Clements.

"Capt. Howard. . ." Emily V. Mason to Kate Mason, Jan. 26, 1835, John T. Mason Papers, Burton.

Pg. 285 "Emily Mason. . ." Sarah McKnight to LL, Feb. 23, 1837, Lyon Papers, Clemens.

"Miss Emily. . ." John B. Murray to LL, June 24, 1838, Lyon Papers, Clements.

"You cannot imagine. . ." Lucretia Lyon to LL, Nov. 13, 1838, Lyon Family Papers, Bentley.

"one of the finest. . ." LL to Lucretia Lyon, Apr. 25, 1839, Stuart, p. 456.

"Mrs. Bonnycastle. . ." LL to Lucretia Lyon, Jan. 1, 1844, Stuart, p. 457.

Pg. 286 "Miss Mason. . ." Sarah McKnight to LL, Dec. 30, 1844, Lyon Papers, Clements.
"Well no doubt. . ." Friend Palmer, *Early Days In Detroit,* p. 778.

Pg. 287 Later life of Emily Mason from Kent Sagendorf, *Stevens Thomson Mason,* p. 421.
"You deserve. . ." Anonymous to LL, undated 1836, Lyon Papers, Clements.
"and she hopes. . ." Frances H. Williamson to LL, May 28, 1838, Lyon Papers, Clements.
"I look upon. . ." LL to Lucretia, Apr. 25, 1839, Stuart, p. 456.

Pg. 288 "I must have. . ." Mignonette to LL, Dec. 25, 1849, Lyon Papers, Clements.
"Pray pardon. . ." Anonymous to LL, Feb., 1850(?), business file, Lyon Papers, Clements.
"You have forbidden. . ." Mignonette to LL, Apr. 10, 1850, Lyon Papers, Clements.

Pg. 289 "as I saw. . ." Mignonette to LL, Apr. 20, 1850, Lyon Papers, Clements.
"How insipid. . ." Mignonette to LL, June, 1850, Lyon Papers, Clements.
"The difference. . ." LL to [no addressee], Sept. 10, 1850, typed copy, Lyon Papers, Clements.
"The Lyons. . ." Baxter, op. cit., p. 380.
"a woman. . ." ibid.

Pg. 291 "I think. . ." Lucius Thayer to LL, Dec. 3, 1845, Lyon Papers, Clements.
Lucius Thayer and Grand Rapids water pipes, Baxter, p. 206.
"life was despaired. . ." G. W. Thayer to LL, Aug. 21, 1850, Lyon Papers, Clements. This
    is also the letter which invites LL to live with the Thayers on his return to Detroit.

Pg. 292 "After bringing. . ." *Biographical History of Northern Michigan,* p. 69-70.

Pg. 293 "a man of. . ." LL to A. G. Ellis, Feb. 20, 1838, Stuart, p. 506.
"The character. . ." Everett, op. cit., biographical sketches, p. 39-40.

Pg. 294 "Established. . ." Farnham's record, Ernest Fisher, op. cit., II p. 237.

Pg. 297 "wish to invest. . ." Edward Lyon to LL, Feb. 12, 1836, Lyon Papers, Clements.

Pg. 298 "I should be. . ." Edward Lyon to LL, Jan. 10, 1839, Lyon Papers, Clements.
"which made them. . ." Edward Lyon to LL, Apr. 17, 1842, Lyon Papers, Clements.
"I have taken. . ." Edward Lyon to LL, May 26, 1842, Lyon Papers, Clements.
"for nearly half. . ." Silas Farmer, *History of Detroit and Early Michigan* II, p. 1218.

Pg. 299 "When his grape. . ." Isabella Swan, *The Deep Roots: A History of Grosse Ile,* p.345.
"We view. . ." Swan, op. cit., p. 345.

Pg. 300 "Homer has. . ." Edward Lyon to LL, Jan. 15, 1839, Lyon Papers, Clements.

Pg. 301 "for no other. . ." LL to the President, June. 13, 1844, Stuart, p. 584.
"I have made. . ." Gaius S. Deane to LL, Oct. 18, 1845, Lyon Papers, Clements.

Pg. 302 "He was a thoroughly. . ." Baxter, op. cit., p. 118.
"came to Michigan. . ." David Fisher, *Compendium of History and Biography of Kalamazoo
    County, Michigan,* p. 128.
"on the Saganaw. . ." Ira Lyon to LL, Apr. 25, 1834, Lyon Papers, Clements.

Pg. 303 "In politics. . ." David Fisher, op. cit., p. 128.

Pg. 304 "has followed. . ." Baxter, op. cit., p. 118.
Pg. 305 "Has the western. . ." Lucretia Lyon to LL, Feb. 28, 1834, Lyon Papers, Clements.
"though Esther. . ." James W. Tabor to LL, Feb. 23, 1836, Lyon Papers, Clements.
Rooms in Lyons, Esther Tabor to Lucretia Lyon, Apr. 13, 1838, Lyon Family Papers,
    Bentley.
"Mr. Tabor. . ." George A. Robinson to LL, Dec. 1, 1837, Lyon Papers, Clements.

Pg. 306 "I am afraid. . ." LL to Lucretia Lyon, Oct. 31, 1828, Lyon Family Papers,
    Bentley.

Pg. 307 "Dressing tight. . ." LL to Lucretia, Apr. 15, 1827, Lyon Family Papers, Bentley.
Invitations, place cards, and inauguration ball invitations in Lyon Family Papers, Bentley.
"Miss Lyon. . ." Obituary in MPHC XXVI, p. 141.
"I am too ignorant. . ." Lucretia Lyon to LL, Feb. 14, 1837, Lyon Papers, Clements.

Pg. 308 "here yet. . ." Lucretia Lyon to LL, FEb. 17, 1846, Lyon Papers, Clements.
Keeping her dress, Lucretia Lyon to LL, Jan. 24, 1841, Lyon Papers, Clements.
"Mr. Coffinberry. . ." Lucretia Lyon to LL, Mar. 31, 1850, Lyon Papers, Clements.

Pg. 309 "a half. . ." Rent account book, Grand Rapids Museum archives.
"Miss Lucretia. . ." Grand Rapids Directory, 1875-76.
"always ready. . ." Dwight Goss, *History of Grand Rapids and Its Industries,* p. 168-9.

Pg. 310 Narrative of Mrs. Caroline P. Campbell is filed with the Lyon Papers, Clements.

Pg. 311 "I have known. . ." LL to Asa Lyon, Nov. 16, 1843, Stuart, p. 565.

Bibliography

Bassett, John Spencer, ed. *Correspondence of Andrew Jackson* (Carnegie Institute: Washington D.C.) 1931.

Bates, George C. "By-Gones of Detroit" *Michigan Pioneer and Historical Collections* XXII, p. 305-404.

Bauer, K. Jack. *Zachary Taylor: Soldier, Planter, Statesman of the Old Southwest* (Louisiana State Press: Baton Rouge) 1985.

Baxter, Albert. *History of the City of Grand Rapids, Michigan* (Munsell & Company, Publishers: New York) 1891.

Biographical History of Northern Michigan. (B. F. Bowen & Co.) 1905.

Bishop, Henry. "The Reason Why So Many Men Are Out of Employment," *Michigan Pioneer and Historical Collections* XXIX, p. 218-22.

Bishop, Levi. "Recollections," *Michigan Pioneer and Historical Collections* I, p. 511-17.

Block, Marguerite Beck *The New Church in the New World* (Octagon Books, Inc.: New York) 1968.

Blois, John T. *Gazetteer of the State of Michigan* (Sydney L. Rood & Co.: Detroit) 1838.

Branch, E. E., ed. *History of Ionia County, Michigan: Her People, Industries and Institutions* (B. F. Bowen & Co.: Indianapolis) 1916.

Brown, E. Lakin, "Autobiographical Notes," *Michigan Pioneer and Historical Collections* XXX, p. 424-94.

Butler, James D. "Tay-cho-pe-rah -- The Four Lakes Country -- First White Foot Prints There," *Wisconsin Historical Collections* X, p. 64-89.

Carter, Clarence Edwin, ed. *The Territorial Papers of the United States* (Government Printing Office: Washington D.C.) 1942.

Collins, Edward Day *A History of Vermont: with Geological and*

Geographical Notes, Bibliography, Chronology, Maps, and Illustrations (Ginn & Co.: Boston) 1903.

Dorr, Harold M., ed. *The Michigan Constitutional Convention of 1835-36: Debates and Proceedings* (University of Michigan Press: Ann Arbor) 1940.

Dunbar, Willis F. *Kalamazoo and How it Grew* (Western Michigan University: Kalamazoo) 1959.

Ellis, J. Dee. *Pioneer Families and History of Lapeer Co., Michigan* (Ellis Publishing Co.: Lapeer) 1978.

Etten, William J., ed. *A Citizens' History of Grand Rapids, Michigan* (A. P. Johnson Co.) 1926.

Everett, Franklin *Memorials of the Grand River Valley* (The Chicago Legal News: Chicago) 1878.

Farmer, Silas *History of Detroit and Wayne County and Early Michigan* (Silas Farmer & Co.: Detroit) 1890.

Field, Reverend George, *Memoirs, Incidents and Reminiscences of the Early History of the New Church* (R. Carswell: Toronto) 1879.

Fisher, David and Frank Little, eds. *Compendium of History and Biography of Kalamazoo County, Michigan* (A.W. Bowen Co.: Chicago) 1906.

Fisher, Ernest B., ed. *Grand Rapids and Kent County, Michigan* (Robert O. Law Co.: Chicago) 1918.

Fuller, George N. *Historic Michigan* (National Historical Assn.) 1924.

Garfield, Charles W. "Theodatus Timothy Lyon" *Michigan and Pioneer Historical Collections* XXIX, p. 481-91.

Gard, Robert and L. G. Sorden, *The Romance of Wisconsin Placenames* (Heartland Press: Minocqua, Wis.) 1988.

Goss, Dwight *History of Grand Rapids and Its Industries* (C. F. Cooper & Co.: Chicago) 1906.

Hemans, Lawton T. *Life and Times of Stevens Thomson Mason the Boy Governor of Michigan* (Michigan Historical Commission: Lansing) 1920.

Hemenway, Abby Maria *The Vermont Historical Gazetteer* (Burlington, Vermont) 1867.

Higgins, F. Hal. "The Moore-Hascall Harvester Centennial Approaches" *Michigan History Magazine*, Summer 1923, p. 415-437.

History of Kent County (Charles C. Chapman & Co.: Chicago) 1881.

History of Oakland County (L. H. Everts & Co.: Philadelphia) 1877.

History of Shiawassee and Clinton Counties (D. W. Ensign Co.: Philadelphia) 1880.

History of Washtenaw County (Charles C. Chapman: Chicago) 1881.

Holloway, F. M. "Hillsdale County from 1829 to 1836 Inclusive," *Michigan Pioneer and Historical Collections* I, p. 171-80.

Holt, Henry H. "History of Michigan's Portrait of General Lafayette," *Michigan Pioneer and Historical Collections* XXIX, p. 298-301.

Hunt, John Warren *Wisconsin Gazetteer* (Deriah Brown: Madison) 1853.

Jerome, Edwin. "Incidents in the Black Hawk War," *Michigan Pioneer and Historical Collections* I, p. 48-51.

Lane, Kit. *John Allen: Michigan's Pioneer Promoter* (Pavilion Press: Douglas, Michigan) 1988.

Lapham, I. A. *Wisconsin: Its Geography and Topography, History, Geology and Mineralogy* (L. A. Hopkins: Milwaukee) 1846.

Leiby, Maria Quinlan. "A Hero and a Governor," *Michigan History*, July-August 1990, p. 32-3.

Leonard, Catherine. *Early History of Lyons*, mss. Library of Michigan, Lansing.

Lowe, Berenice Bryant. *Tales of Battle Creek* (Albert L. and Louise B. Miller Foundation, Inc.) 1976.

Lyons/Muir, Michigan (n. p.) 1976,

Magee, Dorothy M., ed. *Centennial History of Mount Clemens, Michigan 1879-1979* (Bright Future for Mount Clemens Committee: Mount Clemens, Michigan) 1980.

Martin, Morgan L. "Narrative of Morgan L. Martin" *Wisconsin Historical Collections* XI, p. 395-400.

Martin, Mrs. Sophia (Smith) *Mack Genealogy* (The Tuttle Co.: Rutland, Vermont) 1903.

Mollenhoff, David V. *Madison: A History of the Formative Years* (Keendall/Hunt Publishing Co.: Dubuque, Iowa) 1982.

Moore, Charles *History of Michigan* (The Lewis Publishing Co.: Chicago) 1915.

Moses, John. *Illinois: Historical and Statistical* (Fergus Printing Company: Chicago) 1895.

Murdoch, Angus *Boom Copper* (Book Concern: Hancock, Michigan) 1943, reprinted 1964.

Nelson, Anson and Fanny. *Memorials of Sarah Childress Polk* Reproduced from an 1892 original. (The Reprint Company: Spartanburg, South Carolina) 1980.

Nesbit, Robert C. *Wisconsin: A History* (The University of Wisconsin Press) 1973.

Nevins, Allan, ed. *The Diary of John Quincy Adams, 1794-1845* (Charles Scribner's Sons: New York) 1951.

Osborn, Chase S. and Stellanova Osborn. *Schoolcraft -- Longfellow -- Hiawatha* (The Jacques Cattell Press: Lancaster, Pennsylvania) 1942.

Palmer, General Friend. *Early Days in Detroit* (Hunt & June: Detroit) 1906.

Peters, Bernard C. "Early Town-Site Speculation in Kalamazoo County" *Michigan History*, Fall 1972, p. 201-15.

Reber, L. Benjamin. *History of St. Joseph* (St. Joseph Chamber of Commerce: St. Joseph) 1928.

Romig, Walter *Michigan Place Names* (Walter Romig: Grosse Pointe) n.d.

Rosalita, Sister Mary. *Education in Detroit Prior to 1850* (Michigan Historical Commission: Lansing) 1928,

Sagendorph, Kent *Michigan: The Story of the University* (E.P. Dutton & Co.: New York) 1948.

Sagendorph, Kent *Stevens Thomson Mason; Misunderstood Patriot* (E.P. Dutton & Co., Inc.: New York) 1947.

Schmiedeke, J. M. "With Chain and Compass," *Surveying and Mapping* March 1972, p. 63-7.

Shirigian, John. *Lucius Lyon: His Place in Michigan History* University of Michigan PhD Thesis, 1961.

Sibley, James Scarborough *The Sibley Family in America* (Honolulu, Hawaii: 1922)

Smith, Alice E. *James Duane Doty: Frontier Promoter* (State Historical Society of Wisconsin: Madison) 1954.

Soule, Anna May "The Southern and Western Boundaries of Michigan," *Michigan Pioneer and Historical Collections* XXVII, p. 346-390.

Streeter, Floyd Benjamin. *Political Parties in Michigan, 1837-1860* (Michigan Historical Commission: Lansing) 1918.

Swan, Isabella E. *The Deep Roots: A History of Grosse Ile, Michigan, to July 6, 1876* (n. p.: Grosse Ile) 1977.

Thayer, George W. "From Vermont to Lake Superior in 1845," *Michigan Pioneer and Historical Collections* XXX, p. 549-566.

Thayer, George W. "Life of Senator Lucius Lyon," *Michigan Pioneer and Historical Collections* XXVII, p. 404-11.

Tobias, Thomas N. Jr., and Mary Wallace Baker and Barbara A. Fairfield. *The History of Ypsilanti: 150 years* (Ypsilanti Area Sesquicentennial, Inc.: Ypsilanti) 1973.

Trowbridge, C. C. *Personal Memoirs of Charles Christopher Trowbridge as Written for His Kindred* (Published at Detroit) Christmas 1893.

Utley, Henry M. and Byron M. Cutcheon *Michigan as a Province, Territory and State, the Twenty-Sixth Member of the Federal Union* (The Publishing Society of Michigan) 1906.

Van Zandt, Franklin K. *Boundaries of the United States and the Several States* (U. S. Government Printing Office: Washington, D. C.) 1966.

White, C. Albert *A History of the Rectangular Survey System* (United States Department of Interior: Washington, D.C.) 1983.

White, George H. "Sketch of the Life of Hon. Rix Robinson; A Pioneer of Western Michigan," *Michigan Pioneer and Historical Collections* XI, p. 186-200.

White, George H., "A Sketch of Lucius Lyon, One of the First Senators from Michigan," *Michigan Pioneer and Historical Collections* XIII, p. 325-333.

Whitney, Ellen M., ed. *The Black Hawk War, 1831-1832* (Illinois State Historical Library: Springfield, Ill.) 1973.

Williams, B. O., "My Recollections of the Early Schools of Detroit that I Attended from the Year 1816 to 1819," *Michigan Pioneer and Historical Collections* V, p. 547-550.

Williams, Mentor L. "Cooper, Lyon and the Moore-Hascall Harvesting Machine," *Michigan History,* Summer 1930, p. 26-34.

Woodford, Frank B. *Mr. Jefferson's Disciple: A Life of Justice Woodward* (Michigan State College Press: East Lansing) 1953.

Index

Grand Traverse Co. 275
Grandville 216
Granger, Mr. 215
Granger & Ball 214
Grant Co. (Wis.) 51, 191
Grant, Julia 256
Grant, U. S. 256-7, 277
Gratiot County 161
Gratton 274
Green Bay, Wis. 40, 91, 120, 187, 188, 189, 190, 192, 196, 197
Green, C. K. 95, 102
Griffin, John 21
Grigon, Augustine 41
Grosse Ile 300
Grundy, Felix 92, 104, 106
Guiteaux, John B. 217
Gull Prairie 79, 139
Gurnsey, Daniel G. 138
Gurnsey, J. J. 137-8

Haines, Ezekial S. 254
Hall, Amos T. 262
Hall, Frederick 258, 301
Hammond, C. G. 231, 247
Hanse, Andrew 166
Harrington, Benjamin 297
Harris, Israel V. 111
Harrison, William Henry 240, 241
Hart, A. N. 179
Hascall, John 203
Hastings 161
Hastings, Eurotus P. 131, 147, 161
Haswell, Nathan B. 277
Hatch, Junius H. 213
Hathaway, Charles W. 295
Hathaway, Joshua 196
Hathon, A. E. 208
Hayward, Elijah 49
Hazel Green 51
Hefferan, Thomas 311
Hendricks, William 95
Higbee, Isaac Newton 13, 166, 173, 255, 303-4
Hill, William B. 224
Hillsdale 64
Hillsdale County 156
Hinsdill Brothers, Inc. 296
Hinsdill, Chester B. 296
Hinsdill, Henry M. 296
Hinsdill, Stephen 215

Hobbie, S. R. 90
Hodges, Mr. 185
Holland 209
Homan, Julia (Tabor) 306
Holt, Henry 117
Hook Lake 196, 232
Hopkins, Charles W. 265
Horner, John S. 73, 88, 89, 91, 97, 118, 188, 189, 190, 191
Houghton, Douglass 8, 28-9, 45, 220, 222-3, 247, 252, 253-4, 290
Houghton, Jacob 253-4
Howard, Capt. 284
Howe, Philander R. 137, 177
Howell, Andrew 116
Hubbard, Gurdon S. 196
Hubbardston 305, 306
Hulburt, Ansel 219-21
Hulburt, Henry 219
Hulburt, Hijson 219
Hull, William 19
Humphrey, Levi S. 231
Hungerford, O. 254
Hunt, James B. 238, 255
Hunt, Joseph 274
Hunt, Mr. 164, 165
Hunt, Robert H. 274
Hurd, Isaac N. 156
Huron County 162
Huron, Lake 100
Huron River 210
Huston, Hosea 139, 209
Hutchins, Allen 177, 178, 226-9
Hyde, Joseph E. 255

Ingham County 37, 210
Ionia 163, 169, 178, 217, 227
Ionia County 12, 37. 112, 162-3, 168, 178, 185, 212, 228, 238, 293, 297, 301, 305
Iowa County (Wis.) 59, 60, 187, 189, 190
Irish, David 13, 166, 168, 169, 170, 175, 301
Irish, Lenora (Lyon) 13, 166, 168, 169, 170, 207, 301
Irish, Joseph 13
Irish, Lavina (Lyon) 13
Irwin, Judge 189
Isham, Giles 164, 165-6, 168, 169, 199

347

348

* * * * *

Kit Lane, a Michigan native, has spent more than 25 years researching and writing Michigan history. Until 1988 she and her husband, Art, ran the *Fennville Herald* and the *Commercial Record*, weekly newspapers in the Saugatuck area. They are thought to have had the only his-and-hers newspaper combination in Michigan. Other newspaper work includes stints with the *Detroit Free Press, Grand Rapids Press, Birmingham Eccentric*, and *Daily Tribune* of Royal Oak. In addition to a series of small books on western Michigan history, and the compendium-sized *Western Allegan County History*, she is the author of *John Allen: Michigan's Pioneer Promoter*. Between book projects Kit teaches in the Language Arts department of Montcalm Community College, Sidney.

John Allen:
Michigan's Pioneer Promoter

John Allen was a debt-ridden Virginia farmer in 1823 when he left home to sell some cattle -- and vanished. He reappeared in Michigan to begin a remarkable 26-year career in land speculation. He was co-founder of Ann Arbor and touched other settlements including Lawrence, Spring Arbor, Lansing, and Grand Haven. Poor, but still hopeful, Allen left for the California gold fields in 1850.

224 pp., illustrated, index, bibliography, 5 1/4 x 8 1/2
Hardcover (1-877703-17-6) $19.50   Trade Paper (1-877703-16-8) $11.50

WESTERN ALLEGAN COUNTY HISTORY

Thousands of pictures, topical area history, survey of settlements, recollections, and more than 900 family histories.

Hardcover with full color cover painting, 537 pp., index, 9 x 12
(0-88107-122-6) $66.50 (plus $4.50 shipping)

The Day the Elephant Died and Other Tales of Saugatuck
Stories of Saugatuck, unusual, humorous, interesting -- and mostly true.

72 pp., illustrated, softbound, 5 1/4 x 8 1/2 (1-877703-19-2) $5.50

The Popcorn Millionaire and Other Tales of Saugatuck
Celebrity visitors and residents including Susan B. Anthony, Paderewski, Carl Sandburg, Amelia Earhart, and millionaire D. K. Ludwig.

96 pp., illustrated, softbound, 5 1/4 x 8 1/2 (1-877703-20-6) $5.50

Some Stories of Holland Harbor
Singapore: The Buried City
Douglas: Village of Friendliness
Saugatuck; A Brief History, Illustrated
Shipwrecks of the Saugatuck Area
20-28pp., illustrated, softbound, 8 1/2 x 11 $2.00 each

Fennville: The Early Years
Fennville: Village to City
Fennville Area
52-64 pp., illustrated, softbound, 8 1/2 x 11 $3.00 each

By Kit Lane

Include $1.50 shipping and handling for small books, order from:

PAVILION PRESS P. O. Box 250 Douglas, Michigan 49406